Responding to Crisis

*A Rhetorical Approach
to Crisis Communication*

Responding to Crisis

A Rhetorical Approach to Crisis Communication

Edited by

Dan P. Millar
Millar Communication Strategies, Inc.

Robert L. Heath
University of Houston

2004

LAWRENCE ERLBAUM ASSOCIATES, PUBLISHERS
Mahwah, New Jersey   London

Lawrence Erlbaum Associates, Inc., Publishers
10 Industrial Avenue
Mahwah, New Jersey 07430

Cover design by Kathryn Houghtaling Lacey

Library of Congress Cataloging-in-Publication Data

Responding to crisis : a rhetorical approach to crisis communication / edited by Dan Pyle
    Millar, Robert L. Heath.
        p. cm.
    Includes bibliographical references and indexes.
    ISBN 0-8058-4059-1 (alk. paper) – ISBN 0-8058-4060-5 (pbk. : alk. paper)
        1.   Crisis management. 2. Communication in management. 3. Organizational change. I.
    Millar, Dan Pyle, 1938- II. Heath, Robert L. (Robert Lawrence), 1941-

    HD49.R47 2003
    658.4'056—dc21

                                                                                2003052859

Books published by Lawrence Erlbaum Associates are printed on acid-free paper,
and their bindings are chosen for strength and durability.

Printed in the United States of America
10   9   8   7   6   5   4   3   2   1

Contents

1

A Rhetorical Approach to Crisis Communication: Management, Communication Processes, and Strategic Responses

Robert L. Heath
University of Houston

Dan P. Millar
Millar Communication Strategies, Inc., Indianapolis, IN

In recent years, researchers and practitioners have explored the nature, theory, and best practices that are required for effective and ethical crisis preparation and response. The consequences of being unprepared to respond quickly, appropriately, and ethically to a crisis are dramatic and well documented. For this reason, crisis consulting and the development of crisis response plans and protocols have become more than a cottage industry. Agencies devote part of their business toiling for their clients and employers who are in trouble or who want to avert trouble by proper strategic planning. Responding to this challenge, researchers and practitioners want to know best practices of crisis planning and response.

Public relations literature is littered with case studies of organizations which lost brand equity, suffered damage to products, services, and lost issue positions because of inept handling of crises preparation and response. A classic example of crisis damage occurred in 2000 when the actuality and potentiality of death and bodily harm drove Bridgestone/Firestone stock share value to *less than half* of what it had been before the crisis. That crisis cost the company lots money and a ton of consumer good will.

Taking a rhetorical view of crisis events and utterances, this book is devoted to adding new insights to the discussion. The book describes a rhetorical approach to crisis communication. To help set the tone for that description, this chapter begins with a review of definitions of crisis, moves to offer a rhetorical definition of crisis, and then explores the intellectual, theoretical, and best practices implications of this approach to crisis planning and response. The following chapters address unique contributions to a rhetorical view of crisis management by centering their attention on one of the stages of crisis preparation and response: precrisis, crisis, and postcrisis.

CRISIS DEFINED: DAMAGING EVENTS AND TURNING POINTS

A crisis is typically defined as an untimely but predictable event that has actual or potential consequences for stakeholders' interests as well as the reputation of the organization suffering the crisis. That means a crisis can harm stakeholders and damage the organization's relationship with them. This harm to stakeholders and damage to reputation can haunt the organization regardless of its responsibility. The organization must respond in many ways to put the minds of its stakeholders at ease about the organization's responsibility for creating or allowing the crisis to occur. The responsibility issue needs to be put to rest to demonstrate that the organization can regain control over its activities so that the crisis no longer exists or no longer harms stakeholders. The manner in which the organization addresses this responsibility serves as a turning point for it: Respond well and survive the crisis; respond poorly and suffer the death of the organization's reputation and perhaps itself.

With this brief overview, we launch our discussion of crisis by focusing on the bad news day of a company. Having defined crisis in conceptual terms, let's focus even more on the actual character of crisis.

Crisis exists when the media are knocking on your door and you would rather they were not. Crisis exists when employees don't want their friends and relatives to know who they work for while hoping that a different company is looking for persons with their experience and talents. Crisis occurs when customers are looking to your competitors for a better and safer product. A crisis exists when traders are selling your stock in hopes of getting out before the bottom falls out. Crisis exists when stakeholders are calling for legislative or regulatory hearings to regulate and punish the offending organization.

Crisis exists in the new communication technology age—cyberspace—when you read allegations on a Web site or in an email about your personnel, organization, products, or services that are absolutely untrue. Rumors are a special kind of crisis—at times even more provoking in cyberspace. Rumors are often not based on fact but are frequently based on narrow or misinformed interpretations of fact. Such was the case when an Internet rumor alleged that sodium laureth sulfate was a known carcinogen. Actually, this chemical is a sudsing agent used in leading brand shampoos and toothpastes—each named in the email circulated through highly credible family–friendship networks. Web site messages were placed to combat this misinterpretation and disinformation campaign's rhetorical attack. The rumor campaign may have been a case of cybersabotage enacted by a competitor to the name brand products. To combat this attack, advocates provided credible information on the safety of this chemical and discredited the message by demonstrating that it was factually inaccurate. One inaccuracy was that Canada Health had banned the substance; it had studied the chemical and found it to be safe. Another inaccuracy was that the researcher who was alleged to have discovered the carcinogenic nature of the substance simply did not exist. The cybersabotage was a fabrication of fact, but without timely informed response it would have damaged the brand equity of leading products.

Similar characteristics of crisis can be used to recall the bad times experienced by governmental agencies and nonprofit organizations. For instance, you might remember the scandals associated with salary and fees charged by the head of a national nonprofit or by the failure of a governmental agency to respond properly during a terrible hurricane. Each of these crises consists of an event, or series of events, that gives stakeholders reason to believe that the leadership of the organization has lost control of the organization's operations in ways that harm its stakeholders.

Rhetorically speaking, crisis can harm the organization's efforts to create understanding and maintain mutually beneficial relationships with interested parties whose support and good will the organization needs. If unattended or poorly managed, the crisis can prevent the organization from making satisfactory and expected progress toward achieving its mission, because stakeholders and stakeseekers come to doubt the organization's ability or willingness to properly control its activities to assure their health, safety, and well-being. A crisis results in actual or negative consequences for the health, safety, and well-being of others. The organization's reputation is harmed. If poorly managed, the crisis may mature into a public policy issue and affect the organization's ability to compete in the marketplace.

Typical definitions may allude to the communication responses—precrisis, crisis, and postcrisis—but rarely go into detail on that subject. Stressing the strain on organizations' ability to adapt and cope, Barton (1993) defined crisis as "A situation faced by an individual, group or organisation which they are unable to cope with by the use of normal routine procedures and in which stress is created by sudden change" (p. 86). Other views expand the consequences of disrupting routines and creating stress.

- Crisis interrupts normal business activities. Crisis management/communication is a corporate strategy for dealing with a major business interruption.
- Crisis may result from management decisions to implement the organization's strategic plan, such as the crisis resulting from a major layoff of employees. Although the kind of event that results in a crisis can be predicted, the specific time of the occurrence may not be foretold. Some events, such as massive layoffs can be foretold and even timed. One large company, working with a national consulting firm, chose April 1 as the date for announcing to the employees which ones would be laid off. "April Fool—no, you really are laid off!!!"
- Crisis can damage the reputation of the organization and prevent management from accomplishing its mission and strategic plan.
- Crisis can harm the organization's efforts to create understanding and foster mutually favorable relationships with stakeholders.
- Crisis can mature into a public policy issue. Conversely, a public policy issue can become a crisis. Ask the tobacco industry.
- Crisis can weaken the organization's ability to compete in the marketplace.
- Crisis can be described by several characteristics: magnitude, duration, locus of cause, locus of responsibility, emergency response (timely and effective), and restoration/resolution.
- Crisis can result in damage that is actual, an explosion, or merely apparent, as in the case of an unfounded rumor (e.g., the number of cases of a medical problem—such as cancer or asthma—ostensibly experienced by residents who live in a community near chemical plants).
- Crisis often prompts an emotional response by key stakeholders. A crisis evokes emotion because interests are damaged—or at least appear to be (Mitroff & Pearson, 1993; Pauchant & Mitroff, 1992).
- Crisis is an extraordinary event that results in "an unstable time or state of affairs in which a decisive change is impending" (Fink, 1986, p. 15).
- "Crises are characterized by low probability of high consequence events that threaten the most fundamental goal of an organization" (Weick, 1988, p. 305).
- "A critical incident or a crisis is simply a sudden, unexpected event that poses an institutional threat suggesting the need for rapid, high level decision-making" (Paschall, 1992, p. 4).
- Crisis entails events and outcomes about which key stakeholders make attributions regarding cause and responsibility (Coombs & Holladay, 1996). "Crises are threats, meaning that they actually do or have the potential to create negative or undesirable outcomes" (Coombs, 1999b, p.

2). "Crisis management represents a set of factors designed to combat crises and lessen the actual damage inflicted by the crisis" (Coombs, 1999b, p. 4).

- "A *crisis* is a major occurrence with a potentially negative outcome affecting an organization, company, industry, as well as its publics, products, services, or good name" (Fearn-Banks, 1996, p. 1).
- A crisis "is an event that brings, or has the potential for bringing, an organization into disrepute and imperils its future profitability" (Lerbinger, 1997, p. 4).
- Crisis is a strain on the reward–cost balance between an organization and key stakeholders who can work to impose constraints on the organization's activities thereby costing it additional resources (Stanley, 1985).
- A crisis is a major business (organization) disruption which generates intense media interest and public scrutiny (Irvine & Millar, 1998).

Crisis has potential or actual consequences for the organization. Crises come in various shapes and sizes. They have magnitude, duration, and culpability. Crises make others attend to your business.

These definitions feature the dynamics of a crisis, but do not suggest the communication options and functions that are required by a crisis. The next section corrects this slight by stressing that in addition to the preparations that are necessary for a timely and ethical response to crisis, timely, ethical, and strategic message development and delivery are crucial. Thus, we have the rationale for a rhetorical definition of crisis.

A RHETORICAL DEFINITION OF CRISIS

As was emphasized in the previous section, typical definitions of crisis emphasize damage, actual or potential. They focus on consequences for relationships and reputations. They suggest response options and processes that may be needed to combat or abate the damage of the crisis.

A rhetorical definition moves the needle a bit further. A rhetorical approach to crisis explicitly acknowledges that the responsibility for the crisis, its magnitude, and its duration are contestable. It stresses the message development and presentation part of the crisis response. It underscores the role that information, framing, and interpretation play in the organization's preparation for a crisis, response to it, and postcrisis comments and actions. It features discourse, one or more statements made over time.

Central to a rhetorical analysis of crisis is the concept of a rhetorical problem. A rhetorical problem arises when exigencies (i.e., occurrences and statements) call for a statement from one or more persons or organizations (Bitzer, 1968). Organizations and individuals, because of their role in society or in the crisis, are looked to for a statement that is a wise, ethical, and strategic response to a rhetorical problem.

A rhetorical definition of crisis features the communication processes and efforts to co-define meanings that assist persons who are affected—or think they are affected—to prepare for, accommodate to, and recover from the disruptive events. What the event means—how it is to be interpreted— becomes a central rhetorical theme. Corporate spokespersons are expected to make statements that can be thoughtfully considered by others to determine whether they bring closure to the event given what those publics knew about the organization prior to, during, and after the event.

A rhetorical approach to crisis recognizes that each crisis has an actual dimension and a perceived dimension. Some crises are "perceived" to be bigger or smaller than they actually are. One explanation for this difference in perception is the ability of key spokespersons to communicate effectively before, during, and after the crisis. Crisis managers, then, need to think in terms of the technical, managerial, and rhetorical dimensions of a crisis. They need a mind set that motivates them to prepare for the crisis, as well as to prepare others for the crisis. The mind set leads them to respond and communicate during a crisis, as well as after a crisis.

Thus, crisis has two dimensions: technical/managerial and communication. A crisis is created by choices and performances that have technical or managerial dimensions. A plant releases hazardous materials into waterways, as was the case of Coors Brewing Company in Golden, Colorado. In the summer of 2000, a negligent employee released some 70,000 gallons of beer into a stream. The alcohol in the beer killed fish. Separate from the technical or managerial problem is the communication response. Of course, the pollutant and the dead fish had to be cleared from the stream, the technical dimension. A rhetorical approach to crisis asks the following question: What needs to be said before, during, and after a crisis?

Before

A crisis plan is needed to prepare all sorts of persons to know what to do in the event of a crisis. Preparation can entail at least two key functions: looking for and reducing the likelihood that a crisis will occur; and communicating with key markets, audiences, and publics to prepare them for a crisis so that it can be framed and addressed when it occurs. Messages, in this context, may be used to alert persons to the signs of a crisis so they can recognize it and take emergency response measures to reduce its likely consequences for them.

Governmental entities, for instance, may use emergency response messages to alert citizens to the potential for a crisis by warning them to avoid the crisis or act properly if it occurs to minimize its magnitude and duration. A good example of this kind of crisis is severe weather warnings: tornadoes and hurricanes. Companies also can warn and otherwise prepare employees and community members to be prepared for the eventuality of a crisis. For instance, the chemical manufacturing industry acknowledges to its citizen neighbors that an operating problem can occur where hazardous materials are released into the air or water in ways that can affect the health and safety of community members. This warning and the emergency response measures are part of the precrisis planning. These are not only operational plans, but constitute rhetorical statements designed to demonstrate the commitment, trustworthiness, and alignment of company with community interests.

A rhetorical approach to crisis features the messages that are used in advance of a crisis, during a crisis, and after a crisis. This approach to crisis response asks, "What can be and must be said to react in a reasonable, responsible, and ethical way to the concerns of the stakeholders affected by the crisis?"

On the one hand, crisis preparation and response seem simple. The advice might be, "Tell the truth; play the public relations function of the journalist-in-residence and provide the information that will tell the concerned persons what they want and need to know to understand the cause of the crisis, its impact, its likely duration, and the steps being taken to end it."

During

In addition to providing information, the rhetorical approach to crisis preparation and response requires that statements frame the crisis. The latitudes of possible response to the many kinds of crisis is virtually limitless. Response can include blame placing, whether that blame is fairly and accurately assigned. It can entail blame accepting. Some organizations believe that they need to accept the blame, acknowledge the acceptance, and apologize for it. That rhetorical response they expect to exonerate them of the larger responsibility for the crisis. Some practitioners, in this case, believe that apology reduces the likelihood that concerned persons will seek to punish the organization if it apologizes sincerely. Chrysler's acknowledging the odometer fiasco and apologizing for it is one example. By the same token, some cultures (e.g., Japanese business people) *require* an apology for having harmed others.

The time frame of this model can be extended to include message processes that transpire before a crisis occurs. Through information, responsible managements speaking through the voice of public relations to address the reasonable and responsible concerns of stakeholders about the eventuality of a crisis. In some industries, this is a crucial stage of message positioning. Notable examples include the airline industry, electric generating and distribution companies, governmental agencies providing key services to citizens, industries that engage in hazardous manufacturing processes (the chemical and refining industry), and companies that manufacture any product that can adversely affect the health, safety, or environmental quality of people. Industries, nonprofits, and governmental agencies are wise to think about issues of safety (including security), fairness (e.g., the fair treatment of customers), equality (e.g., the equal treatment of residents), and the environmental quality.

The rhetorical approach to crisis raises a second question: What concerns do people have about potential crises that should be addressed? What responsibility does the organization have to address these issues? How can these issues of crisis potential be addressed in ways that do not alarm key markets, audiences, and publics unnecessarily, but give them the information they need to be forewarned and prepared for a crisis. A classic case of such precrisis forewarning is employee safety training and the emergency management warnings and preparations—including evacuation—that can accompany nature's violence such as a hurricane or volcanic eruption.

The sorts of rhetorical choices that are available for use during a crisis is limitless. The advice and best practices are widely debated, for instance, including whether the senior officer of the organization should or must become the chief spokesperson during the crisis.

After

Postcrisis response is narrower in latitude. By the time the organizational spokespersons are working to put the crisis behind them, many of the issues regarding the crisis have been resolved. The debate about the crisis tends to frame the sort of issues that need to be addressed by the organization. Thus, postcrisis, a vital part of the process, entails providing information that demonstrates how, why, and when the organization has put things right as well as what it plans to do to prevent the recurrence of a similar crisis.

Based on this review, we agree that a crisis is a predictable, critical incident, the likelihood of which can be identified but the exact time of occurrence cannot and that it can have negative consequences for one or more organizations. It encourages others to look critically at the organization and therefore requires strategically developed statements that responsibly and ethically address stakeholder concerns, issues, and need for control. This definition builds from the earlier traditional definitions, but adds the dimension that a crisis constitutes a rhetorical problem that needs to be addressed through skillfully developed and delivered messages which respond to the concerns of stakeholders in an ethical manner.

THE STRUGGLE FOR CONTROL

A crisis can be viewed as a struggle for control. Persons who are affected by a crisis look to responsible parties to control their actions or to create actions that reduce the harm of the crisis. If a company has manufactured flawed products that consequently lead to deaths, key markets, audiences, and publics rightly demand that the organization control its operations to end and prevent such occurrences. If the organization fails to do so, these markets, audiences, and publics rightly call on other organizations—often governmental agencies and activists—to force the offending organization to control itself. Punitive responses to the organization can include refusal to buy its products, onerous legislation and regulation, and litigation.

The messages of the organization need to responsibly define the crisis, the actions that need to be taken, the actions that will be taken, are being taken, or have been taken. These messages may also contain information the markets, audiences, and publics need to understand what they should know to form appropriate attitudes and to take actions that reduce the impact of the crisis on them.

This view of crisis assumes that three stages can be used to define the crisis life cycle: precrisis, crisis response, and postcrisis response. The following outline features key elements in this process featuring the stages and cycles to lay a foundation for the chapters that follow. The central theme is that organizations are responsible for their management and communication choices that positively or negatively affect the interests of others. An organization is expected to manage its affairs and not harm others; likewise, it is expected to communicate in ways that supply proper warnings prior to a crisis as well as to offer appropriate responses during a crisis and corrective and restorative actions after a crisis.

A. Precrisis strategies:

1. Management tactics designed to prevent a crisis
2. Management tactics designed to mitigate the impact of a crisis should one occur
3. Communication tactics designed to prevent a crisis
4. Communication tactics designed to mitigate the impact of a crisis in the event that it occurs

B. Crisis response strategies

1. Management tactics designed to exert control during a crisis
2. Management tactics designed to mitigate the impact of a crisis while one is occurring
3. Communication tactics designed to co-define the meaning of a crisis
4. Communication tactics designed to mitigate the impact of a crisis by explaining the crisis, its causes, consequences, and predicted restoration strategies

C. Crisis correction and restoration: Postcrisis response strategies

1. Management tactics designed to restore the organization and its community; management strategies used to restore control
2. Management tactics designed to mitigate or eliminate the negative impact of the crisis
3. Communication tactics designed to retrospectively co-define the meaning of the crisis
4. Communication tactics designed to explain postcrisis restoration strategies—bringing closure to a crisis.

CRISIS AS RHETORICAL EXIGENCY

Earlier, we stressed the notion that a crisis constitutes a rhetorical problem. Bitzer (1968) argued that rhetorical problem results when an exigency demands a rhetorical statement that addresses the problem and seeks to provide a rational, justifiable response to the exigency. A classic version of this view of rhetoric is the problem–solution presentation. A problem demands a solution. In terms of a crisis, either the organization suffering the crisis will achieve control of the crisis events or control will be imposed on the organization.

The rhetorical exigencies created by a crisis center on the organization's actions and statements to regain control of the circumstances, which have been maturing in a crisis. Items in the following list broadly highlight some elements of a crisis that relate to its cause, magnitude, and duration and therefore constitute aspects of the rhetorical problem:

- possible cause of an event,
- factors amplifying the event,
- factors attenuating the event,

- estimated magnitude of events,
- estimated duration of events.

CRISIS AS INTERPRETED EVENTS

Crisis happens. As with all events, they are subject to interpretations. All parties that are affected by a crisis and involved with it tend to seek to interpret it, evaluate it, and draw conclusions about it. This rhetorical problem, then, focuses on the platforms of fact, evaluations (value), and conclusions—even policies—that will be promulgated to achieve restoration, mitigation, and prevention. Such competing interpretations, both within and outside the organization, magnify the challenges that constitute a rhetorical problem.

A variation of this view is to treat crisis as an interruption of a narrative. The story of an organization and the persons whose interests it affects are expected, by those persons, to constitute a story that "continues happily ever after." A crisis interrupts this narrative.

Some elements in the event have narrative implications. A crisis not only is an interruption of one narrative—the normal activities of an organization, but it also begins its own narrative, one that may or may not end happily ever after.

In the context of the narrative, the exigency is to management actions and rhetorical statements that can or must demonstrate persuasively that the organization understands the crisis and has the resources—intellectual, managerial, financial, rhetorical, and ethical—to restore to an acceptable, as opposed to an unacceptable, narrative. Each narrative consists of the dramatization of archetypal organizational roles (Mitroff & Pearson, 1993). *What is the likely narrative outcome of the crisis as it is alleged to be managed by the parties responsible for enacting the crisis narrative?*

Rhetorical approaches to crisis are likely to be expected to address variations of narratives. One is the interrupted narrative. All is going well, and then something goes bump in the dark. A second narrative is "been there, done that." The rhetorical exigency is the recurring crisis—a recurring story of the company having suffered the same or similar crisis before. A chemical manufacturing facility has explosions periodically resulting in deaths. Each of these stories is harder to explain. The bottom line in the recurring story is the organization's inability or unwillingness to exert the control required to prevent the recurrence of these events.

The following elements constitute parts of the organizational story. Each of these factors becomes part of the rhetorical problem and therefore requires responses by the organization.

Scene: Where did the crisis occur? What is the symbolic power of that scene?

Personae: The *dramatis personae*—cast of characters—of this undirected play that leads to, occurs during, and transpires to resolution after a crisis.

- heroes/heroines—persons and factors that attenuated, contained, and restored operations so they did as little harm as possible
- rescuers—specific heroes/heroines that contained the crisis
- enemies—persons and factors that caused or amplified the crisis
- allies—persons who assisted the heroes/heroines
- protectors—agents who acted on behalf of the stakeholders
- villains—agents who acted against the stakeholders
- victims—persons and things damaged by the crisis

Plots and themes: past, present, and future sense of the organization and its ability to perform in ways that meet rather that offend the expectations of key publics.

Viewed in these terms, we can approach the rhetoric of crisis response as being a narrative framed by scene, moved by personae, in which a theme is created and a plot is enacted.

Theme: Each story has a central idea—a theme. What is the theme of this crisis? Is it accurate in the estimation of the organization? Will the organization's thematic account of the crisis—cause, duration, and magnitude—sustain itself against the scrutiny of other interested parties, such as media reporters and even criminal investigators?

Plot: What is the story line that the organization wishes to feature? Is it the same as that told by other stakeholder advocates and adversaries?

These are some of the stock elements of the rhetorical problem that results from a crisis. The elements are offered as suggestions for the sorts of topics, personae, and themes that must be part of the rhetorical planning and implementation of the crisis communicators because concerned stakeholders approach crisis with these themes in mind.

Each of the resulting narratives is framed in the context of other narratives. For instance, one organization, unlike its counterparts, suffers or does not suffer crisis. The narrative of all of the organizations, an industry for instance, is that it has or does not have recurring or repeated crises. In contrast one organization exhibits a narrative that either is better or worse than that of its industry.

In addition to the content of statement made, rhetorical perspectives on crisis preparation and response can focus on communication style—the manner in which it is made. Communication styles are revealed in the audible and written voice of the organization making the crisis statement. Styles are reflected in the visible nonverbal cues of the spokespersons. Style is conveyed in the timing and responsiveness of the communicators. The following list exemplifies the kinds of communicator traits that markets, audiences, and publics use to interpret and evaluate style. The key rhetorical guideline is that style must fit the rhetorical exigency. For instance, if deaths occur from the crisis event, then spokespersons must be high ranking, sincere, and empathic in the statements they make regarding victims. Style modifies and confirms the content of message, a key guideline in rhetoric. Interpretation and evaluation of style is shaped by the degree to which organizational messages:

- demonstrate concern and empathy
- demonstrate compassion
- orient to solutions
- appear poised and confident/competent
- appear responsible and responsive
- reveal open-mindedness and receptivity to comments and criticism

CRISIS AS DRAMATISTIC PENTAD

A Burkian view of crisis would incorporate the perspectives of the pentad: scene, act, agent, agency, and purpose. Burke (1969a) argued that human motives and the discourse related to those motives feature these five key elements and the ratios between them. In some ways this set of rhetorical options is similar to a narrative approach to crisis. It certainly supports that view. It adds, however, another way to look at the elements of a crisis with the primary purpose of disclosing purpose, the reason for the crisis, and the actions that resulted from the crisis.

A quick review of this theme is demonstrated by the scene justifying the act in a crisis. One could argue that military actions, including the casualties of those actions, constitute a crisis which a government needs to manage (Heibert, 1991). The fundamental question in the mind of the public is whether the war (the scene) justified the damage, including loss of life and limb. The crisis management of WWII was based on the definition of the scene as a just war against terrible tyrants. Thus, the loss of life was a justifiable supreme sacrifice for freedom. Lyndon Johnson, on the other hand as President of the United States, failed to define the scene of the war in Viet Nam. He lost the rhetorical definition of the war, and the loss of life. The justification for the war was perceived as unjust: "Hey, hey, LBJ. How many kids did you kill today?" The 1991 Gulf War was just because the scene was painted as invasion and Saddam Hussein was demonized (and the need for an uninterrupted flow of oil).

The elements of the pentad provide a platform from which to view organizational crises:

- Scene: What was the physical and symbolic scene in which the crisis occurred? In what ways, if at all, did the scene create the crisis? To what extent did the crisis result from an inability or unwillingness of the organization to respond in ways that prevented or mitigated the crisis? How does the crisis change the definition of the scene?
- Act: What acts led to the crisis? What kind of act is the crisis? What acts were done to prevent or mitigate the crisis? What acts have been done and not been done since the onset of the crisis? What acts will be done to correct the crisis?
- Agent: Who are the key players in the crisis? What is the relationship between the players?
- Agency: By what means was the crisis created? By what means is the crisis being sustained? By what means, if at all, is control being returned into the crisis situation?
- Purpose: What purposes motivate the persons engaged in creating and responding to the crisis? What motives account for the crisis and the organization's response to it?

The rhetorical exigency occurs when others—especially the media—perform a pentadic analysis (who, what, when, where, why) of a crisis leading to interpretations which are incorrect or counterproductive to alternative interpretations of the causes, effects, and restoration measures.

QUESTIONS THAT FLOW
FROM A RHETORICAL PERSPECTIVE

In the chapters that follow, authors add their insights to establish theoretical and best practices insights regarding what needs to be said, how it can best be said, and when it must be said. A rhetorical perspective focuses on the meaning that is co-created or is expected of the organization in advance of a crisis, during a crisis, and after a crisis. A rhetorical perspective builds on the premise that the organization needs to look to the quality of its performance as the foundation of its messages that are generated in response to inquiries and implied by the nature of the crisis. Then it needs statements that address the key topics and themes from the perspectives of its stakeholders.

News accounts are part of the driving logic that frames the rhetorical situation. Reporters seek information, interpret information, and form evaluations (including attitudes) which motivate them to act. Crises are events or a series of events that are newsworthy. They attract attention to something an organization has done or needs to do. Reporters do not necessarily focus on faults, but their typical view of the scene suggests that some organization needs to address concerns and issues that are on the minds of markets, audiences, and publics. These concerns focus on issues of control and relate to the markets', audiences', and publics' desire to reduce uncertainty about the crisis, its cause, duration, and magnitude. Why did it happen? Who did and will it hurt? How much damage is it doing or did it produce? How long will it last? What is being done to end it?

One of the key elements of a rhetorical response to crisis is the need for interpretation. On the one hand, this crisis response can open the door to "spinning." That sort of interpretative strategy has received substantial attention. It is not what is thought to be the most ethical and effective rhetorical response. Spinning is a strategy that privileges one party in the crisis—usually the focal organization—to give a self-serving interpretation of the facts. Spinning is a rhetorical strategy, but not one that is likely to bear the challenge of being ethical or responsible. Its ethics are limited by the tendency of spinning to mask part of the truth and give a privileged interpretation. Such an interpretation is likely not to be credible and will not sustain itself against media and stakeholder scrutiny. In short, people who are affected by the crisis simply are unlikely to believe—at face value or after more careful scrutiny—the interpretation.

A rhetorical approach to crisis assumes that people will believe the facts when presented and their interpretations. An ethical rhetorical response requires that the messages co-create a meaning that benefits the organization as well as the people who hold and seek stakes from it. It adds value to the relationship between the organization because it fosters trust, openness, commitment, identification, and aligned interests. The value of this rhetorical approach is that it endures because it helps the key players to know what happened or will happened, what actions have been taken, will be taken, or should be taken to benefit the persons whose interests are at stake.

To further define the latitudes of the rhetorical approach to crisis, the chapters that follow address key issues such as these:

- How should the persona of the organization and of the stakeholders be framed? The persona is the reputation conveyed or enacted by the organization that is the centerpiece of the crisis. Of substantial importance is the "second" persona of the targets of the messages (Black, 1970). A message implies a particular orientation on the part of the persons who are expected to interpret, evaluate, and accept or reject the message.

- How should fault be assessed and assigned? Does forewarning change the kind and degree of responsibility? What do markets, audiences, and publics deserve to know about a crisis that is pending, happening, or winding down because of their interests and their relationship with the organization?

- How should the degree of harm or uncertainty created by the crisis be defined and presented? If it is overplayed, people may respond inappropriately, as they may if it is downplayed inaccurately and inappropriately? How can the organization with actions and statements demonstrate its ability and willingness to reduce the uncertainty and establish the required amount of control as a specific response to the crisis?

- What is the magnitude of the crisis? What would or will its magnitude be? How can people be warned and motivated to specific actions as a means for mitigating the crisis if or when it occurs? Does the organization acknowledge the magnitude from the perspective of those affected by the crisis?

- What is or will be the duration of the crisis? How long can people expect the crisis to last? How does each statement help the audience to monitor its duration?

- How can the human element be addressed appropriate to the duration and magnitude of the crisis? How are cultures of the persons affected or to be affected by the crisis a crucial part of the rhetorical problem? If grieving is a vital part of the response, how can the organization credibly and responsibly engage in or facilitate the grieving? How long should the grieving last? What is the role and rhetorical response required of the organization during the grieving period?

- How can identification be restored or fostered so that the relationship between the organization and the affected parties is created, repaired, or maintained? As Kenneth Burke (1969b) argued, the rhetoric of identification is a form of courtship. Before, during, and after a crisis, key organizations need to foster identifications with markets, audiences, and publics. Some companies, such as nuclear generating facilities, implement community communication and emergency response measures. They communicate with persons who live and work near the nuclear generating facilities. They continually notify these people of the emergency response options that are designed to reduce the impact they would suffer in the event of a release of nuclear material. The identification between the organization and the members of the community is a bond of mutual trust, a demonstration that the company is committed to safety, is willing to work with the community to implement safety measures, because the members of the community deserve no less.

- How can the organization engage in the formation and enactment of narratives that include crisis detection and prevention, as well as crisis response and postcrisis consolidation? Crises are inherently narrative. Reporters and interested parties see them as such. Savvy crisis preparation and response experts know that they are very unlikely to control the narrative, but they can treat it as a rhetorical problem. As such, they need to provide information, interpretations, evaluations and actions that add to the eventual resolution of the crisis, which in narrative terms ends, "and they all lived happily ever after."

- What needs to be said to inform the markets, audiences, and publics? This is not as straightforward as it seems. Often crises require technical interpretations that strain the ability of key persons to understand. Such technical explanations are likely to be vetted by the media and other commentators. This information and explanation must be the best available. It needs to be accurate and ethical so that it sustains itself under scrutiny. It needs to be interpretable with the persons who need the information and advice.

- What statements most responsibly, effectively, and ethically convince the affected persons regarding key interpretations and the subsequent actions? Do the messages motivate the appropriate response?

- What messages are needed for collaborative decision making and to demonstrate the organization's willingness and ability to engage in collaborative decision making?

This introductory chapter is designed to review a rhetorical perspective on organizational crisis. As such, it raises questions and provokes issues more than it addresses and answers them. The chapters that follow can be viewed as a series of experts participating in a panel discussion. The challenge to each of the authors is to add depth and breadth of understanding to the analysis of the rhetorical implications of a crisis as well as to the strategies that can be used ethically and responsibly. Central to this analysis is the theoretic perspective that crisis response requires rhetorically tailored statements that satisfactorily address the narratives surrounding the crisis, which are used by interested parties to define and judge it. As a corporate level specialist in crisis response once said, "I can't prevent a story. I can't shape a story. But I can add my information and interpretation to help the story be right, one that people can trust and use to make their own decisions" (personal confidential comment to the authors, May 1997).

2

Exposing the Errors:
An Examination of the Nature
of Organizational Crises

Dan P. Millar
Millar Communication Strategies, Inc.
Senior Consultant
Institute for Crisis Management

Organizational crises have been defined by many authors, including other writers in this book, each seeking to describe the phenomena. Gathering various elements from several definitions leads to a list of characteristics. A crisis:

- suddenly occurs
- demands quick reaction
- interferes with organizational performance
- creates uncertainty and stress
- threatens the reputation, assets of the organization
- escalates in intensity
- causes outsiders to scrutinize the organization
- permanently alters the organization

The problem with most crisis definitions is that they leave the impression that most crises occur without warning, with little or no prior knowledge of the organization. In this sense, the organization can do little to prevent organizational crises from occurring. From this perspective emerge several beliefs about organizational crises which are, at best, distortions and, at worst, are simply not supported by fact.

This chapter examines a few of these beliefs about newsworthy crisis events, beliefs apparent in popular and business press, using a database of negative business news stories maintained by the Institute for Crisis Management (ICM). To accomplish the overall purpose, I describe the information within the database, apply information gained through use of the data, and finish with several conclusions about business crisis events consistent with the data as gathered and analyzed.

METHODOLOGY

Content analysis of business crisis news stories published in various print media comprises the methodology used by the Institute for Crisis Management. Using news stories rather than government statistics, ICM maintains an ever-growing database of more than 80,000 records from the printed press accumulated since 1989 from the Dialogue information service. More than 1,500 sources are captured by Dialogue, including nationally syndicated newspapers (*New York Times, Los Angeles Times, Wall Street Journal,* etc.), business news wire services, business magazines, business newsletters and trade publications, as well as selected regional newspapers (*Detroit Free Press, Louisville Courier-Journal, Indianapolis Star, San Francisco Chronicle,* etc.). Records on business are downloaded and analyzed quarterly. Once downloaded, the stories are examined to assure no duplicates enter the database. Only *original stories* are collected. In this way, one story distributed by the Associated Press appearing in scores of newspapers appears only once within the database. Although this practice misses the impact of multistory coverage it increases both the validity and reliability of the information. The evolution of the ICM database has paralleled the development of electronic databases and software for penetrating them. The improvements have permitted increased accuracy of story identification and decreased collection redundancy.

The database uses Standard Industrial Classification (SIC) codes to locate *types of industries* experiencing crises. With more than 8,000 industrial categories, the SIC system allows for a relatively specific identification of types of organizations reported to have crises in print media. For example, SIC code #6021 identifies "banks," SIC code #6035 classifies "savings and loans associations-federal." By selecting SIC codes #60xx–67xx, ICM can identify the crises in all types of financial institutions: depository, nondepository credit, security and commodity brokers, insurance carriers, insurance agents, brokers and service, real estate, holding and other investment offices. Whereas the database carries reports on business crises around the globe, the primary focus is on institutions within North America.

The search logic governing the selection of the crises includes a second criterion, *impact.* The logic is constructed so that the selection of database records is based on a term identifying a crisis situation and the actual, or potential, impact of the crisis. The item enters the ICM database only if the nature of the crisis is connected to a consequence of the crisis, real or potential. For example, for "fire" or "explosion" to be included in the ICM database, "fatality," or "xxx dollar loss," or "shutdown" (the impact) would have to be connected in the same record.

Two consequences result from establishing impact as a criterion. The database (a) includes only those situations for which negative outcomes to the business have been specified (improving the validity of a "crisis" database), and (b) probably underestimates the number of business crises because it skips stories in which neither the headline nor the descriptors may describe the impact (improving the reliability). The result is a governing logic based on 73 sets of terms, which representatives of Dialogue describe as one of the "most complex and terrifying" search logics they have ever seen.

The ICM database breaks information into *16 categories* of crisIs types as the basis for analysis:

- business catastrophe
- class action suits
- defects/recalls
- environmental damage
- financial damages
- labor disputes
- sexual harassment
- white collar crime
- casualty accident
- consumer action
- discrimination
- executive dismissal
- hostile takeover
- mismanagement
- whistle blowing
- workplace violence

Each type represents a variety of similar events based on language used by the print media to describe organizational crises. For example, the descriptors *accident, blast, earthquake, collide, tornado, flood, derail, hurricane, blizzard, fire, and sink* cluster into the "business catastrophe" crisis type. Each crisis category, then, is comprised of several characteristics.

The database uses the language of the story headline and the content of the story to determine the *degree of unexpectedness* of the crisis event. For example, some crises occur suddenly with no warning—the bombings at Oklahoma City or the Atlanta Olympics, or the terrorists flying 767s into the World Trade Center towers and the Pentagon. Other crises smolder, a little heat apparent but the organization's management is unwilling or unable to rescue the situation before it goes "public"—Mitsubishi's sexual harassment, the tobacco industry's awareness of the addicting qualities of smoking, AT&T's insider trading, Department of Defense and Department of Energy disposal of chemical and radioactive waste, and Enron's shifting certain ventures off the books to hide drag on profitability. In short, the nature of the crisis—sudden or smoldering—can be identified.

The *origin of the crisis* can be identified, for example, *teacher, worker, executive, vendor, customer, activist, investor.* For analysis, the ICM database clusters these terms into three originators of crises: management, employees, other (i.e., external agent–terrorist, natural phenomenon–hurricane, etc.). However, because the several descriptors remain in the database, the "other" category can be subdivided to provide more precise analysis.

Many records in the database also include company names and states in which the crises occurred. Because of the manner in which ICM stores the data, the industry, the region (i.e., state), the company can be identified sharpening analysis of individual events and trends.

Because only original stories appear in the database, the *number of crisis events* can be identified and counted. Also, the number of original stories written about any one event can be counted. As seen later in this chapter, this ability allows for a description of which crisis categories and individual crisis events generated the most "original" news stories within the business pages of the 1,500 news sources monitored.

Finally, *sources of information* specified within the article can be identified as well. Using a variety of terms to capture that information, eight clusters of "sources" emerge from the descriptions of crises: activists, consumers, customers, employees, executives, government officials, judicial personnel including law enforcement officers, and union members and leaders.

The database permits the counting of the number of different crisis categories, the name of the organization, its geographic location (in most cases), the industry, the impact of the event, the number of events, the number of original stories written about the event, the sources of information mentioned in the story, the amount of warning before the crisis occurrence and the primary cause of the crisis.

ANALYSIS OF THE PERCEPTIONS OF ORGANIZATIONAL CRISIS

Perception #1: Business Crises Have Increased Significantly in the 1990s

It takes just a few noteworthy crises to give the impression that the number of business crises has grown. Consider only the year 2000:

- More Deaths Reported in Tire Probe; Safety: Latest summary includes 4 fatalities in accidents since Firestone's August recall
- Oxygen tank mix-up is suspected in 3 deaths. (Carriage-by-the-Lake nursing home, Bellbrook, Ohio)

- Air Panel Fines Power Plant $17 Million Over Pollution; Environment: Violations at Long Beach facility trigger largest penalty ever levied by AQMD. Firm must install state-of-the-art equipment.
- First Nationwide Class Action Lawsuit Filed Against Ford for Economic Damages, Personal Injuries and Death Caused by Improper Placement of Ignition Modules
- Nabisco Becomes a Pawn of Philip Morris's Marlboro Man: Consumers Resist Escalating Kraft Boycott.
- Weed Wizard's makers recall parts that may fly off during use.
- African Americans File $5 Billion Bias Suit Against Microsoft; Plaintiffs Charge Discrimination in Pay and Promotions
- Lucent Fires CEO, Issues Gloomy Sales Prediction; Ouster comes as no surprise because of the company's deteriorating performance
- AT&T Announced Breakup of Company on Worries of a Hostile Takeover Due To Falling Stock Price.
- Actors go on strike, seeking to raise pay for ads on cable TV
- Sotheby's Ex-Chief Pleads Guilty in Collusion; Courts: Auction giant is also expected to admit to one criminal count in case involving price-fixing with officials from its competitor Christie's.
- 22 Women to Split $1 Million Harassment Settlement; EEOC Sees Trend Involving Immigrants
- Northrop to Settle Whistle-Blower Suit; Aerospace: Firm will pay $1.4 million but denies allegations it overcharged the Air Force for B-2 bomber manuals
- Putnam Executive Pleads Guilty to Conspiracy and Wire Fraud, Reports U.S. Attorney
- Crew members of cruise ship charged with sexual assault
- EPA Cites Ventura Foods for Chemical Release Reporting and Record-keeping Violations; Proposes $302,528 Fine.

However, assuming printed articles reveal the extensiveness of crises during any one year, the annual number has remained relatively constant during the 1990s. Figure 2.1 reports the total number of crises for each year since 1990. The number of business crises ranged from a low of 5,891 in 1999 to a high of 8,342 in 1994.

Some years have a higher incidence of crises than others. For example, in 1994, USAir and American Eagle planes crashed, killing everyone on board, GM experienced a strike idling more than 30,000 workers, labor strife continued at Caterpillar, Eli Lilly's drug Prozac went on trial (again), Intel introduced the flawed Pentium chip, and Jack-in-the-Box cooked up *E. coli*.

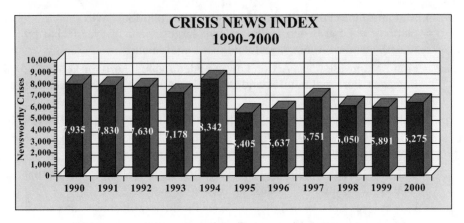

FIG. 2.1. Organizational crises during the 1990s.

Although the annual number of business crisis events has fluctuated but not steadily increased during the decade, significant change within crisis categories has occurred. Figure 2.2 reports the changes in the nature of business crises.

The major shift during the past 11 years has been a *decrease* in the number of environmental accidents, hostile takeovers, mismanagement, and white collar crimes and an *increase* in class action lawsuits and defects and recalls. Workplace violence continues to creep up, as it has throughout the decade, but still accounts for relatively few organizational crises.

Crisis Categories Compared		
(expressed as a percent of the year's crises)	*1990*	*2000*
Casualty accidents	4.8	4.9
Catastrophes	5.5	5.0
Class action lawsuits	2.2	28.4+
Consumer activism	2.8	1.6
Defects and recalls	5.4	16.7+
Discrimination	3.3	3.5
Environmental damages	7.8	1.9–
Executive dismissal	1.3	.8
Financial damages	4.2	4.4
Hostile takeover	2.6	.5–
Labor disputes	10.3	11.0
Mismanagement	24.1	6.3–
Sexual harassment	.4	.5
Whistle blowing	1.1	.7
White collar crime	20.4	9.3–
Work violence	3.8	4.4

FIG. 2.2. Changes in crisis events between 1990 and 2000.

The shift in the categories may indicate several social changes:

- greater attention to potential environmental damages precipitated by the Exxon Valdez accident and subsequent governmental crack-downs on polluters,
- a growing willingness by consumers to seek restitution from and punishment of an organization who sells a defective product or commits some wrong,
- greater attention to procedures which expose an organization to fraud, embezzlement, and other forms of theft.

The federal Whistle Blower Act which became law in the middle of the decade apparently has had little effect on the number of crises caused by informants taking internal problems outside the organization.

The greatest growth has occurred in class action lawsuits. This is an interesting phenomenon because class action lawsuits follow the wrongdoing, or the perceived wrongdoing, of a person or organization. Crisis events that occur after the original crisis, but are related to it, are labeled "aftershocks." The increase in the number of class action lawsuits suggests, then, that the crisis is not over when it's over. Expect the *aftershock* of a lawsuit against the organization.

With changes occurring over the decade, changes between years might be expected and that is the case. The percentages in Figs. 2.3 and 2.4 illustrate that crises occur at different amounts depending on the year. In the

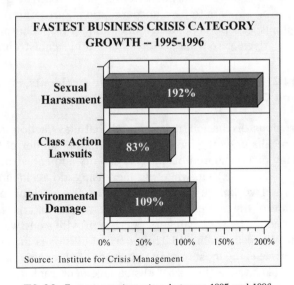

FIG. 2.3. Fastest growing crises between 1995 and 1996.

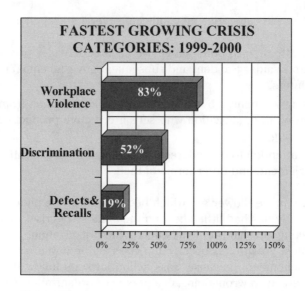

FIG. 2.4. Fastest growing crisis events between 1999 and 2000.

middle of the decade, the years between 1995 and 1996, sexual harassment, environmental damages, and class action lawsuits jumped. At the end of the decade, 1999 and 2000, workplace violence, discrimination, and defects and recalls increased.

Despite changes in the nature of crises during the 1990s, the actual number of crises has steadied, or declined, during the period. The belief that crises are increasing appears to be a misperception. Furthermore, our analysis of the first misperception builds a foundation for dispelling another, that organizational crises arise from accidents and other catastrophes.

Perception #2: Most Business Crises Involve Accidents, Chemical and Oil Spills and Workplace Violence

From the previous discussion, it was found that class action lawsuits and defects and recalls grew the most during the 1990s. Neither of these crisis categories may be considered business accidents and catastrophes, either natural or person-made. But, while not increasing, do accidents, chemical and oil spills, and workplace violence account for the most business crises?

Computation of the percentage of the total number of crises during the 1990s accounted for by each category of crisis provides one way to answer the question. When including all 11 years and all crises in the database, white-collar crime is the most frequent business crisis accounting for nearly 1 in 5 crises (17.2%; see Fig. 2.5). Mismanagement ranks second (13%), closely followed by labor disputes (12.8%). Although casualty and environ-

1. White-collar crime (17.2%)
2. Mismanagement (13%)
3. Labor disputes (12.8%)
4. Class action lawsuits (9.3%)
5. Defects & recalls (8.0%)
6. Business catastrophe (7.1%)
7. Casualty accidents (5.5%)
8. Financial damages (5.0%)
9. Workplace violence (4.4%)
10. Environmental damages (4.3%)
11. Discrimination (4.2%)
12. Executive dismissal (2.1%)
13. (tie) Consumer activism and Hostile takeover (1.9%)
15. Sexual harassment (1.6%)
16. Whistle blower (1.2%)

FIG. 2.5. Rank-order of percentage of all crises during the 1990s.

mental accidents and natural catastrophes do account for many business crises—combined about 1 in 6—they do not comprise the bulk of the crises experienced by organizations.

A second way to address the question of cause is to add across crisis categories to determine the percentage of crises attributed to sudden crises, specifically accidents, catastrophes, and violence. The sudden crises categories include business catastrophes, casualty accidents, environmental damages, and workplace violence. Combined these account for 20% of the total number of crises reported during the decade. Eighty percent of the crises experienced by organizations occurred because of other factors. That is, the problem exists within the organization, may even be known to employees and managers of the organization; for one reason or another it is not resolved before it escapes the organization thereby coming under the scrutiny of the news media, regulatory and law enforcement agencies, and the public. The conditions leading to a crisis linger, smolder for a time, until something causes them to flare. Then, what may have been a controllable business problem, becomes an uncontrolled business crisis.

Another way to address the question of cause is to examine the nature of crises in various industries. Space does not permit more than a couple of examples: health care and higher education.

Notice the differences between crises in the health care industry and all industries (see Fig. 2.2). Although the four highest-ranked crises are the same, the percents differ with health care experiencing high amounts of white-collar crime and mismanagement (see Figs. 2.6 and 2.7).

Whereas the top four remain the same, the percentages differ. Sexual harassment becomes more frequent in higher education than either among all organizations or health care. In short, different industries suffer different

1. White-collar crime (20.4%)
2. Mismanagement (19.4%)
3. Labor disputes (10.7%)
4. Class action lawsuits (8.6%)
5. Casualty accidents (7.7%)
6. Workplace violence (5.6%)
7. (tie) Defects & recalls and appropriate financial damages (4.4%)
9. Whistle blowing (3.8%)
10. Discrimination (3.1%)
11. Executive dismissal (3.0%)
12. Catastrophes (2.4%)
13. Consumer action (2.3%)
14. Sexual harassment (1.8%)
15. Environmental damages (1.6%)
16. Hostile takeover (.7%)

FIG. 2.6. Rank-order of percentage of health care crises during the 1990s.

crises. The perception that organizational crises are most frequently fires, explosions, workplace violence, and chemical spills is wrong; it is a misperception of organizations in crisis.

The answer to the question—Do accidents, chemical and oil spills, or workplace violence account for the most business crises—is no. Most crises are neither accidental nor sudden. Rather they reveal questionable, illegal, or unethical activity by someone within the organization frequently involving other members of the organization or people who routinely interact with organizational personnel. Not only does the problem exist, someone in the organization knows, or has neglected to learn, of its existence. The

1. Discrimination (18.9%)
2. Mismanagement (17.8%)
3. White-collar crime (11.5%)
4. Labor disputes (8.6%)
5. Sexual harassment (6.2%)
6. Defects & recalls (5.3%)
7. (tie) Executive dismissal and Workplace violence (4.7%)
9. Financial damages (4.4%)
10. (tie) Catastrophes and Casualty accidents (4.1%)
12. Consumer action (3.3%)
13. Whistle blowing (1.3%)
14. Executive dismissal (2.1%)
15. Class action lawsuits (1.2%)
16. Hostile takeover (0%)

FIG. 2.7. Rank-order of percentage of higher education crises during the 1990s.

problem is not lack of knowledge, but rather an unwillingness to report the problem or to resolve it.

If accidents and spills fail to comprise the majority of organizational trials then it follows that most crises do not happen in heavy industry.

Perception #3: The Industrial Sectors of Business Cause Most of the Crises

Over the course of the decade, the majority of crises has arisen in the nonmanufacturing sectors of the United States economy, reflecting the overall change from a manufacturing to a service economy. To illustrate that conclusion examine Fig. 2.8, which reports, in rank order, the most crisis-prone industries for the years of the 1990s. By "crisis-prone" is meant accumulating the greatest number of records within the ICM database.

Of the top ten industries, only motor vehicle and aerospace manufacturing would be considered heavy industry. Both of these industries make the list because of labor strife and defects and recalls, not because of accidents, natural catastrophes, environmental damages or workplace violence (see Fig. 2.8). Following from the beliefs that accidents and heavy industry are most involved in organizational crises may be the belief that employees or "natural events" are responsible when most crises occur. This belief is not supported by data.

By clustering the titles of various organizational positions (CEO, chairman, supervisor, employer, worker, employee, operator), the ICM analysis of organizational crises suggests the vast majority are caused by managers not employees or outside agents (see Fig. 2.9). Managers annually cause approximately 3 of 4 crises whereas employees cause roughly 14%, with the remaining 11% caused by "acts of God" or agents external to the organization (i.e., terrorists, activists, competitors).

Why does the belief persist that employees or external agents cause most crises? ICM's conclusion is that belief follows belief in the other misperceptions. That is, accidents, environmental spills, and other crises result from operations. If a person believes these categories account for

1. Banks and other depository institutions	6. Aerospace
2. Stock and bond brokerages	7. Telecommunications
3. Insurance	8. Air transportation
4. Motor vehicle manufacturers	9. Computer software
5. Oil and gas extraction operators	10. Pharmaceuticals
(measured by percentage of incidents recorded in the ICM database)	

FIG. 2.8. Rank-order of crisis-prone industries: 1990–2000.

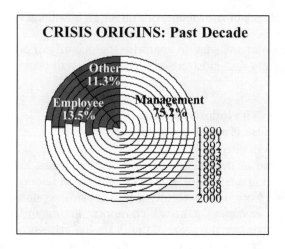

FIG. 2.9. Causes of organizational crises in the 1990s.

most crises, then the belief suggests that a "worker" committed some error. Frankly, few managers "operate" the processes of manufacturing. However, our analysis recommends a different conclusion—management decisions or indecision are the roots of most business crises.

CONCLUSION

The analysis of business crises during the 1990s recommends that three beliefs commonly held about such crises are not based on accurate information. In short, the beliefs are false stereotypical perceptions:

- business crises have not increased but have remained relatively constant
- accidents, spills, and workplace violence are not the dominant crises
- "heavy industry" does not experience the most crises
- employees are not responsible for business crises

Analysis based on the ICM database did reveal the following about crises:

- the nature of crises may be changing from operational to human causes
- smoldering crises outnumber sudden crises
- service industries experience the most crises

- heavy industry crises may involve labor disputes, and design or manufacturing defects
- management, either through poor judgment or criminal acts, causes the majority of crises faced by business

The findings suggest at least two additional comments. First, the misconception of organizational crisis needs to be changed to diminish the sudden, coincidental perception while increasing the smoldering, mismanaged nature of crises. To the justification offered by the analysis in this chapter can be added the observation that most sudden crises, although momentarily disruptive, come under organizational control rather quickly and disappear. What does not disappear quickly, however, may be the consequences of the "sudden" happening—governmental (elected and regulatory) investigation, legal actions and stock value declines, distrust by employees and customers of the company. Furthermore, most smoldering problems can be located and resolved before they flare into uncontrollable crises if the climate of the organization and the means to report them can be created.

Second, the preponderance of smoldering crises suggests that most crises can be prevented if identified and corrective actions taken. Experience leads me to believe that thousands of smoldering crises are resolved in this manner by astute employees, middle managers, and senior executives because the public never hears about them. But to do so requires a shift of managerial attitudes and business cultures. It also requires mechanisms for locating and reporting smoldering crises without endangering the reporter while protecting the rights of the participants until a full investigation can occur.

One start toward reconceptualizing crises and emphasizing prevention is to examine and alter the misperceptions currently held, the central purpose of this chapter.

CRISIS PREPARATION:
PLANNING FOR THE INEVITABLE

Robert L. Heath

Crises are predictably unpredictable. Savvy managements know crises can occur, but they don't know when they will happen. For these reasons, wise managements strive to understand the sorts of crises that could affect their organizations. They plan and prepare for the eventuality of a variety of crises. They take a management view by getting crisis processes and responses into place. Communication crisis planning can even include preparing key stakeholders for the possibility or eventuality that a crisis could happen.

Managements have learned that one size of crisis preparation does not fit all. That theme is emphasized in the chapters in this section. These chapters work together to stress the importance of strategic preparation for crisis response.

This preparation requires understanding the processes of communication as well as considering the kinds of messages that can and will be needed to address various kinds of crisis that may occur. A rhetorical approach to crisis planning and response features the need to understand the alternative channels, publics, and messages that must be approached strategically.

Several premises are examined in this section that can guide and aid executives, including communication managers, as they plan for crisis response by applying the following best practices:

- Organizations need to consider all of the publics that will want timely messages when a crisis occurs.
- Practitioners are wise to advocate the need to develop a crisis response plan, train to implement that plan, and practice implementing it.
- Plans need to be tailored to the unique circumstances of each kind of organization and the types of crises that it might encounter.
- Practitioners are wise to plan for the ways they can monitor the results of their communication and other responses so they can track the success or failure of the response options they are employing.
- Organizational culture should be excellent and lead to responsive, proactive planning and to a sensitive interest in key publics' response to the messages and other crisis response options used by the organization.
- All of what the organization does and says during a crisis enacts its response and will be interpreted as reflecting the character of the organization.
- Each crisis constitutes a rhetorical problem that requires specific and tailored responses.
- Wise practitioners use case studies to help define best practices by learning from successes and failures typical of the organizations they represent and counsel.
- Control is a huge incentive in the planning and response process. However, wise practitioners realize that they cannot control the response of others but that they must provide information and evaluations that help demonstrate the organization's ability and willingness to exert self-control through effective management policies and procedures.
- Crisis planning and preparation is sharpened by practitioners' realization that key publics seek to attribute cause to explain why a crisis occurred and why management responded as it did.
- Planning should address the vulnerability of an organization as well as its strengths. Such is also the case for its ability to create and deploy messages and make other communication responses.
- Collaborative decision making that engages the organization's leadership to develop a comprehensive and useful plan can reduce the conflict that can harm the implementation of the plan.

The chapters in this section open consideration to the following research questions:

- Careful, thorough, and comprehensive planning can increase the likelihood that organizations will suffer fewer threatening crises because they are vigilant.

- Careful planning increases the likelihood that crises will not last as long and be as damaging than if less careful preparation has been made.
- Crisis plans that are more complex offer more responses but also require more training and practice to implement effectively.
- Organizations that are more self-reflective are likely to create and implement a more successful crisis response and communication plan. Such organizations are more likely to develop multiple options and achieve requisite variety.
- Case studies often are used in ways that tend to support researchers' predispositions rather than challenge conventional wisdom and lead to advances in practitioners' and scholars' understanding of crisis planning and response.
- Organizations are likely to suffer less damage from crisis when they are prepared to repair relationships and demonstrate commitment to promote and protect their stakeholders' interests.
- Vigilant preparation can reduce the likelihood of a crisis and increase the responsiveness of the organization to demonstrate its ability to reestablish control over its operations.
- Attribution theory offers substantial promise for understanding in depth how crisis type, communication strategies employed, and stability affect key publics' image of organizations.

Chapters in this section apply theory, explore case studies, and offer best practices that constitute a sustained argument that can be offered to members of senior management who balk at the prospect of budgeting for crisis planning, training, and practice. The underpinning rationale offered here is that strategic preparation fosters responses that reduce the likelihood that crises occur or, if they do, mature to a danger level. Better preparation is cost effective because it reduces the likelihood of a crisis, as well as its impact on the organization. In short, effective planning can be cost effective. This is a lesson many organizations have learned, the hard way.

Effective crisis response planning should be an important part of executives' stewardship. It can help them ethically and responsibly manage the organization's resources. A badly managed crisis can harm nonprofits' fund raising. It can result in lost customers or investors. It can make the organization a less desirable employer. If the organization is a government agency, it can lose taxpayer favor. Planning and response is more than just being a good communicator. Effective planning prepares the organization to be responsible and effective in its communication.

3

Crisis Management: Toward a Multidimensional Model of Public Relations

Don W. Stacks
University of Miami

No corporation is immune from crisis. In 1989 an average of 10 crises annually challenged the management of large American corporations (Mitroff, Pauchant, & Shivastava, 1989). Effective crisis management requires that organizations take a *proactive* stance to potentially dangerous situations, one that allows management to maximize its opportunities and minimize the dangers it confronts. However, most corporations today have yet to adopt an orientation that suggests something different than "the worst will not happen to us, the worst will happen to others" (cf. Mitroff et al., 1989; Wisenblit, 1989). This orientation suggests that at best corporate America is woefully unprepared for a major crisis—one that may face it sooner than planned.

This chapter does not seek to identify crisis management situations. It offers instead a theoretical model based on effective public relations to establish the underlying rationale for dealing with crisis situations. It also recognizes that preparation for crisis is perhaps one of the best survival strategies that any organization can attempt. How an organization communicates its crisis management plan, however, is one area of crisis management that has been neglected, both in terms of descriptive research into past crises as well as theoretical development of crisis management communication campaigns. This chapter, then, proposes a model of communication based on public relations principles that allows for maximum communication of the crisis management plan adopted. Quite simply, it is

37

axiomatic that a plan is only as good as the communication campaign developed for it.

CRISIS MANAGEMENT PLANNING

Crisis management planning is actually a corporate communication plan that seeks to manage various public perceptions of the crisis. An effective crisis management plan is a well thought out campaign that seeks to reduce any negative impact, while generating positive outcomes during a crisis period (Lin, Stacks, & Steinfatt, 1992). Traditionally, "good" crisis management includes three elements: There must be a plan of action, the organization must have early warning systems in place to signal potential crisis situations, and the organization must have a crisis management team in place with the power to act. As many organizations have learned, these elements are minimal; they do not ensure success. To be minimally effective a crisis management plan must be formulated that centers on three critical communication channels: Who does the communicating? Who are the audiences with whom to communicate? What communication channels are to be used in the crisis?

Clearly, focus of crisis management planning should be on communication strategies. However, it appears that *communication* planning within the crisis management plan is not provided major emphasis, other than an identification of the various external and internal channels that should be employed. Empirical studies clearly indicate that although crisis management planning is given priority by corporate America (Fink, 1986; Stanton, 1989; Wisenblit, 1989), very few actually have comprehensive crisis management plans in place (Wisenblit, 1989). Further, current crisis management models are usually unidimensional in nature—they seek to describe the crisis and then put into place a set of guidelines for managing the crisis. Although this model may provide some means of affecting the crisis situation, it clearly falls short of an integrated, proactive model.

TOWARD A MULTIDIMENSIONAL MODEL

In proposing a crisis management model, a number of dimensions must be identified. Thus, an *effective* crisis management model presented takes on multidimensionality lacking from most extant models. Minimally, the model should take into account the type of public relations potentially available for practice. It must focus not only the type of organization itself, but also the interorganizational divisions that must act on the plan. Furthermore, it makes several assumptions that are pivotal to any crisis management model. These are discussed briefly in the following section.

Assumptions

To be effective, a crisis management plan must have an advocate. That advocate must be a member of top management, a member of the management "team." Grunig and Grunig (1992) argued that to be effective communicators, management must include in the boardroom a public relations practitioner. Further, that practitioner must have input to corporate decision making. Thus, *proactive crisis management begins with a communication professional taking part in the development and subsequent dissemination of the crisis management plan.*

An effective crisis management plan takes into consideration the type of organization that will implement the plan. That is, the crisis management plan must tailor its communications based on the way the organization communicates. There are several organizational models that provide different forms of communication, each assuming a different corporate mentality toward communication. Mechanistic models, for instance, tend toward a communication model of downward communication flow with little feedback, whereas organismic models tend to look at communication as a way of satisfying organizational needs and relations. Thus, *effective crisis management needs to take into account the type of organization the plan will encompass.*

Third, even within the organizational system, departments (subsystems) will organize differently, often according to function. Within the mechanistic organization, for instance, upper management must respond from an organizational needs and relations perspective, while those on the line or loading dock are modeled after the traditional mechanistic organizational pattern. Thus, *effective crisis management must take into account not only the organization as a suprasystem* (cf. Stacks, Hickson, & Hill, 1991), *but also as a composite of various subsystems.* The effective crisis management plan must include not only extraorganizational communications, but also internal communications to ensure effectiveness. (This is perhaps the most singular gap in the majority of crisis management plans.)

The type of communication employed must be examined. From an information-processing perspective, certain forms of communication are more effective than others, given specific *a priori* constraints. That is, at times communication is most effective when it travels downward as directives, at other times communication is best when approached as an interactive process. Thus, at times a crisis management plan must be communicated directly, with little or no feedback. At other times it must be approached as a persuasive message, one that reinforces or alters held perceptions of the crisis situation. *The type of communication message, then, becomes a fourth part of our model.*

Finally, the approach the public relations practitioner takes to the public relations function affects how the crisis management plan will be adopted. However, as Grunig and Grunig (1990) pointed out, a good public relations model is one that adapts to changing situations, one that understands both the nature of the organization and its various publics. Thus, *an effective crisis management plan will be communicated via the most appropriate public relations model for its intended audience.*

What does this model look like? Imagine for a moment a cube (see Figs. 3.1 and 3.2). On one face we have the different metaphors an organization may operate under. On a second face we have the different metaphors the organization's subsystems may operate under. On a third face we have the different types of communication possible. On a fourth face we have the different public relations models available. On a fifth face we have the various publics that are to be influenced, and in turn influence the plan. Finally, on the sixth face we have the outcome, the "x" so to speak.

Mathematically, we can state that effective crisis management is a function of five independent yet interrelated variables. Each has the potential to influence the outcome of a crisis, yet all are intercorrelated. Thus the crisis management model might be described as follows:

CM = f{public relations model + communication strategy + affected publics + organizational structure + organizational infrastructure}.

In the following sections we briefly discuss each component—face—of the model.

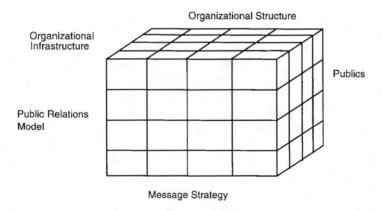

FIG. 3.1. Basic model.

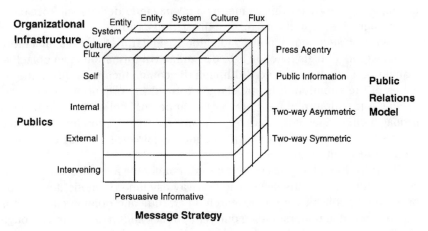

FIG. 3.2. Fleshed model.

TOWARD A MULTIDIMENSIONAL MODEL
OF CRISIS MANAGEMENT

Public Relations.   Based on the previous discussion, it should be obvious that any effective crisis management model must incorporate a public relations component. Furthermore, top management, the "management team," must include the public relations practitioner as one of its immediate members. An effective crisis management model, then, has as a *necessary condition* for success input from its public relations element, as directed by a full member of the corporate management team. This alone, however, will not, nor can it ever, assure effective crisis management. To be effective the crisis management plan must be communicated in an effective manner, one that takes into account the various components of effective communication discussed earlier as basic assumptions to the working model.

Of the several public relations theories posited, Grunig's (1976) may be best suited to the crisis management situation. This theory focuses on both the direction and purpose of communication, yielding four historically developed models of public relations: press agentry/publicity (one-way, asymmetrical), public information (one-way, symmetrical), persuasion (two-way asymmetrical), and relational (two-way symmetrical). Each model is tied to a particular communication function. The *press agentry/publicity* model serves a promotional function; it is a direct conduit between organization and a passive public and promotes a particular point of view. The model focuses primarily on a public external to the organization. Because of this, and a perception that the communication provided is mainly distorted or incomplete, many view this as merely a propaganda device, one that often fosters negative impressions among the various publics.

The *public information* model's function is similar, but focuses on a more journalist function. Its function is to disseminate information in an objective manner to a passive audience. Although the communication reflects the realities of the situation, it is still slanted toward the organization, often reflecting a less than real view of what is happening, but still a step beyond propaganda. It does not, however, prepare an organization for a potential crisis situation, nor does it provide adequate guidance for participation in the management of such situations.

The third model focuses on *persuasion,* employing a feedback look to ascertain message effectiveness. The two-way asymmetric model focuses on persuading publics based on research on attitude and opinion change. It is a step forward in understanding different publics and their needs. Although two-way, it is still unbalanced and depends on some form of strategic positioning from the organization.

The fourth model is *relational.* It seeks a mutual understanding between the organization and its publics. The two-way symmetric model tries to serve a mediator role, focusing not on prediction and control (as does the scientific persuasion function of its asymmetric other) but on a mutual understanding between all publics.

Publics. An effective crisis management plan must segregate its publics. We can divide publics into four primary audiences, three of which impact directly on the crisis management plan. Publics generally consist of the *self* (an internal public, focusing on ethical and honest treatment of the situation by the PR person), the *internal public* (that associated with the organizational chart from top to bottom), the *administrative public* (top level corporate leaders), and the *external public* (further divided into primary and secondary publics based on influence). The self presents the link between the public relations requirements of the organization and the top management team. The administrative public are those individuals who will plan and execute the crisis management plan). The internal public (what Stacks, 1991, identified as an *intervening* public, one that affects not only the total plan but various external and administrative publics) is those affected by the crisis and who must not only carry out the various crisis management plans, but also understand the "big picture." The external public consists of those people whom the crisis communications have targeted (government, business, media, gatekeepers, and so forth).

Most crisis management plans emphasize the administrative and external publics, placing less emphasis on the internal public. Given the purpose of crisis management, this is reasonable, yet shortsighted. *An effective crisis management plan must be communicated throughout the organization if it is to be effective.* Not only must top management understand the larger picture, but those who must suffer through the crisis should also understand what is happening, why it is happening, and how it affects them. Given the competitive nature of the media—and the increasingly sophisticated means for transmitting stories from crisis sites—*all* organizational personnel, from CEO to janitor, have the potential to "tell the organization's story." Thus, all should be briefed about the plan; all should be considered when examining the communication strategy to be employed.

Organizational Structure and Infrastructure. There are any number of different organizational models that describe and predict organizational behavior on a suprasystem level. Perhaps the most appropriate to crisis management, given the emphasis on metaphor in this model, is that of Gareth Morgan (1986). Morgan suggested that organizations operate as one of several different metaphors. The most primitive metaphor is that of the *entity,* the organization as a machine, the traditional model of classical management theory and scientific management. Associated with the machine metaphor is the organization as an organism metaphor, either as an open system approach or as a "brain," a holistic information-processing system. A more advanced metaphor is that of the *system,* the organization as reflected as political or psychic systems that dictate forms of governance. An even more advanced metaphor is the organization as a *culture,* creating an organizational reality through shared perceptions. Finally, there is the metaphor of the organization as a *change agent,* or the organization in a constant state of flux and transformation.

Each of these metaphors describe an organization that interacts with its environment and subsystems differently. Each requires that different communication strategies be adopted in order that any communication in general, and crisis management plans in particular, are communicated and executed effectively. Each metaphor is best suited for one or more public relations models; each treats its publics differently.

The entity model views the organization as a whole. Its communication functions tend toward a marketing or management of communication from top-down perspective. Within this model, however, are different metaphors that focus on how that entity is organized. The most basic of these structures is that of the machine, or what has been labeled as a "scientific management" approach. Here communication is merely a means to an end; feedback is limited or nonexistent. An offspring of the entity model embraces open systems theory whereby organizational needs are identified in a way of establishing homeostasis or balance. This approach adds to the entity a means of self-control through feedback. However, that feedback almost always focuses on maintenance functions or organizational "unity." An extension of the open systems entity is that which compares the organization to a brain. Here the organization is seen as not only reacting to its environment, but also capable of learning through its experiences. It can self-organize and seeks inputs from all parts of the organization. The limiting function, however, is still survival. All entity models view the organization as something static; change, when it comes, comes slowly if at all.

A second metaphor compares the organization to a political system. Here interaction is no longer simple, but is viewed in terms of power and control. Morgan posits two types of systems metaphors. One is political and views all communication as purposive and grounded in establishing power, of creating social order. The political metaphor's impact suggests that organizational ideology may be more important than organizational rationality. That is, the organization is not simply an entity but a diverse set of interests, each of which competes for rather limited resources. Further, an understanding of the political structure rather than the organizational structure provides for message strategies. A second metaphor emerges from that of the political organization: the organization as a psychic prison. This metaphor explores the darker side of the political organization, one which explores the control created by power relationships.

The third organizational metaphor is that of culture. Here organizations are seen as resting on shared meaning systems that create organized action. The organization in effect is larger than its structure and its political systems are contained within the larger culture the organization has created in adapting to its particular spot or niche. Thus, the cultural organization has its own belief systems and way of rationalizing its existence. It creates and lives within its own mythology. The cultural metaphor establishes an organization that is interconnected between its environment and its strategic management; the organization becomes what it is and what it is attempting to do. The culture becomes the function; the culture becomes the product; *the organization empowers itself to be itself.*

Finally, we have organizations as change agents in and of themselves, a transformation model. Change, Morgan argued, takes place on one of three levels. Autopoietic manifestation is where we view change from the viewpoint of our own organization and environment that suggests organizations can change the nature of change through interdependence. Mutual causation focuses on organizational change as a function of interconnectiveness and relationships that shape stability and change. Dialects focus on the generation and reframing of opposites in order to effect change. Transformation, however, is hardly ever predictable; the organizations, as change agents, tend to ignore the basic problems associated with change in the first place (those originating from entity or system or cultural systems or subsystems within the organization). Understanding the logic of change may be problematic; organizations that serve as change agents are better understood after the fact than on some *a priori* grounds.

Even Morgan's metaphorical model is rather simple. At the macro level it suggests that organizations consist of conflicting but orderly subsystems. Taking his model one level down, the same four metaphorical models can be found in any organization, regardless of its adherence to a particular metaphor. That is, even in the machine metaphor there will be divisions, subsystems, departments, or whatever that take on the metaphors discussed as reflecting other organizations.

As far as crisis management is concerned, each must be taken into account when preparing the crisis management plan. Each represents a different public relations problem in gaining not only acceptance but also awareness of that plan. A plan that is not accepted throughout the organization is an ineffective plan. Thus, the ability to communicate the plan's logic, requisite parts, and projected impact on the targeted publics may be inhibited by a failure to account for organizational structure *and* infrastructure.

Communication Strategy. The foregoing discussion identified the major elements of a model of crisis management. Across all elements has been a concern for communication. The final face of the model deals with the message and message strategies to be employed. For the most part message strategy can be viewed as several distinctly different message types. Basically, message strategy should seek to inform or persuade. Informative strategies take into account situations where quick access to information is required or information needs to be disseminated as quickly and widely as possible. Informative strategies often take the form of asymmetrical, one-way communications. Persuasive strategies take into account situations where reinforcement or attitude change is necessary and are either transitional (one-way or two-way with delayed feedback) or transactional and asymmetrical. The message strategy adopted should conform to the public relations model chosen, which in turn should be chosen as the most representative for the particular organizational structure/infrastructure and best for the targeted public(s).

When considering communication strategy, the communication channels must be explored and included in any message strategy. As noted earlier, one of the three elements of a "good" crisis management plan includes the channels of communication through which messages are transmitted. Although most crisis management plans focus primarily on external channels to the detriment of the entire plan, both internal and external channels must considered when developing message strategies. Channel capacity, direction, and load are also important considerations when planning message strategy.

PUTTING THE MODEL TO WORK

Earlier it was suggested that this model of crisis management was best viewed as a cube. Each face of the cube represented a different element or process. This cube can be further defined as a number of cubes, much like the Rubik's Cube puzzle. The model is analogous to the Rubik's Cube in that different parts of the crisis management plan represent different parts of the cube.

In planning for a crisis the model posits that each of the elements or processes needs to be taken into account. That is, once the plan has been developed it must be communicated first through the organization. To effectively communicate the plan, the organization's basic structure, as well as its infrastructure must be identified. Once accomplished, the various publics must be identified and message strategies created. For infrastructure communications it may be best to use a public information-type model; information essential to the workings of most online units is part of an information awareness process. However, it may be that certain divisions are best served via a two-way model, where reinforcement or attitude change is required to implement the crisis plan.

At the onset of a crisis, an automatic press agentry approach may be the best strategy; information might be prepared to let the public(s) know that the organization is working on the problem (and in potential control of that problem). When communicating with employees who need reassurance, such as after a natural disaster, employing a press agentry public relations strategy may be the first of several steps through which the organization seeks to gain control of both perceptual and real problems it may face. Obviously, different organizations will have different structural composition, requiring that messages and delivery systems (public relations models) will vary within and between organizations.

Of particular impact will be the type of communication strategy employed in dealing with external publics. The majority of extant theory and research in crisis management has focused on surveying those organizations with crisis management plans, examining who has been targeted, in what way, and through which channels. Once the organization has been persuaded that a workable crisis management plan exists, the next step is to plan for its execution. Again, the cube model offers potential strategies based on the organizational and public relations needs of that organization. The key component across situations, however, is the need for public relations input at top management, representation on the "management team." This model is predicated on that assumption.

HYPOTHETICAL EXAMPLE

As noted earlier, crises take on many forms. Effective proactive management requires that the public relations practitioner have some model prepared to counter potential crises. The example employs the model in a proactive fashion and, although hypothetical, represents an actual public relations problem.

The organization is a large hospital undergoing expansion. The problem facing the public relations person is that one of the lots used by both patients and staff (to include doctors) is being relocated so that a new parking garage can take its place. The problem is multiplied by the fact that this lot is closest to the hospital (and why the parking garage is being placed there). There are several potential crises facing the practitioner. First, there is the organizational structure associated with large, modern organizations. Second, there is the organizational *infrastructures* associated with the organization. And, third, there are multiple publics, each with their own particular communication problems. The parking lot problem might not sound very "crisis-like," but little events such as these often create very large problems for the organization.

What does the practitioner do? If the practitioner were following the model, he or she would already have taken the organizational "pulse" and identified the organizational structure. It may be a cultural model, one that has in its corporate history simply enacted change without consultation, or it may have assumed that, much like an entity model, that information flows (is open to and read by the affected publics) once it is put in the system. Further, because the organization is complex, its infrastructure will produce its own communication problems. Patients, for example will have their own perspective of the hospital. Medical staff will have their own perspectives on communication. Administrative staff with have yet another perspective. Further, each will have different message channels from which they get their information. The first step, then, would be to identify how each unit perceives itself. The administrative units may operate as an entity model. The medical staffs will be divided into at least two levels: professional (doctors and nurses) and nonprofessional (clerical and assistants), each most likely adopting a different models. The patients will have different perspectives on the infrastructure, depending on a variety of variables that, while not controllable, are predictable: reason for visit, degree of illness, number of prior visits, interaction with administration, medical and staff, and so on.

Understanding the organizational structure and infrastructure then help identify the publics affected. The practitioner is affected, how will he or she react? This knowledge allows the practitioner to predict how others will react. Clearly identifying the internal, external, and intervening audiences will help in assessing message effect. External publics are mostly patients—they must be forewarned about the upcoming changes. How? Often through intervening publics, in this case the doctors and nurses who send them to the hospital, as well as the admissions personnel who set up the initial visit. And there are others, to include the hospital security force. Major predictable problems are going to be with the internal publics, those who have been using the parking lot for years. But, with the hospital, each internal public is also a potential intervening public—talking in elevators on floors about problems can cause small, insignificant problems to quickly become full-blown crises.

Communication strategies will be influenced by both the public relations model employed and the message strategies chosen. (Note: There is no one message strategy, but multiple strategies must be prepared.) Clearly, all four public relations models discussed will be used. A press agentry approach will get the message out to the largest number of people. Examples might be handbills handed out as staff leave work or placed on car windows. Handbill notices may be placed in the cafeterias and waiting rooms. Second, internal and external public information campaigns will seek to get information into the internal media channels (i.e., the hospital's television channel, newsletters, on bulletin boards, memos to department heads, etc.). Press releases will be sent to the local external media (e.g., newspapers, radio and television, local HMOs newsletter articles at the least). The message strategies employed are factual and straightforward, aimed at getting the message out.

Both two-way models will be employed as persuasive vehicles aimed at gaining understanding for why the changes are occurring. The asymmetric model might employ dialogue between an interviewer and hospital administrator about the need for change and the expected outcomes. The product would be transmitted through all possible channels. The symmetric model might employ one-on-one discussions with department heads, and other opinion leaders. The administration might meet with departments to discuss the potential problems and steps taken to reduce them. Two-way communication with patients would be accomplished through the information desk, possibly establishing a "hot line" for parking information, and follow-up calls about their hospital experience that included the parking situation. Obviously, the two-way models would require research—surveys, focus groups, one-on-one interviews—with each of the publics. But all would be planned from the beginning.

This example is hypothetical, but is based on a real problem the author worked on with a real hospital. The real problem was more complex: The nursing staff was in the middle of negotiating a new contract with central administration, who were asking for concessions. The hospital was so large that patients often complained about getting lost, and the parking problem would acerbate it even more so. The public relations administrator's background was in marketing, not management and definitely not public relations. The proactive crisis management plan did not include all that was discussed, the model was just beginning to be developed, but parts were employed. The parking lot was closed, there was confusion and resentment, and there were little "fires" to be put out, but the large-scale crisis did not happen.

SUGGESTIONS FOR FUTURE RESEARCH

The proposed model suggests several lines of inquiry available to the public relations researcher. From a theoretical perspective, is the model truly additive? If so, do any of the elements take precedence over others, should they be "entered" into the equation in a "step-wise" manner or do they affect outcomes equally? The model assumes that failure to account for a particular element reduces outcome, but does that failure zero-out the outcome, if so, is the model multiplicative? And, if so, what are the interactive effects? Statistically, how much variance does the model account for in terms of crisis management planning? Crisis management action? How much variance is accounted for by the individual elements (and potential interactions)? From an applied perspective, how many organizations practice crisis management from this perspective? With what effect? From a systems perspective, how many crisis management plans cover the elements, but fail to account for the hypothesized additive nature of the model? Is the model applicable to public relations in general?

SUMMARY

Although this model has yet to be tested, its intuitive logic is appealing. So, too, is its simplicity. However, as with many models, simplicity yields complexity. Exactly how each element affects others is not clear, nor is it clear how potentially competing strategies will work within the single organization. The model presented here, however, is a first step in attempting to understand the dynamics of crisis management planning and implementation in the modern organization.

4

Constructing Response During Uncertainty: Organizing for Crisis

Teresa L. Holder
Peace College

This chapter presents Weick's (1969, 1979) theory of organizing as a perspective for organizational strategic planning in crisis situations. From an information system's perspective, the response before, during, and after a crisis is connected to overall, ongoing organizational strategy and issues management. Weick's perspective provides a framework of thinking about crisis communications as ongoing issues management.

THE PROCESS OF ORGANIZING

Organizing for a crisis involves behavioral communication cycles—what Weick refers to as enactment, selection, and retention. During enactment, members attend to information by using "rules" and "cycles" to interpret and process ambiguous information. For example, organizations must develop information-processing mechanisms capable of detecting trends, events, competitors, markets, and technological developments relevant to their survival. This concept holds true for departments, groups, or individuals (Daft & Weick, 1984).

For crisis management, *enactment* plays a key role during the preparation phase as an organization plans for or anticipates potential crises. According to the Society of Human Resource Management survey, only half of 5,700 companies included in their survey reported having a crisis management plan in place before September 11 (Kiger, 2001). Kiger concludes that because crises do not happen in a vacuum, preparation has to include wide-range strategies such as how the organization will communicate with internal and external publics even when there may be limited information and resources.

Ostrow (1991) criticized action plans by pointing out they are based on the assumption that crisis evolve to defined scenarios. He argues that although there are certain predictable patterns of how particular types of crises evolve, are handled by the media, and then decline in public interest, crises rarely fit procedural plans. "No 'expert' can predict when information will develop that may make a crisis worse or help resolve it. Nor can they predict who may be motivated to act on the information that may be available, whether in support of or against management interests" (p. 24). Coombs (1999a) pointed out one of the weaknesses of the crisis communication literature is the tendency to be "heavily descriptive." For example, much of the crisis communication literature comes from authors offering simple lists of do's and don'ts or lessons learned from one or more cases, rarely providing "verifiable support for recommendations" (p. 19).

From Weick's (1969) viewpoint, it is not the plan itself, but the *reflection process of planning*, which enables organizations to act appropriately. The implications for planning is that it can best be understood as thinking in the future perfect tense. It isn't the plan that gives coherence to actions. Coherence comes from the fact that when the act to be accomplished is projected in the future perfect tense, the means for accomplishing the act become explicit, and the actions run off with greater coherence. It is the reflective glance, not the plan per se, that permits the act to be accomplished in an orderly way. A plan works because it can be referred back to analogous actions in the past, not because it accurately anticipates future contingencies (p. 161). So, when crises do occur, an organization may be better able to act more quickly and effectively because it has thought ahead to develop some procedural rules for handling the situation and communicating with publics. By projecting into the future, it has "reflected on the past."

Planning requires establishing, monitoring, and maintaining good relationships with all of the organization's publics. Public relations officers of California State University–Northridge cited that their relationship with the media (which was already established) helped them in handling their campus crisis when the earthquake occurred (Fearn-Banks, 1994). Crisis communications specialist Andre Gilman (Soundbites, 1998) is quoted in *PR Tactics*, "from a reputation management standpoint, it's vitally important in a crisis situation to have a spokesperson who can provide factual information" (p. 4). In the company there must be someone who is prepared to present a dependable and reliable corporate personality who can handle the pressure with the media. "If the first time you talk to the media is during a crisis, then something's wrong" (Couretas, 1985, p. 100). Even for large corporations, that personality should be initiated at the local level and established on a continuing basis. Barkley and Evergreen's Crisis TRAK™ program includes a 24-hour hotline card designed on the assumption that companies have to view crisis management as an ongoing process (Stateman, 1997). "The card makes it clear to our clients that we are available 24 hours a day, 7 days a week," according to its president Mike Swenson.

The *selection* phase of organizing requires organizations to decide how to interpret information by relying either on established rules or behavioral cycles. During the pre and postphase of a crisis, an organization can rely more on routine procedures for communicating with its publics. When a crisis occurs, organizations must be prepared to rely more on communication cycles (e.g., multiple channels, greater frequency, and more face-to-face communication) as a way to deal with and communicate ambiguous information. In his evaluation of companies' responses to September 11, Leonard (2001) quoted a manager whose company, Bovis Lend Lease, had to be evacuated from the nearby MetLife building:

> Advance planning was of limited help for this disaster. I did pull down our dusty old disaster recovery plan from the shelf and looked at it. While some of it did help and did give us a framework to operate from, nothing really could've have prepared us for a disaster of this magnitude. (p. 3)

Although ongoing planning helps provide readiness, crisis by its very nature has the element of the unplanned and unexpected, making Weick's idea of selection a necessary part of managing a new situation.

Retention occurs when ways of handling crisis become part of routine organizational procedure. Through the process of planning and training, assembly rules for responding during a crisis become part of organizational memory. Role-playing exercises and actual crisis situations become part of the ongoing process of organizing and modifying policy regarding crisis situations. Leonard (2001) commented that September 11 "tested the mettle" of many employers, but in part, the planning done to anticipate and prepare for Y2K had actually helped prepare companies for the problems created by the World Trade Center disaster. And while no one would want to face again what happened on September 11, the lessons learned will inform how future crises will be handled.

PRINCIPLE OF REQUISITE VARIETY

According to Weick (1969), organizing is directed toward removing equivocality from the information environment. The basic raw data on which organizations operate are informational inputs that are equivocal.

The principle of requisite variety states that very complex or equivocal messages require equivocal communication—behavioral cycles to enact them. This explains why difficult information is more effectively communicated face-to-face rather than by written communication. Face-to-face interaction uses both verbal and nonverbal channels, which help clarify the message or allow the nonverbal to "soften" the blow. Face-to-face interaction also allows for a quicker cycle of acts and interacts to reduce uncertainty. When crisis occurs, uncertainty is very high and that creates a greater need for processing information. For example, Johnson & Johnson's efforts regarding the Tylenol scares were praised even though the company had to correct earlier stated misinformation because information was given quickly and frequently. In contrast, organizational "rules" are effective when simple, routine, unambiguous messages require only uncomplicated processes for enactment.

As stated earlier, although companies may anticipate the types of crises they may face, most companies cannot accurately anticipate what will actually happen. What this means is that what must be said and how it will be said will be unanticipated. From Weick's (1969) perspective, the important thing may be *to simply act or be quick to respond*. Otherwise, an organization may be forced into a pattern of reacting rather than acting, or worse—develop a pattern of defensiveness and inadequate communication. For example, Levine (1993) stated that when news is negative, silence will create disaster. In this situation, she argues, if news leaks, facts will be distorted or omitted. However, if a company is able to release information effectively in a press conference, it has exercised more control over what is said and how the information is presented to the public.

Weick (1969) pointed out that these interlocking behaviors related to information processing will either be characterized by control or chaos. Control can occur when an organization enacts information effectively by managing what is said, when it is said, or how it is said. For example, Dilenschneider and Hyde (1985) recommended procedural control by suggesting a "control center approach." Part of this approach is to have a clearly defined chain of command, which is understood by all employees and a control center designed to provide tactical supervision to manage process.

INFORMATION THEORY AND STRATEGIC COMMUNICATION

The way in which management handles the crisis and its communication responsibilities matters as much as how the event itself is resolved. For example, even after a second Tylenol scare and other drug tampering cases, Johnson & Johnson have still been regarded as effective in crisis management. In contrast, Exxon has suffered in credibility even though the chance of future spills occurring has been reduced and the damage to the beaches addressed (Harrison & Prugh, 1989).

In October 1988, Sybron Chemicals, Inc. faced a crisis when an accidental chemical leak required the evacuation of about 60 nearby residents producing fear and anxiety. Sybron received negative publicity because of this incident as well as other concerns about the plant.

In order to address the problems and become accepted as a responsible trusted "good neighbor," Sybron decided to take immediate and credible action regarding each of the concerns identified by neighbors, local officials, and state regulatory officials. Sybron provided regular reports on its efforts, progress, and intended actions to neighbors, local officials, environmental groups, and the press. As part of its communication efforts, Sybron conducted 300 1-hour in-home interviews (rather than telephone interviews) that provided in-depth information on the real concerns, knowledge, expectations, needs, and views of area residents. Hendrix (1995) stated that this particular strategy may have been among Sybron's most effective as the kitchen table and living room interviews eased fears and anger, encouraged communication, and also presented information about Sybron and its operations. In the process of conducting the in-depth interviews, Sybron communicated that it was really committed to listening and responding to the community. The interviews as well as a computerized 24-hour phone system allowed neighbors to get instant information about the plant and make calls to neighbors in the event of a problem, reducing equivocality of the situation.

TIMING IS IMPORTANT

In all crisis situations, the goal is to reduce uncertainty even in the absence of "information." For example, messages that reassure sincerity, commitment to finding out what happened, willingness to explain, or messages that control rumor, or maintain credibility need to happen quickly (Mallozzi, 1994). Jim Burke of Johnson & Johnson has been praised for his immediate action and ability to communicate concern for consumer safety regarding the Tylenol murders. Although Warren Anderson's trip to Bhopal, India to assess the damage was controversial, from Weick's (1969) perspective, it was "doing something" and perhaps more effective in the long run than taking no action. At least to some, his action communicated concern even though his ability to make a difference was minimal. If a company fails to take action quickly, chaos is likely to occur allowing speculation and rumor to take over.

In addition to action, an organization must *talk* about what action it is taking. Simon (1986) cited a case of a mid-sized, northeastern university which failed to do this when one of the female students was assaulted and raped. Even though the president took quick and appropriate action in meeting with the student in her dormitory along with a follow-up call to her parents, his indecision about whether or not to talk with the local press or the editor of the student newspaper (he didn't) caused him to lose a timely opportunity. He failed to present to the media what steps the university had taken as well as provide input in how the story would be communicated to the public and student body. Although he felt the story had been mishandled, he decided not to approach either newspaper about it. Without any knowledge or input from the university on what actions had been taken, the stories based only on police reports, were sensationalized, according to the president. When a letter (see Appendix A) was sent to parents approximately 3 weeks after the incident, the content was defensive and antagonistic. It also failed to reassure parents or communicate any sadness about the incident (pp. 6–7).

According to Geibel (1996), it is the company's responsibility to fill up the information vacuum. Although most newspaper people are responsible journalists, they are under extreme pressure to meet their deadlines. If an organization doesn't feed the press with the information they need, they'll look for other, less knowledgeable and reliable sources. After the Challenger disaster, "NASA's 24-hour communications vacuum destroyed more than 20 years of excellent media relations" (p. 26).

When Bowater South faced lawsuits for wrongful deaths because of a major accident on U.S. I–75 due to dense fog (created by the emission by Bowater's nearby plant), Bowater failed to handle the crisis when it neglected to bring out all of the facts, which would have helped resolve the issues (Maggert, 1994). Because of the fear of litigation, the company took a defensive stance and silenced their one spokesperson creating confusion for the press and public. When the company was forced to withhold information because of pending litigations, feelings of distrust were created toward Bowater. Also, according to Sheil, Bowater's new manager of public affairs and governmental relations at the time, in the confusion of the crisis, Bowater neglected to say it was sorry for the families who had lost loved ones.

Waste Management, Inc. in Oakbrook, Illinois faced a crisis when it was accused of illegal storing and disposing of wastes. Public disclosure of this significantly impacted its stock market value (it fell $800 million within a short period; Couretas, 1985). After dealing with the crisis, the company attempted to strengthen its communication program by hiring a community relations staff. The new staff was given the task of improving the corporate image with local community groups and leaders by creating an environmental compliance program to eliminate compliance problems. To further improve their image, the company also produced a series of four TV com-

mercials, which aired on network and local public affairs and news programs.

Enactment after the crisis should emphasize follow-up, as outlined in the
crisis plan or suggested by the crisis itself. As business returns to normal,
follow-up communication management can rely more on routine organizational channels and communication vehicles as well as responsive programs or campaigns.

ORDER OUT OF CHAOS: A SUCCESS STORY

Even though they had planned for crisis, when an earthquake hit southern
California on January 17, 1994, California State University, Northridge
(CSUN) encountered a crisis they had not anticipated. The university had a
crisis plan in the event of an earthquake, but they did not plan to be without any access to buildings, telephones, power, supplies, or any communication and information-gathering tools. In the midst of the crisis, the public
relations officers had to reconstruct background information and communicate to appropriate audiences even though they had little information of
their own.

Without even the use of a manual typewriter, the public relations officers
successfully relayed information to the University's various publics following the earthquake. They had to answer the obvious questions students
would ask: Is the campus safe? Where will I park? Where will classes be
held? When will classes begin? Will commencement be postponed? Many
staff members did not know if they still had a job, whether or not to report
to work, when and where to report, or whether the campus was even safe.
See Appendix B for an outline of strategies used by the public relations staff
when the earthquake occurred. CSUN was cited for its effectiveness, because campus officials were able to organize quickly and effectively proc-
essed a great deal of ambiguous information with its various publics.

CONCLUSION

Neglecting to plan for crisis, many organizations are reactive rather than
proactive in dealing with the media and communicating with their publics.
Weick's (1969) model provided a way of analyzing the larger information
system in which crises are managed. The benefit of crisis planning, from
this perspective, may not be that it provides clear-cut answers to all possible disasters, but rather provides a structure by which organizations can
view uncertainty and manage information. Several areas of research are
proposed from this system's perspective:

1. How does crisis planning foster an organizational culture of crisis prevention and responsiveness?
2. What system characteristics enable organizations to resolve crises effectively?
3. Which (and in what ways) are new communication and information technologies effective tools for reducing equivocality during crisis?
4. What types of crisis training make organizations more adept in handling crisis situations?

The model's emphasis on information process also provides a useful perspective for constructing messages and interpreting information during organizational crisis. Examining crisis communication from Weick's theory of organizing contributes toward public relations by placing an emphasis on information process and including crisis communication as part of overall strategic planning.

APPLICATIONS FOR PRACTITIONERS

Prepare for Action

Planning for potential crises helps organizations spring into *action* when crisis does occur. In one of his books, Weick (1979) relayed a wonderful story about a group of hikers who get lost in the mountains and panic because they can't find their way back. At the point of almost giving up, one group member realizes he has a map, which enables them to find their way back. Afterwards, they realize the map was for a different mountain range! The point Weick makes is: When you're lost—any map will do. During crisis, action leads to clarifying and understanding what to do even as the events unfold. As Weick (1979) asserted, it's only by acting that organizations and individuals can begin to make sense of what is happening. Yet, the cardinal rules for crisis communication "Tell it all and tell it fast" and having a prepared statement within 24 hours are often forgotten at the onset of crisis, resulting in textbook cases of what not to do.

Monitor and Reflect on Others' Crisis Situations and Management

When Union Carbide experienced its crisis in 1984 at the Bhopal, India plant, journalists contacted other chemical companies, like Dow, seeking information and explanation. When journalists couldn't get through to Union Carbide for answers, they turned to other companies like Dow who knew they had to treat the crisis as their own.

In February 2002, the last of the Big Five consulting firms announced its plans to separate its firm's accounting and consulting functions. This action is a direct response to Enron's recent collapse. The consulting firms hope to bolster consumer confidence and avoid crisis by association in the aftermath of Enron and Arthur Anderson's relationship with the energy company. They know they simply cannot ignore what has happened.

Recently, in the community where I live and teach, there have been three assaults at one of the other colleges causing some panic and creating uncertainty on that particular campus. What's happening there could easily happen on any campus and requires us to reflect on our own vulnerabilities. Their crisis should cause us to pause and ask, "How well will we have prepared?" and "What will we have done about it?"

APPENDIX A: BROOKE COLLEGE LETTER

[This letter appears in Simon, R. (1986). *Public relations management: A casebook.* pp. 6–7. All names, dates, and places were disguised.]

Dear Brooke Parents:

Many of you have perhaps heard by now, on Wednesday September 20, at 1:30 a.m., a Brooke student was raped just off the campus grounds near the Valley Road gate.

I am writing you to ask your help in convincing your daughter that she should take all precautions necessary to assure her own safety. While we not wish our students to be fearful of leaving their dormitories, we do want them to realize that they must exercise caution. As you know, the campus is large and heavily wooded and it is impossible for us to provide security coverage for all of it at all times. Our security people regularly patrol the roads and walkways through the campus, but they cannot keep all of the property under surveillance constantly.

Our students have been repeatedly told:

1. Not to walk or jog alone at night.
2. To be careful in the woods during the day and stay out of them at night.
3. To travel in groups of three or more at night.
4. To keep their dormitory rooms locked and not prop open exit doors.

As a matter of fact, the very week of the rape, a notice was sent to all students reporting an afternoon incidence of exhibitionism and warning them to take the above precautions.

However, some students assumed that "it can't happen to me." We hope it will not. As has always been the case, our security officers and residential living staff are trying to help assure that it does not by patrolling, counseling, and speaking to students privately and in groups. But we need your help and the cooperation of the students as well.

APPENDIX B

Information-seeking and communication strategies used by CSUN public relation officers after the southern California earthquake

Public relation officers:

- Contacted the coroner to find out if there were any student deaths (in the collapsed apartment building near campus)
- Relayed what information they had regarding the status of campus building face-to-face with reporters who asked
- Obtained cell phones to communicate with media
- Set up tents to be used as a command center for the university president (the primary spokesperson) and her staff
- The PR officers began communicating with the following publics: staff, faculty, visiting faculty for the spring semester, disabled students, foreign students, students who lived in San Fernando Valley, students who lived outside the area, and deaf students
- The university president, Dr. Blenda Wilson communicated with the following publics: the regents, heads of alumni organizations, governor, mayor, and other officials
- Created fact sheets and backgrounders from memory
- Researched destruction, damage and deaths in order to communicate with media and publics
- When it was discovered that two CSUN undergraduates had died in the apartment building (across from campus) which had collapsed, letters were sent to the families and half-page ads in the form of a letter from the president were placed in the *Los Angeles Times* and the local *Daily News* to express sympathy to not only the families and friends of the two students but for all who lost loved ones in the Northridge Earthquake
- Six phones were set up during the first week enabling the public to call in for information. Hotline operators were given scripts that were updated daily with new information for students, faculty, and staff.
- An additional line was set up with recorded information updated daily

- A TDD line was set up for students who were hearing impaired
- PSAs and news releases were released to the media announcing the telephone lines
- Cell phones were used for outgoing calls; phone trees were created to communicate with various internal publics—school deans, department heads, etc.
- A backgrounder called the "General Information Guide" was created which included names of university officers, details and statistics of the earthquake's effect on campus, and other facts about the university
- Reporters were given guided tours as they requested
- The university president announced in a news conference that classes would begin four weeks after the earthquake, followed by full-page ads.
- The student newspaper, *The Daily Sundial*, published its special registration issue at another campus, which provided students with vital information as well as prepared readers with the damage done to the campus.
- The student radio station set up operations in a temporary location created two daily live broadcasts of interviews with various university officials to provide update information about campus
- The University Information Bulletin, normally distributed once a week, was distributed daily in an attempt to disseminate information about the library, mail, counseling, transportation services, etc.
- A letter was mailed to faculty and staff from President Wilson, which reported damage estimates and plans for restoration
- Twenty-two information stations were set up in tents at every major campus entrance point

5

Reframing the Organizational Exigency: Taking a New Approach in Crisis Research

Curt Bechler
Aquinas College

Crisis research continues to develop as an area of concern and interest. How a crisis is conceptualized and perceived shapes the way in which researchers study the exigency and come to understand the organizational response. There are three guiding premises in this chapter: First, scholars working on crisis research have focused on the methods and symbols organizations may use to prepare for and respond to crisis situations. Second, because most of the research has focused on effective crisis response mechanisms and the need for crisis containment, crisis situations have been treated as isolated events rather than necessary correctives that are interrelated with the culture and history of the organization or industry. And third, as the conceptualization of crisis changes, the types of research questions that are salient also change. These questions have implications both for the direction of crisis research and for how public relations practitioners and organizational leaders engage in crisis management.

The crisis literature is replete with studies and suggestions demonstrating the value of both crisis preparedness and planning (Quarantelli, 1988). Much of the information has been garnered from organizational case studies utilizing public information (i.e., in many cases media reports) to gain insights and draw conclusions about an organization's response or lack of response to crisis situations (Bensen, 1988; Berg & Robb, 1992; Frame, Nielsen, & Pate, 1989; Hall, 1991; Ice, 1991; Sen & Egelhoff, 1991; Williams & Treadaway, 1992).

These approaches to crisis communication, however, underscore and emphasize the uncertainty of crisis situations, the negative nature of crisis, and the need to return the organization to the status quo or an improved position. David Hurst (1995) underscored this in his book on crisis and organizational change, when he noted, "Crises and surprises have usually been regarded as dysfunctional" (p. 118). Thus, although many studies give insights into the negative nature of crisis and practical advice concerning the organizational response, these same studies have become the lens that now seems to limit how a crisis can be understood, potentially predicted, and perhaps even valued.

THE STATE OF CRISIS MANAGEMENT RESEARCH

Crisis situations vary in definition and type. They span the globe and differ in magnitude and impact. From gas leaks in Bhopal to gas attacks in Tokyo to oil spills in Alaska, to earthquakes in Los Angeles, organizational crisis situations may be intentionally or unintentionally created. During the last century, particularly the last two decades, organizational crises have continued to grow both in size and number. Crisis situations have threatened the survival of a number of organizations and often the safety of individuals within society. Many large organizations experience crisis situations on an annual basis (Mitroff, Pauchant, & Shrivastava, 1989). As a result, crisis management has become a growing topic of study.

Several prominent definitions identify characteristics of an organizational crisis. Egelhoff and Sen (1992) in their conceptualization of crisis built on a definition by Hayes (1985): "Crises arise when there is a major incongruence between the expectations of a corporation and what happens in the environment" (p. 36). Egelhoff and Sen (1992) differentiated crisis typologies, arguing that unique variables create and define each type of crisis. Billings, Milburn, and Schaalman (1980) discussed the organizational exigency as an event or situation with limited resolution time that could create an important loss for the organization. Hermann (1963) noted that crisis, "(1) threatens high-priority values of the organization, (2) presents a restricted amount of time in which a response can be made, and (3) is unexpected or unanticipated by the organization" (p. 64).

Although crisis situations differ in size and scope, a number of interrelated variables have been identified as occurring in most crises. First, a crisis situation is often unexpected within the organization (Hermann, 1963; Richardson, 1992; Tortorella, 1989; Wisenblit, 1989). Second, exigencies force the organization to change its immediate approach to information processing (Hermann, 1963; Smart & Vertinsky, 1977; Tjosvold, 1984). Finally, as organizations cope with crisis situations those in leadership narrow their communication channels, thus changing the way information is distributed (Hermann, 1963; Tjosvold, 1984). Although theorists differ on the types of phases or stages that mark the evolution of a crisis, many agree that crisis situations seem to have marked stages from development to resolution (Fink, 1986; Slatter, 1984; Sturges, Carrell, Newsom, & Barrera, 1991). The one point (or phase) that has the broadest level of apparent agreement is that crisis situations do have a resolution point (Fink, 1986; Milburn, Schuler, & Watman, 1983a, 1983b; Sturges et al., 1991).

Most of the discussion concerning the organizational crisis has focused in two areas: preparing for the event, and responding to or managing the crisis situation (Quarantelli, 1988). It has been argued that the research surrounding crisis management draws from no established paradigms but can be delineated by two perspectives—the technical and the symbolic (Coombs, 1994). The *symbolic* focuses on the use of language to influence perceptions of the organization and crisis. The *technical* is directed at crisis preparation and planning.

Regardless of how crisis management has been delineated, a number of themes recur. The crisis management plan has been discussed within a variety of contexts (Barton, 1991; Fink, 1986; Flecker, 1990; Hall, 1991; Markwood, 1988; Milburn et al., 1983; Quarantelli, 1988; Sen & Egelhoff, 1991; Seymour, 1991; Smart & Vertinsky, 1977; Sturges et al., 1991; Wisenblit, 1989). Research validates the importance of the crisis management plan, or advanced crisis planning, particularly with regard to product disasters (Wisenblit, 1989). Preplanning allows those responding to the crisis to have a measure of certainty in the midst of chaos. The preparation provides the decision maker with a framework from which to see the crisis, and thus lessens the response uncertainties. However, crisis planning does not offer the organizational leadership any guarantee of successful resolution (Quarantelli, 1988).

The crisis response has also received attention. Communication that explains the crisis or provides meaning to internal and external publics is perceived as being vital for organizational success (Barton, 1990, 1991; Benson, 1988; Coombs, 1995; Egelhoff & Sen, 1992; Fink, 1986; Flecker, 1990; Ice, 1991; Markwood, 1988; Seymour, 1991; Sturges et al., 1991; Tortorella, 1989; Weinberger, Romeo, & Piracha, 1991; Williams & Treadaway, 1992; Wisenblit, 1989). Initially, the crisis literature focused on broad response strategies, but increasingly crisis response strategies are narrowing. This narrowing includes: typologies of crisis situations with specific information-processing characteristics (Egelhoff & Sen, 1992); various types of rhetorical or impression management strategies (Allen & Caillouet, 1994; Coombs, 1995; Hobbs, 1995; Ice, 1991; Williams & Treadaway, 1992); and specific managerial behaviors that may accompany crisis situations (Benson, 1986; Slatter, 1984).

The implicit and often explicit goal that marks the crisis literature and research is the desire to return the organization to the status quo, or better yet to a point where public opinion is more positive after the crisis concerning the organization. Sturges et al. (1991) made this point clear, "Beyond physically coping with the aftermath of a crisis, the objective of crisis management is to influence public opinion to the point that post crisis opinions of any constituent audience are at least as positive, or more positive, or not more negative, than beforehand" (p. 23). A few attempts have been made to link the crisis to the organizational culture—changes in the culture needed prior to the crisis situation or in light of the crisis situation (Hurst, 1995; Mitroff, Puachant, Finney, & Pearson, 1989; Silva, 1995). However, most of the current research focuses on either influencing internal and external publics during the crisis and in its aftermath or on making the correct decision in response to the crisis situation.

Theorists describe in neutral terms the pros and cons of using various public relations and management strategies in their discussion of the pragmatics of crisis. This neutrality demonstrates little or no regard for the ethical implications of assisting an organization in crisis. Egelhoff and Sen (1992) noted in their conclusion that their crisis contingency model, "suggests that firms need to design systems that are within the bounds of the organization's information-processing capability, if they hope to engage in responsible crisis management" (p. 480). Their article is indeed successful as one of the best "attempts to develop a broad contingency theory about corporate crises and crisis management" (p. 479); but, like most articles dealing with crisis, it does not delineate in any detail "responsible" versus "irresponsible" crisis management. Delineations of this nature could lead to a broader understanding of how a crisis is framed and understood.

THE CRISIS AS A NECESSARY CORRECTIVE

When a crisis occurs the immediate *response* most often targeted by researchers is the way an organization can act responsibly and effectively. Image management strategies and crisis management plans provide the organizational leadership with a means to identify successful communication strategies and information processing networks. These plans may return the organization *to the status quo*, but also prompt an improved position in the marketplace. However, this perspective of studying and practicing crisis management implicitly assumes . . . that the organization has a right to life; and that the crisis incident is an isolated event with little or no relationship to a faulty organizational culture.

An example of this type of thinking may be instructive at this point. In a recent study of public relations practitioners (Bechler, 1995), a practitioner was asked: What is your overarching goal in helping a client respond to a crisis? The response was: "The terms are usually stop the bleeding. It is damage control at first. You have to make sure your first actions don't magnify the problem or compound the problem. [The] First thought is to look at all the effective audiences and try to put yourself in their place and find out what they are thinking. [The] Goal is to get back to business as usual and get the whole issue off the table."

One of the problems with current crisis research and practice (as this public relations practitioner unknowingly acknowledged) is not that practitioners and researchers seek to stop the bleeding or help an organization provide a strong first response (the need for organizational assistance during a crisis is beyond question); rather, the point of contention comes in how crisis management is perceived, pursued, and then evaluated. A significant problem occurs when the crisis is viewed only as an obstacle to be controlled, contained, and put "off the table."

This type of conceptualization divorces the exigency from the context of the organizational culture and its corresponding norms, roles, traditions, and values. When this occurs, crisis management or crisis communication may help the organization overcome "a dysfunctional incident" and perhaps even maintain a positive reputation, but never really deal with the internal problems that prompted the event in the first place. A crisis management strategy based on this conceptualization (a one-size-fits-all approach) while providing a short-term solution to the "current" organizational problem, may in fact reinforce patterns that lead to an even greater and potentially more damaging crisis.

This approach (often unintentionally) takes a linear, singular cause perspective (Crisis event > Correct response to the event > Resolution and return to the status quo). By treating the crisis as an isolated event to be dealt with using symbolic and technical strategies, it fails to account for the systemic nature of organizational life. Rarely do events have singular causation, most "incidents" come to life through the organizing actions of numerous individuals throughout the system. Weick's (1988) discussion of organizational sensemaking and the numerous variables involved in responding to a crisis (i.e., commitment, organizational expectations, etc.), exemplifies the multilayered, interrelated nature of organizational life. Thus, individuals within the organization foster a framework where multiple causation is inherent to most crisis situations.

These crisis situations may be provoked through ongoing, interrelated, organizationally rewarded behaviors that are dysfunctional, unethical, and even immoral. The crisis may appear to have singular causation, the death of a founder or an accident of terrible proportions. But, over time (and often through later study), the event is seen as being symptomatic of larger organizational problems. For example, unethical or dysfunctional patterns of leadership may show up only when the founder creates a crisis through death or departure (e.g., Robert Maxwell's suicide and the ensuing financial collapse of his communications empire). Sexist and racist behaviors or standards may be scrutinized only when a crisis brings them to light (e.g., the racist behavior at the Denny's Restaurant in California). Finally, the disregard for product safety ratings and the ongoing filtration of important information may only show up when a terrible accident occurs (e.g., the Challenger accident). These examples of crisis events illustrate the integrated nature of the incident and the organizational system and culture.

In these situations, the event is damaging to the organization, but it may also be of value both on micro (to the organization) and macro (to society at large) scales. Although initially painful, crisis situations can have long-term value. Without crisis, much needed organizational change may not occur, or may be very slow in coming. David Hurst (1995) noted a number of organizations that either developed during times of societal crisis (the Quakers in preindustrial England), or which experienced positive internal change and increased effectiveness as a result of a precipitating crisis (Russelsteel, Nike, Chrysler, General Motors, and G.E., to name a few). He argued that organizations like ecosystems go through a life cycle where crisis is an important and necessary phase in ongoing growth and life.

Research by Frame, Nielsen, and Pate (1989) concerning the organizational change that occurred in a *Chicago Tribune* printing plant reinforces this argument. They studied an ongoing labor crisis within the printing plant. The crisis in this case was the catalyst for increased effectiveness and productivity. Their findings, like Hurst's (1995), demonstrated the potentially transformational nature of an exigency.

In many ways, this view of the organizational crisis is comparable to the perspectives found within the literature on conflict. The research on conflict (Folger, Poole, & Stutman, 1993) has identified a number of variables that could be related to how the organizational crisis can and should be viewed; Conflict is inevitable. Every organization will face crisis. Conflict often brings about innovation. Crisis situations can bring about important institutional changes and much needed innovation. Conflict can further develop and broaden important relationships within the organization. Crisis situations can increase team effectiveness and improve relationships between those within the organization and between internal and external publics. Hurst (1995) provided a fascinating example of this set of outcomes in his discussion of Russelsteel. Although many aspects of conflict are dangerous and dysfunctional, conflict within the literature is perceived to be relationally and organizationally important.

Crisis situations can play a similar role in organizational life, and the literature needs to develop this perspective. By focusing mainly on crisis containment and image management, researchers and practitioners may be encouraging change-resistant cultures to maintain patterns of behavior and communication that are damaging to those without power in the organization and to society as a whole. Reframing the popular view of crisis so that it is also perceived as a necessary and important corrective is a step toward better understanding how organizations can respond effectively to chaotic and harmful situations. Changing the way in which a crisis is understood may also enable the organization to effectively respond to other problematic behaviors that have been embedded and protected within the organizational culture.

A NEW AGENDA FOR CRISIS RESEARCH

If crises are perceived as having the potential to be necessary correctives, then the crisis must be viewed as an integrated, rather than isolated, event. For change to take place, the event itself must be connected to the way in which the members of the institution organize their communication behaviors to reach their goals. Several studies (Bechler, 1994; Glaser, 1994; Hurst, 1995; Kurzbard & Siomkos, 1992; Mitroff, Puachant, Finney, & Pearson, 1989; Silva, 1995) illustrate this. These studies focus on various dimensions of crisis and reach distinct conclusions; but, they (in some cases unintentionally) underscore the same theme: Organizational crisis situations often grow out of the organizational culture.

In these cases, to understand and respond to crisis from a long-term perspective, the organizational members were forced to look beyond the incidents (or precipitating events) to the underlying culture (i.e., values, traditions, rituals, norms, and so forth) that guided the behaviors before, during, and after the crisis. It is important to note that successful organizations in some cases were more prone to crisis due to pushing the envelope of change (see Silva's discussion of this in his book *Overdrive: Managing in Crisis-Filled Times*). Consequently, in studying the corrective nature of crisis, researchers must move beyond just studying the immediate crisis response to a broader perspective that accounts for: (a) how the organizing practices and sense-making behaviors within the institution contribute to the growth and development of the exigency; and (b) how the exigency can help spark a change from dysfunctional or problematic patterns.

Granted, there is a danger in making this argument from case studies. Berg and Robb (1992) noted this danger in a scathing repudiation of using the single case study in a paradigmatic fashion when it comes to judging the effectiveness of a crisis response. However, case studies do give scholars and practitioners helpful insights into organizational activities and histories. These insights are particularly valuable when a common thread is identified from a collection of case studies and when the insights help scholars and practitioners identify new questions that broaden crisis understanding, particularly as it relates to organizational change.

The questions that grow out of these case inquiries interrelate with the issue of how a crisis is perceived and consequently understood. When the crisis is perceived as a singular damaging event, then control, containment, and a return to the status quo becomes the expectation. When the crisis is perceived as an important and potentially beneficial corrective, change within the organization becomes an expectation. Corrections imply that something could be improved upon or that something was problematic. As systems theory demonstrates, for real change to occur the whole must be analyzed and accounted for rather than just a singular part. The result of this interrelationship between the corrective role of crisis and the organizational whole (or the overarching organizational culture and history) is a paradigmatic shift that influences how a crisis is approached, studied, and understood.

Crisis management in this paradigm does not just account for resolution of the event (a homeostatic perspective), though resolution continues to be an important dimension within the process. The focus instead is on a coordinated response that moves beyond the symptoms (i.e., often the event itself) and targets understanding how the crisis became situated within the culture, and the positive changes needed to move beyond the dysfunctional patterns that allowed for the evolution of the event (a pathological perspective).

An analogy may be helpful. When a child is taken to the emergency room for treatment of a loss of consciousness the attending physician first treats the symptoms that may threaten the life of the child, but the doctor does not stop at that point. The physician is concerned both with the symptoms (i.e., the loss of consciousness) and also how the illness came to be sustained. A history of repeated accidents and illnesses that seem to point to problems within the family system would trigger questions about dysfunctional family behaviors and lifestyles. The physician recognizes that restoring the health of the child is of limited value when the family does not recognize or deal with the pathogenic agents that are inherent to the system which created the problem or disease in the first place. If not dealt with, these same pathogenic agents (i.e., lifestyle patterns) will continue to create problems and disease. The loss of consciousness, which instigated the parent's concern, may in fact serve an important purpose in bringing about needed changes in the family system and for the long-term health of that particular child.

In this new paradigm, crisis research questions move beyond understanding an isolated event. This is not to say that all crisis situations grow out of the organizational culture or all crisis situations are necessary correctives. That would simply not be true. A random act of violence in an organization may have few if any links to dysfunctional organizational values or behaviors. But the questions should arise: Does the organizational culture encourage, provoke, or prompt such an attack? Regardless of whether the attack seems to be random or unrelated, it cannot be divorced from the environment out of which it gains life. They are intertwined and interrelated; to understand one you have to be able to study the other.

Crisis Research: A Design Overview

The questions that grow out of this paradigm are not unlike those involved with research on disease and transportation accidents. That is, they are not answered through single case histories or isolated laboratory experiments. Answers to these questions will come from a compilation of information resulting from the use of multiple methods and ongoing organizational analysis. This is a radical change of approach in crisis research. Through categorizing and organizing these cultural elements, significant variables may be isolated and found to be common across organizational boundaries and time frames, thus providing important clues as to how and when a crisis will occur and how it can be used to stimulate needed change within the organization. Questions that seek out these common crisis variables and cultural idiosyncrasies may provide clues that allow for the introduction of a preemptive crisis to stimulate positive change and growth within the organization (for further discussion of this idea of using a preemptive crisis to stimulate change see the discussion in chapter six of Hurst's [1995] book, *Crisis and Renewal*).

Previously, crisis research has been limited to studying the organization after the crisis has already occurred. However, after an exigency occurs the organization may be radically changed and the stress of the events may influence member perceptions of the organization and its past. Consequently, the first step in this research is to begin study on a sample of organizations before a crisis occurs. Mitroff et al. (1989) found crisis situations occurring on an annual basis in many large organizations. If crises are as common as these researchers suggest, several crisis situations should occur within the sample of organizations that have been under study.

The purpose of this research would be to analyze the organizational culture before, during, and after the crisis to see what variables were present at the onset, what types of changes occurred during the crisis, what stimulated lasting change within the organization, and what variables seemed to be central to the crisis process itself. This type of research will also help in understanding what forms of internal crisis communication enhance the corrective nature of the exigency and what types of behaviors impede much needed organizational changes.

The second step in this type of study would be designing a research framework that was easily overlaid on a variety of organizations. The frame (categories of study) would need to be sufficiently broad to have flexibility in studying various types of cultures, but narrow enough to establish comparable data across organizations. For instance in the cultural analysis of Olivet College following an organizational racial crisis (Bechler, 1994), the author suggested five key variables for further study in organizational life: (a) the leadership, (b) the communication networks and norms, (c) the role that the business environment plays in establishing organizational values and goals, (d) the recent history of crisis communication, (e) the legends and stories about the organization that shape public perceptions. These key variables could establish the categories (or frame) to be used across organizations. In each category, questions would be developed on two levels: First, a grouping of fixed-alternate and open-ended questions could be used across organizations to develop a data bank of comparable variables and issues relevant to organizational life regardless of organizational type (for an example of this first level of work with these types of questions see the 1989 work on organizational cultural analysis by Mitroff et al.). Using a survey method, the researcher would gain thin, but potentially generalizable, data from a cross section of organizations.

Second, questions could be designed for specific organizations in order to gain deeper insight into the unique issues central to the organizing practices of the culture. These questions would need to be interwoven with an ethnographic methodology. The researcher would need to be immersed within the organization in order to gain insights into the language and sensemaking practices (rites, rituals, critical events, stories, legends) within the specific culture. In this way, the researcher gains insight (and thick date) into the unique nature of the organization, while also gaining information that may be useful to generalize to a broader population.

As mentioned earlier, these organizational studies would be similar to the health studies of a particular human sample over a period of years (i.e., studies of nurses from a particular school or geographical area over an extended period of time). In this way, the organizational culture is established and profiled through rich layers of data rather than the thin data accumulated through a singular study of a particular culture following a specific incident. This would address two ongoing problems: the problem of organizational access, and issues of multiple causation. When an organization is under crisis, trust becomes a critical issue and consequently, it is difficult for researchers to gain admittance to examine and explore the changes that are occurring within the culture. Organizational leaders and media are prone to provide information that assigns a singular cause for the crisis. Thus, researchers may have a distorted perspective of the crisis based on limited access. When a positive relational history is established, trust lessens as a factor, access becomes easier because key informants have already been established prior to the crisis, and rich data gathering becomes much more likely.

These are neither short-term approaches to crisis research nor are they easily completed studies. But, this approach to research moves crisis management beyond maintaining the social and organizational status quo with no regard for the disenfranchised or for society as a whole. Because studies would be ongoing, the management of the moment would be compared across time thus providing reference points that are less likely to be influenced by the media or managerial portrayal during that particular crisis incident. Decision-making becomes "contextually" understood rather than "incidentally" understood. That is to say, the decision is viewed from the historical cultural context, rather than from the narrow frame of the particular incident in time.

These types of studies move beyond a "control, contain, and get-it-off-the-table" mentality, and offer the potential for new insights into the nature of organizational life during critical moments. The longitudinal nature of these studies should also provide key insights into what types of variables blend to help provide lasting positive (or negative) change in response to organizational crises and dysfunctional behaviors. Often, the insights gained through short-term studies of success stories are tempered by later organizational failure. Because the time of study is short, the researcher does not realize that the "wise" decisions being made, which seem to lead to bottom-line financial success and good crisis management, may in fact be the very factors that demoralize and drain the organizational culture. Consequently, at the first economic downswing the organization may be prone to failure.

Viewing institutional communication, decision making, and change through the historical cultural lens helps ascertain what variables truly led to beneficial change and what variables provided short-term change but with disappointing long-term results. This is a key component for this research paradigm—moving beyond looking at what brings about momentary homeostasis to looking at the pathology of organizational life.

SUMMARY

The organizational crisis has been studied from the perspective of how to contain and control the possible damages and outcomes. Public relations practitioners and communication researchers have found various strategies that have worked with a measure of success in responding to organizational crisis situations. These strategies, however, have come with little discussion concerning the limitations of their uses. The "one-size-fits-all" approach to crisis has not considered the possibility of unethical and dysfunctional organizations surviving and maintaining patterns of behaviors that are problematic.

The organizational exigency may provide both the organization and society as a whole with a necessary corrective that creates change and innovation in dysfunctional and problematic organizational cultures. Thus, the crisis may be an important step to deconstructing problematic organizational behaviors that over time have become "acceptable" and embedded within the culture. This interrelationship between the crisis and the environment within which it develops becomes the object of study and research.

The research questions in this new paradigm are focused on understanding the longer term perspective of how the organizational culture is linked to the crises. Although immediate organizational response is important, it is not the central issue of study. This type of research agenda may answer significant questions concerning the role of specific cultural variables in the creation, and potentially the prevention, of an organizational crisis. Thus, scholars and practitioners may be able to further assist organizational members in the task of effectively communicating before, after, and in the midst of chaotic times.

6

Burkian Counternature and the Vigilant Response: An Anticipatory Model of Crisis Management and Technology

Bolanle A. Olaniran
David E. Williams
Texas Tech University

The works of Kenneth Burke include a strong ecological concern and an explanation for that concern. Burke's motive provides a framework from which crisis management personnel can evaluate their organization's potential for disaster. The concepts of hierarchy and the scientific rationalization create the theoretical basis for the anticipatory model of crisis management.[1]

Inherent in Burke's dramatism is the inevitable and unavoidable drive for perfection. This drive is particularly visible in the continual efforts to improve technology that continues to permeate our society. Recognition of the desire to perfect technology is at the heart of the anticipatory model of crisis communication. The anticipatory model recognizes our natural desire to create and rely on technology. The model positions crisis managers to recognize the fallibility of technology and continually seek signs of potential disaster in an effort to prevent crisis escalation.

At the heart of Burke's human dramatism is the natural drive for perfection. Burke (1989) defined the human being as being "rotten with perfection." As human beings, Burke explained, we place ourselves in numerous hierarchies (economic, social, etc.) and we have a natural desire to improve our position by climbing those hierarchies. As Ruekert (1982) noted, "in a most general sense, hierarchy is any kind of order, but more accurately, it

---

[1]For complete figure of the model see Olaniran and Williams (2000, p. 491).

is any kind of graded, value-charged structure in terms of which things, works, people, acts, and ideas are ranked" (p. 131).

Our position in these hierarchies creates an uneasiness, which Burke (1954) referred to as a psychosis or hierarchic psychosis. The psychosis arises as individuals find themselves struggling with the desire to increase their position in the hierarchy while simultaneously fighting to prevent their decent in the order. The psychosis is intensified when we realize we frequently cannot explain the difference between our present level and the next level in the hierarchy.

"So every hierarchy, which is a 'good' in that it makes orderly what otherwise might be chaotic, is a 'goad' in so far as division into higher and lower is inevitable whenever there is ordering, and such division makes inevitable the hierarchic psychosis and categorical guilt engendered spontaneously by any 'social order' " (Ruekert, 1982, p. 132).

We recognize from Burke's discussion of hierarchy that numerous types of social ordering are inevitable, unavoidable, and all encompassing. Furthermore, the hierarchy creates a desire to succeed or perfect one's position in the order. This drive, or rottenness, for perfection has specific consequences with reference to technology (Clark, 1994). The crisis manager must be ever-mindful of the human propensity, but inability to perfect technology. No matter how sophisticated or fail safe the engineering, the crisis manager cannot assume that failure (and crisis) are impossible.

In *Permanence and Change*, Burke (1954) revealed the three great rationalizations humans use to make sense of their world. Magic was the first rationalization. This allowed people to seek a knowledgeable person (magician, wizard) who would have the power to control nature. Later, humans developed a second orientation, which allowed them to explain or control human actions. This orientation was religion and focused on control of human behavior to please a greater power. Science was the third rationalization according to Burke. While all three are currently present in our culture, Burke warns that science is by far the most dominant.

The scientific orientation has manifested in an attempt to control nature with technology and machinery. Although still caught in a hierarchical drive for perfection, we have developed a dependency on technology with the belief that when perfected, machines can fulfill all of our needs.

> If one pursues the implications of Burke's system one finally comes to what Burke calls the total anthropomorphizing of nature. Man, who is, in Burke's marvelous phase, "rotten with perfection," has not just added language and symbol-systems to the non-verbal world from which he began. In following his own genius to the end of the line, he has transformed nature into symbol-systems and has used his great gift for symbolic action and the creation of

symbol systems to develop a technology (a symbol system if there ever was one) that is so resourceful it is liable to perfect itself and destroy the natural world before man can develop counter-measures against his own creation. (Ruekert, 1982, p. 273)

The Burkian vision of the human drive to perfect technology explains how humans have inadvertently created damage to the earth. The earth has been changed by human development more than by any other animal (Burke, 1984). The result is what Burke calls counternature—nature plus human intervention.

The Burkian concepts of hierarchy and technology combined with his views on technology and counternature create for the crisis manager a perspective that puts forewarning and anticipation at the forefront. From the Burkian perspective, crisis management does not view technological disaster as a possibility but as a process, that has been underway for decades. This perspective also forces the crisis manager to see his or her organization as part of an ideology that maintains and promotes technological superiority and dependence. The manager must be vigilant of their own organization's use of technology but also the larger role of technology in society.

Whereas the pessimistic conclusion of this perspective might be an abandonment of technology, the crisis manager must instead take a more critical view toward the handling of potential crises. From this perspective it is important for crisis personnel to recognize that the technology used and being developed by their organization carries with it a deceptive ethos because of the belief that it has "developed" beyond that which was used by their predecessors. Although the improvement is likely genuine, it is still an instrument of symbol use, which further removes humankind from its natural condition. Crisis personnel, therefore, find themselves in a dilemma in which improved technology can also mean decreased control over its consequences.

Burke's perspective from counternature establishes the need for crisis management teams to focus on anticipation and vigilant decision making. To counter the inevitable doom to come from overreliance on technology, crisis managers can critique the use of technology through anticipation, vigilance and control. Anticipation is a key to the emergent model as the perspective guides one to view an organization's use of technology as a situation that will have high crisis potential based on the lack of control over machinery. Control, however, must be established in decision making through vigilance. The model suggests that sufficient anticipation will help provide vigilant decision making. Having established the need for an anticipatory perspective through an examination of Burkian counternature, we now move to the components of the model.

COMPONENTS OF THE ANTICIPATORY MODEL

Industrial crises, such as Firestone, Chernobyl nuclear disaster, Exxon Valdez oil spill, Bhopal toxic chemical leakage, and Johnson & Johnson Tylenol tampering are organizational crises with the common denominator of technology. As industrialized nations attempt to improve productivity and profitability, they sought the aid of modern technologies. Dependency on technology has become problematic as some corporations have become complacent with the idea that technology has approached perfection. The complacency heightens a rather crucial problem, the failure to plan for crisis. Some organizations hold the assumption that with the installation of sophisticated technologies, the probability of failure is reduced or eliminated completely. However, evidence has shown that technology or computer breakdown is one of the most frequent types of crisis experienced by Fortune 100 companies (Mitroff, Pauchant, & Shrivastava, 1989).

Furthermore, some organizational decision makers believe that no matter what their crisis management efforts are the potential for catastrophic accidents is imminent. A majority of the senior management officials in the surveyed Fortune 100 companies reported it will take a major disaster to get them to prepare for crises (Mitroff et al., 1989). Perrow (1984) underscored this view of crisis in his work "normal accidents," where he indicates that some systems (technology) with catastrophic potential possess elements of risks regardless of the attempts to make them safe. At the same time, the financial burden and low probability of technological crises lead to inadequate preparation for crises as technologies based on low immediate occurrence of a breakdown creates the illusion of safety. Olaniran and Williams (2000) noted that this line of reasoning about technology allows most organizations to focus on post-facto crisis management. Therefore, this chapter utilizes the anticipatory model of crisis management (Olaniran & Williams, 2000) to underscore the need for anticipation in crisis prevention or de-escalation of adverse crisis consequences. In doing so, the chapter examines a case of crisis management that could benefit from application of the anticipatory model of crisis management.

ANTICIPATORY MODEL OF CRISIS MANAGEMENT AND TECHNOLOGY

The decision to incorporate modern technology in any organization is almost certainly based on cost–benefit factors. According to Sethi (1987) a focus on potential benefits is a justification offered for applying dangerous technologies. Many stakeholders are unaware of dangers they are being subjected to in using these technologies. Furthermore, overemphasis on benefits blinds organizational leaders against imminent dangers to the relevant environment of such technology application. Consequently, decision makers fail to avert the impending disaster. The key issue, however, is not whether technology will fail but when and how it will fail. Therefore, answering the questions of when and how technology will fail may be a key to solving the puzzle of effective crisis management and prevention. To answer these questions we look at the assumptions of the anticipatory model.

The Anticipation Factor

In their anticipatory model, Olaniran and Williams (2000) draw from the work of scholars such as Mitroff and Kilmann (1984) and Weick (1988). They subscribed to the claim that although one may not be able to prevent all tragedies from occurring, prevention should be a primary concern (see Mitroff & Kilmann, 1984). Similarly, they drew from the "enactment perspective" (i.e., Weick, 1988), which focuses on the prevention of impending error in an attempt to reduce the magnitude of those errors when they occur.

In essence, the anticipatory model suggests that while human errors cannot be completely eliminated, attempts should be made to put in place programs that enhance prevention of errors. Similarly, Sethi (1987) argued that one can anticipate nearly all the "unthinkable" before they become a reality.

First, it is assumed that the less attention devoted to understanding the nature of a crisis the greater the tendency for a crisis to escalate. Furthermore, Weick (1988) warned that "the very action which enables people to gain some understanding of these complex technologies can also cause those technologies to escalate and kill" (p. 308). Consequently an understanding of the technology along with its organizational and social environment is essential. Technologies are fallible because they are designed by humans, thus, subject to human error. A majority of industrial disasters are linked to combination of human and technological errors (Olaniran & Williams, 2000; Shrivastava, 1987; Shrivastava & Mitroff, 1987; Shrivastava, Mitroff, Miller, & Miglani, 1988; Weick, 1988). Following is a brief explanation of the critical components of the anticipatory model.

Understanding

Understanding in the model suggests having a thorough knowledge of conditions, situations, or events that could signal potential for danger. It is believed that understanding can not be complete without two relatively similar concepts: enactment and expectations. Enactment is defined as a process in which a specific form of action is brought about (see Smircich & Stubbart, 1985). Weick (1988) extended enactment to include consequences imposed by a given action. Olaniran and Williams (2000) however, contend that "anticipation" of crisis in itself is action because it constrains the choice an organization makes based on given information. They argue that decision makers must look ahead to anticipate opportunities, threats, and weaknesses in their environment and then take appropriate actions. Furthermore, both action and inaction results in different (i.e., crisis) outcomes.

Expectations

Expectations represent assumptions people make about certain events or objects. Assumptions made about an occurrence determine whether or not an error results in a crisis of catastrophic proportion. In essence, assumptions by decision makers about technologies represent a critical element and a starting point in crisis prevention. Olaniran and Williams (2000) noted that assumptions at times bring about self-fulfilling prophecies. For example, they argued that when organizations assume that a technology is fail safe, they often relax safety measures as unnecessary and not preventive-worthy. Thus the ensuing crisis potential from such oversight increases as decision makers engaged actions that are only consistent with their assumptions (see Perrow 1984; Weick, 1988).

While the anticipatory model emphasizes precrisis management activities, other components within the model also address the importance of active engagement during crisis. This includes the concept of "control." Control is multifaceted in the model in that it addresses how well organizations are in command of crisis situations. Control is measured in relative terms including, the organization's, stakeholders and relevant environments (e.g., public, consumers, and victims) perception. The notion of control revolves around the ability to implement an effective crisis management program including information dissemination, media relations, etc. along with flexibility to make changes when necessary (i.e., rigidity).

ANTICIPATION AS A VIGILANT RESPONSE TO CRISIS

Enactment and expectation in the anticipatory model are crucial in crisis prevention, but do not automatically represent a vigilant response. Therefore, the following section addresses other concerns relevant to vigilant decision making. It stands to reason, however, that expectation and enactment processes are interdependent. Expectations determine actions, which also determine where an organization places its emphasis (e.g., preventive or postcrisis mode).

The vigilant decision-making process also suggests that decision makers ought to move through the decision making process in an efficient manner by carefully analyzing the situation, setting goals, and evaluating the outcomes (Hirokawa & Rost, 1992; Williams & Olaniran, 1994). Thus, decision making centers on both internal and external communication behaviors in an organization. These two communication behaviors are not mutually exclusive. The integration model (Kreps, 1990) illustrates this notion. The internal communication process helps direct organizational activities focusing on maintenance of stability and structure whereas external communication focuses on bringing about change that establishes a decision path for an organization.

Organizations have more control over internal than external communication processes. External communication variables like legal, social, political, and economic indices are outside the direct control of most organizational decision makers. Consequently, external communication often directs internal communication. Notwithstanding, while external communication creates friction and stress, organizations must not be reactionary, but rather proactively anticipate them. Furthermore, the vigilant decision making is better facilitated under a stress-free environment. Therefore, it is imperative that vigilant crisis management teams proactively anticipate external communication factors, by keeping up with legal governing bodies, social factors, economic indicators, political factors, media effects, and other relevant organizations affecting their operations. With these factors, decision makers must then select appropriate internal communication to be adapted to their crisis program. Such a focus will help organizations in selection of appropriate strategies. For example, organizations have the options of choosing from rigid versus liberal policies, control versus empowerment, and personnel selection and training. Because anticipating crisis focuses on prevention, it helps to reduce uncertainties when crises occur. Thus, a careful monitoring of external communication coupled with the appropriate internal communication significantly enhances vigilant crisis management within an organization. Anticipating crises then constitutes a vigilant response only when the process has managed to scrutinize all the unthinkable potential causes of technological failures/distresses. Shrivastava et al. (1988) referred to this process as identifying the "triggering event"—specific factors identifiable according to place, time, and agents. Triggering events may have low probability of occurrence, nevertheless they still poses threats of major disaster (Kates, 1977). Therefore, small technological glitches must be discovered to prevent their exponential escalation. Inasmuch as stress accompanies all crises, the goal is to reduce the level of stress in crisis management. In an effort to facilitate a stress-free environment while creating a vigilant anticipatory model of crisis management the elements of rigidity and control need attention by decision makers.

The focus on anticipation shares a concern for detailed insight, which is amplified by similar public relations research in risk communication. Renz (1992) briefly described risk communication as "any communication about uncertain physical hazards" (p. 1). She further explained that risk communication should consider of primary importance both the publics who would be involved and the messages created for them. The concern for detail in risk communication involves a thorough recognition and announcement of the environmental risks and possible consequences of different technological options a company or government is considering. A goal of risk communication, therefore, might be that no environmental impact from technology catches the public unaware. The anticipatory model shares this concern for the discovery of details. However, the proposed model shifts the focus from the consequences of technological failure to expectation and prevention of a crisis.

Rigidity

Rigidity consists of the degree of inflexibility that is built into a particular action or process. Thus, the degree of rigidity that is exercised by a decision maker could determine how vigilant a crisis response is. Weick (1988) illustrated the notion of rigidity by looking at the relationship between enactment and commitment. He indicated that as actions become "public" and "irrevocable" they become difficult to change and that these actions also become more "volitional," which in turn makes their explanation more tenacious. This view is consistent with that of the Vigilant Interaction Theory that argues that how individuals view a problem, available options, and consequences will determine the quality of the choices made (Hirokawa & Rost, 1992).

Tenacious justifications involving rigid explanation about certain actions (Salancik, 1977) could be advantageous in crisis situations for clarifying ambiguity and confusion (Staw, 1980). Furthermore, justification provides structure for maintaining accurate views and analyzing available options (Weick, 1988). The challenge with rigidity is it creates a blinder that prevents consideration of competing alternatives. In such cases, one fails to acknowledge that a decision or explanation provided could adversely intensify or resolve crises. For instance, organizational decision makers are often convinced that as long as a regulatory standard for technological upkeep is maintained they are absolved of liability. When this happens, decision makers may fail to recognize that deaths or losses attributable to their organizational crises may not be dismissed on the basis of simple adherence to minimal safety standards, because different rules and factors come into play depending on the member of the relevant environment affected. Some scholars addressed this concern suggesting that organizational responsibility in crisis situations should be decided based on the extent to which a crisis could have been anticipated and prevented (e.g., Buckey, 1984, 1986; Mitroff, 1986; Sethi, 1987).

Control

Control represents another factor that may influence the vigilant response to a crisis in both a positive and negative manner. Control is viewed as the degree of influence that organizational members have at their disposal. The control is often elusive because it has to do with individual perception especially when the influence is "indirect" in nature, which is often the case. Control influences crisis in the sense that it affects how individuals respond to crisis situations given the action taken. For instance, if individuals see themselves as having the ability and authority to do something about a crisis, it is more likely that they will take action. Thus, ability and authority go hand in hand and constitute empowerment, which could extend to a vigilant response in crisis management.

Empowerment or empowering organizational members in crisis management programs provides opportunity for those members to be able to exercise control in their behavior by exploring their abilities. It is believed that if people are given the opportunity to handle a variety of issues (expanded roles) based on their expertise, they will be willing to do more than when restricting them to their formalized job descriptions. Weick (1988) argued that when people think they can do more, they pay more attention to their surroundings and issues, which leads to greater ability to control and cope with their environment. When organizational members are empowered or have greater control, they are able to respond quicker to crisis-triggering events as they unfold. In contrast, individuals with specialized expertise will have a narrow focus that could prevent him or her from seeing the incident as a crisis triggering event, thus, miss a chance to prevent a crisis (see Olaniran & Williams, 2000; Perrow, 1984).

Giving organizational members, greater control suggests the need to redistribute control within an organization. Top level organizational members should be willing to relinquish some of their control to the lower level members, which could be accomplished by facilitating a cooperative climate and working relationships among members (Kreps, 1990). Individuals who are closer to the proximity of triggering events should be allowed to attend to the situation rather than waiting for others in another part of the organizational echelon for approval to take action (see Olaniran, 1993; Perrow, 1984, Tabris, 1984). Although this stresses decentralization contrary to the centralized information dissemination that is prevalent in crisis management literature, the two are not necessarily in contradiction. Centralization as stressed in the literature addresses information and actions geared toward individuals who are external to the organization such as the public and the media (Shallowitz, 1987). Given the need for consistency, centralization is prudent. However, decentralization of information and action is stressed because of the internal focus of crisis prevention, and centralization given the different constituents and job responsibilities will only complicate issues by delaying actions (see Tabris 1984; Quarantelli, 1988).

Decentralization emphasizes the importance of career path in organizations and their crisis management. Weick stresses that decision makers who move up the organizational ladder via technical ranks usually possess hands-on experience and the expertise to sense trouble-shooting needs in the technological environment. In addition, this experience could help decision makers recognize the need to let people closer to the source of the problem attend to it. Another implication is that there may be a need to restructure organizational management promotion and tenure policy. For instance in an organization susceptible to crises it may be beneficial for management to promote people with technical expertise into decision-making positions when those positions are available (see Shrivastava & Mitroff, 1987; Weick, 1988).

More significant is the effect of both rigidity and control on the interaction patterns within organizations. Excessive rigidity and inappropriately distributed control can result in one of the following faulty decision-making schemes: (a) failure in recognizing positive qualities of alternate decision options, (b) overlooking critical negative aspects of a decision choice, (c) exaggeration of positive aspects of a decision option, and (d) overestimating negative consequences of a decision option. Therefore, crisis decision processes resulting in one or more of these problems will hinder the decision outcome, whereas avoiding these problems would facilitate vigilant decision making (Hirokawa & Rost, 1992). The following section presents Ford and Firestone cases and attempts to illustrate how the anticipatory model could have helped the companies avoid their crises. Implications for practitioners are explored. Specifically, the case is used to identify how failure to use proper anticipatory measures resulted in problematic crisis response efforts.

CASE OVERVIEW

The Ford–Firestone Fiasco. On August 9, 2000 Ford and Firestone announced the recall of 6.5 million Firestone tires. The affected tire series are the 15 inch 235/75/15 ATX, ATX II, and Wilderness after the National Highway Traffic Safety Administration (NHTSA) opened formal inquiry in May regarding tread separation from tires relating to 88 deaths (see Reuters, September 13, 2000; http://biz.yahoo.com/rf/000912/n12377774.htm). In addition to the initial 6.5 million tire recall, another 1.4 million tire recall was announced about a month later. Also, NHTSA linked 29 more deaths to the tire blowouts, thus bringing the total of fatalities to 148 including three deaths occurring after the August recalls (Nathan, 2000; Skrzycki, 2000). The figure also increased the injuries figure from 500 when last reported on October 17th to 525, while other complaints mount from 3,500 to 4,300. NHTSA is still investigating the cause of the tire failures and whether to extend the recall. Although most of the tires are fitted to Ford's sport utility vehicle (i.e., Ford Explorer model), other vehicles are also linked or identified in the recall:

- 1996–2000 Mercury Mountaineers
- 1991–2000 Ford Rangers
- 1991–1994 Ford F-Series
- 1991–1994 Ford Broncos
- 2001 Ford Explorer Sport Tracs
- 1994–2000 Mazda B-Series
- 1991–1994 Mazda Navajos

IMPLICATIONS FOR ANTICIPATORY MODEL OF CRISIS MANAGEMENT

Ford and Firestone's tire crisis is selected because of the potential lessons it illustrates in application of the anticipatory model of crisis management. This case also illustrates the implication of inadequate control crisis management. The overarching question that faces both Ford and Firestone is whether the massive tire recall, especially the fatalities resulting from it could have been prevented. The response to this question is clear from the following explanation. It appears there is precedence for tire malfunctioning and recall guiding the two companies. More specifically, Firestone was previously involved in a huge tire recall in the 1970s when millions of its "Firestone 500" steel-belted radials were recalled after NHTSA found the tire defective in which the company paid half a million dollar fine for knowingly marketing tires that would fail government test. As for Ford, it became part of the crisis through guilt by association and the possibility of being a contributing factor in roll-overs that occurred after tire separation from its Explorer. Along with several consumer complaints in and outside the United States, is a company document released by the congressional investigators. The document indicated a high incidence of vehicle roll-over after a tire blowout or tread loss that had not been detected for other vehicle brands: Toyota, GM, and Chrysler all have significant presence in this market segment (Grimaldi & Skrzycki, 2000, p. E01). This information, at least, suggests a probability of imminent danger facing the company, its customers, and the need to enact a crisis prevention program.

Given warning signals and a history of tire problems, one would think that Ford and Firestone would both develop a plan to handle such crises. Instead, both companies focused more on avoidance, excuses, and blame shifting decision-making strategies. Case in point is Firestone's attempt to shift the blame on Ford Motor Company regarding the Ford Explorer design contributing to the problem. For instance, congressional investigators released a May Firestone memo where company officials in Venezuela said that there had been no tire-related deaths in Grand Blazers there and concluded that the Explorer must be specifically prone to roll over. However, Bradsher (2000) indicated that no agency in Venezuela collects national traffic death figures. In the United States, insurance industry data suggests that Explorer owners have a below-average rate of rollover deaths compared to other midsize SUVs but a higher rate than midsize cars.

Furthermore, a Firestone spokeswoman said that tread separations were the most common problem in radial tires and could be linked to any of several factors, including road hazards, warm weather improper repair and underinflation, rather than a manufacturing defect. Ford countered with its own allegations that Firestone tires were simply poorly made and unreliable (i.e., Toyota Land Cruisers, Neon, and a Blazer). Ford claimed they had photos of vehicles that crashed in Venezuela after Firestone tires failed (Bradsher, 2000; Grimaldi, 2000). The blame shifting continued when Firestone attempted to scapegoat one of its plants in Decatur, Illinois. It suggested that tire quality lapsed because the plant used replacement workers when there was a strike.

Notwithstanding blame shifting, accusations, and counter accusations between Firestone and Ford, documents showed that Ford was warned about tire tread problems. Cletus Ernster III (a Houston resident and an Explorer owner) indicated that he sent Ford a certified letter dated November 24, 1998 explaining his treacherous experience when the left-front tire of his Explorer peeled off. In his letter he requested that Ford take action to save lives of the millions of owners and families riding the Explorer but he received no response. Ernster was not alone, a flurry of other customers indicated that they called Ford customer relations department to complain about similar incidents to which the company responded that they were unable to assist on the matter. Ford executives also stated they had no idea the tires were dangerous until the summer of 2000 (Audi & Dixon, 2000).

There were so many warnings, and red flags that provided windows of opportunity for effective action. The free press points to 5,000 pages of government and court documents showing that customers, dealers, and attorneys for victims and their family tried to warn Ford that the tires were dangerous. When Ford finally accepted the possibility of defective tires abroad by replacing tires in Saudi Arabia and Venezuela in 1999, Ford continued to tell American customers that the same set of tires were safe until federal regulators launched a formal investigation this spring. Then, Ford finally demanded that Firestone hand over crucial U.S. claims data from which it took only a few days to confirm what others have been trying to tell them for years.

Regarding control, both Ford and Firestone failed to communicate to the public that they have a major problem and that they are doing everything in their power to address the problem. As a matter of fact the companies are accused of being more interested in settling lawsuits in private than in admitting the real problem and danger that looms in public (Audi & Dixon, 2000; Grimaldi, 2000; Ranalli, 2000). In the first instance, the executives from both companies did not announce the recall until after NHTSA had launched a probe regarding the deaths. They demonstrate lack of control by waiting until an official investigation is launched by the regulating agency before announcing the recall. This lack of control is further embedded in Ford CEO Jacques Nasser's blame shifting and scapegoating tactics that contend that every time Ford presented Firestone with problems from foreign consumers, the tire maker insisted there were no tire defects in the United States or overseas. Nasser also told congress that Ford is a "data-driven" company, and did not have reliable data from Firestone for years, thus, the problem went undetected. Lampe (his counterpart from Firestone) on the other hand, responded by stressing the Explorer's propensity to roll over after tire burst (Dobbyn, 2000). Nasser's self-projection as a data driven company and its accusations about Firestone lead one to doubt the automaker's sincerity in addressing the issue. Specifically, one has to wonder whether Ford asked Firestone for "claims data" which would have been the proactive way of dealing with the crisis. This question is also pertinent because by the automaker's admission, it did not ask Firestone for the crucial claims data that led to the recall until summer 2000 because Ford claims that it had no reason to believe there was a problem in the United States. It would appear that a data driven company would pay more attention to its data collecting and analysis. In terms of the anticipatory model, Ford should have been more vigilant in determining the cause(s) of the tire separation problem at the first complaint. The customer relations department is there to stay in touch with consumers and pass on information to the management as feedback to be used in behavior or activity modification. Unfortunately this was not the case.

Events following the recall did not do much to help the situation and the company's public image. Vines (a Ford spokesperson) suggested that Lawsuits and letters do not count as data in his statement "are we supposed to run down the hall screaming every time there is a lawsuit and say, We have a problem" (Audi & Dixon, 2000). This is a major error and evidence of lack of preparedness and anticipation of crisis. Emphasis should be made in all crisis plans to expect and anticipate potentially explosive questions and develop a plan to defuse the explosiveness. Vines' comment represents common mistakes decision makers make when they allow frustration and stress accompanying crisis to get the best of them. All the more reason to develop a prepared plan and practice response efforts so the information is second nature to all practitioners. On anticipation, one must also wonder what prevents Firestone from not volunteering the claim data to her long-term business partner? It seems like the prudent thing to do is to acknowledge the problem or potential problem (expectations) and bring in motion a plan to address the problem jointly with Ford or independently. The failure to do so, risks Firestone's public perception that the company has something to hide and therefore, it must be guilty whether it is or not. A consumer analysis manager indicates that the majority of the public sees the problem as a Firestone problem where the level of trust for the company stands at 17% on August 18 in comparison to the Ford's 70% (Holstein, 2000).

During crisis, an organization must leave nothing to chance. More importantly, it must refrain from any indication that it puts greater emphasis on money or cost of solution than the safety of its consumers and other stakeholders. The complex nature of the relationship between Firestone and its Japanese partner Bridgestone added to the lack of control issue. Kaizaki (Bridgestone President who ran Firestone from 1991–1993) indicates although tearfully, after the recall that he was first aware in May of tires being linked to a high number of accidents due to the company's headquarters in Tokyo being slow to respond to reports of the accidents. In another explanation, Kaizaki provided the excuse that the accidents may also be attributable to the inability to use Bridgestone's method in United States with its sister company Firestone (Gibbs, 2000). Bridgestone and Firestone fared poorly in their ability to convey to the public that they were in control and to present the company's story in a convincing and persuasive manner. First, is the silence of Bridgestone until September. Second is the lack of believability of the explanation. Both gave the impression that the company was unsympathetic to the multiple stakeholders' concern, and that the sincerity of the apology was questionable. Some level of training may help in this regard; however, the crisis period is not the time to provide the training or to determine whether a CEO has had sufficient training to help ease the company out of its trouble (Small, 1991). Crisis anticipation should help a company to review or conduct a crisis audit and provide ample opportunity to correct a potential problem by providing additional training when necessary.

John Scanlon (a senior V.P. at Daniel Edelman, Inc.), stated that large companies such as Bridgestone-Firestone and Ford are known to be rigid by exhibiting a "monolithic bureaucracy" tendency that is slow to act (Small, 1991). All CEOs communication style confirmed this tendency. It appears that information is either not flowing through appropriate channels or was simply not available. Blaming and burden shifting are convenient strategies often employed when one is not willing to accept an alternate view or responsibilities. All these strategies fall short of Ice's (1991) recommendation that calls for rhetorical strategies, which de-emphasize both technical and financial issues, but focuses on safety and humanitarian aid to stakeholders for repairing relationships and image with the public during crises.

Another challenge includes disagreements as to how to handle the recall. Three months before the August 9th recall, Ford Venezuela executives attempted to absolve themselves of any responsibility for the rollover accidents. According to an internal memo, the Ford Venezuela president rejected a proposal that both companies should share blame. Instead, the president insisted that Firestone handle the replacement of tires through its dealer network and tell the Explorer owners that the tires were to blame (Fix, 2000). When both companies finally decided to recall on August 9th, there was a disagreement on how to handle the announcement as to whether to make the announcement with or without entertaining questions from the media. According to Fix (2000), Firestone finally recalled the tires in Venezuela on September 4th but without admission that the tires were defective only that they were mislabeled. Similarly in the United States, Ford's Nasser tried to shift complete blame on Firestone tires and told the congress that the delayed recall is to be blamed on Firestone (Fix, 2000). However, Audi and Dixon (2000) alluded to company memos indicating that both companies were hesitant to recall because they were concerned about notifying the Department of Transportation (DOT).

Another bone of contention during the recall is the tire pressure. Firestone's then CEO Ono, recommended on August 9th to Ford to notify SUV owners to increase tire inflation pressure from 26 p.s.i. to 30 p.s.i. to give owners additional safety margin for deflation (Fix, 2000). However, it was not until late September before Ford decided to notify owners. Tauzin (House Rep LA and an Explorer owner) referred to this as "a couple of years and a hundred lives too late" (Fix, 2000). Ford insists that its recommendation for inflation pressure had nothing to do with safety problems. However, documents show that some of Ford's officials were not so sure, as Ford's own data confirm the risk (Audi & Dixon, 2000; Fix, 2000; Pickler, 2000). Litigants were quick to argue that both Firestone and Ford know all along that underinflation increases the chance of tire separation. One of the attorneys contend that "the automaker knew that steel-belted tires leak air, and that consumers who have their tire checked just once every 3,000 to 5,000 miles when they have their oil changed could have been unwittingly driving on tires with as little as 20 p.s.i." (Audi & Dixon, 2000). The late rec-ommendation did not bode well for either of the two companies and espe-cially for Ford, as this creates the impression that the companies have no regard for safety of their customers, more importantly, human lives in gen-eral. This impression was confirmed as Tauzin accused and criticized Ford for not testing the recalled tires under real-world conditions. Ford used Ford 150 pickup (a smaller vehicle) equipped with same type of the recalled Firestone tires in 1989 to simulate Ford Explorer (see also Bradsher, 2000).

Additionally, upon the recall, the companies face massive supply prob-lem for replacements. The companies were caught off guard after the recall as there were no plans in place to ensure that there would be enough tires to meet the replacement need. The company claimed it accelerated tire production by air lifting tires from factories in Japan to accommodate indi-viduals who want to replace their tires quickly (Aldrich, 2000; Reuters, 2000). It was not until after public outcry that companies allowed competi-tors to provide replacement tires (Aldrich, 2000). Four months after the re-call, tire replacements were yet to be completed. It is noteworthy that the lack of preparedness and NHTSA pressure on the companies resulted in the decision to recall. Consequently, a series of events and actions following the recall appears to be unplanned, unorganized, hence resulting in errone-ous, at times cover-up remarks that heighten and escalate the crisis further. With the anticipatory model in place most of the problems encountered by the companies could have been predicted with a well thought out plan ready to address them. However, the absence of this plan left both compa-nies scrambling not only for tires but also for answers and the greater sur-vival of their brands.

Noted earlier, it is generally imprudent to discuss financial costs during a crisis. It is however necessary to put things into perspective relative to the anticipatory model of crisis management. More than 6.5 million tires have to be replaced not counting the cost of the campaign to restore a posi-tive public image. Ford had to shut down plants for 2 weeks in order to rout the tires meant for Ford Ranger and Explorer for replacements. The 2-week shut down costs Ford production of 15,000 Rangers and 10,000 Explorers as sources of profits. In addition 6,000 hourly workers were given temporary lay off notices, although Ford still had to pay them 95% of their base pay during the layoff, under the union contract along with sharing the cost of tire replacement with Firestone (Nissen, 2000). According to Bridgestone costs relating to tire replacements and lawsuits are estimated at $900m for the cost of replacement and pending lawsuits (Nathan, 2000). The lesson here is that while anticipatory crisis programs costs money, and lots of it, failure to have crisis plans in place costs even more. Companies stand to lose or spend more money in cleaning up after the crisis. Thus, money spent enacting the anticipatory crisis model is money well spent.

There are plenty of warnings (from technological and human errors) to allow the companies to install an anticipatory model of crisis. Evidence of safety risk dated back to 1997 when Paul Wright (Technical Branch manager of a Ford dealership in Saudi Arabia) wrote both Firestone representatives in Saudi and Ford's regional office in Dubai on October 24, 1997. The memo reads, "As you know this concern goes back to mid-1997 when we first notified you of this concern. I have to state that I believe this situation to be of a safety concern which could endanger both the vehicle and more importantly the user of the vehicle" (Audi & Dixon, 2000; http://www.auto.com/autonews/why6_20001006.htm). It was not until May 10, 1999 that Ford decided to send a task force consisting of Firestone officials to the Middle East to determine the cause of the problem. Other memos worth noting include the following: One dated June 23, 1999 (more than 2 years after the first complaints from the middle East) indicates the frustration of a car dealer in Oman:

> It is very pathetic that our Explorer customers are losing lives because of the Firestone tires. We regret to inform you that in spite of many discussions and inspections we had on the subject so far, no action has been taken either from Ford side or from Firestone side to sort out the problem by actually replacing tires on affected vehicles.

Another memo followed a week later from the same source with an angrier tone:

> We have been informing Ford Motor Co. about the fatal accidents. The news of fatal accidents on explorer is spreading rapidly and customers are scared to buy Explorers. (Audi & Dixon, 2000; http://www.auto.com/autonews/why6_20001006.htm)

The Firestone and Ford case proves that technology and human errors are often involved in crises situations. The increasingly interactive complexity involved in technological design increases the potential for crises. For example, its is a known fact that despite increased performance of the steel belted radial tires the technology also allows for pressure leakage that when goes unchecked creates potential hazards to vehicles and their occupants (Audi & Dixon, 2000; Fix, 2000). Thus, vigilant decision making would include a crisis management plan that anticipates such potential sources of crises and deals with them before they grow into major catastrophes. The anticipatory model of crisis management suggests the possibility that crises could be held in check through an understanding of preconditions and instituting action plans to counteract the precondition effects. The importance of this fact cannot be overstated, given that instituting action against crisis preconditions could simplify tasks while also subduing potentially catastrophic crises. Weick (1988) indicated that task simplification is important when one considers the fact that stress accompanies all crises but with less effect on simple task performance and that many crises escalate due to the secondary effects of stress-induced crisis decision making. Task simplification effects could be realized when one prepares for occurrence of one major disaster such that when faced with a crisis, even when the crisis differs from the one anticipated, one can draw some useful information from the anticipated crises (Mitroff, Pauchant, & Shrivastava, 1989).

LESSONS LEARNED AND BEST PRACTICES

The 6.5m tire recall by Firestone and Ford provides lessons on how to, and how not to handle a crisis in today's high tech and informational savvy consumer era. The Firestone and Ford debacle offers three lessons including timing, rigidity, control, and media relations as addressed by the anticipatory model of crisis management, especially when dealing with relevant environment. Each of these are addressed next.

Timing. Although Ford would like to foster the impression that they moved swiftly to address the crisis, both companies missed a critical window of opportunity to deal with the problem. It should not take 2 years after the first event to begin investigation into the cause of tire separation and vehicle rollover. At the same time, companies need not wait until after the onset of federal investigation and 88 deaths from the accidents before deciding to recall. In crises, timing is everything! Although a company does not want to jump to conclusions about crises, lateness and indecisiveness are far worse. According to a brand strategist, "Consumers simply make emotional judgment that a company has or has not accepted responsibility for a problem" (Holstein, 2000).

Control. The failure to act decisively drove potential buyers, and the general public in need of information, to Internet chat rooms seeking answers. The danger to chat room information is that they are usually full of rumors and innuendoes that are hard to combat as everyone tries to present his or her opinions pretending to be expert when they are not. Thus, accuracy of the information in chat rooms while often difficult to verify is nonetheless believable to participants. The companies lost control of information and information that was released faced with greater public and media scrutiny. The companies also lost control as they engaged in finger-pointing and blaming, which damaged a century old relationship between them. Both parties sought to protect their own interests in attempt to defend their brands instead of working together to present a coherent and sympathetic front to the consumers and potential customers (Audi & Dixon, 2000; Holstein, 2000).

Rigidity. Hanging on to tradition and old ways of doing things may not serve companies in times of crisis. The rigidity demonstrated by both companies can be traced back to the insistence of Ford that Firestone is solely responsible for the problem. Grimaldi and Skrzycki (2000) indicated that a 1986 memo written by the company's policy and strategy committee pointed to their success in defeating several auto safety standards and avoiding criminal penalties. The memo reads

> Through the efforts of a broad-based industry coalition led by Ford we were able to delete the criminal penalty provisions, modify the vehicle side-impact requirements, and limit the vehicle crash worthiness proposal to DOT coordinated research project. If a bill emerges from the congress in 1986, we expect it to be in a form that we would find acceptable. (p. E01)

Although Ford did not comment on the memo it did acknowledge that the auto industry opposes some safety measures including air bags, at the time (Grimaldi & Skrzycki, 2000).

At the same time, Firestone insisted that Explorer's design and owner's failure to inflate tires properly contributed to the rollover. According to Aaker (Prophet Brand strategist) arguing that "it isn't our fault" even though one may be right, from a branding point of view, is catastrophic. Holstein (2000) suggested this is the reason why a majority of surveyed potential customers indicated that they attributed primary fault to Firestone. Perhaps, also worth mention is the fact that Firestone responded to its two crises similarly with failure to accept responsibility and forced recall both in 1978 and in 2000 (Evans, 2000). Although using a similar strategy by itself may not be faulty, it must be done with adjustment to the environment. A notable difference is the fact that the last time Firestone was involved in a major recall, the news of the recall spread much more slowly (Holstein, 2000). The society and stakeholders today are not the same as they were 22 years ago. Perhaps the single factor that has most changed and complicated crisis management in the recent years is communication technology which has removed the sole monopoly formerly enjoyed by traditional media and organizations by redistributing power to general public (e.g., Computers and Internet). As such, it is harder to restrain consumer outrage than in the pre-Internet era.

Media Relations. The rule with media is for the company to control information. This can only be achieved by developing good relationships with media personnel before it is needed (Olaniran & Williams, 2000). During crises, these relationships become valuable, as members of the media are likely to help present the organization's messages as accurately as possible based on the established trust. One must also be aware that because the Internet aids in magnifying consumer concerns, it is more pressing for organizations to proactively present its story utilizing this media. One of the key things that Ford did well was utilizing both traditional and nontraditional media (i.e., TV and Internet) in getting its message across (Charny, 2000). Although it is essential to get the message out as swiftly as possible, it is equally important to work at resolving the problem quickly. The longer a crisis continues to be the focus of the headlines the harder it is to manage the crisis as a company is more prone to make mistakes (Holstein, 2000). Furthermore, it is essential to come clean to the media and the public regardless of how damaging the information. It is better that stakeholders hear it from the company than from a different source. The less forthcoming a company is the greater the risk it faces as media scrutinize dirt and self-serving information from whistleblowers and disgruntled individuals who may have a dispute with the company. For example, Alan Hogan (a former Firestone employee and a whistle blower) informed the media about the recklessness and disregard for safety at Firestone's Wilson plant. He indicates that he witnessed Firestone's management using "dry stock"—a combination of steel belts and rubber that should have been discarded because they were no longer tacky—were continually recirculated into production (Meyer, 2000). He offered further damaging evidence by indicating that Firestone attempted to make the useless materials useful again by swabbing the tire's steel with a "benzene" compound (i.e., glue). Hogan's claim was given merit when a few months later both Firestone and Ford investigations suggested that tire separation can be linked to the glue/adhesives coming apart (Healey, 2000; Pickler, 2000; Reuters, 2000). Today's media are quick to find individuals with damaging evidence and the issue is not *whether* they will find them but *when*. In other words, it is only a matter of time before a cover-up attempt blows up in the face of a company. Allowing the media to dictate one's strategy during crises is a bad decision.

In conclusion, periodic safety inspections and maintenance audits of products, technologies, and environments for vulnerability analysis and assessment to identify potential crisis is called for (Shrivastava & Mitroff, 1987). Specifically, it is indicated that the most vigilant way of responding to crises and eliminating their catastrophic nature is by reducing interactive complexity design in a system; which implies paying attention to the interactions of human, technological, and general management factors which exacerbate crises (Shrivastava & Mitroff, 1987; Weick, 1988). No additional warnings should be needed to convince decision makers that their organizations are vulnerable to technological failure and that anticipation is the key to managing the risks of technological crises.

7

Reasoned Action in Crisis Communication: An Attribution Theory–Based Approach to Crisis Management

W. Timothy Coombs
Sherry J. Holladay
Eastern Illinois University

A consistent theme in communication research is that situations are an important influence on the selection of communication strategies (Bitzer, 1968; Black, 1965; Metts & Cupach, 1989; Ware & Linkugel, 1973; Wilson, Cruz, Marshall, & Rao, 1993). It is reasonable, therefore, to assume crisis communication should be affected by the crisis situation. Such a connection can produce valuable insights for practitioners. By understanding how crisis situations recommend or restrict crisis communication options, a crisis manager can plan ahead. By knowing which crisis response strategies fit with which crisis situations, a manager can assess the potential utility of his or her communication options. A crisis manager is better prepared for crisis communication when she or he knows which response fits best with a given crisis situation. Three points must be addressed to understand how to match crisis response strategies with crisis situations: development of a list of crisis response strategies; identification of crisis types; and creation of a link between the crisis response strategies and crisis types.

A number of rather extensive lists of crisis response strategies have been developed (Allen & Caillouet, 1994; Benoit, 1995a; Hobbs, 1995; Ice, 1991) and various researchers have proposed systems for categorizing crisis types (Egelhoff & Sen, 1992; Pearson & Mitroff, 1993). The first two points have been addressed. Unfortunately, there has been limited progress in linking crisis response strategies and crisis types (Coombs, 1995; Hobbs, 1995). The linkage is critical for generating practical insights because it informs practitioners as to the relative value of each crisis response strategy in his or her crisis situation. Understanding the interplay between crisis situation and crisis response strategy improves a crisis manager's preparation. By providing guidelines for crisis response strategy selection, crisis managers can respond more quickly because they are better prepared to craft a response. The neglect of the linkage can be traced to a failure to develop a theory-based connection between the crisis response strategies and the crisis types. The two lists tend to be developed separately and lack a theory-driven basis for integration. One of the great advances in public relations education has been the movement from accepted wisdom and "seat-of-the-pants" thinking to reasoned action. Students are taught principles, grounded in theory, which recommend certain courses of action when confronted with a public relations problem. Public relations moves from mere hunches to reasoned action. Crisis communication needs to move in the same direction. A theory-based model provides crisis managers with guidelines for reasoned action—provides reasons for the selection of crisis response strategies. This chapter reports on research which serves as the foundation for expanding crisis communication theory by developing a theory covering the use of crisis response strategies.

When a crisis hits, organizations must respond. One aspect of crisis communication can be improved by understanding how to best use crisis response strategies to protect the organization's reputation. Our Situational Crisis Communication Theory (SCCT) is an attribution theory–based approach to crisis communication. As presented in this chapter, SCCT seeks to develop a system of guidelines, which can be used to maximize the reputation protecting effect of crisis response strategies. This chapter reports extant and new studies that were conducted to test key ideas proposed by SCCT. The chapter begins with an explication of the SCCT model, moves to a discussion of the results of the various studies, and concludes with an examination of the implications from this line of research.

AN ATTRIBUTION THEORY–BASED APPROACH OF CRISIS MANAGEMENT: SCCT

Fusing attribution theory into crisis management is an effort to build crisis communication theory. More specifically, the research line presented here represents the foundation of a distinct theory of crisis communication. To understand the approach it is important to begin by explaining its attribution theory roots. Next, the application of attribution theory to crisis management and communication is developed. This second section identifies the propositions which required testing.

Attribution Theory Background

Attribution theory serves as the foundation for linking crisis response strategies and crisis types. Attribution theory is premised on the belief that people make judgments about the causes of events. People commonly use three causal dimensions when making attributions: stability, external control, and personal control/locus. Stability reflects whether the cause of the event happens frequently (stable) or infrequently (unstable). If someone repeats the same mistake it is stable, but it is unstable the mistake is unique or rare. External control indicates whether the event's cause was controllable or uncontrollable by some other person. If another actor controls what happens to a person, there is strong external control in the situation. Personal control assesses whether the event's cause is controllable or uncontrollable by the actor. This is the idea that the person can control his or her own fate in the situation. Locus reflects if the event's cause is something about the actor or something about the situation. An internal locus reflects something about the person, whereas external locus reflects something about the situation (McAuley, Duncan, & Russell, 1992; Russell, 1982; Wilson et al., 1993). Because research consistently demonstrates a substantial overlap between personal control and locus, it is suggested that the two causal dimensions be taken as one dimension (Wilson et al., 1993). Both personal control and locus reflect the intentionality of an act. High personal control and a locus in the actor create perceptions of intentional actions by the actor, whereas low personal control and a locus in the situation foster perceptions of unintentional action.

The judgments people make about these three causal dimensions influence their feelings and behaviors toward the actor (Weiner, 1985; Weiner, Perry, & Magnusson, 1988; Wilson et al., 1993). The messages a person creates can shape how others perceive the three attribution dimensions and how the messages can affect the feelings created by the attributions (Weiner et al., 1988). Communication can be used in attempts to influence a person's attributions, or the subsequent feelings attached to those attributions.

SCCT: Propositions and Research Directives

Logically, a crisis is an event for which people/publics seek causes and make attributions. More specifically, people evaluate organizational responsibility for a crisis when they determine the cause of a crisis. The more publics attribute crisis responsibility to an organization, the stronger the likelihood of publics developing and acting upon negative images of the organization. Greater attributions of responsibility lead to stronger feelings of anger and a more negative view of an actor's/organization's image (Weiner, Amirhan, Folkes, & Verette, 1987).

Organizational crisis responsibility should be perceived as strongest when the cause is stable (the organization has a history of crises), external control (controlled by others outside of the organization) is low, and personal control/locus is internal (the crisis originates from within the organization). When a crisis event is repeated (stable), publics should be more likely to attribute responsibility to the organization. Attributions of low external control indicate that the crisis was not under the control of groups outside of the organization and, thus, the crisis should not be attributed to external agents. Attributions that entail an internal locus/personal control suggest that the organization could have done something to prevent the crisis. Such attributions indicate that the organization could have prevented the crisis and knew that preventative measures could have been enacted. By meshing attribution theory and crisis communication, a set of testable propositions have been established as well as a research directive. We now consider the propositions and research directive.

Organizational crisis responsibility should be weakest when attributions suggest the locus of causality is external (the crisis originates from outside of the organization) and the cause is unstable (the crisis is an exception in the organization's performance history). Attributions reflecting strong external control and low personal control/external locus suggest that factors outside of the organization prompted the crisis.

Crisis Responsibility Proposition. As attributions of personal control/locus intensify, stakeholders attribute greater crisis responsibility to the organization in crisis.

Crisis types can be grouped according to attributions of personal control/locus. Crisis guru Ian Mitroff (1988b) is a outspoken advocate of grouping crises. By forming crisis clusters, crisis teams can construct one basic crisis management plan for each crisis cluster instead of one plan for each and every individual crisis type an organization might face (Mitroff, Harrington, & Gai, 1996). Although not amenable to becoming a proposition, how crisis types using an attribution approach is important to determine. Hence, we have formulated a research directive that should be investigated along with the propositions.

Cluster Research Directive. What clusters of crises emerge when external control and personal control are used to group crisis types?

Perceptions of crisis responsibility are related to the reputational damage inflicted by the crisis.

Organizational Reputation Proposition. Reputational damage increases as perceptions of crisis responsibility grow stronger.

Crisis responsibility becomes the link between the crisis types and crisis response strategies (CRS). One objective of crisis management is to prevent or lessen reputational damage to an organization (Barton, 1993; Benoit, 1995; Pearson & Mitroff, 1993; Sturges, 1994). A reputation is a valuable commodity for an organization. The reputation is linked often with such important factors as stock prices and recruitment (Fombrun, 1996). Hence, a reputation is worth protecting. If communication can alter publics' causal attributions or affect feelings created by these attributions, crisis response strategies could be used to prevent or to reduce reputational damage. Ultimately the potential reputational damage of crisis situation will recommend the selection of crisis response strategies, a point we develop further shortly. Basic informational needs must be met before the crisis manager tries to shape the organization's reputation among its key stakeholders. The first priority is to disseminate the information stakeholders need to protect themselves from harm (Sturges, 1994). Once the basic information needs are addressed, a crisis manager can turn to reputational concerns in his or her messages.

Crisis response strategies have been arrayed along a defensive–accommodative continuum. Defensive CRSs seek to protect the organization at the expense of the crisis victims. Accommodative CRSs make protecting the victims the top priority (Marcus & Goodman, 1991; Siomkos & Shrivastava, 1993). Table 7.1 places a set of commonly used CRSs on the defensive–accommodative continuum. The CRSs in Table 7.1 can be divided into three postures: deny, diminish, and repair. A posture represents a set of strategies that share similar communicative goals. The postures and strategies were derived from an analysis of the crisis communication response literature.

The *deny* posture represents a set of strategies that claim either no crisis occurred or that the accused organization has *no* responsibility for the crisis. If there is no crisis, there can be no organizational responsibility for a crisis. The *diminish* posture reflects a set of strategies that attempt to alter publics' attributions by re-framing how publics should interpret the crisis. Crisis managers might try to place distance between the organization and responsibility for the crisis. The *repair* posture encompasses a set of strategies that seek to improve the organization's image in some way. Crisis managers might encourage publics to judge the organization more positively or less negatively.

SCCT focuses on the symbolic dimension of crisis response strategies (what an organization says and does after a crisis). The symbolic function uses communication in attempts to influence how stakeholders perceive the crisis and the reputation of the organization in crisis. The CRSs are

TABLE 7.1

Postures and Crisis Communication Strategies

Postures	Strategies
Deny	*Clarification:* denies the crisis happened and reinforces the denial by explaining why the event could not have happened. Pepsi explained away the syringe scare of 1995 by clarifying how it was impossible to have a foreign object stay in the can during bottling.
	Attack: levels charges against the accusers to prompt the accusers to stop making charges.
	Shifting blame: admits a crisis event did occur but places the blame outside of the organization.
Diminish	*Excuse:* seeks to minimize responsibility for the crisis event. A crisis did occur, the organization is involved, but bears little of the responsibility for the crisis.
	Deny intent: say the organization did not mean for the crisis to occur.
	Deny volition: argue that the organization could not control events leading to the crisis.
	Justification: accepts responsibility for the crisis but attempts to limit the negativity associated with the crisis.
	Minimizing: argues that a crisis created little or no damage and/or poses little or no threat to stakeholders.
	Comparison: argues that the crisis is not as bad as similar crises.
	Big picture: places the crisis in a larger context and argues that such crises are the price that must be paid for reaching some larger, desirable goal. NASA placed the Challenger disaster within the context of the need to explore space.
	Misrepresentation: argues that the crisis is not as bad as others make it out to be.
Repair	*Suffering:* notes that the organization is also a victim in the crisis.
	Bolstering: reminds stakeholders of the good deeds an organization has done in the past. An organization might remind publics of past charitable work as a form of bolstering.
	Praising others: uses flattery toward a stakeholder to win that stakeholder's approval of the organization.
	Compensation: offers stakeholders gifts designed to counterbalance the crisis.
	Corrective action: seeks to restore the crisis situation to normal operation and/or promises to make changes which will prevent a repeat of the crisis in the future (Benoit, 1995). An organization tries to restore order as soon as possible after a crisis—return to normal operations. The organization also may change policies and/or procedures in order to reduce the likelihood of the crisis repeating itself.
	Apology: has the organization accept responsibility for the crisis and ask stakeholders for forgiveness.

matched to crisis types according to attributions of crisis responsibility. Greater attributions of crisis responsibility require more accommodative CRSs to better protect the organizational reputation. Organizations must do more to help victims as attributions of their crisis responsibility intensify.

Crisis Response Strategy Selection Proposition. Crisis response strategies that are matched to the crisis type will produce more positive organizational reputations than mismatched CRSs.

Stability is the third basic dimension of attribution theory. For organizations, their performance history is one form of stability. Performance history has two components: past crises the organization has suffered and the quality of relationships with stakeholders. An unfavorable performance history, past crises, or poor relationships with stakeholders indicates the crisis is part of a pattern of behavior—the crisis is stable. A favorable performance history would produce the opposite effect. The stability of a crisis will intensify the reputational damage of a crisis.

Stability Proposition. A history of crises intensifies perceptions of crisis responsibility and has a negative effect on organizational reputation.

Summary

This section explained how attribution theory can be applied to crisis communication and management. As part of the explanation, four propositions and one research question were identified. These propositions and Research Directive must be examined to determine the viability of an attribution theory–based approach to crisis management. Theory building requires the testing of propositions to determine whether or not they are accurate reflections of the phenomena.

STUDIES TO TEST SCCT

SCCT makes a number of assumptions about crises and how people react to crises. The primary assumption is that crisis communication strategy selection should be influenced or guided by the characteristics of the crisis situation. This section reviews extant and new studies designed to test the basic assumptions associated with SCCT. We begin by reviewing the basic idea behind the approach and discussing the measures used in the studies. Then, the results relevant to the research question and four propositions identified in the previous section are examined.

Basic Approach and Measures

The crisis communication strategy(ies) a crisis manager selects should be contingent upon the crisis situation. A crisis category system that can be tied to the earlier set of crisis communication strategies is needed. It would help to better prepare crisis managers for responding to the crisis. Attribution theory provides the materials necessary to create a category system that permits such a linkage. Let us return to the three dimensions of attribution theory. In every crisis, publics will have the ability to make judgments about external control and locus/personal control. Publics can generate both types of attributions from a description of the crisis. Not all crises have readily identifiable stability (performance histories). Publics have a short memory for most corporate activities, except those that are especially deplorable (Birch, 1994; Druckenmiller, 1993). Moreover, not all media reports about a crisis provide the relevant performance history (stability) as a context. Hence, the most appropriate category system will draw upon the external control and personal control/locus dimensions of attributions. We return to performance history when we consider factors that can intensify attributions of organizational responsibility.

The research studies involved two elements: the crisis scenarios and the dependent variable measures. The pool of crisis scenarios included:

1. accidents, two cases;
2. natural disasters, two cases;
3. workplace violence, one case;
4. legal violations (organization caught violating some law or regulation), two cases;
5. purposeful risk (an organization takes an action it knows will place publics at risk), one case;
6. product tampering, one case;
7. protest by some angry stakeholders, two cases;
8. product recall caused by a technical error (machine caused), one case; and
9. product recall caused by human error (a person performing his or her job incorrectly), two cases.

Product recall was divided into technical and human error because previous research suggests that people may perceive the two types of errors differently (Lerbinger, 1997).

The dependent variables included reputation, external control, personal control/locus, stability, and severity. Respondents' perceptions of organizational reputation were measured using a 10-item scale adapted from

McCroskey's (1966) measure of character. Character may not be the perfect measure for reputation. Still, character is important to public relations since credibility is essential to the effective practice of public relations (Baskin & Aronoff, 1992). It is preferable to identify key reputation dimensions and to have publics evaluate each dimension (Denbow & Culbertson, 1985). However, the need for consistency between scenarios prevented the use of such dimensional reputation measures in this study. The Revised Causal Dimensions Scale (RCDS) from McAuley et al. (1992) was used to measure attributions of personal control/locus, external control, and stability. Three to five items were used to measure each of the four dimensions.

Crisis Cluster Research Directive Study One

According to Russell (1982), the fundamental attribution error occurs when researchers assume respondents will perceive causes in the same way the researcher sees them. This warning is relevant to how we conceptualize crisis types. Although we can speculate on the attributions generated by different crises, this is only conjecture until people are asked how they perceive a crisis. Furthermore, it is assumed that these crises can be grouped into identifiable crisis types. These concerns are reflected in the crisis cluster research question:

> RQ: What clusters of crises emerge when external control and personal control are used to group crisis types?

If characteristics of a crisis situation suggest the most effective type of crisis communication strategy(ies), one must first know how people really perceive crisis situations. It would be folly to construct the rest of the approach without examining its foundation. Cluster analysis is an effective way to determine how attribution theory can be used to create groups of crisis types. The cluster analysis informs us about how people perceive each crisis type and which crisis types are perceived similarly.

The respondents were 270 students from the Midwest and Southeast. One hundred and fifty-two students were female (56.3%) and 118 were male (43.7%). Their ages ranged from 17 to 55 ($M = 21.98$, $SD = 5.06$). Each respondent was given one of 14 crisis scenarios and asked to complete a questionnaire after reading the scenario.

Results

A cluster analysis was used to divide the crisis types into identifiable groups. The analysis sought the smallest number of clusters in which locus and external control provoked differences between clusters. A four-cluster solution proved to be the simplest structure approaching this goal. The

TABLE 7.2
Analysis of Variance for Crisis Clusters

Crisis Dimension	Four-Cluster Solution			
	Cluster 1	Cluster 2	Cluster 3	Cluster 4
External Control	3.14_a	6.37_b	4.21_c	4.59_c
Locus	3.13_a	4.59_a	8.06_b	6.31_c

Note. Within any row, means with different letters differ at $p < .05$ or better by an LSD follow-up procedure.

analysis of variance revealed that locus and external control were effective in distinguishing between the resulting clusters. Table 7.2 summarizes the analysis of variance results.

The natural disasters crisis cluster is characterized by a strong external locus and weak external control. This cluster should generate the weakest perceptions of organizational responsibility since no one could control these events. The product tampering cluster is characterized by a strong external locus and strong external control. The strong external locus serves to mitigate organizational responsibility. However, the action was purposeful by an external agent and the organization should be prepared to defend itself from such actions. Thus, publics might be willing to attribute some organizational responsibility for not being better prepared to prevent the crisis. The accidents cluster is characterized by a slightly external locus and minimal external control—near the center of the graph. This cluster includes accidents, workplace violence, protests, and technical error recalls. These are things that "just seem to happen" and are not intentional. This cluster should produce minimal perceptions of organizational responsibility. The transgression cluster represents purposeful wrong-doing by an organization and is characterized by a strong internal locus and weak external control. This cluster includes purposeful risks, legal violations, and human error recalls. These crises should produce the strongest attributions of organizational responsibility.

Crisis Cluster Research Directive Study Two

Later research demonstrated that external control did not contribute significantly to explanations of crisis responsibility or organizational reputation and it was dropped from SCCT (Coombs, 1998). A second study was performed to determine which crisis clusters would form when external control was omitted. A total of 13 crisis types were used in the study:

1. rumor, false and harmful information about an organization is circulated;
2. natural disaster, naturally occurring environmental events;
3. malevolence/product tampering, organization is attacked by an external agent;
4. workplace violence, former or current employee attacks current employees on the job;
5. challenge, some group claims the organization is operating in an immoral or inappropriate manner;
6. technical breakdown accident, equipment or technology failure causes an industrial accident;
7. technical breakdown product recall, equipment or technology failure results in a defective product;
8. megadamage, a technical error accident that creates significant environmental damage;
9. human breakdown accident, human error triggers an industrial accident;
10. human breakdown product recall, human error leads to the production of a defective product;
11. organizational misdeed with no injuries, management knowingly places stakeholders at risk but no serious injuries occur;
12. organizational misdeed management misconduct, management knowingly violates regulations or laws; and
13. organizational misdeeds with injuries, stakeholders are placed at risk and there are injuries.

External control and personal control were replaced by crisis responsibility as the clustering factor. Crisis responsibility was selected because crisis responsibility was shown to be isomorphic with personal control and it is central to how SCCT assesses crisis types and selects the appropriate crisis response strategy (Coombs & Holladay, 2002).

RQ: Which clusters will emerge from the 13 crisis types when crisis responsibility is used as the cluster factor?

The respondents were 130 students from the Midwest and Southeast. Eighty-three were female (64%) and 47 were male (36%). Their ages ranged from 18 to 54 ($M = 21.8$, $SD = 5.40$). Each respondent was given two of the 13 crisis scenarios and asked to complete a questionnaire after reading each scenario.

Results

A cluster analysis was used to divide the crisis types into identifiable groups. The analysis sought the smallest number of clusters in which crisis responsibility created differences between clusters. A three-cluster solution proved to be the simplest structure. The first cluster was called the "victim" cluster and contained natural disaster, rumor, workplace violence, and product tampering crisis types. This cluster produced minimal attributions of crisis responsibility.

The second cluster was called "accidental" cluster because the crisis types were unintentional. The accident cluster included challenges, mega-damage, technical breakdown accidents, and technical breakdown product recalls. This cluster produced moderate attributions of crisis responsibility. The third cluster was called "preventable" cluster because all the crisis types involved knowingly violating laws or regulations, knowingly placing stakeholders at risk, or involving human errors that could have been avoided. The preventable cluster included human breakdown accidents, human breakdown product recalls, and the three variations of organizational misdeed. This cluster produced very strong attributions of crisis responsibility (Coombs & Holladay, 2002).

Crisis Response Strategy Selection Proposition

Two separate experiments were conducted to test for the effect of matched and mismatched crisis response strategies on reputational damage. The two experiments cover crises types from all four of the crisis clusters. Experiment 1 examines the transgression and accident crisis situations while Experiment 2 examines just the natural disaster and tampering/terrorism crisis situations.

Experiment I

SCCT seeks to match crisis communication strategies and crisis situations. The belief is that elements of the situations produce certain attributions and that these attributions represent organizational responsibility for the crisis. In turn, the stronger the attributions associated with organizational responsibility, the more likely the organization is to suffer reputational damage. Crisis communication strategies are used to reduce either (a) the attributions associated with organizational responsibility or (b) the negative feeling generated by those attributions. Therefore, a matched crisis communication strategy (one derived from the model) should protect an image better than either no response or just any response. It is the strategic, not random, use of communication that protects an organizational reputation from damage (Allen & Caillouet, 1994). The SCCT model posits that a matched crisis communication strategy should protect an image better than merely providing information or randomly selecting any crisis communication strategy.

> H1: Subjects in the matched strategy condition will hold more positive organizational reputations than those in the no response or mismatched response condition.

Subjects. The respondents in this study were 231 undergraduate students enrolled in communication courses at a Midwestern university. About 43% were male and 57% were female. The respondents ranged in age from 18 to 48 years ($M = 22.49$, $SD = 2.49$).

To test the three hypotheses, the experimental design included the manipulation of three factors: crisis type, performance history, and crisis response strategy. Two crisis types were used, accident and transgression. The difference between accidents and transgressions is intentionality. Accidents are unintentional while transgressions are intentional. In the scenarios, each crisis was presented as either a one-time or multiple-time occurrence. A one-time occurrence reflects a more positive performance history (i.e., the crisis is an isolated incident) while a multiple-time occurrence reflects a more negative performance history (i.e., the crisis is one in a series of crisis events). This two-level manipulation was intended to reflect the organization's performance history.

Crisis type and performance history were crossed to create four basic crisis scenarios. The scenarios were based on actual, lesser known cases but the information was adapted to fit the needs of the study. Next, one of three response types (no response, matched response, and mismatched response) was added to each of the four cases. The no response condition included only the case description with no mention of any organizational response beyond providing information about the crisis event. The matched response condition used a match between the crisis type and the crisis response strategy provided by the SCCT model of crisis management. The mismatched response condition also added a crisis communication strategy. However, the mismatched response scenario used a crisis communication strategy which was not recommended by the SCCT model of crisis management. Thus, each of the four cases had three response options, resulting in a total of 12 crisis scenarios. Table 7.3 summarizes the crisis situations and the responses.

Tests of Hypothesis. In order to examine Hypothesis 1 organizational reputation was analyzed using a 2 (crisis type: accident and transgression) × 3 (organizational response type: no response, matched response, and mismatched response) ANOVA. As expected, the results revealed significant main effects for crisis type [$F(1, 230) = 30.14$, $p < .0001$, eta$^2 = .12$] and re-

TABLE 7.3
Crisis Types and Response Options for Experiment 1

Crisis Type	Response Condition	Crisis Response Strategy
Accident	No response	Just information
	Mismatched response	Deny intent only
	Matched response	Corrective action
Transgression	No response	Just information
	Mismatched response	Minimization
	Matched response	Corrective action and compensation

Note. For each of these six scenarios, stability (stable and unstable) was manipulated resulting in a total of 12 scenarios.

sponse type [$F(2, 230) = 7.67$, $p < .0001$, eta^2 = .07]. To assess pairwise differences among the three levels for the main effect for response type, the Scheffe follow-up procedure ($p = .05$) was performed. The results indicated that reputation assessments for the matched response ($M = 3.15$) differed significantly from both the no response ($M = 2.63$) and the mismatched response ($M = 2.63$). Hypothesis 1 was supported by the findings. The Crisis Response Strategy Selection Proposition held for accident and transgression crisis types.

Experiment 2

Experiment 2 builds on Experiment 1 by examining the two remaining crisis clusters—natural disasters and product tampering. Performance history was not examined in this experiment since Experiment 1 established its role in intensifying reputational damage. As with Experiment 1, the matched response conditions are expected to protect/enhance the organizational reputation best.

H1: Subjects in the matched strategy condition will hold more positive organizational reputation than those in the no response or mismatched response condition.

Subjects and Design. The respondents in this experiment were 106 undergraduate students enrolled in communication courses at a Midwestern university. About 47% were male and 53% female. The respondents ranged in age from 18 to 46 years ($M = 22.31$, $SD = 2.42$).

Experiment 2 involved the manipulation of two factors: crisis type and crisis communication strategy. The two crisis types were natural disasters (e.g., tornadoes, floods, earthquakes, and so forth) and product tampering. The main difference between natural disasters and product tampering is ex-

TABLE 7.4
Crisis Types and Response Options for Experiment 2

Crisis Type	Response Condition	Crisis Response Strategy
Natural disaster	No response	Information only
	Mismatched response	Shifting the blame
	Matched response	Deny volition
Tampering	No response	Information only
	Mismatched response	Suffering only
	Matched response	Suffering and corrective action

ternal control. Both involve events external to the organization but some external actor can control tampering—she or he decides whether or not to tamper, whereas no one can control a natural disaster.

The crisis types were used to create two basic scenarios. Descriptions of equal text length were written for the two scenarios. Next, one of three response types (no response, matched response, and mismatched response) was added to each of the two cases. Following Experiment 1, the no response condition included just the case description with no mention of any organizational response beyond providing information about the crisis event. The matched response condition used a crisis communication strategy recommended by the SCCT model of crisis management. The mismatched response condition used a crisis communication strategy not recommended by the model. Table 7.4 presents the crisis types and the crisis communication strategies. Each of the two crisis types had three response options resulting in a total of six crisis scenarios.

Results

In order to examine Hypothesis 1 organizational reputation was analyzed using a 2 (crisis type: natural disaster and tampering) × 3 (organizational response type: no response, matched response, and mismatched response) ANOVA. The results revealed a significant main effect for crisis type [$F(1, 99) = 10.26$, $p < .005$] but no significant main effect for response type [$F(1, 99) = 2.04$, $p = .13$]. Hypothesis 1 was not supported, there was no significant difference in reputation scores between the different crisis communication strategies for either the natural disaster or the tampering crisis type. The Crisis Response Strategy Selection Proposition did not hold for product tampering and natural disaster crisis types. Both crisis types had strong organizational reputations after the crisis (natural disaster $M = 4.13$ and product tampering $M = 3.70$). It could be that with such strong organizational reputations the crisis response strategies could have little effect.

Stability Proposition

Performance history is one manifestation of stability and can be divided into crisis history and relationship history. When an organization has a history of crises, an individual crisis becomes part of a series of crises and should be perceived as more stable than a crisis that has happened only once. The greater the perceived stability of a crisis, the stronger perceptions of organizational responsibility should be (Griffin, 1994). The more publics perceive an organization as responsible for a crisis, the stronger a crisis' negative impact on the organization's reputation should be.

Crisis History Study

Crisis history refers to whether or not an organization has had similar crises in the past. When an organization has a history of crises, an individual crisis becomes part of a series of crises and should be perceived as more stable than a crisis that has happened only once.

> H1: Organizations in the favorable crisis history (low stability) condition will generate lower perceptions of crisis responsibility and stronger perceptions of organizational reputation than organizations in the unfavorable crisis history (high stability) condition.

Subjects.   The respondents in this study (Coombs, 1998) were 518 undergraduate students enrolled in communication courses in a Midwestern university. Fifty percent ($n = 259$) were female and 50% ($n = 259$) were male. The respondents ranged in age from 18 to 50 years old ($M = 22$, $SD = 4.35$). Accidents and organizational misdeeds were the crisis types used in the study. Each crisis type had two history/stability conditions: no history of crises/ low stability, and a history of crises/high stability. The crisis types and history conditions were crossed to create four basic scenarios.

Test of Hypothesis.   Hypothesis 1 was examined using separate one-way ANOVAs for accidents and organizational misdeeds. Performance history was used as the independent variable and crisis responsibility and organizational reputation were the dependent variables. The organizational misdeed analyses were significant for crisis responsibility [$F(1, 168) = 8.19$, $p < .005$] and organizational reputation [$F(1, 169) = 7.30$, $p < .01$]. The accident analyses were significant for organizational reputation [$F(1, 112) = 8.41$, $p < .0005$] and crisis responsibility [$F(1, 112) = 6.53$, $p < .02$]. The hypothesis was supported. Table 7.5 summarizes the means from the one-way ANOVAs. For both accident and organizational misdeed crisis types, the Stability Proposition held true (Coombs, 1998).

TABLE 7.5
Crisis Stability Means

Stability Conditions	Organizational Reputation		Crisis Responsibility	
	Accident	Transgression	Accident	Transgression
One-time crisis	3.48	2.52	1.99	3.18
Repeated crisis	3.10	2.14	2.35	3.44

Relationship History Study

Relationship history is the nature of the interaction between the organization and its stakeholders. A favorable relationship history is reflected in good works by the organization while an unfavorable one is characterized by conflict and failures by the organization to fulfill obligations to stakeholders. If a crisis is part of a pattern of "bad" behavior (unfavorable relationship history), the crisis should be perceived as more stable.

> H2: Respondents in the unfavorable relationship history will attribute greater crisis responsibility to the organization and will hold more negative organizational reputations than those in the favorable or neutral conditions.

Subjects. The respondents in this study (Coombs & Holladay, 2001) were 174 undergraduate students from a Southeastern university. Sixty-one percent ($n = 106$) were female and 39% ($n = 68$) were male. The respondents ranged in age from 18 to 25 years old ($M = 21$, $SD = 1.25$). A human breakdown accident crisis type was used as the stimulus. There were three crisis relationship conditions: favorable, the company was rated highly as a place to work and was involved in helping the community; neutral, no relationship history information provided; and unfavorable, the company was rated low as a place to work and failed to support the community.

Test of Hypotheses. ANOVAs were used to test for the effect of relationship history (independent variable) on organizational reputation and crisis responsibility (dependent variables). The results revealed a significant main effect for relationship history and crisis responsibility, $F(2, 165) = 4.87$, $p < .05$, $eta^2 = .04$, power = .68. Post hoc analyses found that the unfavorable relationship history condition ($M = 3.68$) attributed greater crisis responsibility to the organization than the favorable ($M = 3.26$) or neutral ($M = 3.30$) conditions. There was no significant difference between the favorable and neutral conditions. A significant main effect was found for relationship history and organizational reputation too, $F(2, 165) = 34.19$, $p < .001$, $eta^2 = .32$, power = 1.00. Post hoc analyses found the unfavorable relationship history condition (M = 2.92) produced significantly lower organizational reputation scores than the favorable (M = 3.53) or neutral condition (M = 3.51). There was no significant difference between the favorable and neutral conditions. Because the unfavorable relationship history conditions drove the results, Coombs and Holladay (2001) called the findings the "velcro effect." The relationship history is like velcro, it attracts additional reputational damage much like velcro attracts and snags pieces of lint and cloth.

Crisis Responsibility and Organizational Reputation Propositions

Three separate studies have examined the key relationships of crisis responsibility–personal control/locus and organizational reputation–crisis responsibility (Coombs, 1998, 1999; Coombs & Schmidt, 2000). Table 7.6 provides a summary of the correlations for the variables. All three studies found moderate to high correlations for crisis responsibility–personal control/locus and organizational reputation–crisis responsibility. The crisis responsibility–personal control/locus relationship correlated at between .41 to .73. The crisis responsibility–organizational reputation relationship correlated at between –.35 to –.67. The correlations indicate the Crisis Responsibility and Organizational Reputation Propositions are viable.

Limitations

Although the experimental task (reading crisis scenarios) may at first appear to be somewhat artificial, reading scenarios is not necessarily dissimilar from reading newspaper accounts of a crisis. The average person probably has minimal exposure to the details of crisis cases. Similarly, the audience may know little about the company prior to its receipt of publicity following an incident.

TABLE 7.6
Correlations for Crisis Responsibility–Personal Control/Locus
and Organizational Reputation–Crisis Responsibility

	Study		
Variable	Coombs, 1998	Coombs, 1999	Coombs & Schmidt, 2000
Crisis responsibility and personal control/locus	.73**	.54*	.41**
Organizational reputation and crisis responsibility	–.67**	–.35*	–.40**

$^*p$ = .05. $^{**}p$ = .01.

CONCLUSION

It is becoming increasingly important for organizations to assume a pro-active stance by formulating a crisis plan to manage the uncertainty associated with a crisis (Barton, 2001). Although having a crisis plan in place is important, it is equally important that crisis management be grounded in theory. Crisis managers should use reasoned action when selecting among possible organizational responses. The ideas presented in this chapter represent a move toward a systematic, theory-based approach to crisis communication. Developing the theory should improve crisis preparation. Crisis managers will have lists of crisis response strategies, crisis situation factors to consider, and guidelines for matching the two.

This chapter described SCCT and a program of research designed to test empirically ideas derived from the model. The first step in this research program was to apply the concepts of external control and locus, two concepts derived from attribution theory, to group crisis types. Four clusters of crises were identified using the dimensions of external control and locus. The clusters hold promise for understanding how aspects of the crisis and concomitant attributions lead stakeholders to perceive crises in systematic ways. This initial set of crisis clusters was replaced by a set based upon crisis responsibility. A new set was required as external control failed to contribute significantly to SCCT (Coombs, 1998) and personal control was found to be isomorphic with crisis responsibility (Coombs & Holladay, 2002).

SCCT proposes that different communication strategies should be more effective at preserving organizational reputation for different crisis types. The assumption underpinning this approach is that communication that is matched to the situation should be more effective than communication that does not take situation into account. Three specific postures (deny, diminish, and repair) and specific organizational responses (communication strategies) were identified then matched to the situations (crisis types). The matches were driven by the tenets of attribution theory and the demands each crisis places on the crisis managers.

The studies reported here draw on crisis cluster results and attribution theory by investigating factors thought to affect organizational reputation, including communication strategies, the organization's performance history (stability), and crisis severity. Two experiments were dedicated to the Crisis Response Strategy Selection and Stability Propositions. The experiments examined how crisis type, communication strategies, and stability were associated with the organization's image. Experiment 1 used accident and transgression crises and manipulated stability (Coombs & Holladay, 1996). The results indicated that communication strategies derived from the proposed situational model were more effective, in accident and transgression crises, at preserving a favorable image than no response and mismatched strategies. Accidents produced less reputational damage than organization misdeeds, presumably due to the stronger attributions of internal locus (i.e., organizational intentionality) generated by organizational misdeeds. A positive performance history (stability) was associated with a more positive reputation than a poor performance history. Performance history (crisis history and relationship history) was found to affect attributions of crisis responsibility and the organizational reputation. Both the unfavorable crisis history and relationship history resulted in people attributing greater crisis responsibility to an organization and increasing the reputational damage from the crisis. Unfavorable performance history creates a perception of stability for the crisis—the event is part of a pattern of "bad" behavior rather than an isolated event. Performance history appears to provide a context from which to interpret the current crisis and organizational response.

Experiment 2 focused on natural disaster and tampering cases. For these two crisis types, communication strategies were not found to be associated with reputation. A matched response was no better than a no response or a mismatched response at preserving organizational reputation. It seems likely that both of these types of crises are perceived as having very little organizational responsibility and inflict minimal reputational damage. As a result, there is little opportunity for the communication strategies to affect the reputation. Because the image is still very positive for these two crisis types, it is hard for communication strategies to have a significant impact on the organizational reputation. It also is possible that the result was an artifact of the particular scenarios used in this study. As expected, organizational reputation measures were significantly more positive in the natural disaster case compared to the tampering case.

Results from three extant studies addressed the Crisis Responsibility and Organizational Reputation Propositions. These studies were reviewed to determine the possible existence and strength of relationship between crisis responsibility and personal control/locus and crisis responsibility and organizational reputation. The moderate to high correlations between the variables support the viability of both propositions.

The research reported here represents first steps toward the development of a comprehensive theory of crisis management/communication based on attribution theory. These studies are the initial attempts to test components of the theory. Not all possible response strategies have been tested. One specific case and response strategy was used as an exemplar for each of the four crisis clusters. In order to offer more confident generalizations, there is a need to conduct additional studies with different specific exemplars and strategies. Replication and extension of these ideas are needed.

Best Practices

SCCT has utility for crisis management. It can be used as a framework from which to examine past cases (both successes and failures; e.g., why Exxon's posture failed to resonate with the perceptions of the public). The framework also may be applied in the testing of hypothetical cases. It can benefit crisis managers by serving as a template for formulating crisis plans. Crisis plans are useful because they reduce response time in crisis by developing options or rules before the crisis hits. Similarly, this model offers guidelines for selecting crisis communication strategies, thereby reducing the time spent developing and selecting such strategies during a crisis.

Crisis managers can use the results of the attribution theory–based approach in planning as well as responding. Crisis management plans save time by providing guidelines for critical decisions. Crisis managers save time when they do not have to make decisions from scratch—they have established decision making criteria and identified decision options. SCCT provides a list of potential crisis response strategies and recommendations for how to match the CRSs to the crisis situation. These guidelines can be integrated into the crisis planning process and made a part of an appendix to the crisis management plan.

Crisis managers benefit from theory-driven advice. The crisis managers learn why certain options are better or worse than others. Situational Crisis Communication Theory provides informed guidelines for the use of crisis response strategies. Crisis management efforts can become more effective when crisis managers utilize theory-based guidelines. Whether in planning or responding, crisis managers can benefit from an attribution theory–based set of guidelines for using crisis response strategies.

8

A Model for Crisis Management

Jennifer L. Borda
University of New Hampshire

Susan Mackey-Kallis
Villanova University

A bad public image has the power to make or break even multibillion-dollar corporations. A crisis can tarnish the most positive of corporate images, even that of an organization with well-established name recognition. Defending an organizational image during crisis requires a great deal of effort and skill. Yet, despite tremendous growth in the field of crisis management, the communication literature is filled with anecdotal evidence of what corporations and public relations professionals, with a limited scope of expertise and relying on their specific crisis experience, have done when faced with a crisis. As a result, what emerges in the literature are numerous "models" or prescriptions successfully applied to a small number of individual cases. This chapter presents a model developed and grounded in a review of the literature on crisis communication. The model's heuristic value is then demonstrated by application to examples of both successful and unsuccessful crisis management in the context of two corporate crises: the Alcan Chemical Explosion and the Dow Corning Breast Implant Cover-Up.

A crisis is any event "which seriously interferes with the operation of the organization and which can be regarded as unwelcome by those involved" (Wragg, 1992, p. 265). Companies are prey to a broad range of crises, both human-made and natural, such as tampering with a product, discovery of criminal activity, unwanted or hostile takeover, loss of an important customer, environmental accidents, recalls, and operator error. In recent years, efforts to control corporate crises, or crisis management, has matured as a public relations function and grown into a specialty area. Reasons for this development include: the growth of electronic media as the primary source of news; the increasing speed and capability of the media to acquire information, due to technological advances in research such as databases; the growth of special-interest groups and their proficiency in staging media-oriented events; and the expansion of instantaneous global communication capabilities (Birch, 1994; Reinhardt, 1987). Because a common factor found in all of these components is the speed of information transmission and reception, news of a crisis can spread so quickly that it can potentially paralyze top management before they can effectively control the crisis situation. As a result, fear of crises and the need to control them have escalated to previously unforeseen levels in business and industry.

Despite tremendous growth in the field of crisis management, the majority of the literature in this area provides anecdotal evidence of what corporations and public relations professionals, based on a sometimes limited scope of expertise, have done when faced with a crisis. The problem is lack of a model that has been tested and refined to apply to most cases.

A review of the research in communication and public relations, combined with the communication and public relations literature's recommendations for crisis management, is the basis for the descriptive model that follows. In order to demonstrate the model's heuristic value, the chapter also applies portions of this model to two case studies representing both successful and unsuccessful crisis management responses. Because the literature on crisis management is written by both in-house public relations experts and by outside consultants, however, there are often shifts in the views expressed. Despite these insider–outsider shifts in perspective, no major differences were found between the steps advised by experts within organizations and those advocated by experts hired as consultants. Before developing the model, we begin with a brief discussion of the role of communication in crisis management.

THE ROLE OF CORPORATE COMMUNICATION IN A CRISIS

Most communication scholars agreed that, "Image is something that a communicator creates" (Grunig, 1993a, p. 126). In large and small corporations, the public relations department is usually responsible for a corporation's image. To keep the positive image a corporation may have worked years to create, quick and effective action must be taken at the onset of any problem, because a crisis can tarnish even the most positive image of an organization with well-established name recognition.

Depending on the magnitude of the particular crisis, the response of the organization will vary. Because every step from the onset of the crisis to its outcome becomes crucial, however, organizations or crisis management teams should avoid making "seat-of-the-pants" decisions. Time, effort, and effective communication are essential to managing a crisis, and as Gibson (1991) noted, defending an organizational image requires a great deal of effort and skill.

Research has shown that communication is central to the list of universals that organizations should consider when addressing a crisis situation. In the early 1960s, for example, John Marston (cited in Hallahan, 1993) introduced a program known as RACE (Research-Action-Communication-Evaluation), which includes communication as one of the four central components. Years later, a similar program was devised by Hainsworth and Wilson (1992) that also proposed communication as one of the four basic elements in a model composed of research, planning, communication/implementation, and evaluation. Both Marston and Hainsworth and Wilson also cite communication as central to all phases of crisis management. During the research phase, for example, decisions need to be made based on sound, socially responsible business principles (Cutlip, Center, & Broom, 1985). The role of communication is a fundamental part of these decisions, as well as a critical element in the preservation of the corporate image. Adept communication is also crucial to good planning, which involves setting goals and objectives that allow the corporation to resolve the crisis at hand. Once the crisis heats up, the most important task is, of course, the communication phase—"conveying a company's message in a coherent, disciplined and organized fashion" (Werner, 1990, p. 30). If handled properly, this communication "can reduce the chance of escalation, limit interference with normal business operation and contain damage to the company's operation and bottom line" (Kaufmann, Kesner, & Hazen, 1994). Effective communication also will limit legal liability and significantly aid in the maintenance of a respectable corporate image. What emerges from the literature is the overall importance of communication in crisis management and the realization that proficient communication is essential to every step in crisis planning.

The following model of crisis management (Fig. 8.1), which emphasizes the role of communication in the organization, focuses on the literature's recommendations regarding the steps companies and public relations firms should take for successful crisis management in the pre-, present-, and postphases of a crisis.

CRISIS MANAGEMENT: BEFORE THE CRISIS

As a result of the fast-paced world of crisis information, most crisis management experts advise public relations practitioners to prepare for a crisis long before one hits. Many crisis management researchers agree there are a number of steps an organization can take before a crisis actually occurs

CRISIS MANAGEMENT MODEL

I. Before the Crisis

PREPARE	PLAN	PUT IT TO THE TEST

* Create A Crisis
  Management Team
	* Create a Message
	  Action Plan (MAP)
		* Test the Plan

* Gain Management Support For A Crisis Plan	* Define target audiences	

* Identify Corporate
  Vulnerabilities
	* Establish techniques needed
	  to communicate the message	

* Train Employees	* Assign responsibility	
* Complete Pre-crisis Preparations		

II. During the Crisis

GATHER	PACKAGE	DELIVER
* Do Background Research	* Disclose All Information	* Get Your Message Out Quickly
* Designate A Spokesperson	* Tell the Truth	* Be Assertive With the Media

* Define Short- & Long-Term
  Problems
	* Put Yourself in the Other
	  Party's Shoes	

	* Show Concern	

III. After the Crisis

EVALUATE	CONGRATULATE	CONTINUE TO CONTROL

* Evaluate the Crisis
  Management Campaign
	* Congratulate Employees
	  Within the Organization
		* Prepare for Continuing
		  Media Coverage

FIG. 8.1. Crisis management model.

(Katz, 1987; Umansky, 1993; Werner, 1990). According to Katz (1987), "Crisis communications need not be an amorphous service provided under emergency conditions, a mad dash by practitioners to respond to the latest media inquiry. Instead, it can and should be part of a systematic, practiced approach, put into place long before the 'wolf' ever comes to the door" (p. 46). The extra time spent during crisis-free periods preparing for possible situations will save critical moments that may be needed later to successfully manage a crisis. The object of a crisis plan is to develop a methodical framework for action that will contain most crises before they get out of control (Umansky, 1993). The time before a potential crisis hits should be used for preparation, planning, and putting a crisis management strategy to the test.

Preparation Phase

In the preparation phase, time should be spent on creating a crisis management team; gaining management support for a crisis plan; identifying corporate vulnerabilities; training employees; and completing precrisis preparations.

Create a Crisis Management Team (CMT). To help alleviate some of the burden on the organization, many companies have opted to employ crisis management teams to handle potential crisis situations. According to the expert majority opinion, appointing this team before the crisis strikes is usually more efficient, due to the limited time during a crisis for decision making. Once a crisis management team is assembled, it becomes the team's responsibility to keep up-to-date information about every aspect of their particular organization.

According to Umansky (1993), isolating a multidisciplinary task force assures that competent individuals will be there to handle the crisis so others can concentrate on the day-to-day running of the organization. According to Kaufmann, Kesner, and Hazen (1994), "a crisis management team (CMT) should be composed of people who are creative, knowledgeable of the business, powerful (having the authority and responsibility to make decisions and allocate resources quickly), and able to bring a variety of unique perspectives to bear on solving the problem" (p. 38).

Gain Management Support for a Crisis Plan. Once a crisis management team is in place, the team's primary goal, from a public relations point of view, is to gain management's support for a crisis plan. An informal study conducted in the mid-1980s revealed that top company executives respond to crises with a relatively universal order of behavior. Media relations often appeared last on the list of these executives' initial concerns, despite the fact that the media often get word of the story before any other group (Lukaszewski, 1987). Due to the inconsistency between how top management and public relations professionals think about crisis management (although this may be changing in the more media-conscious 21st century), most models suggest gaining top management support for a plan.

Identify Corporate Vulnerabilities. A third step in precrisis planning that emerges from the literature is identifying corporate vulnerabilities. Katz (1987) advised talking to top-level managers, technical personnel, and even outside sources to discover potential troublespots. He suggests asking questions such as: *What are our greatest risks? How likely are they to oc-*

cur? Who will be affected? How serious will the consequences be? Umansky (1993) proposed extending this process by asking, "In my wildest dreams, what three things would never happen to this company?" (p. 33). He further recommends including these worst case scenarios in your plan. Katz (1987) also stressed the importance of including an issues assessment program to identify, prepare for, and resolve issue-related problems before they become emergencies. This may require research and monitoring public-opinion trends, trade literature, special-interest groups, and the media on all issues that are related to the organization.

Train Employees. Umansky (1993) advised, "invest in the *people* who will carry your corporate identity and deliver your message through times of crisis. Give them all the training they need—and then some" (p. 33). In addition, many experts stress the importance of establishing positive employee relations within the company and enlightening people involved in the corporation about the implications and facets of a potential crisis situation. This is a crucial step because employees are the foundation of any business or corporation. Sklarewitz (1991) suggested notifying receptionists and other personnel where to direct reporters' inquiries or setting up rules (e.g., no one is permitted to take outside calls or to call out during a crisis). Dilenschneider (cited in Eisenhart, 1990) recommended training people to be sensitive to crisis techniques, including media training and how to deal with regulatory agencies. Moreover, Werner (1990) advised making sure everyone is familiar with the company's "Message Action Plan" (discussed in the next section) and can complete their responsibilities competently.

Complete Precrisis Preparations. In addition to training employees in crisis preparation, various articles urge companies to complete as much of the communication effort as possible before a crisis happens. Media packets containing information about the business, biographies of key individuals, and photographs should be prepared in advance (Brown, 1990). Additional time-savers range from crucial preliminary efforts, such as setting up an information hotline, to simple tasks, such as making sure there is a stash of take-out menus in the meeting room to keep energy levels up (Mitchell, 1993). Reinhardt (1987) stressed evaluating the organization's current media and community relationships. Crisis communications begins by establishing and building solid day-to-day community and media relations before a crisis ever occurs. Such positive relationships ultimately pay off when a company really needs them.

Plan for the Crisis

When a crisis strikes an organization, many outside influences can hinder its ability to get its message out effectively—the most important task in managing a corporate crisis. These influences include confidentiality, time limitations, stress, and the possibility of emotional decisions taking precedence over logical ones (Werner, 1990). According to Lawrence Werner (one of five public relations executives recruited to assess the communications and public relations challenges posed by the Exxon Valdez oil spill), an important element of the planning process in crisis management involves designing a Message Action Plan (MAP).

Create a Message Action Plan (MAP). The MAP communication matrix combines all elements of a public relations or communications plan into a single, easily read document that helps assure a company's key message will be conveyed in a coherent, disciplined, and organized fashion in times of crisis. It allows for quick understanding of what must be accomplished when, how, and by whom. Werner (1990) emphasized that a MAP—created while time and sanity are abundant—reduces a crisis to its most basic components, provides an easy reference for the crisis management team, and helps keep crisis management on schedule when there is not a lot of time to think.

Werner (1990) implied three central requirements of a thorough MAP: It must define the target audiences for the company's message, develop the proper techniques to communicate the message, and assign responsibilities for these tasks.

Define Target Audiences. The first element of a MAP focuses on the target audiences or publics. Robert Dilenschneider, a leading crisis management advisor, concluded there are four primary audiences to be reached in a crisis: employees, politicians, the mass media, and stock market analysts. Although he admits that in some crises the immediate community, environmentalists, and the Red Cross are important factors, the primary four are the company's lifeblood. He explained why each of these four groups are important:

> politicians [because they] can make the crisis a lot worse and cause you big problems in state capitals or Washington. The media, because if they don't get the story right, they are put in a hell of a position and could misreport. The employees because without them, you can't solve the problem. Finally, analysts are key to your stock price. You really have to hit them all at once. (Eisenhart, 1990, p. 86)

In creating a MAP, Werner (1990) advised listing every group to be targeted in the public relations effort in order of importance. Deciding importance before a crisis hits prevents time wasted by second-guessing the list when the crisis explodes. He further suggested listing the concepts to be communicated to these target audiences. This requires developing the messages to be conveyed to internal and external audiences. Umansky (1993) recommended deciding what consumers, staff, investors, buyers, the media, legislators, and other regulatory agencies should know absolutely and positively about the company throughout a crisis. Umansky (1993) also advised including messages that cut to the very core of the organization's corporate mission, culture, and identity. Once the messages are established, the second step of a good MAP is to ensure that messages are communicated quickly through proper channels.

Establish Techniques Needed to Communicate the Message. Once the company's target audiences are defined, the MAP should list all techniques that will be used to communicate the company's message to these groups. Werner (1990) noted that public relations executives need to think broadly about this category. Examples of communication strategies used include press releases, media packets, other publications and printed materials, audio and video communications, personal contacts, and paid media advertising.

Reinhardt (1987) advised that it is crucial to set up areas needed for these activities in advance. Various experts within the literature advised designating a conference room for the crisis management team that includes access to a private phone line, fax line, copiers, and a secretary, if possible. Reinhardt (1987) recommended designating a news center within the crisis headquarters from which the company can constantly feed the media information. She wrote, "Provide telephones and typewriters for their use. And select a spot for television interviews—away from the scene of the disaster and without company identification in the shot" (p. 44). This prevents the media from digging up information on their own, and possibly reporting an incorrect version of the story.

Assign Responsibility. The third element of a successful MAP assigns the person or persons responsible for each task. Clarifying who is in charge makes tasks easier to handle during the crisis and prevents missed opportunities and deadlines. Werner (1990) suggested setting up a timeline for how quickly these tasks need to be accomplished and making those deadlines the company's or public relations agency's priority during the crisis.

What emerges from the literature on crisis management is that the advantages of setting up a communications matrix, such as a MAP, greatly outweigh the efforts needed to construct one. This simple document keeps everyone involved focused on the important communications strategies and the objectives to be achieved. As Werner (1990) concluded, the result is a more controlled effort, reduced inefficiencies, and more productive performances from everyone working on the crisis.

Put the Crisis Management Plan to the Test

Test the Plan. The final step in precrisis preparation, once a plan has been established, is to put the company to the test. Umansky (1993) suggested using professionals and outside firms, if necessary, to simulate a crisis to see if the system works. Repeating these drills over time will help the company to cover many hypothetical crisis situations. Testing is essential, because even the most carefully thought out plans must be re-evaluated and refined. For example, Monsanto, a major chemical manufacturer, holds crisis drills several times a year. During one drill, Monsanto found that the fire department's radios no longer operated on the same frequency as their own radios (Stanton, 1989). Learning a lesson like this during a practice run can free up precious time during a real crisis, and in the case of Monsanto, might even save lives.

Most experts agree that the key to crisis survival is proper preparation, planning, and testing of the plan. This precrisis phase of crisis management, however, is only the beginning. Every crisis is different and no single plan provides all of the answers. Nowotny (1989) explained that the best defense in a crisis situation is to stay on your toes. Therefore, the next section of this chapter discusses steps to be taken during an actual crisis situation. These are the techniques communication scholars and public relations professionals suggest following in order to keep the crisis under control and to keep the company's or client's image intact.

CRISIS MANAGEMENT: DURING THE CRISIS

According to various public relations professionals, three of the most important steps in creating a corporation's public relations campaign are the *gathering, packaging,* and *delivering* of information. This process can be found across the board in the drafting stages of any good public relations campaign. Given the prominence of these steps within the public relations discipline, it is not surprising that they also offer efficient guidelines for constructing a public relations campaign during a crisis situation. Each of these three phases in crisis management—gather, package, and deliver—and the various steps involved in each, are discussed in this section.

Gathering Relevant Information

The process of creating a public relations campaign always begins with the gathering of all information relevant to the client or the company involved. Any consultant intent on shaping the public's perception of a corporation first must know that corporation and the crisis at hand inside and out. This also applies to any in-house crisis management team. What emerges as essential in the information-gathering phase of crisis management are researching the background of the crisis, designating a spokesperson during the crisis, and defining the short- and long-term goals for managing the crisis.

Do Background Research. Before meaningful recommendations can be provided during a crisis, the crisis management team must understand both the background of the situation and the scope and dimensions of the organization's or client's position. After receiving the initial crisis alert and before the first meeting with the client or the company's top management, Croft (1992) recommended developing a list of possible actions, based on a preliminary understanding of the problem and the team members' experiences in similar situations. Croft recommended asking as many questions as possible about the situation, such as: *Who is responsible for the situation? What is the historical background? Where are support and opposition likely to come from? What position has the media taken, if any?* and *What damage could your company suffer from the situation?* (p. 31). Based on the information found in such a meeting, Croft suggested revising the action plan if necessary and establishing any new priorities. If time permits, he advised holding a brainstorming session with staff members outside of the crisis team to receive feedback from other perspectives.

Designate a Spokesperson. Katz (1987) argued that a crucial part of managing a crisis is appointing one spokesperson to present a unified message about the crisis. Additional literature recommends designating a clear-thinking and articulate person with a solid grasp of both the business and the key message the company wants to convey. If that person is the CEO, a back-up person should be appointed to represent the CEO if she or he is away at the time. This decision is fundamental because this person is going to be the symbol of the company, and she or he must have the ability to present the best aspects of the company until the very end.

The first "public relations rule of thumb is that in a crisis situation, the corporate spokesperson should reach the media first" (Murphy, 1991, p. 125). Public perception is a very important factor if a corporation is going to win its crisis battle. Getting word to the public from a reliable or recognizable source gives the public reassurance.

Define Short- and Long-term Problems. It is critical to immediately define the short-term problem and the long-term effects of the situation. Umansky (1993) urged asking the question, "Where does senior management want to stand in a day, in a week, in a month, in a year?" (p. 34). One place to begin identifying these problems is opinion polls. Actions and messages employed in a crisis must fully account for the attitudes of the company's key audiences (Katz, 1987). By tapping into what the public is thinking and feeling, a company can avoid basing their actions solely on what the media is saying, and concentrate on what people really perceive as the problem. In addition, Theus (1993a) recommended listening carefully to the company's critics and then following their suggestions if appropriate.

Packaging Critical Information

Once the crisis has been defined and the problems established, the crisis team needs to create the messages it wants to convey to the organization's various audiences. This part of the process involves packaging the previously gathered information in order to have it reflect the company's mission and display its image in a positive light. Among all the various suggestions regarding the packaging phase of crisis management during a crisis, four guidelines seem to emerge across the literature: disclose all relevant information, tell the truth, be prepared to counteract any negative publicity that may be generated by opposing parties or watch groups, and show concern for victims of the crisis.

Disclose All Information. When giving information to the media, the literature stresses honesty, accuracy, and full disclosure. Conventional wisdom seems to be that the media will uncover the whole story anyway, and left to do the dirty work themselves the coverage will probably end up lasting longer and dragging the crisis out further. Hal Warner, director of crisis management for a leading New York public relations firm, recommends that organizations inform audiences to the best of their knowledge, even if that knowledge is limited (Maynard, 1993). He advised, "You may not be able to say much, but you can say something. If all the facts aren't there, get out and say so" (p. 54). Experts also advise a company not to disclose information that is beyond their realm of experience. There are few attributes more important to a company than its credibility, and getting involved in areas where there is a lack of experience and speculating about what you do not know is a quick way to lose it (Lurie, 1991). Therefore, the literature suggests calling in other professionals if necessary, such as consultants and investigators, to prevent losing credibility by disclosing information about which the company lacks considerable knowledge.

To aid in the monitoring of when and how information should be disclosed, a specialized subgroup within the crisis management team should be responsible for regulating crisis information. Kaufmann et al. (1994) noted that this subgroup should consist of a minimum of three members: a lawyer to regulate the legal implications of disclosed information, a public relations professional to oversee the effect of disclosed information on the company's image, and a member of senior management who can supervise the disclosure of information and make the final decision regarding the lawyer's and the public relations practitioner's suggestions.

Tell the Truth. People want to hear the truth from a company. A 1992 survey by the Porter Novelli public relations firm found that the leading causes of anger about crises were when the company involved refused to accept blame or responsibility, when the crisis could easily have been avoided, when the company supplied incomplete or inaccurate information, and when the company placed corporate profits ahead of the public interest. Ninety-five percent of those surveyed said they were more offended by a company's lack of honesty than by the crisis itself (Maynard, 1993).

Put Yourself in the Other Parties' Shoes. According to Croft (1992), if the organization's crisis is the result of a specific party's actions, such as a workers' union, a regulatory agency, or a special interest group, it is helpful to try on the other parties' shoes. It is also beneficial to know the concerns of the key publics involved in the crisis. Katz (1987) advised, "Company messages and actions in a crisis must fully account for the attitudes and opinions of its key audiences. A mechanism must be put into place as part of your crisis planning to sample quickly the opinions of these publics" (p. 46). Croft (1992) stressed, "An experienced public relations practitioner may be guiding the other party's media campaign. In such cases, you should make every effort to anticipate and counter these efforts" (p. 30). In addition, he advised, "take a careful look at your client and probe for policy weaknesses, unfortunate corporate activities or past behavior that may attract negative media coverage" (p. 30).

Croft (1992) also recommended either preparing a counterattack or diluting what you anticipate will be the other party's media effort with a comprehensive campaign of your own. This kind of forethought helps the company prepare for a "wildcard"—a totally unexpected, bizarre, or often incorrect item of information leaked out by an opposing force (Pinsdorf, 1991).

Show Concern. As soon as the crisis breaks, public relations experts agree it is imperative to show concern. Pinsdorf (1991) advised, "Treat survivors compassionately. Provide them with as much information as possible. Keep them informed about the investigation of the incident" (p. 31). She also suggested, "Don't let possible legal liabilities interfere with presenting a human face" (p. 31). By presenting a human face, people are more likely to think of an organization as trustworthy. If the company points fingers and assigns blame, people will regard the company as defensive and guilty. John Hall, Ashland Oil's chairman and CEO, advised, "If the public perceives you are truly sorry and that you genuinely want to do the right thing, they will usually forgive you rather quickly" (Kaufmann et al., 1994, p. 30).

Deliver the Crisis Response Message

The final step in crisis management involves recommendations for the delivery of the crisis-response messages. The delivery of the organization's message will have the greatest impact on the success of the campaign, as well as on the public's perception of the corporation after the crisis. According to the literature, the two steps essential to delivering this message, while preserving the corporation's good image, are communicating the message quickly and controlling the media.

Get Your Message Out Quickly. According to the literature, giving the who, what, how, when, why, and where as quickly as possible is crucial to a company's crisis management objectives. Letting the story dribble out only prolongs the agony, and results in new and potentially damaging headlines with each dose of new information. Dilenschneider advised, "You can't go much beyond a few hours because if you do, you demonstrate that you're out of control and don't know what you are doing" (Eisenhart, 1990, p. 86). Reinhardt (1987) advocated designating someone to be on call for the press 24 hours a day and delivering the corporation's messages directly, without depending on intermediaries.

Be Assertive With the Media. The literature recommends that companies be the first to inform their audiences of what is being done to remedy the situation. Mitchell (1993) warned against waiting for the media to begin reporting the recovery from a crisis, since a recovery does not make news, whereas a disaster does. She suggested using this opportunity to find human-interest stories and pitching them to the media (1993). This also will portray the company as sensitive, understanding, and people oriented. By providing a fast and complete communications blitz, a company can usually provoke the media into losing interest, which may allow the story to fade away quickly. Reinhardt (1987) cautioned against trying to be promotional in press releases or interviews during the height of a crisis, however, as there will be plenty of time to sell an organization's virtues once the dust has settled.

CRISIS MANAGEMENT: AFTER THE CRISIS

After the crisis has passed, the crisis management team's first instinct will most likely be to forget the whole thing and move on to new business. However, crisis management does not end with the conclusion of the crisis. According to the crisis management literature, the crisis management team should always be looking for ways to prepare for the next crisis by *evaluat-*

ing, congratulating, and *continuing to control* the situation. This final phase of crisis management includes evaluating the crisis management campaign used during the actual crisis and making improvements for next time, bolstering morale by letting employees know that their work did not go unnoticed, and continuing to monitor and control media coverage of the story.

Evaluate the Crisis Management Campaign

After the immediate crisis has passed, various articles recommend an evaluation period. Reinhardt (1987) had this advice: "The emergency team should reconvene to review the organization's contingency plan. Be candid. Recommend improvements and point out vulnerabilities" (p. 44). Dilenschneider suggested talking to the press in order to find out weaknesses in the campaign and how things could have been done better (Eisenhart, 1990). The literature advises preparing a detailed summary of how the plan operated, mistakes made along the way, and things that could have been better prepared for in advance (Katz, 1987; Reinhardt, 1987; Umansky, 1993; Werner, 1990). The team can then use this information to revise and improve the plan for the next time a crisis may occur.

Congratulate Employees Within the Organization

Katz (1987) noted, "Crises pass, but their effects often linger" (p. 47). The morale of the organization is almost always shaken during a crisis, therefore a crucial postcrisis effort is needed to bolster the spirit of the company's employees and everyone involved in managing the crisis. Trahan (1993) asserted, "Make sure to say 'thank you' because you need people to get your job done" (p. 32). Dilenschneider added, "You need to look for winners in a crisis—those who have done a really super job—and physically reward them. You need to make them winners in front of employees, the press, and the community. You need to turn the crisis into a celebration, so to speak" (Eisenhart, 1990, p. 87).

Continue to Control the Situation

Although a company may ultimately survive a crisis, it may be some time before the media accepts this reality. Birch (1994) warned that the story "will run again and again. When a public inquiry begins and when it finally reports, when the legal actions start and, if it is a quiet news day, on the anniversary of the initial crisis, and sometimes each year thereafter" (p. 34). The team should be prepared for this response and have reaction statements ready to counteract negative publicity. By predicting this coverage and intervening, the company can have a significant influence on the substance of these reports.

The three steps previously outlined: evaluating the campaign, bolstering morale within the organization, and preparing for continued media coverage complete the model of crisis management. As illustrated in the model, the initial concern of the company's public relations department—or an agency working for a client—is to have a concise, easy to follow, comprehensive plan before a crisis hits. In the second stage, during the actual crisis, it is important to maintain focus on the company's centralized message, address the cultural values of the company and the public concerned, and make sure that the message is communicated quickly with concern and compassion. During this phase, it also is important to disclose all relevant information, tell the truth, and broadcast plans for remedying the situation. Hal Warner urged, "A company's action in a crisis can be summed up in one phrase: 'Do what is right.' Ask yourself, if it were my family, my home, my community, is this what I would want done?" (Maynard, 1993, p. 54). Finally, after the crisis is over, the literature recommends evaluating an organization's MAP and preparing for the next time. Success or failure in crisis management hinges on the company's performance. A best effort will be well recognized, and the image that the company has worked so hard to create will remain intact.

The following section demonstrates the value of the preceding model through a review of two case studies. The crisis management campaigns of Alcan Smelters and Chemicals Ltd. and Dow Corning are summarized and discussed in terms of how closely their crisis management efforts complied with the *gather*, *package*, and *deliver* guidelines advocated in the "during the crisis" phase of the management model. Due to limited information supplied in these case studies regarding the pre- and postcrisis efforts of the corporations, the analysis focuses mainly on their actions during the crisis. Alcan represents a corporation whose crisis management strategies closely resembled those outlined in the model and, by contrast, Dow Corning represents a corporation whose crisis management campaign differed from the model's guidelines.

CASE STUDIES

Undoubtedly, all crises are not the same, because each is influenced by various factors—many of which are uncontrollable and unforeseeable. Although the perceived severity of each crisis may vary, what remains constant is the threat that specific crises can pose to organizations. The analyses of the following case studies from Alcan and Dow illustrates how successful crisis management was achieved through adherence to the *gather*, *package*, and *deliver* guidelines of the crisis management model. Specifically, the case studies show how the handling of these two crises, the near-seamless response to "The Alcan Explosion" and the less well-handled "Dow Corning Breast Implant Cover-up," supports the usefulness of the crisis management model developed from our review of the communication and public relations literature—and the significant consequences of not adhering to such a model.

The Alcan Explosion

The 5-day-long crisis suffered by Alcan Smelters and Chemicals Ltd. began just minutes after the freak explosion of a contracted ship in La Baie, Quebec on March 11, 1990. The Pollux, a Norwegian vessel, was contracted by Alcan to transport spent pot lining—a by-product of aluminum production. The corporation's crisis management skills were quickly put to the test as news reports, which surfaced within 15 minutes of the explosion and speculated on the possibility of deaths, toxic emissions, and environmental damage, threatened to undermine public confidence in the corporation's ability to handle the crisis (Bouchard, 1992).

As a result of the blast, two foreign seamen were killed instantly and eight people were injured. The unfortunate incident was caused by a buildup of oxides contained in the pot lining, which become volatile when exposed to water. It was later determined that deckhands had covered the air holes with plywood to avoid inhaling ammonia vapors emanating from the pot lining inside the ship, which led to the blast (Bouchard, 1992).

"According to Canadian law, from the moment the explosion occurred, jurisdiction for the port transferred automatically to the federal government. However, it was still Alcan's crisis" (Bouchard, 1992, p. 45). Alcan immediately took charge and initiated the creation of two crisis teams to handle the threat of further danger and to handle public communications. The first group, consisting primarily of Quebec police, environmental personnel, transport officials, and Alcan environmental specialists and engineers, was responsible for ensuring public safety measures and abrogating the threat of a second explosion. The second team, composed primarily of public relations professionals, was charged with reversing negative public opinion surrounding the crisis.

In addition to the concerns already expressed by the media and the industrial town of La Baie, the possibility of a second explosion and the need to transport hazardous waste through La Baie's main street further complicated Alcan's crisis situation. The communication crisis team was faced with deciding which information to disseminate to the public. Working from past experience, the public relations specialists on site advised full disclosure, and during the first news briefing 2 hours after the explosion, the truth of the incident was told. An Alcan spokesperson continually presented a reassuring image during informational broadcasts throughout the crisis. This crucial decision on the part of the team, combined with the speed of their actions, strictly adhered to the package and delivery steps of the crisis management model—and resulted in Alcan's favorable perception by the media and the public.

Once the communications team had grouped to deal with the crisis, they began defining the short- and long-term problems of the crisis. They established their primary objective as allaying the anxiety that had been generated in La Baie among town residents and Alcan and port employees. The long-term goal was to assure that all parties involved would be promptly compensated for any damages or inconveniences suffered, a gesture that would begin to restore Alcan's image in the community. The team worked quickly to console employees and the general population regarding their future safety. By the second day, teams from the property department were estimating damages and accepting claims made by La Baie residents. By developing these objectives, the company successfully determined the immediate concerns of their publics (by placing themselves in the shoes of the other parties involved), anticipated their feelings, showed their concern, and acted to rectify the situation. These actions, in addition to promptly defining the problems caused by the crisis, successfully emulated the steps specified in the gather and package phases of the model.

Alcan's full disclosure of all aspects of the situation continued throughout the 5-day crisis. The communications team kept the 340 port employees directly informed of events through a telephone chain (before they were disclosed to the media, whenever possible) and reporters were kept informed through two daily full-scale news briefings, regular news bulletins and continuous contact with Alcan public affairs staff (Bouchard, 1992). These briefings were also aired over cable television, reaching 80% of La Baie's population and providing viewers with first-hand information about the developing situation.

Another goal of the communications team was monitoring media and public feedback in order to stay abreast of evolving aspects of the situation. "The communications unit took appropriate action to inform key publics on an ongoing basis, striving to anticipate shifting public concerns and stay one step ahead of the company's detractors" (Bouchard, 1992, p. 44). This allowed the team to continue their background research throughout the crisis, try on the other parties' shoes, and prepare for any situation that might arise.

The Alcan crisis communications team also was extremely effective in their handling of the media—providing a fast and complete communication blitz, which provoked the media into losing interest. Alcan initially brought in several outside experts, which added to their credibility and "as a result, reporters did not question the explanation of the explosion, the appraisal of risks to the population, nor the actions taken to deal with the continuing danger" (Bouchard, 1992, p. 45). The corporation's public affairs department monitored all media so that the company could adjust its messages accordingly. "The crisis team was in virtual control of the situation. There were no surprises in the evening newscasts or the morning newspapers" (Bouchard, 1992, p. 45).

The immediate crisis ended on the fifth day when emergency crews were finally able to open a second ship's hold with remote-controlled hydraulic jacks. By the close of the initial 5 days, management of the disaster was considered successful. By keeping open communication, responding to key publics' concerns, and building credibility, Alcan managed to save their reputation and promote a positive image in the aftermath of a deadly explosion. By following the recommendations of the *gather, package* and *deliver* phase in the crisis management model, the communications unit also was able to avert the equivalent of a public relations explosion which, in the world of corporate reputations, can be just as fatal.

As the previous reviews of the Alcan corporation's crisis management efforts illustrate, utilizing the *gather, package*, and *deliver* guidelines for crisis management resulted in a productive handling of the crisis and the preservation of a positive corporate image. By contrast, a case study of the crisis management strategy employed by Dow Corning shows how this corporation did not follow the model's guidelines during a crisis. This may have accounted, in part, for their unsuccessful handling of "The Dow Corning Breast Implant Cover-up."

The Dow Corning Breast Implant Cover-up

In 1991, Dow Corning, the world's largest manufacturer of silicone-gel breast implants and the leader in what was estimated to be a $300 million U.S. breast-surgery industry in the early 1990s, was hit by one of the worst crises in the corporation's life. The company came under growing criticism for failing to disclose knowledge of the health hazards caused by the breast implants they manufactured, and for the reckless endangerment of the lives of thousands of women who received these implants nationwide. What began as a lucrative business spawned from the growing popularity of cosmetic surgery swiftly transformed into a public relations nightmare of drastic proportions. According to Michigan crisis-management consultant Gerald Meyers, "this was a textbook case of crisis mismanagement. The company has been playing a hardball defense all the way, and that is a surefire formula for failure" (Chisolm, 1992, p. 42).

In December 1991, a federal district court jury in San Francisco awarded $8.6 million to a woman who claimed she was suffering from an autoimmune disease resulting from her breast implants. "In a stunning blow to the company, the jury also found that Dow Corning acted with fraud, malice and oppression, because of its failure to disclose information about the implant's hazards. Company executives reacted to the ruling with outrage and blamed the finding on 'sensationalist' media reports" (Chisolm, 1992, p. 42).

As mentioned in the crisis management model, the public is often more offended by a corporation's lack of honesty than by the crisis itself. This consensus worked against Dow Corning for years as reports of hidden information and cover-ups continued to leak into the press. Public outrage increasingly focused less on the growing evidence of health risks posed by the breast implants and more on the perception that Dow Corning had known of the potential hazards of its product for more than 20 years (Rumptz et al., 1992).

Although Dow Corning did not successfully adhere to any of the guidelines laid out in the crisis management model, one of the most blatant violations was their public relations team's failure to release vital information regarding breast implants. Soon after the 1991 court settlement, and despite the company's efforts to prevent their publication, hundreds of pages of internal Dow Corning documents used in the case were released (Chisolm, 1992). The documents, which would cause substantial damage to the corporation, indicated that: Some employees had known as early as 1971 that the manufacturer lacked sufficient scientific data to guarantee the implants health safety; Dow Corning had paid millions of dollars in out-of-court settlements to keep claims about health risks secret; and warnings of the need for more thorough testing by Dow company scientists had been repeatedly ignored.

Additionally, the company failed to show concern after numerous implant-induced health complications were revealed, they refrained from any public action, and they misled rather than worked with regulators, physicians, and federal watch groups. All of these acts represent a violation of advice suggested in the crisis management model; namely full disclosure of information, telling the truth, showing concern, and anticipating the actions of key publics. In fact, even the corporation's proactive actions turned out to be destructive. In mid 1991, Dow Corning set up a toll-free hotline to address breast-implant questions and concerns. This line was shut down by the FDA in early 1992, however, because the information Dow Corning provided to callers was either "false or used in a confusing or misleading context" (Chisolm, 1992).

In 1992, newly appointed CEO Keith McKennon, who specialized in crisis-issues management, supervised the public release of sensitive Dow Corning documents dealing with the safety of the devices, as well as a proposal to pay for the removal of the implants for low-income women (Chisolm, 1992). These actions, although well-intended, came too late to rescue the corporation's declining image in the minds of consumers. "Dow Corning has actively covered this issue up, they are reckless and they have a reckless attitude about women," claimed Dr. Sidney Wolfe, director of the Public Citizen

Health Research Group in Washington (cited in Chisolm, 1992, p. 43). For years, under former CEO Lawrence Reed, the company had failed to show concern for thousands of women with serious health problems resulting from breast implants by assuring them and their doctors that implants were safe, essentially placing the corporate interest before public responsibility.

In sum, the public relations effort of Dow Corning failed on all accounts. The corporation neglected to take a proactive stance immediately following the first public outcry regarding health risks. Dow failed to release factual data as soon as it became available or appoint a credible spokesperson. Finally, the corporation did not demonstrate sympathy for victims of implant-imposed health problems, cooperate with key publics, or publicly rectify its behavior (Rumptz et al., 1992). The corporation reduced its credibility by covering up its mistakes with out-of-court claim settlements. It met media inquiries with defensive allegations and consistently committed actions deemed unsympathetic by the thousands of women adversely affected by this crisis.

The preceding review of Dow Corning's unsuccessful crisis management campaigns lends further support to the heuristic value of the *gather, package*, and *deliver* steps of the crisis management model. Dow, deemed unsuccessful in its crisis management campaign, went against the *gather, package*, and *deliver* guidelines detailed in the model. The corporation's failure to efficiently gather background research, package its message, and deliver it quickly and effectively to the public and the media was a contributing factor in the unsuccessful management of the breast implant crisis.

CONCLUSION

The tragic events that occurred at Alcan and Dow Corning—as well as the innumerable and well-publicized crisis events not included in this study, such as the Pepsi syringe-tampering crisis, the AT&T blackout, and the Source Perrier contamination scandal—made the unthinkable, the unimaginable, and even the inconceivable, a reality for these corporations. For the public, they were frightening events with horrific images that shook many people's faith in "Corporate America." For the media, they were incredible stories to cover and remarkable people to investigate. But for the corporations involved, they were crises that could have meant the end.

All of these crises posed serious public relations problems to their prospective organizations, and some, like Dow Corning's breast implant cover-up, still do so to this day. But why did they happen? As Seeger (1986) pointed out in his analysis of the NASA Challenger disaster, "while by nature a crisis is an unanticipated event . . . certain organizational conditions may increase the probability of a crisis occurring" (p. 154). These conditions, coupled with poor crisis management before and after the crisis, and failure to follow the *gather*, *package*, and *deliver* guidelines during a crisis, adds to the severity with which the crisis is perceived by the media, the government, and the public, thus resulting in potential threats to an organization's future.

Although it is undoubtedly impossible to determine whether or not the crises experienced by Alcan and Dow Corning could have been avoided, it is possible to ascertain whether or not they could have been handled better. In looking at the literature on crisis management, we discovered several key factors that continually emerge as necessary for successful crisis management. Alcan, in their more successful crisis management campaign, implicitly followed the steps detailed in the gather, package, and deliver section of the model. This corporation maintained open and honest communication with the public, kept the key public's interest their primary concern, used a proactive stance, and utilized three different enterprising strategies: keeping a visible corporate spokesperson, providing quick initial communication about the crisis, and being assertive with the media. Moreover, Alcan also disclosed all pertinent information, told the truth, and showed concern for victims of the crisis.

With the explosion of technology, response time to crises has shortened dramatically. It is possible, however, for crisis teams to use the technological advances to their advantage. As a result of modern information science, there are many new, fast, and accurate resources that can assist crisis teams in developing an effective solution to their problems. Some key crisis fighting devices include fax machines, video news releases, voice and electronic mail, satellite communication, desktop publishing systems, specialized databases, and the Internet. These devices are solutions that speak to "the need to bring people together rapidly, wherever they are" (Calloway, 1991, p. 87) since "fast responses to crises depends on having 'just-in-time' information" (p. 85). Although speed is developing as a key factor in the successful outcome of crisis situations, as these case reviews have indicated, speed is not enough. Crisis management communications is now emerging as a science rather than an art and, although no one can predict when or where a crisis will occur, there are some guidelines that organizations may find useful when dealing with specific crises. Although not "tested" on an actual organization, these guidelines—emerging from a review of the communication and public relations literature on crisis management—offer a model of successful crisis communication that may be of use to public relations professionals, communication scholars, and experts in business and industry.

ACKNOWLEDGMENTS

The authors wish to thank Carrie Dunn, Melissa Kraus, and Jennifer Shvanda for help with earlier drafts of this chapter.

Patterns of Conflict Preceding a Crisis: A Case Study Analysis

Martha Dunagin Saunders
University of West Florida

Not every crisis falls in the same category as the highly visible catastrophes of the Exxon Valdez oil spill or Tylenol poisonings. Some equally devastating organizational crises, such as labor walkouts and consumer boycotts emerge from the social/cultural milieu. The primary difference between them lies in how quickly they hit.

The onset of crises can be said to fall into two broad classifications, *anticipated* and *unanticipated* (Hoff, 1984). The unanticipated crisis often falls into one of the following categories:

1. acts of nature such as hurricanes, earthquakes, and epidemics;
2. intentional acts such as product tampering, bomb threats, or hostage-taking; and
3. unintentional events such as explosions, fires, and chemical leaks.

In contrast, the anticipated crisis is characterized by slowly developing conflicts such as labor unrest, sexual harassment, and product boycotts. These conflicts are eventually touched off by a triggering event (Mitroff, 1988b) to erupt into a full-blown crisis. The insidious nature of the anticipated crisis makes it less amenable to control and thereby potentially more damaging.

The adage, "You can't plan a crisis but you can plan for one," exemplifies the thinking among many professionals that you can't do much about crises except manage them once they've happened. Examinations of unanticipated crises dominate the literature. Public relations textbooks focus primarily on media handling in the midst of crisis. Crisis plans most often include structures for handling the unanticipated crisis. To date, the anticipated crisis remains relatively unexplored by crisis researchers. This is unfortunate, because the very nature of the anticipated crisis makes it amenable to proactive measures. Good issues management techniques may play an important role here. Lauzen and Dozier (1994) conceptualized issues management as "the transformation of raw data or information into intelligence" (p. 166). In other words, good issues management enables an organization to deal with a problem situation before it becomes crisis. Mitroff (1988b) established a strong connection between issues management and crisis through his identification of signal detection as the first stage of crisis management. He concluded that most triggering events are preceded by detectable patterns which, when analyzed correctly, alert decision makers as to the likelihood of a crisis.

In this chapter, I examine the role of communication in an anticipated-type crisis—the pilot walkout at Eastern Airlines. I show how detectable patterns of communication could have been used to anticipate a massive organizational crisis. Case study analyses of this nature are useful toward theory building because they provide observations grounded in actual organizational efforts aimed at solving actual organizational problems.

A CASE STUDY

Eastern Airlines' Pilot Walkout

In February 1986, the 58-year existence of Eastern Airlines as an independent company came to an end. Following years of turmoil, Eastern was sold to Texas Air Corporation (TAC), a holding company that owned Continental Airlines, People Express, and New York Air. A period of severe employee unrest followed. In March 1989, a strike against the airline was called by the International Association of Machinists (IAM) and was supported by both the Transport Workers Union (TWU), representing the flight attendants, and the Air Line Pilots Association (ALPA). A week later, Eastern filed for bankruptcy and its management fought to retain control of the company in the face of furious resistance from labor, and rapidly diminishing confidence among its investors.

Four years later, bankruptcy court judge Burton Lifland ruled that Frank Lorenzo, the brash corporate raider who had acquired Eastern for his Texas Air empire, was unfit to run the company. Lifland appointed a trustee for the airline. One final effort for order failed, and on January 18, 1991, the company folded its wings for good.

Industry analysts agree that the solidarity of the unions, *especially the support of the pilots,* contributed greatly to the defeat of Frank Lorenzo. ALPA attorney, Bruce Simon, was quoted as saying: "Lorenzo is not in a position to set wage patterns in the industry anymore. . . . There has been a mood in this country over the past decade that you can beat up on unions and get away with it. The message here is that maybe you still can, but not in the airline industry. That is a major victory."

The "victory" referred to by Simon seems somehow less grand when one considers that most of the 42,000 people employed by Eastern when Lorenzo acquired it were put of out of work. The industry may have been rid of a monster when Frank Lorenzo lost power, but the price paid by the people of Eastern was dear.

The pilots' efforts during the conflict were surprising to some observers. *The New Republic* (Fairlie, 1989) reported:

> Traditionally, commercial airline pilots do not strike. They consider themselves professionals. Many have military backgrounds, and observe a military ethic and even etiquette. Yet . . . as management—labor relations at Eastern came to a crisis, it was the pilots who took a full-page advertisement in *USA Today* listing the reasons why Texas Air is not "fit, willing, and able" to operate Eastern. (p. 21)

Indeed, Eastern's management underestimated the extent of the pilots' discontent. Yet, to many of the pilots, the conditions under which they were having to work at Lorenzo's Eastern were intolerable. They viewed the new owners as callous brutes, intent on despoiling the airline. Emotions ran deep. One pilot reflected the apparent views of many when, in response to a 1987 survey (*two years before the strike*), he responded gallantly:

> [I am] greatly affected by current problems. I make less money than other pilots, but most of all I feel that the public thinks I work for a second class outfit. This is not true! Eastern Airlines has always been a great company to work for and I hate for people not to realize this. (p. 37)

The events leading to the pilot walkout at Eastern in 1989 were tumultuous, and the decision to support the IAM's strike was difficult, but as one former Eastern copilot commented, "We did what we thought we had to do. The eyes of an industry were on us. We were being cannibalized by our own parent [Texas Air]. Too many people were suffering. It wasn't about money or days off or anything like that. For us, walking out in support of the machinists was a point of honor!"

Patterns of Conflict

Could the tragedy at Eastern have been avoided? History cannot be relived, but speculations may be based on certain patterns which could have been detected at the time. In my analysis for *Eastern's Armageddon: Labor Conflict and the Destruction of Eastern Airlines* (Saunders, 1992), I used a theory of communication and social change as a framework for detecting these patterns. Bowers and Ochs' (1971) theory of the rhetoric of agitation and control has been used frequently as a tool for observing social conflict of the kind which occurred during the civil rights movement in the 1960s, or the anti-Vietnam War activities of the 1970s. Its usefulness as a gauge for measuring intergroup communication during organizational conflict emerged during the course of my research on Eastern's crisis.

Applying the Theory

To examine the process of conflict escalation surrounding Eastern's pilot walkout, I analyzed the content of (a) news stories involving the pilots or issues of interest to the pilots from January 1986 to January 1991; (b) articles gathered from *The Falcon*, Eastern's internal newsletter; (c) *Eastern Pilot's Checklist*, a newsletter developed by the Eastern pilots' Master Executive Council in 1987; and (d) virtually every letter, memorandum, and video directed to the pilots by both company and union sources. My examination of the patterns of conflict between Eastern's pilots and management relied heavily on the Bowers and Ochs theory.

In their book, *The Rhetoric of Agitation and Control* (1971), Bowers and Ochs identified three primary aspects of conflict: *rhetoric, agitation,* and *control*. Rhetoric, as defined by Bower and Ochs, extends beyond traditional definitions to include nonverbal communication (e.g., carrying signs, shaking fists). Specifically, the authors referred to rhetoric as "the rationale of instrumental, symbolic behavior" (p. 2). The unit of analysis for the content analytic portion of my study, the rhetorical event, was based on this definition.

"Agitation exists," according to the authors, "when (1) people outside the normal decision-making establishment (2) advocate significant social change, and (3) encounter a degree of resistance within the establishment such as to require more than the normal discursive means of persuasion" (p. 4). The communication behaviors of the pilots of Eastern Airlines, as they attempted to effect changes within the company, fell within this definition. Control refers to the "response of the decision-making establishment to agitation" (p. 4). For the purpose of my study, all communication by Eastern's management regarding the company's pilots or issues of concern to the pilots were considered examples of control behavior.

Bowers and Ochs identified specific strategies that agitation groups often adopt in their attempts to bring about change, as well as strategies employed by establishments to resist that change. These categorizations were especially useful in framing my research.

From the perspective of theory, the pilots and management of Eastern were faced with a number of behavioral options as they addressed the conflict resulting from the acquisition. According to Bowers and Ochs, agitation (the pilots') activity could fall into one of nine categories, or strategies, of communication behavior:

1. Petitioning: Normal methods of solving problems. Tactics include phone calls or meetings with management.
2. Promulgation: Seeking to win social support. Tactics include informational picketing or press releases/press conferences.
3. Solidification: Takes place within the group to reinforce cohesiveness among members. Tactics include songs, slogans, rallies, symbols, in-group publications, buttons, bumper stickers.
4. Polarization: Based on assumption that anyone who isn't for us must be for the establishment. Tactics include the use of flag issues and flag individuals for exploitive purposes, derogatory jargon.
5. Nonviolent resistance: Deliberately breaking laws or rules considered unjust. Tactics include rent strikes, hunger strikes, sit-ins, and boycotts.
6. Escalation/confrontation: Attempts to make establishment apprehensive. Tactics include threatened disruption, nonverbal offensive, dressing strangely, expressing sentiments offensive to the establishment, verbal obscene deprecation, non-negotiable demands, nonverbal obscenity, and token violence.
7. Gandhi & guerrilla: Presenting two groups of agitators: some committed to nonviolent resistance and some committed to destruction of the establishment.
8. Guerrilla. Tactics include physical underground attacks.
9. Revolution.

Bowers and Ochs (1971) began an explanation of control (management) strategies available to an organization by pointing out principles governing the stance taken by an establishment. That is, establishment leaders must assume that any given instance of agitation will result in the worst possible outcome. Establishment leaders must be prepared to turn back any attack on the establishment (p. 40).

The authors maintained that when an establishment is confronted with a proposal for change, it can adopt one of four rhetorical strategies:

1. Avoidance. Tactics include counterpersuasion (talks with the agitation leadership in an attempt to convince them they are wrong); evasion (often called "buckpassing" and "runaround"); postponement as a method of deferring decision making; secrecy with a rationale (declining to respond to a request for change by appealing to a higher principles, i.e., national security); and denial of means (preventing agitators from having the physical means to carry on their cause).

2. Suppression. Tactics include harassment, banishment, and purgation.

3. Adjustment. Tactics include sacrificing personnel, changing the name of the regulatory agency, incorporation of some of the personnel of the agitative movement, and incorporation of parts of the dissident ideology.

4. Capitulation, or total defeat.

In order to predict outcomes during specific instances of agitation and control, Bowers and Ochs first isolated three variables for agitation and control. The authors then manipulated those variables in an effort to explain what apparently takes place in real agitative situations (p. 136).

According to their model, the variables critical to agitation are actual membership, potential membership, and rhetorical sophistication. Actual membership includes the number of members considered active within an agitative group. The authors argued that this number always starts out small and that large actual membership probably does not exist in an agitative movement. Potential membership depends on the strength of the agitative group's ideology and the number of people in the society who may be receptive to that ideology. Rhetorical sophistication is the extent to which agitative leaders know and use basic principles of rhetoric (p. 137).

Variables critical to control are power, strength of ideology, and rhetorical sophistication. *Power* is described as either referent or expert. Referent power is power over a person when that person relates to the individual or group in power. Expert power is the kind of power that attracts influences because of a particular skill or knowledge in some area which interest the influencee. By *strength of ideology*, the authors mean that the establishment's ideology is logically consistent and empirically valid. If this occurs, the establishment remains strong. Logical consistency means that everyone in the system shares the same set of values. The authors recognize vertical deviance type of agitation which occurs in situations when the agitators have no quarrel with general value system of the establishment (p. 137).

In the Eastern Airlines scenario, actual membership, or the number of active members in the agitative group, was small initially. Potential membership was considered high, in the case of the pilots, because of the possibility of the pilots' union combining efforts with the other major unions. The *rhetorical sophistication* of the pilots became evident in their ability to attract and maintain media attention, a well as to launch their own publications and telecommunications network.

The Eastern establishment possessed a high level of referent and expert power, logical consistency in the form of unity, coherence of beliefs within a value system, as well as rhetorical sophistication through a complex network of corporate communications.

On the basis of these variables, Bowers and Ochs (1971) developed a set of generalizations in an effort to predict the outcomes of agitation situations. One of the generalizations, which suited this analysis, occurs when the three variables are balanced between agitation and control. When this happens, the establishment will almost always successfully avoid or suppress the agitation (p. 141).

This happens because the establishment holds the advantage in legitimate power (p. 7). Legitimate power, somewhat complex in definition, occurs when an individual or group perceives another as having a sort of social contract or charter over them. Through this position, the establishment can assert influence. Legitimate power is held by the establishment in every organization and is, in fact, a defining characteristic of the establishment (p. 13).

Analysis

The decline of Eastern Airlines, from the acquisition by TAC to the strike, fell into three general phases. I called phase one, The Resistance. During that period employees frantically resisted the acquisition of the airline by a company headed by a man believed to be brutal to employees. Phase two, Relative Peace, showed the pilots appearing to be back to business as usual. Phase three, The Rebellion, erupted furiously as the pilots allied themselves with the other unions in an attempt to shake free from a perceived oppressive management.

It was in phase two that important patterns emerged that could have been used to predict the later behaviors of the pilots. Unfortunately, these patterns were either undetected or ignored by management. Although appearing subdued to the public, the pilots were engaging in the agitation strategy of solidification. This important strategy takes place within the agitating group and includes tactics designed to produce or reinforce cohesiveness among the members. Tactics such as songs, slogans, rallies, symbols, in-group publications, buttons, and bumper stickers are used at this stage to solidify members of an agitating group. This was a crucial strategy for the agitation leaders at Eastern. Historically, the pilots had little opportunity to form cohesive groups because of the nature of their work. On an ordinary work day, the Eastern pilot would arrive at work, board a plane with two other pilots of different rank, and fly to a destination. Upon his return, he would file his report and go home. With the exception of cockpit conversation (all of which was tape recorded), there was no opportunity to pilots to discuss issues as a group. This made them needful of solidification techniques and vulnerable to propaganda.

An indicator of solidification, an Eastern pilots' newsletter began publication in an attempt to galvanize pilots' emotions. The publication invited pilots and their spouses to express their feelings and provided one of the few forums for pilot input throughout the crisis. Each issue included a family awareness column designed to keep up the spirit on the homefront. This inclusion of pilots' families was to continue throughout the upcoming crisis. The November 1987 issue included an open letter to Eastern pilots and their spouses from a concerned pilot's wife: "If family awareness and communications committees are not geared up pretty soon, we'll all be goners in our attempts to salvage EAL and keep Frank Lorenzo from selling us way, way short!"

The slick, 16-page newsletter contained emotion-laden headlines. One headline, "It's Not Over 'til It's Over," borrowed the often quoted Yogi Berra line to introduce an editorial encouraging the pilots to gear up for the "long haul," and to make some effort toward overcoming any ill feelings toward the other employee groups.

"The Bottom of the Morality Barrel," blasted an article in Eastern's company newsletter that was critical of the pilots. Another in the November 1987 issue headlined an editorial calling Lorenzo "an absentee landlord who has bought into a viable operation, looted it, and then blamed the tenants for the slum-like conditions he created.

By this time, all of the pilots who could have bailed (by retiring or going to another airline) had done so, leaving those remaining with few choices. From a theoretical perspective, actual and potential membership of the agitative group was increasing, primarily as a result of the flag issue of safety. One pilot reflected on the issue in his response to a 1987 survey (Saunders, 1988): "I'm not a member of ALPA, but I'm with my fellow pilots all the way. Why you ask? Because the son-of-a-bitch [Lorenzo] is trying to kill me!" This remark appeared among responses to a 1987 survey of pilot communication needs.

The 1987 survey concluded, among other things, that the pilots shared strong perceptions of crisis. In spite of high levels of perceived constraint, they continued to communicate actively—perhaps even avidly. They sought information form a variety of sources but trusted relatively few. They were suspicious of mass media reports because they feared the company's advertising dollar could "buy" favorable coverage.

It is important to note that until this point, the external public was largely unaware of the conflicts at Eastern. One can only wonder what, if any, efforts management was making toward a meeting of the minds between the groups. None seem evident. Management's credibility was poor, and eroding fast.

Careful attention to solidification strategies, most notably through the pilot newsletter and Family Awareness programs, laid a strong, cohesive foundation, which was to serve the Eastern pilots well over the coming months. In addition, the company's tough posture precluded any conciliation and contributed to the pilots' sense of powerlessness. These combinations contributed to the rebellion of 1988 and subsequently to the walkout. During this phase, the pilots *passed a point of no return* in their efforts to unseat what they perceived as unacceptable management. Ironically, management never took them seriously. In fact, on March 4, 1989, 3 days before the strike, one of Eastern's chief pilot managers was asked, "What if the pilots don't come to work—who will fly?" To this he answered, "I don't think that will happen."

The lesson from the preceding analysis is this: Although analysts have noted that labor wasn't the biggest problem Eastern faced when Texas Air acquired the company in 1986, it soon became so. The company's biggest mistake was in cutting the employees out of the process and ignoring the clearly threatening patterns of behavior that followed.

QUESTIONS FOR FUTURE RESEARCH

Traditionally, commercial airline pilots do not strike. They consider themselves professionals. *How, then, do we explain their willingness to join with the other labor groups and fight to unseat management?*

A possible response rightly points to the effectiveness of Eastern Pilot's Checklist in stirring up emotions among the pilots. Remember, too, that many of these men were Vietnam-era pilots who were still smarting from the perceptions of having "lost" a war. In addition, Frank Lorenzo had provided to be a formidable foe of organized labor through is reorganization of Continental Airlines. The eyes of their comrades throughout the industry were on these pilots, as pilots form other airlines feared for their own salaries and jobs. There were considerable pressures on Eastern's pilots to fight Lorenzo with whatever means they had at hand.[1] Future researchers may wish to focus on the role of solidification techniques in intraorganizational unrest.

A former member of Eastern's corporate communications staff has been quoted as saying, "Management never thought the pilots would walk out. In fact, they laughed at the suggestion that those guys would jeopardize their

---

[1]Ironically, some of the Eastern pilots ultimately sued ALPA for reneging on promises made to them (i.e., employment with other airlines) if they followed through with the strike.

big paychecks. Boy, were they ever wrong!" *How is it that upper management completely misread the firmness of the pilots' resolve?*

It would seem management was using the past to predict the future. Prior to this event, the pilots had usually led the way toward concessions with management. This time management underestimated the pilots' resolve. It is also evident that upper management was not listening to front-line communicators. Decision making seemed to grow more cumbersome and the company neglected to respond promptly to employee concerns. Future research may include the attentiveness of corporate decision makers to messages from front-line or boundary spanning employees.

What persuasive tactics were employed by management and employee groups? To what extent were they effective? It was quite evident that pilot leaders understood their constituency. Strong polarization techniques and the emotion-laden "war" messages increased the fervor of the cause. On the other hand, management publications rarely addressed issues the pilots had raised. Instead, they clung steadfastly to the counterpersuasive tactic of "running a more efficient airline."

The role of propaganda and persuasion in organizational rebellions would provide a useful addition to our understanding of employee crises.

II

CRISIS RESPONSE: THE TIME TO SPEAK

Robert L. Heath

Imagine the feeling experienced by an airline public relations executive on the morning of September 11, 2001. You have credible news that one of your airplanes crashed into the World Trade Center. You rush out of a meeting to see what is happening. Televisions are on in the office area. You arrive just in time to see a second plane hit the other tower. You have picked up rumors on the way to your office that this may be the work of terrorists.

You begin to implement your crisis plan. You realize that the plan did not anticipate this eventuality. Will the plan be sufficient to get you through the morning, the day, the week? Little do you know how difficult the next several days will be. Little do you realize that your planes will be grounded. All aircraft that are not authorized by the U.S. Military are grounded. Thousands of passengers are stranded. A safety issue has matured into a customer relations issue. It is about to become a financial issue. What a morning this has been. What a month this will be. So goes the life of persons who develop crisis plans, craft the messages, and respond to inquiries. Messages are posted on Web sites. They are sent via e-mails. Telephone calls are answered. Executive speeches to employees need to be written. A crisis is a time to speak. "No comment" is dysfunctional, even when you really have as many doubts as to the truth as your stakeholders have.

One view of crisis response stresses the need to supply information. Beyond the "mere" facts, often, is the need to interpret those facts. Metaphors are central to human thought. People think with the metaphors that operate between them and objective reality. Crisis response is metaphorical. It deals with the perspectives embedded in terministic screens. It helps to form and repair identifications. It creates, sustains, and repairs relationships by joining the organization and its stakeholders into co-created meaning, shared narratives.

The chapters in this section offer variation and theme of the proposition that crises are interrupted narratives that require strategic responses to present themselves in a positive narrative, by their statements and their corrective actions. Several premises are examined in this section that can guide and aid executives, including communication managers, as they respond to crises by applying the following best practices:

- Social reality is constructed by many voices, which may compete with one another to have the final say. Best practices suggest that one consistent theme needs to be voiced by the organization, tailored to the information and evaluation needs of its various stakeholders.
- Crisis narratives are archetypic. Some archetypes are positive; others are negative. Strategic responses are wise to realize these alternative interpretations and work to prove they are positive and refute the allegations they are negative, or overcome negativity through proactive changes.
- Strategic responses to each crisis should address the metaphors that are used by each group of stakeholders to assess the crisis.
- Each crisis generates one of more interpretative narrative. The focal organization needs to understand and adapt to these narratives, especially insofar as they may be in conflict.
- Each narrative is not only a means by which each group of stakeholders interprets the crisis but also forms the basis of their identification with or against the organization's narrative of the crisis.
- Analysis of the dialogue surrounding a crisis can be sharpened by giving attention to the narrative elements that emerge as various groups interpret the crisis.
- Narrative response to crises results not only from the interpretative frames generated by the dialogue but also by the ensemble of players who cooperate and compete for specific narrative interpretations.
- External or internal events give rise to the crisis and constitute the facts and factors that will be interpreted and evaluated as the crisis runs its course. Responses to the crisis must be centered on the identity of the organization and framed in terms of the social construction of the event.

- How each crisis is named determines the social construction frames that are required by the persons crafting the response.
- One assumption is that a crisis challenges an organization to grow and change for the better as a means for correcting the conditions that led to the crisis. The organization needs to be able to tell the story of organizational change.

The chapters in this section open consideration to many research questions about the communication strategies for crisis response, including those that follow:

- Each crisis is an interrupted narrative. Corrective actions and statements are likely to reduce the duration and magnitude of the crisis if they demonstrate that the new narrative leads to an even more responsive and ethical organization.
- Each set of stakeholders uses its idiosyncratic metaphors to understand and evaluate a crisis. Researchers can uncover where metaphors are compatible or competing as an organizational representative speaks to explain, justify, create understanding and identification with its stakeholders. For instance, responding to the September 11, 2001 crisis, President George W. Bush can use the term *terrorist* to characterize those who planned and perpetrated the attack on the World Trade Center and the Pentagon. To some stakeholders this term is appropriately identifying. To others it offends. They might even recall that during the American Revolution, some colonists were called "terrorists" by British sympathizers. How do metaphors unlock or close the thinking of the persons who evaluate a crisis?
- Researchers can investigate the types of narratives that are used to explain crises and the extent to which conflicting narratives divide some stakeholders from others in regard to the way in which each crisis is understood and evaluated.
- The ability of the management team, including communication professionals, to understand the forces shaping the social construction of a crisis and to respond appropriately and ethically will predict the duration and severity of the crisis.
- The extent to which responses are scripted appropriately and ethically predicts the duration and magnitude of each crisis.
- If the story of organizational changes after a crisis begins demonstrates that the organization is ethical and responsive to the expectations of its stakeholders the duration and the magnitude of the crisis will be less.
- If the crisis results from the enactment of a specific narrative, the corrective actions and statements must remain true to the theme of that narrative.

Chapters in this section apply theory, explore case studies, and offer best practices that constitute a sustained argument that crisis is an archetypic narrative. People experience reality through various narrative frames. Crises, for this reason, are interrupted narratives and require actions and statements that respond ethically to the narrative interpretations that result from the dialogue motivated by the crisis.

10

Metaphors of Crisis

Frank E. Millar
Debra Baker Beck
University of Wyoming

"My boss is always in a crisis mode with his finger poised just above the panic button," says an employee. A university president, describing the institution's fiscal condition, asserts that "we are not quite at crisis, but we are severely challenged." Americans are told we have a "crisis of will" in dealing with our social, economic, political, and ecological problems. What is meant by the term *crisis*? What images and emotions are induced by this word? The term *crisis* seems to induce feelings of fear associated with an equivocal situation. But what is crisis that it is associated with equivocality, and what is equivocality that it is associated with crisis? These questions are explored in this chapter.

The word *crisis* evolved from the Greek word "krisis" indicating a "turning-point of a disease" (Oxford Dictionary of English Etymology, 1982, p. 229). The turning-point may be initiated by a decision (the legislature cutting the university's budget), judgment (Americans seem too apathetic and individually oriented to become involved in social problems), or event (the panicky boss searches for the inevitable error). However instigated, the turning-point indicates that some threshold has been breached (or is about to be crossed) such that a "turn," typically for the worst, is occurring or is eminent. Imagine yourself at a dead end on a country road where you can only turn left or right and you do not know whether either path will get you back on the desired direction. You are in an equivocal situation, at a turning-point that evokes dis-ease—uneasiness, anxiety, discomfort, and confusion.

ASSUMPTIONS

The purpose of this chapter is to explore the metaphors used to describe crisis. This exploration assumes that the way people think about reality is "fundamentally metaphorical in nature" (Lakoff & Johnson, 1980, p. 3). Metaphors are not just frilly words nor poetic phrases nor catchy linguistic slogans. Rather, "metaphor resides in thought, not just in words" (Lakoff & Turner, 1989, p. 2). Metaphor is a thought process before becoming a language process (Ricoeur, cited in Gerhart & Russell, 1984; Wilden, 1987). Metaphorical constructions are conceived of as "the main characteristic and organizing glue of . . . mental process" (Bateson & Bateson, 1987, p. 30). As such, metaphorical thinking occurs in every communication system whatsoever and not just in human language games (Wilden, 1980). The ways humans make sense of experience are shaped by the metaphors used to categorize, classify, and name circumstances. Although the map is not the territory, as Korzybski (1958) asserted, mapping is the territory of interest herein, because maps constrain coherent interpretations of observed territories. Interpretations, in turn, guide actions as well as justify and legitimize the actions enacted in particular situations.

This chapter also assumes that communication is the process within which social reality is constructed (Cronen, Johnson, & Lannaman, 1982; Krippendorf, 1989). All social systems are necessarily communication systems (Luhmann, 1986) and all communication systems are necessarily social systems (Duncan, 1968). Humans "live *in* communication" (Pearce, 1989, p. 196). To say that humans live in communication is to assert that the process per se is formative; what is formed is the shape of our interactions and our meanings about them. The content of the meanings constructed is what we call reality; this content is fundamentally a metaphorical construction.

Humans are rarely aware of either the formative characteristic of communication or the fundamental metaphors used to construct a reality. We tend to conceive of communication as something we do to each other rather than as an evolutionary process constructing us, collectively and individually. To the extent we think of the communication process at all, we often liken communication to a tennis match where players sequentially "hit" (speak) "balls" (words) "at each other" (the players exist independent of each other and the game) on a "court" (a conference room) according to a set of "official rules" prescribing how tennis is "played" (who can ask questions, assert conclusions, give orders), how "scoring" occurs (points are awarded for adroit statements) and who "wins" (whose assertion was accepted). In contrast, the view assumed here frames communication as an evolutionary process enacting people who cannot choose to participate only how, just as we cannot choose to breathe only how as long as life continues. As an evolutionary process, communication is ongoing (not localized on a court, but continually enacted), imperfectable (there is no official rule book existing independent of the process), relational (messages are contingent on previous messages so that messengers are constructed relative to each other) and emergent (regularized patterns of interacting unfold during message enactments in various settings).

Similarly, we rarely think about "basic conceptual metaphors" of "purposes are destinations," "states are locations" and "events are actions" (Lakoff & Turner, 1987, p. 52) structuring our thoughts. (By the way, this lack of awareness is fortunate since it saves massive amounts of time and energy.) For instance, "getting ahead" (purpose as destination) is known by being in front of others (state as location) and is arrived at by issuing orders which others obey, making larger bank deposits, parking in named spaces, and negotiating golden parachutes (events are actions). This chapter, however, asks the reader to think about (state) how thinking occurs (activity) to assess whether other ways of making sense might be more beneficial (purpose).

Whatever else humans do, we tell stories. We are inveterate storytellers and these stories (re)construct our realities (Brown, 1987; Eisenberg & Goodall, 1993; Pearce, 1989). Our stories about experience simultaneously construct our interpretations of experience and perpetuate the interpretations constructed; our stories are reflexive constructions so that the observer is always included in the observations constructed (Ashmore, 1989; Harre & Gillett, 1994; Krippendorf, 1989). Put another way, our stories are largely self-fulfilling and self-validating interpretations. Humans come to "see" that which they "believe" will be seen; "we see things the way they are because of our" stories, (theories, myths; Gerhart & Russell, 1984, p. 10). "Believing is seeing" is a much more accurate description about human thought processes than is the phrase "seeing is believing" (Weick, 1979).

If "believing is seeing" were not a general, accurate description of human thought processes, then training, education, reading, discussions with others, brainstorming sessions, and other ways of "opening" one's mind to alternative interpretations would be of no use. This book would not be written. Notice that the phrase "opening one's mind" presumes a container metaphor for understanding "mind" A mind is a container that can be opened so that other stuff (thoughts) can be put "in" it or that stuff already in the container (memories, stories, habituated rules of sense making) can be rearranged, structured differently, organized into new forms, patterns, or shapes. And notice, too, that to say a person is closed-minded asserts both that new thoughts cannot be put in this container and that rearrangement of existing thoughts does not occur. The closed-minded person does not learn (or understand, or change, or adapt) because "believing" (state) has closed off other ways of "seeing" (activity) so that alternate interpretations are not examined and existing ones are defended (purpose). We return to this container metaphor shortly for it is a very common means of making sense of crises as well as many other events and states.

In sum, we impose an interpretive structure on events and then assert that the structure was imposed upon us. Humans are habitually entrapped in the linguistic prison of their own making. Reality is not found, discovered, or uncovered rather a reality is created, constructed, produced. A primary "key" to the lock of our linguistic prison cells is the choice of metaphors used to create the cell's boundaries.

METAPHOR

A metaphor is here defined as a relation of similarity (Wilden, 1980). Although metaphorical thinking occurs before the acquisition of language, as linguistic constructions metaphors are "abstract qualities perceived as similar from dissimilar phenomena" (Brown, 1987, p. 12). "The essence of metaphor is understanding and experiencing one kind of thing in terms of another" (Lakoff & Johnson, 1980, p. 5). Understanding an unfamiliar event, object, person in terms of a familiar event, object, person is creating a relation of similarity between the unfamiliar and familiar. These similarity relations are based on predicates, on observable actions in particular locations. Events are actions and "no metaphor can ever be comprehended or even adequately represented independent of its experiential basis" (Lakoff & Johnson, 1980, p. 19). Without context, there is no meaning (Bateson, 1979).

Ortony (1975) emphasized that linguistic metaphors are useful expressions because they evoke compact images of events *without* itemizing all the details. This compactness "enables the predication of a chunk of characteristics in a word or two that would otherwise require a long list of characteristics" (p. 49). The characteristics chunked are actions. Second, metaphors often express the quiddity or "essential quality" of an object, person, or event from the speaker's point of view. Finally, metaphors evoke more vivid, multisense images of events because they are closer to perceived experience (Ortony, 1975; Weick, 1979). They are closer to lived experience because metaphors stem from the infinite actions occurring in interactional contexts. These infinite actions, interactional dynamics and contexts of interaction are all evoked by compact, vivid metaphors expressing the essential quality of the experience from the observer's point of view.

Syllogisms in Grass

Bateson (1987) claimed that metaphor is the "organizing glue" holding mental processes together. In discussing the fundamental function of metaphor in mental processes, Bateson used the following example, which he called "syllogism in grass" (p. 26).

Grass dies;

Men die;

Men are grass.

Capra (1988) referred to these as "Bateson's syllogisms" and that label is used in this chapter.

Bateson's syllogisms are the structure of metaphors forming the relation of similarity between two or more objects, events, persons. The structure or form of Bateson's syllogisms is not to be confused with the structure of "logical syllogisms" characterizing deductive reasoning and rational thought. The logical syllogism, called "syllogism in Barbara" by Bateson (1987, p. 26), manifest the following form (or structure).

Men are mortal;

Socrates is a man;

therefore, Socrates will die.

Logical syllogisms depict the relation of contiguity (Wilden, 1980) between class (men) and member (Socrates). Such syllogisms are the indispensable tool of deductive reasoning for they make explicit (mortality) what is implicit in the class term (men). In analogous fashion, Bateson's syllogisms make explicit what predicates (actions) are used to form the similarity relation (die in the above example). Logical syllogisms focus on class–member relations, on what attributes are imposed on the member when grouped in a particular class. But where did the class term itself come from? Bateson's answer is that the class (or category) was created from comparing predicates, from forming a relation of similarity between activities of disparate events or objects. In the earlier example, both men and grass form the class of living systems because both die. Ortony's (1975) *compactness, quiddity, and vividness* stem from the similarity of actions in context.

Bateson's syllogisms are not logical in either the everyday or technical sense of the term. These structures *are not intended* to be logical. Rather, these metaphorical structures are intended to describe how images are formed, how classes or categories or concepts are created, how relations of similarity are constructed, how mental processes might operate. The structure (or form) of Bateson's syllogism is an answer to the following double question: What is thinking that it is fundamentally metaphorical, and what is a metaphor that is fundamental to thinking? Bateson's answer grounds class formation in the interacted experience (the communication process is formative) rather than in language. However, with language acquisition, the ability to describe the infinite nuances of our interactional experiences is increased tremendously as is our capacity to be deceived.

Each of Lakoff and Turner's (1989) three basic conceptual metaphors used to make sense of experience are illustrated in the following Bateson's syllogisms.

Destinations direct actions;
Purposes direct actions;
Purposes are destinations.

Locations distinguish;
States distinguish;
States are locations.

Actions create affects;
Events create affects;
Events are actions.

Destinations delimit pathways;
Purposes delimit pathways;
Purposes are destinations.

Locations demarcate places;
States demarcate places;
States are locations.

Actions regulate relationships;
Events regulate relationships;
Events are actions.

Human conceptual structures are, therefore, fundamentally metaphorical. But every way of "seeing" is also and always a way of "not seeing." Every and any metaphorical construction actively evokes some images and actively negates others. For example, thinking of male–female relations as a "battle"—as in the "battle of the sexes"—actively negates thinking of these relations as a "dance" or a "garden" or a "song" even though each of these other framings are sometimes offered. Let's turn, then, to some metaphors habitually used to describe crises in order to better understand our understandings of crises and how actions proceed "naturally" from those understandings.

CRISIS METAPHORS

A fairly thorough but informal analysis of printed material (newspapers, magazines, textbook case studies) yielded a wide variety of metaphors about crisis expressed by both individuals involved in and reporters writing about these events. Some of these were quite colorful, such as the "circus" metaphor (Rainie, 1993) used to describe the 1993 clash between cult leader David Koresh and the Bureau of Alcohol, Tobacco and Firearms agents near Waco, Texas. Note the Bateson syllogism implicit in the use of "circus":

Circuses display tragic (high-wire acrobatics) and
comic activities (clowns' chaotic activities);
Waco displays tragic (killing children) and
comic activities (agents' chaotic activities);
Waco is a circus.

Whether this metaphorical characterization is empirically accurate or fair to either governmental agents or members of Koresh's compound is *not* the issue of concern. Rather, the focus of this exploration is on how expressed metaphors constrain understanding of the events, activities, and purposes described.

The vast majority of metaphors used to describe crises fell into two primary categories—war and container. A third category, disease metaphors, was also observed, but not nearly as much as expected given that the term crisis originally referred to a turning-point in a disease. This third category will not be explored except to point out that "to be diseased" or "sick" is a state, consisting of several actions (coughing, sneezing, aching, bleeding, etc.) resulting in unintended or unwanted destinations (bed-ridden, doctor's office, hospitalization, death). A few Bateson's syllogisms that vividly compact our understanding of disease are listed next.

Disease harms;	Disease inflames;
Crisis harms;	Crisis inflames;
Crises are diseases.	Crises are diseases.
Disease debilitates;	Disease frightens;
Crisis debilitates;	Crisis frightens;
Crises are diseases.	Crises are diseases.

War Understandings

The use of war metaphors was by far the most frequently observed. Some examples are:

1. The proposal to change federal grazing fees was described as a "war on the West." (White, 1995, p. A1)
2. The Philip Morris suit against ABC was depicted as a situation where "both sides are girding for battle" with a "battalion of more than 20 mostly non-smoking lawyers" gathering for the fight. (Freedman & Stevens, 1995, p. 1)
3. The LA riots following the Rodney King verdict were a "rebellion" or an "uprising." (Whitman & Bowermaster, 1993, p. 36)
4. Insurance agents opposing the entrance of banks in their industry were claimed to be "fighting a desperate defensive battle"; however, the insurance agents had "managed to shield themselves" by becoming "a grassroots army" so that "a confrontation looms again this fall with agents mobilizing against legislation." (Wilke & Scism, 1995, p. A1)
5. The aftermath of the Oklahoma City federal building bombing looked "like an atomic bomb" had been dropped and the day care children killed "were at ground zero." (Leland, 1995, pp. 50–51)

There are several Bateson's syllogisms implicit in these compact, vivid wordings. Each describes activities in the state of war and thereby unfolds the purposes of war so that the essential quality of crisis is understood as war.

Wars destroy;
Crises destroy;
Crises are wars.

Soldiers fight;
Employees fight;
Employees are soldiers.

Rebellions confuse;
Crises confuse;
Crises are rebellions.

Armies mobilize;
Companies mobilize;
Companies are armies.

Bombs devastate;
Crises devastate;
Crises are bombs.

Shields protect and defend;
Armies protect and defend;
Armies are shields.

Wars conscript;
Crises conscript;
Crises are wars.

Generals order;
CEOs order;
CEOs are generals.

Wars require heroics;
Crises require heroics;
Crises are wars.

Enemies attack our territory;
Crises attack our territory;
Crises are enemies.

Several other syllogisms describing similar actions could be created within the war metaphor. But all of them, to varying degrees, entail unnamed predicates that presume an adversarial relationship between interacting systems. An "us versus them" polarity is pictured so that the only perceived choices available involve fighting. One fights in order to "win" or to avoid "losing." To avoid losing is to defend and self-defense is the single most legitimate reason for fighting, for going to war. Winning a war, of course, entails maintaining or gaining resources, lands, and materials and reinforces pre-existing beliefs so that converts are likely to enlist. Losing a war, on the other hand, means that resources, lands, materials, believers, etc., are no longer in one's control (they have been "lost") and that the pre-existing beliefs must have been wrong or in error. Giving up one's beliefs results in a loss of identity so that one must fight to defend one's identity as well as material resources. There is simply too much at stake in a war.

The compact vividness of war metaphors serves various functions for the organization. The declaration of war induces employees to work harder, faster, and longer than in normal times (i.e., the declaration of war helps "rally the troops"). Given the "troops" are motivated to act, the corporation's resources and employees can be effectively and efficiently mobilized to "win" or at least avoid losing. Second, a war metaphor also implies that someone is "in charge" and there is some semblance of structure at a time when it is desperately needed. Regardless of how chaotic events may appear "in the trenches," wars are fought according to rules and strategies designed by someone (e.g., generals, CEOs, presidents, etc.). Third, the "us versus them" polarity inherent in the war metaphor suggests an identifiable "enemy" against whom strategies are plotted and violent actions are directed. The "enemy," of course, is depicted as treacherous, untrustworthy, and undeserving of the moral standards applied to "us." Thus, we "good guys" can fight with a clear conscience—the self-validating nature of human dynamics. Finally, depicting a crisis as a war is especially advantageous in the beginning when the costs of war (crisis) are inevitably underestimated and swift victory is assured (Blalock, 1989).

The disadvantages of the war metaphor are the flip side of its advantages. First, declaring war may blind us to other courses of action that are less costly and more beneficial to all parties. Second, perpetual use of the war metaphor instills a siege mentality where one is consistently looking for enemies. If one persistently looks, one will find enemies whether or not they existed before being identified—the self-fulfilling nature of human dynamics. Third, wars are stressful environments and prolonged states of stress are debilitating, fatiguing, and harmful to participants. Expressing warlike metaphors when these do not appear accurate or necessary to others decreases the respect others manifest toward the speaker or writer (e.g., no one liked working for the boss with his finger consistently poised above the panic button and quickly learned to discredit his comments and directives, referring to him as the "schizoid chipmunk"). Fourth, there is a general assumption that an enemy is some sinister force or person or corporation acting against the well-being of our company. This assumption can be especially problematic when the sinister person is one of "us" or when focusing on outside forces blinds us to internal dynamics that created the crisis. Finally, declaring war on another makes it difficult to reconcile sentiments and return to "normal" relations after the crisis has passed. Reconciliation is especially difficult when one goes head-to-head against individuals or organizations with whom one must later resume normal relations. Whether one is the "victor" or the "conquered," postcrisis relationships will be troublesome.

Container Understandings

The second most common image of crisis was the container metaphor. Even more than the war metaphor, the container metaphor highlights the "loss of control" aspect of crisis because no one is perceived to be momentarily "in charge" and therefore we don't know what to do nor where we are going. The following phrases all indicate that what was contained is no longer "in" the container and a state of dis-ease has emerged.

1. "From the epicenter of Normandie and Florence, the violence rippled outward" was one description of the 1992 LA riots. (Matthews, 1992, p. 34)
2. The 1992 United Way controversy "left the nonprofit world reeling" with reports "about Aramony's luxurious condominiums, limousine service and high-expense-account lifestyle." (Cipalla, 1993, p. 29)
3. Drexel Burnham Lambert's difficulties were depicted as a "creeping crisis" that "sent shock waves" throughout the community. (Gottschalk, 1993, pp. 6–7)
4. A spokesperson for the poultry industry asserted that "our first priority was to begin steps to stop the flow of misinformation in the media" after a "60 Minutes" broadcast was critical of the industry. (Gottschalk, 1993, p. 61)

Imagine a container, any container—a cardboard box, a beer mug, a reservoir, a fenced parking lot, a building, a six-lane freeway. Any and all containers distinguish what is "inside" from what is "outside." Further, activities "inside" are regulated and controlled, states are prescribed and proscribed, and purposes are known. Regardless of the amount of materials, persons and energy occurring "inside" the container, the contained is distinguished from and not permitted to enter its environment except through prescribed pathways and methods (e.g., a box is unwrapped by the intended recipient; a mug is tilted into the mouth so the beer can be swallowed; cars are channeled out of the parking lot through a gate; etc.). Crises happen when either: (a) an "outside" agent or event damages the container's boundaries (e.g., an iceberg breaks the hull of an oil tanker, an airplane crashes into a motel, a squirrel eats through the protective wrapping of a co-axial cable and turns off electricity to the suburbs, a computer hacker sells company secrets to competitors, a dam breaks, an earthquake demolishes a building, unfunded federal mandates bankrupt a small company, an OSHA ruling requires expensive alterations); or (b) an "inside" dynamic or agent implodes the contents beyond their distinguishing boundaries (e.g., a change in company policy incites a "sit down strike," information is leaked to the press, a decaying bridge pillar finally gives way sending many vehicles into the river below, a rotting water main floods the streets, a smoke alarm warning triggers people to jump out of windows, routine practices result in age discrimination lawsuits, normal reporting practices fail to inform executives of faulty products).

In general, activities and states are readily viewed as containers (Lakoff & Johnson, 1980). For example, we easily state that "he is immersed in studying" (activity), repetitively ask "how did you get into consulting?" (activity), assert that "she has fallen in love" (state) or that "he is in a funk" (state). The war metaphor is itself a container framing because the state of war is known by "the actions and other activities that make" up a war; these activities and their by-products are conceived of as constituting a war, as "*in*" or "*emerging from*" a state of war (Lakoff & Johnson, 1980, p. 31). The activities (shooting) and by-products (death) of the state of war constitute its essential quality (Ortony, 1975). The event of war is the activities of war.

Similarly, characterizing crisis with a container metaphor emphasizes that the unequivocal has become equivocal. A turning point has emerged such that a qualitative change of state has occurred. That qualitative change of state from "normal" to "abnormal" is the quiddity of crisis described by container metaphors.

Tidal waves destroy;	Poisons kill;
Crises destroy;	Crises kill;
Crises are tidal waves.	Crises are poisons.
Leakages pollute;	Bombs explode;
Crises pollute;	Crises explode;
Crises are leakages.	Crises are bombs.
Chaos frightens;	Disorder confuses;
Crisis frightens;	Crisis confuses;
Crisis is chaos.	Crisis is disorder.

Notice how easily we associate a change from a desired state (the contained) to an undesired state (the uncontained) with crisis—the normal has become abnormal, the routine no longer operates, the expected did not happen, the ordered has become disordered, the patterned has become random. Hence, crisis is associated with a loss of control, with breaks from the routine, with the turning point (or threshold) from order to disorder. And once a state of disorder has occurred, we can no longer predict the consequences of actions, our habitual ways of making sense and predicting effects of our actions no longer are effective so that we don't know what to do, think, feel. "All is lost," we say. We become fearful, frustrated, and uncertain; feelings of powerless and hopelessness emerge.

Any change of state induces fear even if the new state (container) is desired (e.g., marriage, promotion, winning a lottery, having a child). These new, though desired, states evoke fear because the activities and their by-products that constitute the new state (the new container) have not yet been experienced. The many unnamed predicates enacting the new condition can only be hinted at, longed for, hoped for (i.e., the quiddity of the new state is not vivid, but blurred, hazy, dreamlike). Further, once we experience the activities "in" the new container, our evaluations of the new state invariably are altered; parenting is "even more rewarding then I had hoped" says the new mother, or "being the boss is not all it's cracked up to be" exclaims the recently promoted director. The pattern one knows (container) is the pattern one knows (vivid, compact images of the activities' essential quality). Changes in the known pattern are inevitably avoided, hesitatingly entered, actively resisted, cautiously enacted. Perhaps we should associate crisis with any turning point (entering a new container) rather than just entering an unwanted container (a diseased state) or being "outside" of any known container (chaos).

SUGGESTIONS FOR PLANNING CRISIS MANAGEMENT STRATEGIES

The container metaphor of crisis is especially useful for thinking about how to prepare for a crisis. Crises are inevitable. Unexpected events occur. We can predict with certainty that the unpredictable will occur and that unintended, though frequently predictable, consequences of carefully crafted plans will happen. Although we cannot know the precise activities that will constitute the unexpected, we can anticipate the general shape of many activities constituting our responses to a crisis. Information must be gathered quickly and disseminated to relevant audiences. Materials must be mobilized in nonroutine ways. Employees must be induced to work harder, faster, and longer than normal. By preparing for the crisis, we can manage its dynamics and decrease the probability that even more disastrous effects will evolve. The following steps take time and are best done over several sessions in a workshop or retreat setting. A consultant may be necessary to facilitate the performance of these steps.

1. Generate metaphors: Assemble a planning group involving people from throughout the organization. (Members from different units or levels have varying, but equally valuable perspectives, particularly those in frontline positions.) Ask group members to express metaphors of crisis. The metaphors created should concern how the crisis works, what activities are included in the overarching image. The use of Bateson's syllogisms is especially useful in making explicit these activities.

2. Discuss the metaphors: Group members explore the various images generated, asking how the metaphor was constructed, what else is included in the image, what detailed predicates might be made explicit within the metaphors expressed. Consider whether metaphors used by internal groups might differ from those assigned by others (e.g., the media, customers, gov-

ernment agencies) and whether these varying perspectives contribute further to the crisis.

3. Brainstorm: Using the metaphors generated, imagine what a crisis would look like, feel like, what would be going on "in" the conditions imagined. List what activities are required, what states (emotions, feelings) are likely, and what purposes (goals, objectives) are inherent in the images generated.

4. Generate practical actions: Given the vivid, compact images constructed, suggest actions that could contain unwanted consequences. List several activities that could be initiated that "counter" the unwanted effects of crisis. Do not evaluate the effectiveness and costs of these actions yet, just enumerate them.

5. Evaluate contingencies and commit: Commit to strategies that are workable within your setting and conduct a small scale experiment simulating how these activities fit together. The simulation will inevitably result in other by-products that can now be used to refine the crisis management strategy. Develop, circulate, and discuss the organizational crisis communication plan with all stakeholders. Each individual should understand the plan's basic strategies, why they were developed, how they serve the organization, and how he or she fits in.

CONCLUSION

This chapter explored how we think about crisis by focusing on the entailments of the two most frequent metaphors framing understandings of crises—war and container. The entailments were made explicit with Bateson's syllogisms and Lakoff and Turner's three basic conceptual metaphors. These two devices were used to demonstrate how thought is fundamentally metaphorical and how thoughts are constrained by the metaphors constructed to make sense of experience. Further, these two mental exercises were offered as useful ways for keeping your mental habits in shape, for toning cognitive muscles, for energizing interpretive routines and massaging tired, linguistic joints.

Although we have no direct data, we would expect that the war metaphor is proffered more by reporters of crises, whereas the container metaphor is expressed more by participants in crises. The war metaphor is more dramatic; the essence of drama is conflict and the quintessential conflict is war. The container metaphor, on the other hand, highlights the sense of confusion, the feeling of powerlessness stemming from being out of bounds, the loss of control and uncertainty experienced by those in a crisis situation.

The war metaphor condenses the crisis into a morality play of us versus them, of good guys and bad guys, and thereby encourages a nonreflexive morality that blames someone else or the omnipotent forces of nature for the crisis. The container metaphor, however, is not so simplifying for a more reflexive morality is suggested. Clear distinctions between good guys and bad guys are not indicated; rather, a sense of we don't know what we are doing or where we are going is evoked. Thus, who to blame becomes a secondary (or irrelevant) matter to be addressed by subsequent historians, if at all, because our own habituated routines may have provoked the crisis. The unknown, this sense of not knowing what to do when, can be much more frightening, debilitating, and fatiguing than facing a known enemy. An identifiable "cause" of the crisis, regardless of how powerful or treacherous, is easier to fight than the unknown, especially when the unexpected is a by-product of our own actions and we become the enemy.

The unknown is by definition harder to write about. The unknown is unknown because there are no viable similarity relations to more familiar circumstances; the unknown lacks purposes, locations, and activities because it is disordered, uncontained, unregulated, and uninterpretable. Hence, observers of crisis situations are more apt to express the war metaphor because that interpretation provides purpose to events by locating the story in an understood and understandable framework. This hypothesis directs future examinations on the metaphors of crisis by offering a key to unlocking the linguistic prisons of diverse inmates.

11

Telling a Story: A Narrative Approach to Communication During Crisis

Robert L. Heath
University of Houston

Once upon a time, members of a family, as is typical of families, were surprised by a loud crash in the family room. The older members of the family rushed into the room to see what had happened. They discovered the youngest member of the family standing in the midst of shattered glass, spilled water, and a broken flower arrangement. The *routine family narrative* had given way to a *crisis narrative*. (Or is the breaking of vases a typical family narrative?) The parents asked in unison, "What happened?" The child enacted a crisis response narrative by saying—one of the following, "I don't know how that happened, it just fell over"; "A ghost must have knocked the vase over"; "The dog jumped after a fly and knocked it over"; or "I broke it and I am sorry." As is so often the case, as narratives change from the routine to the different, some person must come forward in the midst of what might be or actually is a crisis and tell a story that in the judgment of key publics puts that event right.

A crisis event constitutes a rhetorical exigency that requires one or more responsible parties to enact control in the face of uncertainty in an effort to win key publics' confidence and meet their ethical standards. A crisis is a predictable event that occurs at an unexpected time and threatens the well being of stakeholders and stakeseekers (key publics); it challenges the ability of the organization to enact the narrative of continuity through constructive change to control the organization's destiny. Control assumes order. People desire order and predictability that lead to positive rather than negative outcomes. This search for order is a rhetorical exigency; it takes the form and substance of a narrative, a series of statements that is expected to present a factually accurate, coherent, and probable account for the event and its proper resolution.

This chapter extends these principles into a theoretically based rationale for public relations—crisis response. It connects the principles of narrative theory to the standard news story, the media, and lay public response to a crisis. The narrative of each crisis results in meaning co-created by the organization, many commentators, and key publics who seek a rational explanation of the event. This theory of crisis response extends the application of narrative theory and can help define and guide the best practices of crisis response.

THE NARRATIVE CHALLENGE

Telling a story is a culturally typical response to crisis. The story told may be a response by the person associated with the event—an ostensible or potential crisis—who is expected to report to others why the narrative has changed from routine to crisis, who or what is responsible for that change, and what will be done to resolve the narrative—maintain or reestablish control of the organization's operations. The strategically preferred progression in this analysis is from routine narrative, to crisis narrative, and back to routine narrative. The crisis story may be part of the narrative of the organization (which is part of the narrative of the operations of all organizations) and sets into place its past, its present, and perhaps most important its future. As well as the story provided by the organization's spokesperson(s) during the crisis, other stories may surface: media reporters, governmental officials, other involved organizations, activists, and other publics.

Archetypal Narrative of Oil Spill. The Exxon Valdez oil spill occurred in Prince William Sound, Alaska, on March 24, 1989. That drama continues more than a decade later as Exxon works to foster a pro-environmental persona, to attribute the causes of the event to various characters, and to establish its story of the event as the shared social reality people recall about the spill. Narrators in this crisis include environmental groups, media reporters, Alaskan officials, federal officials, Exxon personnel, and company supporters and opponents. Each public has a different narrative, sometimes quite at odds with one another. This dramatic spill motivated new legislation that imposed unlimited liability on companies that transport environmentally harmful material along the U.S. coast.

Archetypal Narrative of a Toxic Chemical Release. On December 3, 1984, methyl isocyanate (MIC) leaked from a holding vessel in a Union Carbide chemical plant operating in Bhopal, India and killed more than 3,500 people and resulted in more than 200,000 injuries. Union Carbide portrayed itself as a victim of the operating constraints placed on it by a foreign government. A contrasting narrative was enacted by India's Supreme Court in February 1989 when it ordered Union Carbide to pay $470 million in damages.

Capturing a narrative relevant to the Union Carbide crisis, Rosenblatt (1984) observed: "If the world felt especially close to Bhopal last week, it may be because the world is Bhopal, a place where the occupational hazard is modern life" (p. 20). This observation captured the narrative concern of residents who could legitimately fear that if something happened to others in their circumstances it could happen to them. What fueled public interest was not only the magnitude of the tragedy, but also the fact that the narrative featured a U.S. firm that was manufacturing the same lethal chemical in this country. Keeping alive the narrative theme basic to the Bhopal tragedy, media reporters and environmental critics recalled the narrative theme of earlier chemical disasters: Texas City, Texas in 1947; Saveso, Italy in 1976; Beziers, France in 1977; and BASF factory failures in 1921 and 1979. Discussions of classic crises make an issue so salient that the likelihood of government intervention substantially increases.

A prescient *Wall Street Journal* reporter, Terence Roth (1984) speculated that because of Bhopal "the chemical industry may be facing a fresh wave of legislation to tighten controls on uses of such lethal substances" (p. 4). Reflecting competing narratives, editorials debated the value of chemicals to protect lives and promote food production (Boffey, 1984) versus their potential harm to the health and safety of citizens who live near facilities where chemicals are manufactured (Beck, Greenberg, Hager, Harrison, & Underwood, 1984; Diamond, 1984; Grier, 1984). The outcome of that narrative debate was increased government regulation, the Emergency Planning and Community Right-To-Know Act, section three of The Superfund Amendments and Reauthorization Act of 1986 (commonly called SARA Title III).

The Exxon Valdez and Union Carbide incidents underscore how smoldering issues become inflamed once they are graphically publicized. These archetypal crises suggest that they—the public interpretation, evaluation, and reaction—are narratives—enacted stories that can lead to serious issues that have management consequences (Heath, 1997).

This realization provokes a paradox. If one were to advise public relations practitioners that their public response to a crisis is the telling of a story, they might shudder at the thought that they were being counseled to engage in falsification, assuming that a story is a fib—a lie—to spin the truth. Nevertheless, careful analysis justifies the conclusion that all crisis communication is narrative, the telling of a story designed to lead interested publics to conclude that the organization is willing and able to shoulder responsibility for its activities and their consequences as well as maintain or regain control over its operations. If the story lacks probability and fidelity, concerned citizens are likely to desire to force the organization to control itself or risk having control imposed on it by other agencies.

That conceptual framework raises questions that have practical and research applications. Persons who engage in providing information to the media need to remember the narrative approach typical of news reporting: what, who, when, how, why, and where. In crisis response, some narratives work better than others. The rhetorical options that organizations' spokespersons can exercise seem to be constrained by the various narratives that are relevant to each crisis. All parties interested in a crisis may have different views on what narratives are appropriate and expected. For these reasons, this analysis in this chapter grows out of the desire to know which rhetorical options spokespersons have and what constraints limit the responses they can make as the organizations they represent struggle to regain control over their operations and practices—the daunting challenge of crisis communication.

NARRATIVE: A COMMUNICATION PERSPECTIVE

How central is narrative to the human experience? Kenneth Burke (1983b) answered that question this way:

> Surrounding us wordy animals there is the infinite wordless universe out of which we have been gradually carving our universes of discourse since the time when our primordial ancestors added to their sensations *words* for sensations. When they could duplicate the taste of an orange by *saying* "the taste of an orange", that's when STORY was born, since words *tell about* sensations. Whereas Nature can do no wrong (whatever it does is Nature) when STORY comes into the world there enters the realm of the true, false, honest, mistaken, the downright lie, the imaginative, the visionary, the sublime, the ridiculous, the eschatological (as with Hell, Purgatory, Heaven, the Transmigration of Souls, Foretellings of an Inevitable wind-up in a classless society), the satirical, every single detail of every single science or speculation, even every bit of gossip—for although all animals in their way communicate, only our kind of animal can gossip. These was no story before we came, and when we're gone the universe will go on sans story. (p. 859)

If, as Burke reasoned, story is basic to human existence, we are challenged to explain the role of story in public relations, in this case—crisis response.

Researchers and public relations practitioners study and engage in (or counsel) communication response during crises. They examine how persons caught up in a crisis can and should design messages and respond to media and other investigative inquiries in ways that are ethically and rhetorically sound. One answer to that problem grows out of analysis that reasons that life is narrative and humans can best be characterized as storytellers who think and live in terms of the stories they tell (Fisher, 1985, 1987, 1989).

Narratives are a way of thinking, a way of ordering the events of the world which would otherwise seem unpredictable or incoherent. As people order the events of their world into meaningful patterns, those patterns—scripts and themes—express their values and guide their actions. However, not everyone thinks and acts in the same way. Viewed this way, narrative analysis assumes that people choose among competing stories that account for a given event. Thus, the question is often not whether narrative, but which narrative is best?

What is a narrative? "A narrative generally is recognized to be a way of ordering and presenting a view of the world through a description of a situation involving characters, actions, and settings" (Foss, 1996, p. 400). At first glance we may think of a story—a narrative—as nothing more than a descriptive recounting of events. It is more. "A narrative, as a frame upon experience, functions as an argument to view and understand the world in a particular way, and by analyzing that narrative, the critic can understand the argument being made and the likelihood that it will be successful in gaining adherence for the perspective it presents" (Foss, 1996, p. 400).

Through narratives, people structure their experiences and actions. Narratives give meaning to the world. Through stories, the world and people's actions reflect a logic that explains what happens, why it happens, who makes it happen, when it happens, and how people should respond to these events. Narratives express a set of preferences, the values of the persons who ascribe to those narratives. The world of human events is understood in terms of a thematic logic that begins with "once upon a time" and progresses through "and then she said to him," and resolves into "and all ended well for both." For businesses, a narrative might be "and after that the company had to file for bankruptcy." The desired resolution of a story would be "and all ended well."

Scripted logics allow people to create and share a variety of social realities—zones of meaning. Stressing this point, Gergen and Gergen (1988) concluded,

> Narratives are, in effect, social constructions, undergoing continuous alteration as interaction progresses. The individual in this case does not consult an internal narrative for information. Rather, the self-narrative is a linguistic implement constructed by people in relationships and employed in relationships to sustain, enhance or impede various actions. It may be used to indicate future actions but it is not in itself the basis for such action. In this sense, self-narratives function much as histories within society do more generally. They are symbolic systems used for such social purposes as justification, criticism, and social solidification. (p. 20)

Narratives give people the scripts and perceptual structures they need to identify with and understand the events, actions, and expectations of one another. Narratives embed beliefs, attitudes, and values as ideologies that reflect and guide people's judgments and evaluations. Narrative content and theme allow people the means for coordinating their actions with and predicting the actions of one another. For this reason, savvy public relations persons need to be aware of, consider, and use the several available narratives to predict how key publics may or will react to the events of a crisis and media reporters' accounts of them. Public relations practitioners come to realize that some stories work as the basis for explaining and justifying a set of circumstances related to a crisis, and others do not.

Narratives have substantial rhetorical potency because they are a conventional and convenient means for understanding the theme that runs throughout a series of events—including a crisis—or a set of similar crises such as airline crashes. Narratives simplify; even when they are profoundly incorrect, they nevertheless have the ability to facilitate the attribution of motivation. Narrative is fraught with motive because even—or especially—as children, people learn that the characters in stories respond to and enact motives. The story makes sense because it expresses why people did what they did—why events occurred as they did. For instance, if we say that a major automobile company allowed avarice to motivate cutbacks in safety design so that the cost of a few lawsuits was factored into the marketing of a line of automobile, that narrative is likely to ring true (be predictable given the corporate—free enterprise narrative) (Heath, 1994).

The apparent truth in that case is not exclusively the facts that are presented or assumed to be true, but the commonplace reasoning that such facts are likely to exist because they are the substance of that narrative. Even if key facts do not exist, people are prone to believe that they do because they are inherent to the narrative that people use to interpret an event or action. Because of the attributional richness of narratives, one sentence can explain why a crisis occurred: "Management places profit above safety." If that narrative dominates a key public's thinking, the response by corporate spokespersons, for example, when explaining the safety record and attempting to repair the company's reputation for corporate responsibility must acknowledge the "corrupt corporation narrative," its attributional bias and performance expectations.

Narrative is a vital way of segmenting and giving meaning to the events of people's lives, which occur one at a time and would seem random, unpredictable, and meaningless if they were not viewed as the enactment of some coherent story. Even though each person enacts the episodes of his or her life—one step at a time, life has meaning because themes give it continuity. Each step is meaningful because it is an episode in the enactment of some ultimate principle, as Burke (1969a) reasoned: "[I]f the fate of our hero is developed through a succession of encounters, each of these encounters may represent a different 'principle,' and each of these principles or stages may so lead into the next that the culmination of one lays the ground for the next." "If one breaks down a 'dramatic idea' into acts of variously related agents, the successive steps of the plot could be reduced to corresponding developments of the idea; and the agent or scene under the aegis of which a given step was enacted could be said to represent personally the motivational principle of that step." Each plot has the sense of being ultimate, featuring a principle that guides and motivates each act. "Ultimate vocabularies of motivation aim at the philosophic equivalent of such narrative forms, with a series of steps that need not precede one another in time, but only 'in principle' " (p. 197).

Narrative is a perfect framework for understanding the past, knowing what is occurring in the present, and projecting action and events into the future. "Time is critical because transactions have no meaning outside of their historical contexts: The expectations attendant upon an interaction moment are crucial for understanding the meaning of that interaction" (Eisenberg, 1986, p. 89). Through their efforts to help create and enact narratives relevant to their activities and missions, businesses engage in symbolic processes to represent themselves and define their boundaries (Cheney, 1992; Cheney & Dionisopoulos, 1989; Cheney & Vibbert, 1987). Basic to those definitions, representations, and enactments are narrative plots, characters, events, and themes. Each narrative gives a particular definition to the events of an organization's enactment. Narratives define and prescribe.

A zone of meaning is a social reality that some persons share but is different from the social reality of other persons (Heath, 1994). Convergence results when individuals use the same narratives—the same zones of meanings. Divergence results from people thinking, judging, and acting in accord to different narratives. If a group of people share narratives, they identify (merge) with one another (Burke, 1969b). If the narrative of one group differs from that of another group, division rather than merger occurs. For example, environmentalists have different narratives (as zones of meaning) than do oil companies such as Exxon, which suffered the Valdez crisis, or chemical companies, such as Union Carbide. Once an oil spill occurs, for instance, environmentalists and other key publics will use the operable and relevant narrative that is unique to that event—as a zone of meaning—to interpret and evaluate it. Organizational spokespersons who provide an account of an event should realize that what is said is presented and interpreted as a narrative. It is interpreted by and compared to the predicted, expected narrative each key public thinks is relevant to the event.

For this reason, the narrative of one group can be a counterstatement and perhaps a corrective to the narrative of another group. If, for instance, the narrative of a crisis presented by an organization's spokesperson is rejected because it differs from the narrative believed by some key public, the awareness of that reaction can lead to a correction and change of the narrative used for that explanation and for the actions of the persons in the organization. Behavior and opinions are tested and become meaningful through what people do and what others say and do in response. Narrative enactment is inherently dialectical. Each narrative is likely to encounter some conflicting, competing narrative. The narrative of the orderly family is often strained, for instance, by the rebellious narrative of adolescence. Such is the case, Burke (1983a; Deetz, 1982) reasoned, because knowledge is dialectical, "(a) one acts; (b) in acting, one encounters the *resistance to one's purpose*; (c) *one learns* by suffering the punishment dealt by such resistances" (pp. 22, 26). By taking on and enacting a story, people are likely to encounter converging or diverging narrative accounts of the evaluations, actions, plots, and themes that are relevant to that event.

Although people use narrative to frame what they say, think, and do, not all people see the same events through the same narrative. A set of events: A person commits a crime and is punished by society. In this case, Burke (1932) reasoned that we might approach this criminal and the attendant punishment "from the vocabulary of sufficient grace, whereby we look upon his [or her] transgressions as a deliberate choice of 'evil' where he [she] might as well have chosen 'good,' so that we make our prison justice 'retributive.' " How the criminal is perceived and treated is different if the attribution of motives is based on a different narrative, "if we approach him [her] from the vocabulary of determinism, whereby his [her] transgressions become 'symptomatic' and justice becomes rather a matter of prophylaxis and reclamation. Here we see the destiny of thousands dependent upon a mere shift of terminology" (p. 312) or different narrative.

Another set of facts: A person is fired and then commits suicide. As a narrative, those details are too barren to be satisfying; for that reason, people look closer to explain why this person, at that time, committed the particular act. Thus, Burke (1932) mused,

> one man [woman], dismissed from a job, but having a Marxian "configuration of meanings," will fit his [her] particular fate into a larger social progress, and so feel resentment rather than humiliation, and may perhaps organize an ominous hunger march; another, similarly dismissed, and with only the older pioneer configuration, the doctrine that ability will out, takes his [her] dismissal simply as evidence that he [she] was insufficiently endowed, and so may slink out of existence with a few pilfered sniffs of the gas company's gas. (p. 312)

Thus, people are narrative critics; those who respond to events as spokespersons or reporters need to be mindful that publics use narratives idiosyncratically. The narrative a company or governmental organization opts to account for a crisis might not be rhetorically adequate to the task because it is incompatible with the narratives used by those who pass judgment on the crisis.

Brummett (1995) recognized the necessity of using discursive, expositional rhetoric to work through detailed analysis. In addition, however, he championed the power of narrative as he characterized public relations as "the practice of telling and managing stories that are told about people, institutions, and groups" (p. 24). He thought that "A shift to a rhetoric structured around narrative is a move around the flank of the discursive roadblock of respectable rhetoric. Every group has a story to tell, even if every group cannot, does not, or will not use expositional argument or statistical proofs" (p. 24).

Viewed this way, narrative serves as a rationale for communication practices because it is intimately connected to the ways that people think and act. Scholars and practitioners of crisis communication can use the components of narrative to better explain, prescribe, and critique spokespersons' crisis responses. If public relations persons think they can (or must) supply a story to account for what happened before or during, as well as what might happen after a crisis, they need to understand their rhetorical options framed by the rhetorical exigencies of specific types of crisis. First, people need to recognize that crisis response entails the telling of a story—the enactment of a crisis narrative. The next consideration is the critical and strategic selection of the specific narrative account for and report on that event—a daunting public relations challenge.

NARRATIVE: COMPONENTS OF CRISIS COMMUNICATION

Narratives are the basis for how organizations are enacted, interpreted, and responded to (Heath, 1994). A crisis shifts the narrative being enacted by an organization from one of routine events to one that is not routine. (Or, perhaps, crises are part of the narrative relevant to the organization.) For this reason, crisis is a narrative event that demands unique and strategically appropriate rhetorical enactments. What is needed, then, by those who wish to understand and practice crisis communication is a sense of what critical judgments are made in response to an organization's account of some crisis.

The simplistic response to that rhetorical exigency is: Tell a truthful story. That prescription assumes that all parties operate out of the same interpretative frame—zone of meaning. The previous section in this chapter demonstrated that is not a likely, reasonable, or savvy expectation. What does knowledge of the components of the narrative perspective offer to guide the study and application of crisis response communication?

Crisis occurs when an organization or industry has experienced or is experiencing what they or key publics interpret as a series of events that fit the crisis narrative. A narrative crisis is a matter of the perspective of each key public. For instance, an organization may not believe that it is suffering a crisis although key publics believe that a crisis has or is occurring. A key public may employ a narrative perspective that assumes that some dramatic shift in the routine narrative of the organization constitutes a crisis. That dramatic shift might be an event that is perceived to be out of the routine, one especially that involves or portends substantial harm. A crisis narrative assumes that when some extraordinary event occurs—especially one that produces or portends dire consequences—the organization is obliged to respond and account for itself. This rhetorical problem prompts crisis response.

A competing view of crisis narrative is one used by a key public that incorporates such events into the narrative of the organization. For instance, an environmental group may employ a narrative of chemical companies that features the likelihood of a series of crises, such as oil spills or releases of harmful chemicals. In both cases, the narrative of a crisis leads key publics to believe that as a result of events that have occurred or are occurring the responsible organization must gain, regain, or maintain control of its operations because they affect others. Control is a dominant societal archetype, a narrative that is assumed to guide each organization's enactment. The narrative of business or governmental operations assumes orderliness and benefits rather than unpredictability and harm. Thus, the first question: *Is an event occurring which others interpret as a crisis narrative?*

The second question: *If a crisis exists, what rhetorical response is appropriate?* People use narratives to attribute cause and motive to the events—including crises—that occur. The response to an event is dictated by the scene where that event occurs. What act is appropriate to each scene, asked Burke (1969b). Narrative analysis allows for many focal points of critical judgment and strategic response in regard to a crisis. If narratives frame people's interpretations of and responses to events, the question to be addressed is which narratives become operable in each event. (a) Any narrative can be compared against other narratives of the same type; for instance, a narrative of one product recall crisis can be compared to and framed according to narratives of other product recalls. (b) Any crisis narrative can be compared against and framed according to the larger narrative of the industry or governmental agency to which the member that is suffering a crisis belongs; for instance, the petrochemical transportation industry interpreted the Exxon Valdez in the context of the narrative of thousands of safe trips (this discharge of crude oil was atypical) whereas environmental groups interpreted it as a predictable act by a traditionally irresponsible industry. (c) The narrative of a crisis used by one group is compared against and framed according to the narrative of that organization (or industry) as held by each key public; for instance, anti-fur advocates see the selling and wearing of fur and the crises their activism causes through a different narrative than is used by the customers of the industry.

The third question: *As enacted, what components of a narrative are operable in a given crisis?* If life—personal and organizational—is a lived narrative, the enactment of activities exhibits narrative elements: Narrators, auditors, plot, theme, characters, events, location of the act, acts, relationships, personae, scripts, communication plans and message design logics, and decision heuristics (Heath, 1994). In each crisis and the response to it, key publics focus on the narrator(s) (person(s) who tells the story), auditors (persons who hear the story—actual or attributed audiences), plot as transformation of events and acts into themes, characters (persona as archetypal roles), location of the crisis, narrative response, events of the crisis and response to it, and the relationship between the narrator, characters, auditors. Each drama has scripts. How well do the scripts used by the characters fit the drama? Is the drama as scripted routine or different? Is routine enactment or different enactment the best rhetorical response to the exigency? Does the narrative response fit the decision heuristics of the key publics?

If control is a key element of crisis, the narrative enacted by the key players—those responsible for the crisis and its resolution—must respond to key publics' need for a return of control by the responsible organization. The fourth question: *Does the narrative enacted by the organization responsible for the crisis demonstrate that the organization has not lost control or that its efforts will restore or achieve control; is the resolution of the story satisfactory to the key publics?* This question not only constitutes the rationale for the rhetorical exigency of the event and the selection of the message design logics and scripts, but it is also vital to the planning and explanation of the past and future operations of the organization. A crisis raises concerns about the ability of the organization to plan and operate in ways that maintain or restore control over its actions and build or maintain mutually beneficial relationships with key publics. A crisis response narrative may require that the organizational narrator explain why the event occurred and how the organization has or will operate to restore control. This narrative raises the question of why did the operations fail to achieve or maintain control. What characters and events led to the crisis? If the past operations were inadequate to sustain control, the rhetorical exigency focuses on what operations will be implemented to achieve control.

As enacted, the narratives of the organization responsible for the crisis and other narrators' accounts of the event become a drama. Narratives are evaluated by their ability to "display brevity, avoid contradictions, demonstrate unities of direction and purpose, and integrate the credibility of narrators, authors, and speakers" (Lucaites & Condit, 1985, pp. 103–104). Narrative is sequence. It is a way of knowing what happened—of explaining and attributing motive—over time. It is a way of acting in the immediate and of projecting actions into the future. Narratives are judged based on their integrity and their transformational ability.

The fifth question: *What criteria are used to judge the integrity of a narrative*? The rhetorical integrity of each narrative is based on probability and fidelity, vital "considerations for judging the merits of stories, whether one's own or another's" (Fisher, 1985, p. 349). Narrative probability is a judgment of the extent to which a story holds together, rings true, and is free from internal contradiction. Narrative fidelity refers to the weight of values, good reasons, consideration of fact, consequence, consistency, and the degree to which a story has bearing on relevant issues. Narratives, especially those enacted during a crisis, give audiences, both internal and external to an organization, the chance to know (test hypotheses) which accounts are reliable and whether the organization, if at fault, will properly atone for its mistakes and take responsibility to understand what led to the crisis and take actions to prevent its recurrence.

Narrative probability includes an assessment of a range of events that precede the crisis event and extrapolate into the future. For that reason, a crisis response that merely includes details of the present misses the rhetorical exigency of addressing the past, present, and future. Even if the organizational spokespersons limit themselves to the present, they will find their key audiences do not. Those audiences ask a range of questions, inherent in a narrative. What kind of people allowed this event to occur? Are they the sort of persons who can bring order and control to what seems to be a crisis? These two questions suggest the event does not occur in a vacuum. The reputation of an organization enhances or haunts its crisis account and response efforts. This logic needs to be considered, because Fisher (1987) reasoned, one of the components of narrative probability is *characterological coherence.* "Coherence in life ... requires that characters behave characteristically. Without this kind of predictability, there is no trust, no community, no rational human order" (p. 47).

A second aspect of narrative probability is *argumentative or structural coherence* (Fisher, 1987). Each narrative has a logic—a coherent set of principles. People know and use that logic to interpret the integrity of a story. Thus, if people suffering a crisis have been irresponsible, the prediction is that because carelessness is their character they will continue to be careless. Claims, by organizational spokespersons, to the contrary are unlikely to assuage the disbelief felt by key publics. Of related critical importance is the need for the presentation of a story that is intrinsically believable because the events and the characters related to those events need to exhibit argumentative or structural coherence.

A third criterion of narrative probability is *material coherence* (Fisher, 1987). People know many narratives. They use them (by type) to determine whether any one presentation of a set of events deserves their confidence and concurrence. Children's accounts of any event are judged by their parents against the knowledge of previous events. If a child has told the truth in the past, that narrative lends credibility to each current account of a crisis. Likewise, any account by a child is compared to the narratives known to the parents (some first hand) that are analogous. The account by an organization experiencing a crisis will be compared by key audiences against similar narratives—either by this company or those that are relevant to this event. If that account lacks material coherence, the spokesperson will either suffer a lack of persuasiveness or be expected to prove why the comparison is appropriately different.

In addition to narrative probability, Fisher (1987) reasoned that narratives are judged by their ability to demonstrate narrative fidelity. The critical standard for judging fidelity is that of the logic of good reasons: "matters of *fact, relevance, consequence, consistency, and transcendental issues*" (p. 48). Facts must be verifiable. Those that are presented must be relevant, and relevant facts cannot be omitted. Consequence is a standard by which key publics consider the likelihood and desirability of believing some account. The facts presented are judged by the extent to which they are consistent with those key publics know or expect to be true. Finally, any key public wants to know whether what has, is, or will be done meets its standards of propriety and desirability. Here we are confronted with standards of human value. What value implications are implied by the account of events and the measures taken by the company?

An example: John Hancock Mutual Life Insurance Co. paid a $1,000,000 fine for misleading consumers into thinking that the policy they purchased was designed to be savings for college or retirement; in fact, the policies were life insurance. The company agreed to change its advertising copy and police the actions of its agents more closely. The transcendent value used to determine whether a crisis exists is "honesty." The narrative coherence of this event brings to mind the concern: If the company has demonstrated dishonesty in the past will it become honest? Knowing that kind of narrative logic was likely to be invoked, the company blamed its agents, which engaged in what the company called unauthorized activities. Also fingered in the account was an outside advertising agency (Fine of $1 million, 1996). Do key publics want to do business with an insurance company that cannot control the activities of its employees, agents, and advertising firm— one that controls their actions in ways that customers do not believe are fair and safe. Blameplacing as a narrative response seems not to absolve the company, which is expected to enact the narrative of control, based on

the transcendent value of doing good business—enacting a mutually beneficial interest with its customers.

The sixth question: *What narrative structure leads through a set of events—
past, present, and future—to transform the organization from an apparent or actual loss of control to the implementation or regaining of control?* As Mumby
(1987) reasoned, "Political reading of narrative draws attention to the relationship between narrative structure and the process of interpretation" (p.
113). Narratives consist of sequences which "are constructed through
means other than time—by a theme, a character, or a quality, perhaps"
(Foss, 1996, p. 400). Narrative structure is more than the temporal presentation of events, scripts, and character development. The key to narrative
structure is the principle—often an expression of value—that is developed
by what the characters (including narrators) say and do in response to one
another and to the scene and the events that occur there. By interpreting
this transformation or having it interpreted for them, key publics attribute
values and motives to the actions they witness.

Doesn't a story exist as a set of temporally ordered events? Yes—and no.
In addition to a chronology, other structures and thematic developments
are possible—even probable. Stories must have order. As enacted by organizations, they must lead to order—a resolution that has coherence for the
auditors. A story is the enactment of order, through the dialectic of what
happened during the crisis, what is learned from what happened, and what
will be done in the future based on what has been learned. Narrative is a dialectic, Burke (1969a) observed, "a process of *transformation* whereby the
position at the end transcends the position at the start, so that the position
at the start can eventually be seen in terms of the new motivation encountered enroute" (p. 422).

A crisis exists until some resolution has brought control to the circumstances and events that aroused concern on the part of key publics. In this
way, terms and events relevant to a crisis and the comments on it progress
through "transformation" (change) to "consummation" (resolution). Crisis
narrative can be viewed as "a *development* or *transformation* that proceeds
from something, *through* something, *to* something" (Burke, 1942, p. 15).
Transformation results from the way the dominant symbols modify one another. For instance, the offending organization may claim that new regulatory restraints will harm it and the well being of others; in contrast, the relevant regulatory agencies may build its case on the need for constructive
restraint in the best interest of others.

Transformation may involve the interaction between the individuals involved in the crisis and the symbols that define the scene, act, agent,
agency, or purpose (Burke, 1969a). A crisis narrative of a chemical plant explosion brings forward commentary on the persons who caused the problem, were harmed by it, and responded to it, such as emergency personnel.

These acts occurred in and defined a scene, were done by agents, using an appropriate or inappropriate agency (means for conducting the act), and with a purpose. This set of events is expected to create a transformation from the event (even prior to it) when disorder occurred and control was lost or tested to a point of resolution when control is restored.

Transformation is thematic, the enactment of some principle or set of values. Transformation is created through the development of a cycle of terms, the essence of which is some sense of order. As Burke (1966) explained, "In such a cycle of terms that imply one another, there is no one temporal succession. You can go from any of the terms to any of the others. For instance, you can with as much justice say either that the term 'order' implies the contrary term 'disorder,' or that the term 'disorder' implies the term 'order' " (p. 59). The structure of narrative, including a crisis narrative, results from the transformation of ideas which consists of an arc achieved by moving from principle A to principle I made possible by a progression of statements that feature a unifying theme O. For this reason,

> narrative form (as in a play) in its necessary progression from one episode to the next is like the stages from A to I along the arc. But as regards the principle of internal consistency, *any* point along the arc is as though generated from Center "O." And the various steps from A to I can be considered as *radiating* from generative principle "O," regardless of their *particular* position along the arc of the narrative sequence. (p. 59)

The publics affected by or cognitively involved with a crisis focus their attention on the generative principle and use each of the steps or stages in the development of the narrative as points in the arc to determine what principle is being developed. To examine the rhetorical strategies in this vein, we can recall some of the events of the Exxon Valdez crisis which began (A), at least as a news event, with the vessel running aground and beginning to spill its environmentally harmful cargo. B in the progression could be the first account by the company. Examining this progression, Williams and Olaniran (1994) found that Exxon began (B) by placing partial blame for the accident on the weather, the principle of burden sharing. Failing to restore a sense of control with that strategy, Exxon opted for the strategy (C) of blame placing, focusing attention on third mate, Gregory Cousins and Joseph Hazelwood, captain of the Valdez. The third strategy (D) was to accept blame for the crisis and initiate a set of actions that were predicted to lead to clean up and restoration of Prince William Sound. Even after this decision, Exxon seemed prone to go about business as usual without enacting reports of steady and wise progress. The company, perhaps too confident of its technical skills, wanted to act alone, to be solely responsible for the clean up. The problem, however, the unwillingness of the company to exert control by accepting blame. Perhaps, too much influence in the decision making rested with corporate legal counsel, which tends to prefer a crisis response that avoids accepting blame. The paradox in that regard is the balance between accepting responsibility for the event (if that is the narrative fidelity and probability) and moving to demonstrate willingness and ability to achieve control. Failure to accept responsibility (if responsibility must be accepted) portrays the organization as being a victim that cannot exert control because it does not assume that it made an error in the first place.

Each person, each event, each statement, each reaction—all that is done that has narrative quality is a symbol to be interpreted by members of each key public witnessing the crisis through its idiosyncratic narratives. Key episodes constitute the development of an idea as stages of transformation. Each act foretells other acts. Each statement implies those that will follow. And "the unfolding of each transformation prepares for the next, as the removal of one card from a deck reveals the next one immediately beneath it" (Burke, 1966, p. 62). These events may seem disjointed and even chaotic, but if that is the case, those perceptions result from the attributions of key participants who are applying that narrative to interpret the events and the responses that are occurring. The expectation of all key players in the event (as participants or witnesses) is some meaningful outcome, the enactment of resolution. "It is only by some measure of *uniformity* that a structure of expectation can arise at all" (p. 63). Uniformity of crisis response results from the theme that runs through the interlocking enactment of each episode and from episode to episode.

Any narrative, reasoned Burke (1965), can take one of three dominant forms: progressive, repetitive, and conventional. Progressive form advances an idea through syllogistic or qualitative development. In a narrative, syllogistic progression of premises forces conclusions, as framed in the following narrative theme: Industrial accidents only occur because companies are unwilling to spend the money to prevent them so executives can earn higher bonuses. Company X has just suffered an industrial accident. Therefore, the executives of company X are more interested in their bonuses than in safe operations.

A qualitative progression would deal with attributions made about character, for instance: Honest and ethical managements take credit for crises as well as the successes of their organizations, whereas dishonest and unethical management only take credit for the good and place blame for the bad.

Repetitive form relies on maintenance of principles under new guises, as illustrated by the following statements. *Two years ago*, this company touted a new product that had to be discontinued because the regulatory agency found out that the supporting evidence had been falsified. *Last year* the company executives engaged in illegal insider trading. *This year* the executives of the company are threatening to clear cut massive amounts of its ancient forest timber holdings if the government does not pay a premium to buy the timber land. *For these reasons*, this company can be predicted to suffer an endless string of crises because it will not restrain itself; it deserves governmental intervention into its operating procedures.

Conventional forms feature development—repeated enactment—of standard themes, for example: Last year this company was accused of false advertising; this year the company is being charged with false advertising; the company will always engage in false advertising. People know how to interpret these organizational dramas because they know the standard forms: If X characters and Y plots then Z outcomes. The importance of this analysis is not story content per se, but the fact that form gives meaning and logic to the content.

CRISIS RESPONSE AS NARRATIVE: PROSPECT AND QUESTIONS

The critical question in crisis response is whether in a specific crisis event, the narrators (representatives of the organization and other communicators) co-create a narrative that favors or disfavors the interest of the organization as it fits into the narrative of society and as it works to build or maintain mutually beneficial relationships with its stakeholders and stakeseekers.

1. Is this event one that is accurately interpreted as a crisis, exhibiting the characteristics of a crisis narrative? Is the apparent reason for the crisis, the true reason? What actor—even nature—is culpable or the cause of the crisis? What acts led to the crisis? What actions will about bring its resolution? Will that resolution foster the mutual interests with key publics?

2. Given these persons and factors regarding the crisis, what is the likely narrative outcome of the crisis as it is alleged to be managed by the parties responsible for enacting the crisis narrative? This line of questioning is relevant, for instance, because the crisis encountered by Johnson & Johnson was based on the fact that it was a victim rather than the perpetrator of the events that led to the crisis provoked by product tampering. The evidence of a crisis is the actual, ostensible, or apparent failure on the part of some actor to achieve the control its stakeholders and stakeseekers expected of it.

3. What theme is being enacted by the persons who are centrally involved in creating and responding to the crisis? If a company, activist group, or governmental agency is making planned changes that are predicted to lead to short- and long-term positive outcomes, that is a skillful planning and

management narrative. If the crisis reveals mismanagement and the absence of wise operating controls, that narrative requires external efforts to force control onto an organization that lacks it.

4. What narrative theme characterizes this particular crisis and defines or calls for a particular enactment? Lerbinger (1986) argued that crises can be distinguished by type: Events that result from some mistake in the use of *technology* (explosion at a chemical plant) or technological advance that portends an uncertain future (development of heart transplant capabilities), *confrontation* between representatives of an organization and its critics, or as a result of *malevolence* on the part of an organization (use of humans as medical guinea pigs) because its actions violate acceptable ethical standards or constitute unethical acts against an organization undeserving of such attack, as was evidenced by the terrorism against the government building in Oklahoma City. Is this a victim crisis narrative or a crisis where the central organization is culpable? Is this a widely anticipated event or one that caught people off guard? Having a devastating earthquake in California or Japan is a crisis, but not one that surprises people. When the Exxon Valdez ran onto a reef, that was not only a surprise to much of the public, but one made more so because of assurances by the members of the petrochemical industry that such an event would not occur due to the careful controls that would be implemented to prevent such an event—a means for leveraging governmental support for the project. What is also interesting in the Exxon Valdez case is the fact that many thousand safe cargo trips had occurred—and even more have occurred since—giving the impression that this a narrative of safe, rather than unsafe, operation.

5. Do the personae of the organization and the key players fit the narrative being enacted? For instance, one debated question is whether the CEO or other major management figure should make a dramatic appearance at the scene of the crisis. If the persona of the company and the chief officers is one of openness, visibility, and community involvement, we expect its officers to make an acceptable apology. If the organization and its officers have exhibited the opposite persona, becoming visibly involved the crisis explanation may alter the narrative typical of that company to the point that it lacks fidelity and probability. If an airplane crashes in the Far East, senior officials are expected to make moral and community atonement that demonstrates that they assume responsibility for the events that led to the crisis. If someone commits suicide as a part of the event, that is more likely to be expected as a moral statement in Far East companies—probable to the narrative—than is a similar gesture for U.S. airline personnel (Pinsdorf, 1991).

6. What script should be used to account for the crisis and the response to it to return the organization (and the community) to the previous narrative or to create a new narrative for the organization based on the events, personae, and theme of this crisis? The script for each event is the product of

the personae of the key persons and organizational entities involved and the themes that each set of players are enacting and expected to enact. Part of the fidelity of the script is the extent to which the event is defined and the particulars are reported by the spokespersons for the primary organization in ways that seem to fit the event as it becomes known through the accounts of others, such as media reporters, governmental investigators, and other interested parties. Is the script used to explain the crisis one that has narrative probability—exhibits a sense of coherence, internal consistency, and probative force—a logic that conforms to this kind of event? For some time, a mere apology was a scripted response that seemed to set things right. But as was demonstrated by the response of the Hispanic community to Howard Stern's reaction to Tejano music star Salena's murder, an apology is insufficient atonement, especially given the insincere persona of Stern. An apology assumes sincere atonement, a character trait that must be consistent with the persona of the central character in a crisis. One narrative theme relevant to crisis is that some atonement must be made to enact the proper narrative. Atonement could be an explanation of the management changes that decrease the likelihood of recurrence, it could be a resignation or firing of a high official who is responsible for the events, it could be a large financial expenditure through remediation of the environment, for instance, and a punitive fine exacted by the judicial system. One inherent weakness in the use of the apology script is its failure to reduce the concern persons have for the organization's ability to enact the expected amount of control.

CRISIS RESPONSE: BEST PRACTICES

The previous sections have articulated a narrative rationale for crisis response and raised questions relevant to the rhetorical exigencies inherent in crises. This section prescribes some best practices that arise from the logic of the previous sections.

1. Frame crisis response as an extended series of statements that span the sequence of events from the routine, to crisis, and to the return of routine.
2. Feature the principle ("O") of control by the client organization throughout the transformation of statements about the crisis.
3. Connect with and correct (add or subtract) the content of the narratives that develop; don't assume that you can control these narratives or promote only one narrative but must co-create narratives with other narrators. Recognize and adapt to archetypal narratives that are emerging in the interpretation of this crisis and the attribution of its causes and the responsible parties' motives.

4. Demonstrate that you know what happened, what was learned from what happened, and what will be done to correct the situation and prevent its recurrence.

5. Foster the development of one narrative (even with strategic variations relevant to key publics) that accepts and features the principles of control and responsibility that is exerted in the mutual interest of the various publics.

CONCLUSION

This chapter embraces and seeks to extend the rationale and practice of theorizing about crisis management, preparation, and communication as narrative. Given the nature of narrative—especially as a cultural archetype, this rhetorical approach has the potentiality to inform crisis planning, management, and communication activities in a way that is coherent and systematic. It allows for persons who are engaged in crisis planning and response to sense the narrative thematic continuity that is expected of the organization and to imagine the narrative events (such as terrorism) that could occur—because they are possible or probable narratives. The facets of narrative offer a coherent way of thinking about the kinds of statements—the scripts that are available, criteria for judging them, and the sorts of persons who can reasonably use those lines to enact a coherent organization than has or will regain control over its events.

One last example: On March 23, 1994, A Texas Eastern Transmission Corporation pipeline erupted in Edison, New Jersey. Texas Eastern was a subsidiary of Panhandle Eastern Corporation (now part of Duke Energy). Natural gas exited the pipeline and entered a 1,000 unit apartment complex. The flames from the fire caused by the eruption could be seen in New York City, 20 miles away. This event was even more dramatic because it was the first time in history that a pipeline erupted in a residential area. Hundreds of people nearly lost their lives, and they did lose prized possessions during the fire. This was a crisis; lawsuits and punitive damages were a substantial threat. Public opinion turned against the company initially because of the assumption that typical of all companies this one had cut costs and thereby allowed its facilities to deteriorate to an unsafe level. This would have been the typical narrative, but it was not. Proving that was the challenge facing the company.

Once they became aware of the explosion and fire, senior executives (management, operations, and public affairs) went to the scene and began the enactment of responsible executives expressing and exhibiting concern for the human loss and seeking to set things right (return to control). The objectives of this team and the crisis response effort were these, in order of priority: Take care of human needs, cooperate with investigators to determine the cause of the incident, and return the line to safe operation as soon as possible. These characters and their scripts were met with the predictable counterstatement: doubt, criticism, and threat of lawsuits.

Company executives responded to the human needs within their limits by supplying financial support to people whose property had been harmed by the fire. The company cooperated with federal, state, and local officials to determine the cause of the accident. (The pipeline had been damaged by persons while burying a vehicle to avoid having it repossessed.) Rather than taking onto itself the sense of returning control to the operation of the pipeline, company executives yielded to the government officials involved, especially the local mayor, who needed to enact their role in returning or achieving control of the pipeline operations. This enacted partnership gained approval for the restoration of pipeline service—21 days after the explosion. The crisis response was the enactment of the narrative of community cooperation to restore control and public safety.

This analysis reinforces the assumption that narratives are cultural archetypes, means by which people account for, understand, predict, and seek control over events that occur in their world. Narrative—as enacted by a crisis response and communication team—gives us means for understanding, interpreting, and critiquing the response in a manner than is coherent and systematic. It allows the critic and practitioner a framework by which to view the organization and its rationale as a part of society.

Informed Organizational Improvisation: A Metaphor and Method for Understanding, Anticipating, and Performatively Constructing the Organization's Precrisis Environment

Miriam R. Finch
Xavier University

Linda S. Welker
Northern Kentucky University

Discussion of organizational crisis communication tend to focus on analyses of the communication actions that occurred during and after the crisis event. That these discussions are relevant cannot be disputed. In 1987, crisis management researchers Mitroff, Shrivastave, and Udwadia concluded that it's no longer a question of whether a crisis will occur, but rather a question of "when, how, what form will it take, and who and how many will be affected?" (p. 291). More recently, given the tremendous surge in all types of organizational crises, including most notably violence in the workplace (see Boxer, 1993; Deming, 1991; Fisher & Briggs, 1989; Graham 1992; Herman, 1992: Russell, 1989; Thomas, 1992; Thornburg, 1992), it is evident that the state of preparedness of an organization to handle crisis situations is critical to the health of the organization and its individual associates. The typical way for an organization to address potential crises is by having corporate communication specialists, alone or in conjunction with top management, construct a crisis communication plan. The document is then distributed to what are considered to be key individuals. Our concern here is twofold. First, Ong (1993) warns us of the dangers of relying solely on a written document:

Writing fosters abstractions that disengage knowledge from the arena where human beings struggle with one another. It separates the knower from the known. By keeping knowledge embedded in the human lifeworld, orality situates knowledge within a context of struggle. (pp. 43–44)

The question then becomes, does total reliance on a document decontextualize information to the degree that it renders it obsolete, exacerbates the situation, or at the least compromises its effectiveness in the human lifeworld of the organization? Note, we are not proposing the elimination of crisis communication plans. Instead, we are suggesting that we can most fully appreciate their usefulness when we recognize and account for their limitations.

Specifically, it is our assertion that utilizing the talents of corporate communication specialists solely to produce and act on written crisis communication documents actually underutilizes those talents. The ability of the corporate communication specialist to identify, articulate, and synthesize crisis concerns can enable organizational members to generate evolved dialogues which heighten awareness and contextualize crisis issues. Because by nature many crises occur within organizational "white space," these dialogues provide members with the fluidity needed to better anticipate and respond to situation-specific, unscripted contingencies. In other words, the dialogical process can help generate an interpretive framework from within which organization members can engage in a collective sensemaking effort. Furthermore, even with the increase in crisis events, many businesses and corporations still do not have crisis plans in place. Those that do have plans in place concentrate their energies primarily on actions to be taken after a crisis event occurs. But as Sturges, Carrell, and Newsom (1991) contended, a postcrisis emphasis can actually result in the escalation of the crisis.

Weick (1988) supported this view, arguing that actions taken during a crisis situation become part of the crisis itself and serve to either escalate or de-escalate the crisis. In other words, if the actions taken during a crisis situation are successful (i.e., if they result in defusing the crisis), then those intervention activities in fact become part of the crisis situation as one would describe it from the point of intervention.

Crisis situations, however, are by nature equivocal, and therefore it is not always clear which course of action will result in a successful resolution of the crisis and, in fact, alternative courses of action may produce equally successful results. It is also possible that the chosen intervention may serve to escalate, rather than de-escalate the crisis. Individuals who must respond in crisis situations often have their sensemaking abilities stretched to the limit; the less adequate the sensemaking process the more likely it is that intervention will serve to escalate the crisis (Weick, 1988). This dilemma was described by Weick as follows:

> To sort out a crisis as it unfolds often requires action which simultaneously generates the raw material that is used for sensemaking and affects the unfolding crisis itself. (p. 305)

Weick explained that it is less likely that situations "determine appropriate action than that 'preconceptions' determine appropriate action" (appropriate as determined by the individual) (p. 306). In other words, individuals choose courses of action based on preconceptions they hold. Sometimes these preconceptions result from prior experience with a similar crisis, but more often they result from a general perception about how one should act in a crisis situation combined with the expectations and constraints they perceive to exist within their organizational environment.

Perhaps more disturbing, Barton (1993) maintained that our preconceived notions concerning how one should act in a crisis situation often come from witnessing role models (e.g., friends, relatives, teachers, and public figures) respond to crises that have little if anything to do with our own work-related crises (p. 189). Multiply those preconceptions with the number of individuals involved in the crisis or with the management of the crisis situation, each with his or her own unique life experiences, knowledge, and resulting preconceptions, and the situation is ripe for chaos. To compound the problem, in the heat of the crisis, as individuals are socially constructing the meaning of events (i.e., as they are trying to make sense out of what is occurring or has occurred), they are often unaware that their decision-making processes, as well as the decision-making processes of others, are based on assumptions stemming from preconceptions that may or may not be appropriate for the given situation.

Again, crisis situations are by nature equivocal. The manner in which individuals address the equivocality is influenced by several antecedent conditions. First, the higher the initial equivocality of a crisis situation, the more individuals rely on experience or knowledge-based preconceptions to guide sensemaking and ultimately their decision-making processes. Second, the way individuals act or react to equivocality is influenced by their interpretations of cultural norms and expectations which they perceive to exist in the organizational environment. Third, critical elements that influence these conditions are either present to some degree or absent from the relationships that exist between and among employees and management. They include trust, comfort level, warmth, openness, and bonding communication (Braverman, 1991; Overman, 1991). The composite of these antecedent conditions coupled with what are perceived as here-and-now relevant situation-specific cues guide discursive, nondiscursive, and performative behaviors.

It is our contention that a theory-based perspective of crisis communication processes must consider these antecedent conditions as constituting necessarily the starting point for crisis analysis. It is here where we discover whether organizational processes are loosely or tightly coupled, and where we can discern the extent to which organizational actors in crisis situations may be called upon to devise unscripted courses of action. For to effectively enact their parts in crisis situations, organizational members must be able to improvise—to depart from the organizational script that is played out in "normal" routines. But unlike improvisational actors, the organizational ensemble needs to work toward a collaborative understanding of desired organizational outcomes. We believe it is possible to reach this collaborative understanding through a process we call "informed organizational improvisation."

INFORMED ORGANIZATIONAL IMPROVISATION

Informed organizational improvisation can create a repertoire of possible general behaviors, the spirit of which may be enacted in specific organizational situations as needed, including highly equivocal crisis situations. Thus, rather than ad libbing *ex nihilo*, organizational members performatively construct a unified vision by developing collaborative perceptions of outcomes, which they may move toward and from which they can draw on in times of high equivocality.

Originating in the world of drama, improvisation is an ensemble theatrical activity in which a group sets out to solve a predicament with little or no inclination as to how to accomplish it. In essence, they allow the performance crisis to determine the scene (Spolin, 1963, p. 384). Improvisation expands participants' abilities to perceive and reduces the need for intense and specific scripted preparation. It rejects the constraints of tightly scripted responses prescribed by others who have not lived in that particular moment.

Although improvisation may be thought of as a game, or as play or a play-making activity, it is an activity, nevertheless, which has serious intents and specific procedures. It is not randomized behavior, but the creation of an enacted environment. Improvisation is team effort in which members of the team have the potential of developing extraordinary unity, cohesion, and mutual awareness. Improvisational performers use all of their senses in communicating with one another in a fully embodied exploration and creation of dramatic outcomes. In our particular application, improvisational performers are organizational members in search of appropriate responses to pre-emergent or emergent organizational crises.

The value of providing organizational members with the opportunity to engage in this structured discovery process becomes evident when one considers that individual beliefs, anticipated outcomes, and preconceived notions about how one should act in any particular organizational situation for the most part lie buried in a person's subconscious. Although we are surely conscious (at a surface level) of certain expectations, procedures, and policies (such as those articulated in crisis plans), nevertheless, much of our knowledge of self, others, the organization, and the environment rests beneath our cognitive awareness. Because many of our sedimented preconceptions and prereflective insights reside in the intuitive domain, and because we reflexively draw on them to guide us in the heat of crisis, we assert that informed organizational improvisation provides us with a vehicle to get to the intuitive domain, thereby increasing the effectiveness of our sensemaking abilities.

We may better understand this intuiting process by considering the experience of persons who, in the midst of some kind of crisis or dilemma, suddenly arrive at the correct solution to the problem—as if out of nowhere. *How* they arrived at the solution may seem like a mysterious revelation—a revelation they probably would like to experience again when another crisis occurs. But if an effort is not made to understand the process by which they arrived at the insight, whether or not it can be repeated in the future is left to chance, and certainly cannot be shared with others. As Weick (1979) asserted, the analysis of any socially constructed reality requires that actors "attain at least a partial consensus on the meaning of their behavior and that they look for patterns that underlie appearances, actions, and events" (p. 165).

We believe that the performative concept of informed organizational improvisation forms a serviceable theoretical basis and valuable method for understanding communication before, during, and after a crisis event. By engaging in improvisational activities, organizational members can begin to become more cognitively aware of their own preconceptions, which in turn can provide the raw materials needed for generating the dialogues necessary for reaching consensual agreement. As a structured but unscripted activity, it also enables organizational members to generate new insights, creative configurations, and collaborations. Most importantly, inasmuch as improvisation is a fundamentally phenomenological process, it enables the "intuitive grasping of the essences" of a situation, not by passively waiting for the answer to come, but through a "strenuous, active search that makes possible the intuiting" of the essential, meaningful configurations of data hidden in the subconscious (Polkinghorne, 1983, pp. 42–43). It empowers organizational members to take a proactive role in crisis preparation, and provides them with a collective knowledge base for managing and reflecting upon actual crisis events.

Consequently, informed organizational improvisation may be conceptualized both as a metaphor and as a method. As a metaphor, informed organizational improvisation offers organizational members a theoretical model for understanding organizational activity before, during, and after crisis events. As a method, informed organizational improvisation provides organizational members with the imaginative capacities and behavioral skills needed to respond creatively and effectively before, during, and following crisis situations. In other words, these operations suggest both a theoretical representation and a practical training mechanism.

Informed organizational improvisation is a fruitful process in which "combination of individuals mutually focusing and mutually involved creates a true relationship, a sharing of fresh experience" (Spolin, 1963, p. 24). That which has been deconstructed, analyzed, experimented with, tried on, tested and re-tested is now reconstituted. A new structure emerges through collaborative enactment that is far better than any constructed by a playwright or solo author. As Spolin puts it,

> Here old frames of reference topple over as the new structure pushes its way upwards, allowing freedom of individual response and contribution. Individual energy is released, trust is generated, inspiration and creativity appear as all the players play the game and solve the problem together. (p. 24)

Informed organizational improvisation is a reflexive method useful for excavating and releasing sedimented beliefs about the way things are in an organization, for making perceptible otherwise hidden attitudes about organizational members and their relationships, and for identifying prereflective preconceptions. Informed organizational improvisation enables organizational participants to move presuppositions from the subconscious to the conscious, to validate or invalidate the "truthfulness" or "accuracy" of those preconceptions, to reify or strengthen cogent beliefs, attitudes, and inclinations, to alter or eliminate erroneous biases, and to uncover and make tangible that which is imperceptible to oneself and to others.

To fully explain the method of informed organizational improvisation, we look first at the general concept and technique of improvisation as a performance paradigm. Second, we show how we have incorporated this technique into our method of informed organizational improvisation for use in organizational contexts, specifically, in precrisis exploration.

IMPROVISATION AS A PERFORMANCE TECHNIQUE

The process of improvisation, according to Clark (1971) involves a three-stage process: absorption, interaction and conflict, and resolution and patternmaking (p. 6). What follows is a description of each of these stages.

Absorption. Absorption is a "relatively passive stage" (Clark, 1971, p. 14) in which the group members are presented with a performance problem and then attempt to acquire as much information about the particular situation as possible. Improvisational participants commonly ask questions such as: What has happened? Who is involved? and Where does/did the scene take place? In other words, in the absorption phase the who, what . . . when, and where are discovered by (and, in some cases, provided for) improvisational performers. The improvisation situation involves the establishment of a predetermined scenario within which the participants are to operate in order to solve a performative problem. In organizational terms, improvisational problems may be as simple as handling an intraoffice conflict or as serious as handling a breach of corporate security.

During this stage, group members collect information about the environment that will subsequently allow them to project themselves into the situation and thus to perceive how it feels to be in a particular situation. As Weick (1979) asserted, however, "the concept of an *enacted environment* is not synonymous with the concept of a *perceived environment*" (p. 164; emphasis added). Improvisational participants will learn what it is like to be in this situation by fully participating in it rather than by simply discussing or reading about it. In this absorption stage team members take stock of the resources available to them. They ask: "What do we already know?" "Where can we go to find out more information?"

According to Clark (1971), performers also are concerned with "meaning" in the absorption stage of improvisation. They ask: "Now that we have the 'facts,' what do they mean?" Improvisational performers break down the situation; they de-construct the scene in order to examine and make sense out of the experience. Performers look beneath surface meanings for subtext—hidden meanings or situational infrastructures. According to Weick (1993), "improvisation is largely an act of interpretation rather than an act of decision making" (p. 361). Improvisational performers are interpretive artists who must be must be able to comprehend the complex circumstances confronting them:

> A great dramatist is great because with very few words he [sic] can create a vast space of exploration, and much of that space lies underneath the words. The greater the play, the more profound and significant is the sub-text, and to get at it it is necessary to have a group trained to bring its collective resources to bear on the mining operation necessary. (Clark, 1971, p. 3)

This mining operation is critical for exploring the intuitive domain and thus increasing the effectiveness of the sensemaking process.

Interaction and Conflict. The second stage of group improvisation is pivotal and involves interaction and conflict. It is during this stage that the "How" question is opened up for exploration within the group. Since *how* the participants are to solve the organizational problem is not prescribed, the team must discover it. They do so through collective experimentation. In this stage, the ensemble confronts the situation at hand, "engages with it, conflicts with it, seeks out every crevice and penetrates it" (Clark, 1971, p. 8). By engaging in improvisational exercises, the team investigates possible responses. This trial and error method, which involves spontaneous physical movement and extemporized dialogue, enables the group to explore the conditions necessary for the crisis situation to be resolved.

This stage of interaction may be ripe with conflict. During this stage, the improvisational performers may uncover opposing attitudes, contradictory beliefs, varied and possibly conflicting styles, and even contesting notions of desired outcomes. In fact, according to Clark, "the function of a good leader is to arrange an atmosphere that will allow all the relevant conflict to emerge" (p. 36). Once again, we *expect* that *relevant* conflicts will emerge during this stage. As in any experimental situation, it is far better that conflicts emerge within the relatively safe environment of the "laboratory" rather than have them emerge during the "actual" performance.

While moving through the interaction and conflict stage, improvisational team members may find themselves hampered by feelings of defensiveness which, in turn, may impede their abilities to concentrate on their performance objectives. For instance, they may be afraid of the unknown, insecure about their improvisational abilities, or self-conscious about or uncomfortable with the revelations that may surface. Improvisational practitioners have devised several techniques to aid improvisational participants in such circumstances. For example, team members may be given what is called a "Point of Concentration (P.O.C.)—a chosen or agreed upon object or event on which to focus" (Spolin, 1963, p. 388). Participants use this point of concentration to help them keep focused despite the fact that circumstances and specifics of the scene (and their feelings while in it) are shifting and changing around them. According to Spolin, the point of concentration supplies control, a constancy that counters the potentially damaging consequences of disordered inventiveness:

> Just as the jazz musician creates a personal discipline by staying with the beat while playing with other musicians, so the control focus provides the theme and unlocks the [participant] to act upon each crisis as it arrives. (p. 23)

By focusing on a specific detail in a multifaceted organizational crisis situation, the participants become totally absorbed in the scene and achieve results that incorporate the intuitive as well as the cognitive domain.

Resolution and Pattern Making. Improvisational participants reach the third stage of resolution and pattern making when they begin to discover their situational *throughline of* meaning (Stanislavski, 1948). On the literal, scripted stage, performers are presented with a throughline of action. Also known as the "dramatic spine" (Wilson, 1980), it defines the goal toward which they are striving. Performers who have a clear sense of their throughline are those who are best able to adjust to the unexpected (e.g., a dropped line, a missed cue). They are so thoroughly familiar with and focused on the desired dramatic outcome they are able to quickly and effectively fashion their responses to adjust to that situation and to reach that outcome.

In contrast, the organizational ensemble, because of the high degree of equivocality associated with crisis situations, has only a simple, general throughline-bringing the crisis to a successful resolution. Thus, a great deal of energy must be expended to generate a more specific, consensual throughline of action. To that end, participants might ask questions such as: "What is it that I as a participant in this scene want?" "What does the organization want?" or "What is my driving force?" "What is the organization's driving force?"

During this third stage, the participants must find a "pattern that will allow all the material coming from [the situation] and the group to find a relationship" (Clark, 1971, p. 11). In other words, the group must collaboratively generate a way of organizing and responding to the situation that is both true to the situation and the individuals involved. Throughout the second stage, the group sampled a variety of interaction patterns—performatively constructing their reality on a trial basis. Now, during the third stage, performers must select from among alternative patterns that which best settles the problem. In organizational terms, this is the stage in which participants select the crisis response (from among alternative patterns generated through performance) which is most suitable to the particular crisis situation.

Earlier we noted that the manner in which an individual responds to the equivocal crisis situation is influenced by three antecedent conditions: experience and or knowledge-based preconceptions; interpretations of cultural norms and expectations; and the interpersonal quality of the relationship that exists between and among associates and management. It is our belief that participants who engage in the informed organizational improvisation method will gain more knowledge and understanding of individual and group predispositions to crises by uncovering the raw materials necessary for effectively addressing crisis events.

In addition, the fully embodied enactment within which they participate provides a relatively safe environment wherein essential precrisis self-disclosure can occur and empathy for and appreciation of the diversity that exists within individuals can be nurtured, increasing the communicative quality of their on-going relationships. The importance of this precrisis exploration cannot be overstated. As Hart and Burks (1972) asserted, "an understanding of and a tolerance for individual complexity and diversity is a necessary prerequisite to making wise rhetorical decisions" (p. 76). In the event an actual crisis unfolds, it is essential that organizational members be able to "gel" quickly to effectively deal with the inherent equivocality present in those emergent situations.

INFORMED ORGANIZATIONAL IMPROVISATION METHOD

To engage in this integrated process of discovery and problem solving, groups may participate in a basic five-step method: (1) Identifying the Crisis, (2) Assembling the Improvisation Team, (3) Selecting and Assigning the Duties of the Facilitator, (4) Enacting the Scene/Solving the Crisis, and (5) Interpreting the Outcomes/Reflecting Upon the Process.

Identifying the Crisis. Organizational participants should engage in initial (as well as on-going) discovery session(s) in which group members generate lists of potential crises they believe they could encounter within their organization. Crises of all sorts may be considered, including personal, interpersonal, fiscal, and environmental crises. The range and scope of crises should be limited, however, to that which the organizational members may realistically be responsible for or involved with (i.e., those with the highest probability of occurring). Concerns and influences of both internal and external constituencies may be considered by the improvisation team. Note: The crisis list may change as groups regularly engage in this exploratory process.

Assembling the Improvisation Team. Improvisational participants should be grouped into teams of approximately four to eight members. Others associated with the organizational unit may serve as audience members and rotate into subsequent improvisational team configurations.

Selecting and Assigning the Duties of the Facilitator. A designated improvisation facilitator is an integral member of the improvisation activity. The facilitator role would best be filled by a communication specialist (either internal or external to the organization) trained in the informed organizational improvisation method. Nevertheless, whomever is designated as the facilitator must be able to give up authority to become less of a leader and more of a side-line encourager. The facilitator will help the group select the scenario to be enacted and then begin the exercise. Throughout the explorations, the facilitator will unobtrusively remind participants of their objectives. This improvisational role is very challenging because it simultaneously calls upon the person to process multiple stimuli generated within the group while helping participants focus on their points of concentration.

Enacting the Scene/Solving the Crisis. Along with the help of the facilitator, the improvisation team will select a particular crisis from among those generated through discovery. A two to four sentence scenario will be developed within which the group articulates three situational components: (1) the place the action is occurring (Where), (2) the persons involved in the crisis situation (Who), and (3) the problem to be solved (What).

The team then proceeds to solve the problem while audience members watch and the facilitator guides the improvisation. The length of time that the group will need to solve the problem will depend on several variables: the complexity of the scenario, the amount of information already available to the group, the group's cohesiveness, the abilities of the improvisational participants to effectively interact with one another, and the ability of the group to uncover and address individual and group goals.

It is here that the three-stage process of improvisation begins to unfold. Some groups may reach Stage three within one improvisation session; other groups may take several sessions to arrive at that stage. Even if multiple sessions are needed, this structured, cumulative method will enable the group's interaction to move toward the project objective. Throughout the process, members should be free to involve their whole selves in a total environment. As Spolin (1963) put it, "[T]otal individual involvement with the event or project makes relationships with others possible" (p. 24). By participating freely without expecting to be judged, informed organizational improvisation participants free their intuitive knowledge—"knowledge which is beyond the restrictions of culture, race, education, psychology and age" (p. 19). Here preconceptions, taken-for-granted assumptions, and conflicting points of view emerge and are examined, providing additional data to assist the group in reducing the equivocality of the situation and increasing the possibility that the group will make more informed decisions when choosing among alternative patterns of action.

Interpreting the Outcomes/Reflecting Upon the Process. When the group completes their improvisation session, they may examine and reflect upon the evolved dialogues produced through the enactment. This feedback may come from audience members who have observed the interaction; it may come from the facilitator who has been guiding the improvisation; but it must certainly be primarily generated from the improvisation team members themselves. During this hermeneutic process, participants may ask such questions as: "How successful were we at solving the problem?" "What did we learn about the situation from this exercise?" "What did we learn about ourselves in this process?" "What did we learn about the organization?" What did we learn about our perceptions of the organization? "What did we learn about our perceptions of the nature of crisis?" For future reflection and analysis, organizational members may want to record the insights gained through their critical reflections.

CONCLUSIONS

The method of informed organizational improvisation can benefit organizational members in several ways. It enables groups to generate a repertoire of desired outcomes toward which they may move in particular crisis situations. Participants are more able to adapt and adjust to the group's needs as determined by anticipated crisis situations sublimating their personal needs in favor of group needs. Over time, informed organizational improvisation participants can develop a strong sense of interdependency and improve their ability to work cooperatively toward the accomplishment of group goals.

Further, the cohesion that results from this heightened sense of interdependency will serve groups who may find themselves in crisis situations not previously explored through improvisation. At the onset of an unanticipated crisis, improvisational participants will be more prepared to work with their teams to solve the crisis. Ideally, by having participated fully in the informed organizational improvisation process, they will have come to better know and trust one another. They will have developed an ability to focus on solving the problem, to generate a consensual, situation-specific throughline of action, and to identify individual and organizational superobjectives. They will have learned to more fully express themselves and to better understand the communicative cues of others. They will be less self-conscious and more group conscious. Moreover, because they have already identified many of their preconceptions, they will be able to function in a more informed environment. They will be able to enact a solution that takes these preconceptions into account—embracing those that ring "true" and are pertinent to the situation at hand, rejecting those that are not.

Finally, regardless of the type or method of preparation, organizational crises will occur. We do believe, however, that informed organizational improvisation provides a theory-based method for understanding critical elements present in antecedent conditions that directly influence the manner in which individuals respond in crisis situations. As a method, it has the potential to reduce precrisis equivocality, thereby effectively improving the sensemaking abilities of participants who may one day find themselves in crisis situations.

13

A Symbolic Approach to Crisis Management: Sears' Defense of Its Auto Repair Policies

Keith Michael Hearit
Western Michigan University

Jeffrey L. Courtright
Illinois State University

> *On June 10th, the California Bureau of Automotive Repair made charges concerning the practices of Sears Auto Centers in California.*
>
> *With over 2 million automotive customers serviced last year in California alone, mistakes may have occurred. However, Sears wants you to know that we would never intentionally violate the trust customers have shown in our company for 105 years.*
>
> Ed Brennan Chairman and Chief Executive Officer
> Sears, Roebuck and Co.
> —Brennan (1992a, p. 8G)

So responded Sears' Chairman and Chief Executive Officer Ed Brennan to allegations that Sears Auto Centers had a fraudulent policy by which its customers regularly paid for repairs that they really did not need—in some cases more than $500 worth of repairs. The allegations plunged Sears into a public relations crisis that threatened to damage its image of trust (Benoit, 1995b; Fisher, 1992a, p. D1). This loss of trust subsequently made vulnerable the economic viability of its auto repair business, which saw a 15% drop in the 2 weeks that followed the allegations (Sears Opens Ad Assault, 1992, p. A10).

Furthermore, if the crisis was not resolved quickly, it was likely to cause even more drastic consequences for the Chicago-based retailer: The California Department of Consumer Affairs could revoke permanently Sears' license to do automotive repair work in the state (Fisher, 1992a); and other states, among them New Jersey, New York, and Illinois had begun inquiries into the integrity of Sears Auto Center's repair practices (Fisher, 1992b).

In order to contest the charges and forestall drastic outcomes against the company and its reputation, chief executive Ed Brennan chose to respond with what crisis communication scholars label an *apologia*, a discourse of defense in which issue managers offer a "defense that seeks to present a compelling, counter description of organizational actions" (Hearit, 1994, p. 115). This *apologia* took the form of a full-page newspaper advertisement in which Brennan defended the company and presented Sears' side of the story (Sears Places Ads, 1992). Sears' advertising firm, Ogilvy & Mather, also prepared 2-minute network radio spots and a 60-second television advertisement for broadcast during morning and evening news programs (Sears Opens Ad Assault, 1992).

Many current public relations and management approaches to crisis management deal with crises primarily as a media relations stratagem (Briggs, 1990; Howard & Matthews, 2000; Meyers, 1986, Pines, 1985; Reinhardt, 1989; Seitel, 2001). Although such approaches offer helpful advice to use to manage crises, they typically neglect the substance of what is said. Pines (1985), for example, counsels would be crisis managers to "retain control of the story" (p. 18), yet he offers little insight into how to frame such responses. Conversely, our purpose here is to provide a rationale and explanation for the study of crisis management from a communicative perspective, using the case of Sears as an exemplar. Subsequently, we argue for a conceptualization that locates all crisis management as crisis communication management, because crises are both created and resolved communicatively. Said another way, we assert that communication, rather than being one variable in the crisis management mix, actually constitutes the nature and experience of the crisis itself. To support this claim, we first address some definitional issues as to what constitutes a crisis, noting the relative failure of some crisis researchers to account for the communicative component of crises; second, we argue that a communicative approach to the study of crisis management is rooted in a social constructionist framework, and use the case of Sears to develop the implications such a perspective holds for the understanding of crisis management; and finally, based on this position, we offer some lines of direction for future crisis management research that emanate from this approach.

CURRENT CONCEPTUALIZATIONS OF CRISIS MANAGEMENT

There does appear to be a fair amount of agreement as to what defines a crisis for an organization. Most scholars characterize crises by their infrequent and unpredictable nature. Crable and Vibbert (1986), for instance, described a crisis as "a rare kind of situation" (p. 254), created by both internal and external agents (Hearit, 1994; Mitroff & Kilmann, 1984). Crises are also characterized by their short response time—and often count innocents as their victims (Crable & Vibbert, 1986; Hermann, 1963; Perrow, 1984; Sen & Egelhoff, 1991). Also featured in many definitions is the fact that crises threaten the most basic goals of an organization—its reputation, its financial viability, indeed, its very survival. Weick (1988) aptly and cogently summarized these ideas when he concluded that crises are "characterized by low probability/high consequence events that threaten the most fundamental goals of the organization" (p. 305).

Although there is a recognition that crises do have a random quality, there is a parallel line of research acknowledging that, although crises are unusual and may appear random, they are in many ways "normal" and, hence, predictable. This viewpoint, rooted in the work of Perrow (1984), argues that given the intersection of human beings with systems that feature complex technology, and the numerous ways that systems interrelate, accidents (or in this vernacular, crises) are inevitable. Consequently, organizational officers can and should prepare for crises.

The relative unanimity that characterizes this line of inquiry has unfortunately not resulted in a research tradition that can be described as fully developed. Rather, one strand of crisis management research tends to be "how to" case studies that seek to explain what can be gleaned from a certain attempt at crisis management, be it a positive result, as in the case of Tylenol (Benson, 1988; Snyder, 1983), or negative, as in the case of Exxon (Small, 1991). Other extant scholarship is just beginning to arrive at a theoretical understanding of crises (Coombs, 1999b; Egelhoff & Sen, 1992; Hermann, 1963; Lerbinger, 1997; Seeger, Sellnow, & Ulmer, 1998; Sen & Egelhoff, 1991; Taylor, 2000; Ulmer & Sellnow, 2000; Weick, 1988).

Of particular concern in much of the public relations and management literature is the lack of an emphasis on the role of communication in crisis management; only a few essays account for this critical component (Benoit & Lindsey, 1987; Benson, 1988; Hearit, 1994; Ice, 1991; Williams & Treadaway, 1992). At best, most approaches tend to treat communication as one variable among many. Hermann (1963) and Billings, Milburn, and Schaalman (1980), for example, noted that crises force a change in how organizations communicate: They reduce the number of channels used to collect and disseminate information. Sen and Egelhoff (1991) viewed communication as one aspect of a calculus that must be considered to successfully manage a crisis. Other analyses, such as Marcus and Goodman's (1991), while featuring the role of communication, do so in an unnecessarily objectivist manner: In their discussion of crisis management, they correlate crisis communication with stock value, yet they use "signal theory" to examine "the changes in investors' expectations in response to the *signals sent* by management" (p. 283, emphasis added). Similarly, Sherrell, Reidenbach, Moore, Wagle, and Spratlin (1985) noted that, in responding to negative publicity, "negative word-of-mouth is subject to the least control by the firm, [and] contains the most 'noise' of all the channels of communication . . ." (p. 16). These materialist approaches do not account for the fundamental, constitutive role that communication plays in crisis management, and, as such, reflect fundamentally flawed assumptions about the nature of communication.

The anterior inquiries are rooted in a conceptualization of crisis communication as information transfer. This approach comprehends communication as a "conduit" through which meanings are "transferred" from one person to another (Axley, 1984). Also called the information engineering approach (Eisenberg & Goodall, 1993), this perspective perceives communication to have a relatively objective (i.e., informational) character to it. Language in such a perspective *contains* meanings and is a reasonable *representation* of reality. Thus, this approach views effective communication to occur when there is a reasonable similarity between the message sent and the message received; in a phrase, there is message fidelity. Such an opinion is found in Snyder's (1983) description of the Tylenol case; he argued that "[u]ltimate communication effectiveness, however, can be measured by the "degree to which message receivers are motivated or persuaded to *act* in accord with the sender's intent" (p. 29).

In terms of crisis management, this perspective sees crises as objective events whose meaning is both predetermined and self-evident, and suggests a rule-based response with a limited degree of communicative options. Such a response is based on a calculus of the type of crisis and the degree of organizational culpability (Egelhoff & Sen, 1992).

Because the "facts" speak for themselves, from this objectivist notion an organization's primary communication challenge is to speak in a clear and effective way. Such a perspective suggests that companies avoid common crisis management mistakes such as Sears made. Media analyses concluded that Sears' initial response failed because it attacked its accuser instead of taking a consumer perspective that offered evidence that the charges of unnecessary repairs were false (Stevenson, 1992). The role of communication from this conceptualization is summarized best by Murray and Shohen (1992) who, in arguing that Johnson & Johnson's crisis communication management in the Tylenol tampering scare has become the "gold standard" on which all other crisis communications are judged, asserted: an "[a]ppropriate and caring response to the public is the single most important part of crisis management. By providing the facts in a timely fashion, the window of speculation and the opportunity for misinformation are reduced" (p. 15).

A SOCIAL CONSTRUCTIONIST APPROACH
TO CRISIS MANAGEMENT

The aforementioned scholarly analyses describe crises in a manner that implies a stimulus–response conceptualization in which some external force acts upon a corporation and to which the organization subsequently reacts. Consider, for example, the deterministic implications of a "triggering event" (Barton, 2001; Billings et al., 1980). As a result, many researchers tend to describe "crises"—however unintentionally—as events that are more objective than subjective in character. Current understanding as to the nature of language and the sociological manner in which it is used suggests there is much more latitude in the creation and resolution of crises than current conceptualizations imply.

Social reality is socially constructed through language (Berger & Luckmann, 1967; Orr, 1978; Searle, 1995). Rather than being a vehicle that transfers information from one person to another, communication is the process whereby meaning is created and agreed upon. Orr (1978) summarized the assumptions that drive the social constructionist approach:

> Groups create and sustain their versions of reality through symbolic interaction; that is, consensually validated symbols define reality and truth for their validating communities. Knowledge is, therefore, rooted within socially derived symbolic structures. Rhetoric as symbolic advocacy is a constituent element in the social construction of reality; even a scientific community's version of reality depends on rhetoric. (p. 263)

By referring to a scientific community, Orr makes the point that even those communities that view their work to be most-closely associated with that which is "objective," communicatively construct their social world. Similarly, although crisis managers' options appear few and relatively fixed (and hence, subject to an objective equation), crisis management is a distinctly communicative phenomenon in which participants construct the meaning crises hold.

Crises are terminological creations conceived by human agents, and consequently, are managed and resolved terminologically. As such, instead of being one component, communication constitutes the quintessence of crisis management. Some may object to this notion that a crisis is a terminological construction, arguing (rightly) that an explosion is not terminological, but very real. Yet the manner in which an explosion is described, investigated, and made sense of, is a terminological construction. Thus, whereas all crises may not be initiated by human agents, all are created socially by human symbolic intervention. In other words, issues become crises because someone makes them crises (Crable & Vibbert, 1985).

This conceptualization, then, suggests the need for revision to the aforementioned definition of crisis. A crisis is a name placed on a predictable series of events, created by external or internal agents or events, over which an organization initially has little physical or *terminological control*. The act of naming a situation a "crisis," whether it be done by crisis managers or the media, results in a context in which a whole host of actors react in identifiable and readily anticipated ways; in Orr's (1978) words, the term crisis is a "consensually validated symbol" (p. 263). Only when corporate actors, media, or governmental officials agree to label a problem a "crisis," for example, do they respond to it as such.

Some would construe this stance to assert a standard of "truth" rooted only in consensual agreement. Orr (1978) responded that such a conclusion "may be good sociology but it is questionable epistemology" (p. 268), for an epistemologists asks, " 'Are our agreements about the truth true' " (p. 268)? That is, while consensual agreement is compelling evidence in developing the legitimacy of a truth claim, alone it is not sufficient.

It should be noted that the social constructionist position that we are advocating does not obviate the existence of an "objective reality." Attempts to offer competing views of reality do not preclude the presence of an objective reality, for such are attempts, however flawed, to reach that ideal, and are disciplined by that ideal (Orr, 1978). This fact is illustrated every time rhetorical critics seek to expose the motives of rhetors and explicate their use of language, oftentimes revealing a grammar of deception. Furthermore, if there is no hope for an objective reality then there really is no basis on which scholars can present an assessment and critique.

An emphasis on a terminological approach to crisis management suggests a number of critical implications. First, crises are characterized by competing "proto-definitions." These proto-definitions represent the conflicting interpretive schema offered by participants in a crisis drama, and the proto-definition that becomes accepted will impact the method of resolving the crisis. In the case of Sears, for example, the charge by the director of the California Department of Consumer Affairs carried with it the assertion that Sears automotive repair centers, due to their commission-based pay structure, routinely recommended repairs on vehicles that did not need them (Yin, 1992). In a word, the Attorney General defined Sears' practice as one of "fraud." Sears, conversely, offered a number of competing definitions until it found one that resonated with consumers. First, Sears denied all charges—it defined the allegations as "politically motivated." Dirk Schenkkan, a San Francisco lawyer who represented Sears, maintained that the charges were an effort by Jim Conran, the director of California's Department of Consumer Affairs, to forestall the state from eliminating his department due to a budget crunch. Schenkkan alleged:

> He is garnering as much publicity as he can. If you wanted to embark on a massive publicity campaign to demonstrate how aggressive you are and how much need there is for your services in your state, what better target than a big, respected business that would guarantee massive press coverage? (Fisher, 1992a, p. D1)

Such an attempt for Sears failed; it did not address consumers' concerns about the integrity of the automotive centers and their policies. Consequently, public opinion forced Sears to try a second, and more successful, track.

Given the mounting evidence, Sears could not deny the repeated press coverage of instances of individuals and confederates who sought basic repairs and faced larger repair bills for parts that were not worn out. One such narrative was reported by *The New York Times*:

> One of our undercover operators was told that the front calipers on his car were so badly frozen that the car would fishtail if the brakes were applied quickly.... The calipers on that vehicle were in fine working order. (Fisher, 1992a, p. D13)

More such narratives surfaced (Yin, 1992). Sears had little choice but to become more conciliatory; it offered another proto-definition that sought to explain what had occurred, one that was more consumer oriented. The retail giant responded:

> You rely on us to recommend *preventive maintenance* measures to help insure your safety, and to avoid more costly future repairs. This includes recommending replacement of worn parts, when appropriate, before they fail. This accepted industry practice is being challenged by the Bureau. (Brennan, 1992a, p. 8G, emphasis added)

In effect, Sears said that it did not defraud customers; rather, it helped them to engage in "preventive maintenance." This was a positive account that interpreted the meaning of the "facts" of the case: that customers received more work done than originally intended. Furthermore, it offers a positive terminological connotation: Sears had helped to ensure the safety of its customers. This proto-definition offered Sears a more solid communicative framework by which to resolve the crisis. In effect, a social constructionist approach suggests there is a degree of latitude as to what constitutes "the facts" in any crisis management situation; it is only as they are provided context that their meanings become clear.

Second, a social constructionist approach suggests that crises are only as serious as issue managers, be they media, corporate, governmental, or interest groups, make them. Consequently, a conceptualization of a crisis as socially constructed suggests that issue managers are wise not to use the term *crisis* unless absolutely necessary, because, like the term *war* in a social policy context, *crisis* creates expectations of swift consideration and positive resolution (Zarefsky, 1986). Former President George H. W. Bush, for example, was lauded widely because he did not turn the death of Col. William Higgins, one of the hostages held by Islamic extremists in the 1980s in Lebanon, into a crisis as President Reagan did with the death of William Buckley (Power, 1989). Bush displayed measured concern, but did not use language that elevated the significance of the event to a crisis status.

Similarly, organizations and their surrogates should exhibit caution before they describe nagging organizational problems as crises. To label an event or problem as a crisis conveys a sense of urgency; it suggests that the situation is out of control and implies that sacrifice may be needed in the quest for immediate attention and resolution (Vibbert & Bostdorff, 1992). As such, an event labeled a crisis may induce media, public officials, and corporate actors to work together in an effort to resolve the crisis. For example, given the potential public health concern in the Tylenol tampering crisis, the media and the FDA in many ways acted as partners that helped Johnson & Johnson communicate to the public concerning the safety of Tylenol capsules (Benson, 1988). However, had evidence revealed that Johnson & Johnson was responsible for precipitating the events that led to the crisis, a definition of *crisis* would have caused media as well as governmental authorities to question critically how the company had allowed the situation to degenerate into a crisis.

Finally, a social constructionist approach suggests that the language proffered by crisis managers is a critical object for exploration, for definitions are not neutral but strategic: They create reality (Cox, 1981; Zarefsky, 1986). Issue management researchers have long claimed that definitions are arguments (Crable & Vibbert, 1985; Heath, 1997)—witness the contrasting argumentative claims and terminological universes of pro-life vs. pro-choice. In assessing the constructionist approach, Kneupper (1980), consequently, suggested that argument has a close connection with the social construction of reality, for it is through argument that our definitions of reality are challenged and subsequently changed, or reified and left unchanged. Certainly, words have a denotative, meaning that is neutral; but to affix that name to a person, object, or event, makes a strategic claim about the world. Is one who does not spend much money smart, thrifty, cheap, or a miser?

Naming and object or event is a persuasive act largely determined by the attitude of the one who labels.

Not only is the act of naming suasory, but so is that of renaming. Two communicative techniques bear this out. Stevenson (1944) illuminated the use of persuasive definitions that occur when communicators use the positive connotation of a term while they redefine it to increase its precision. The presence of the word *real* often is an indicator of this communicative shift. In this way, an apologist that employs this technique might assert that "the *real* crime here is. . . ."

Sears used persuasive definition in its attempt to manage the crisis. As noted, it used the proto-definition of "preventive maintenance"; in the next sentence, the company sought to define persuasively exactly what that phrase meant. Brennan (1992a) wrote: "This includes recommending replacement of worn parts, when appropriate, before they fail" (p. 8G). Sears reaps the terminological consequences of a "preventative maintenance" program, while using redefinition to limit the actual meaning of the phrase.

A second technique used by crisis managers that warrants consideration is the use of dissociations. Perelman and Olbrechts-Tyteca (1969) noted that dissociations are an argumentative technique whereby communicators seek to break links (i.e., they bifurcate a unitary concept). In such an instance, an individual or an organization argues that current understanding is an opinion, and not reflective of "true reality." In the case of Sears, the company dissociated itself from those abuses that it could not argumentatively redefine. Certainly there were instances in which automotive centers did step over the line, and to argue that they did not would have caused Sears to suffer even more serious credibility loss. Consequently, Sears engaged in an act/essence dissociation in which the company admitted that some wrongs probably had occurred but that they were in no way representative of the essence of how Sears conducts its business. The company admits:

> With over 2 million automotive customers serviced last year in California alone, mistakes may have occurred. However, Sears wants you to know that we would never intentionally violate the trust customers have shown in our company for 105 years. (Brennan, 1992, p. 8G)

In other words, Sears admits that simply on a statistical level, with more than 2 million customers, some abuses were likely—an observation consumers are likely to agree with; yet a few mistakes (the act) should not be seen as representative of a retailer with a successful 105-year record (the essence). Furthermore, to ensure the mistakes do not happen again, Brennan announced at a press conference that Sears had changed its employee compensation policies that had precipitated the crisis (Patterson, 1992).

Although crises are terminological creations, there are limits to the degree of redefinition that is possible. In the case of Sears, for example, the company reached a settlement with the State of California in which Sears continued to deny "intentional wrongdoing" yet was compelled to pay California $3.5 million for the cost of the investigation, and was forced as well to develop a $1.5 million training program for mechanics and distribute 933,000 $50 coupons to customers who might have been wronged (Collingwood, 1992).

SOCIAL CONSTRUCTIONIST IMPLICATIONS FOR FUTURE CRISIS MANAGEMENT RESEARCH

A social constructionist approach therefore carries with it a number of implications as to the study of crisis management. This final section seeks to draw from scholarship in communication and rhetorical theory to propose a research direction rooted in this perspective. We first propose a typology of crises rooted in a generic imperative; and, second, we propose a series of research questions that seek to identify the primary challenges in crisis management research.

Currently, scholars have a variety of typologies from which to choose (Egelhoff & Sen, 1992; Mitroff & Kilmann, 1984; Newsom, Turk, & Kruckeberg, 2000). We do not wish to propose yet another schema; rather, we contend that crisis research in the discipline of communication has traditionally followed three distinct lines, all of which feature a different motive (Burke, 1945/1962).

In drawing from public relations theory, crisis management has historically focused on those kinds of crises in which external forces *act* upon an organization—be it in the form of terrorism (e.g., either political or consumer), catastrophic events (e.g., an earthquake or flood), or some unexpected sociopolitical action (e.g., changes in regulation) [Mitroff & Kilmann, 1984]. This primary axis of inquiry has revolved around those instances in which an organization is largely considered not to be responsible for the harm that has befallen it. Here scholars have sought to identify the communication techniques used by crisis managers to successfully resolve the crises. Notable studies of these kinds of crises have been undertaken by Benoit and Lindsey (1987), Sherrell et al. (1985), and Benson (1988), who studied the tampering of Tylenol packages, as well as noteworthy efforts that include, but are not limited to, Egelhoff and Sen (1992) and Billings et al. (1980).

Apologetic crises, on the other hand, are the result of charges leveled by corporate actors (e.g., media or public interest groups) who contend that an organization is guilty of wrongdoing. This area of study, rooted in rhetorical theory, views the individual or corporate actor (Burke's *agent*) to bear primary responsibility for the crisis that has befallen it. Crises such as these often necessitate the deliverance of an *apologia*—a justificatory form of discourse that may or may not offer an apology (Hearit, 1994; Ware & Linkugel, 1973); such was the focus of this analysis as it related to Sears. This "apologetic" variation on the traditional conceptualization of crises suggests that, contrary to conventional wisdom, the first step of crisis prevention is not external (e.g., determination of what psychopaths may be thinking) but internal (Mitroff & Kilmann, 1984). Notable research in this area has been conducted by Dionisopoulos and Vibbert (1988); Hearit (1994, 1995a; 1995b, 2001), Courtright and Hearit (in press), and Benoit (1995a, 1995b), who articulated the varied message strategies available to corporate apologists.

A third line of research on catalytic crises is drawn from issue management theory. This form of crisis occurs when an organization attempts to strategically create a crisis in an effort to achieve organizational advantage. Here an organization, rather than waiting for potential threats from the external environment to materialize, deliberately creates a crisis itself—a form of affirmative action (Crable & Vibbert, 1985). Vibbert and Bostdorff (1992), for example, analyzed the efforts of the Insurance Information Institute in its efforts to strategically create a lawsuit crisis in order to bring about public policy reforms that represented the interests of the insurance industry. Bostdorff (1991) has extended this idea to foreign policy discourse used by governments.

A social constructionist approach to the study of crisis management is eminently critical. If crises, and those who seek to manage crises, function in a symbolic universe in which they seek to strategically define their actions, then it follows that crisis researchers must above all be critics as well as analysts who seek to unmask or deconstruct the realities proffered by crisis managers. Four areas of crisis management warrant consideration.

First is the role of media: How are crises reported? Smith (1992) noted that most disaster reporting focuses on discrete acts and fails to provide a context for the story. To what degree can this be said of organizational crisis reporting? Similarly and relatedly, to what extent are media officials willing participants in the social construction of crises due to their propensity to couch their news stories in dramatic forms that feature conflict between heroes and villains—a natural script for a crisis scenario (Campbell, 1991; Epstein, 1973)?

As it relates to the nature of crises, are there similar scripts that crisis managers follow? That is, do most companies follow Sears' lead and first deny forcefully, and then later admit that "some mistakes were made?" Also, what is the role of symbolic guilt? Do participants in a crisis drama find themselves in a guilt–victimage cycle that must be played out, as part of a crisis that will not end until symbolic "blood" is shed and repentance is demonstrated (Burke, 1931/1968)? Conversely, what patterns of crisis management do companies that are not accused of wrongdoing follow?

Third, inasmuch as social constructions require a community to construct them, inquiry into the ideological substrata that inhere in this form of crisis management is necessary. To what degree do people treat corporations as persons rather than institutions? Is there a managerial rationality myth that suggests companies can "learn" from crises in order to prevent their further recurrence (Conrad, 1992; Hearit, 1995a)? This area is almost completely unexamined as it relates to the study of crisis management.

Finally, there exist certainly a number of ethical aspects to crisis management that warrant consideration. Marcus and Goodman (1991), for example, noted that when accused with wrongdoing, those companies that deny all wrong find their stock price holds firm; conversely, those that admit responsibility face a devaluation of their company. Bradford and Garrett (1995) reached the opposite conclusion. What, then, is the ethical response for those companies operating in the new millennium who would seek to be socially responsible in their management of corporate crises?

CONCLUSION

Crises are by their very nature communicative and their resolution is fundamentally communicative as well. This chapter has attempted to explain the theoretical underpinnings of a communicative approach to the study of crisis management. In so doing, it has attempted to serve as a corrective to those who take a variable approach to crisis management and instead offers an approach which views communication as constitutive in crises management.

14

Telling the Story
of Organizational Change

Shirley Willihnganz
Joy L. Hart
Greg B. Leichty
University of Louisville

Human beings are storytellers (Fisher, 1984, 1987) and recent work in organizational communication has examined how stories are used to understand, explain, and manage corporate life (Feldman, 1990; Hart, Willihnganz, & Leichty, 1995; Gabriel, 1998; Martin & Powers, 1983; O'Connor, 1997; Peters & Waterman, 1982; Wilkins, 1983). Within this line of work, organizations are "storytelling systems" (Boje, 1991, 1995), where the meaning of organizational life is created and recreated through the telling and retelling of stories. Narratives form the basis of organizational culture—"an open-ended, creative dialogue of subcultures, of insiders and outsiders, of diverse factions ... the interplay and struggle of regional dialects, professional jargons, generic commonplaces, the speech of different age groups, individuals and so forth" (Clifford, 1983, pp. 136–137).

This chapter examines the stories managers in a small manufacturing firm told to help them cope with crisis and change. We address what Heath and Millar (chap. 1, this volume) refer to as an "interrupted narrative" where a "strong" (i.e., shared) culture pervades an organization "and then something goes bump in the dark." In this case, that bump was the owners' retirement and the transition to new management. Our analysis centers in the struggle for control, a common means by which to view crisis (Heath & Millar, chap. 1, this volume), that ensued as these events unfolded. As we tell the saga of this organization, we explore how participants used stories to identify and enact the crisis.

ORGANIZATIONAL STORYTELLING

We begin with the proposition that human beings are primarily symbol users (Burke, 1966). Whatever, their substance, actual events are named, categorized, and understood through language. Within this view, organizational life is understood symbolically (Tompkins, 1987) and organizations can be studied in terms of language use. Language is the organizing locus of human symbolic experience; language therefore creates organizations and illuminates our understanding of them. As Putnam and Fairhurst (2001) pointed out, storytelling is an example of an ethnography of speaking: It is "a specific type of discourse event that is more than talk; it is a way of encompassing the everyday routines of organizational members" (p. 92). According to Eisenberg and Goodall, "the search for meaningful orders of persons and things begins with what those persons say to each other, and the meanings of those things" (1993, p. 117). These symbolic creations lead us to think, act, and behave in certain ways. This dual ability of symbols to name the unseen and then through the naming create possibilities and constraints on future action, is well illustrated by how organizational stories are used. Stories help constitute culture at the same time that they are cultural artifacts.

Although the study of organizational storytelling is a relatively recent phenomenon, organizational stories themselves are not. From folk tales such as Johnny Appleseed, or Paul Bunyon and his Blue Ox, to more modern organizational legends such as Horatio Alger, John Henry, Jim Casey (UPS founder), and Colonel Sanders (Kentucky Fried Chicken), stories have been used to define success, teach values, and express truths about work life. Organizational stories function as meaning-making devices for organizational members (Barnett, 1988; Feldman, 1990; Gabriel, 1991, 1998; Hansen & Kahnweiler, 1993; Rumelhart & Otony, 1977; Smircich, 1983; Turner, 1986) and storytelling technique is used to highlight important aspects of organizational life (Kanter, 1977; Manning, 1977; Roy, 1960; Terkel, 1974).

It is not surprising that organizational stories are considered to be a key cultural artifact. They're useful for organizational members because they are highly accessible—you don't need to be an expert in anything to understand them. Stories are told at all levels of an organization; they are widely distributed instances of organizational communication (Martin & Powers, 1983). They're well remembered, and a strong socializing agent for newcomers (Barnett, 1988; Martin, 1982). According to Rumelhart and Otony (1977), stories are problem-solving schemata; Martin (1982) noted the morality play elements of organizational stories. Organizational participants' judgments of story effectiveness are grounded in the historical and cultural roots of the organization. Stories form a shorthand cultural code, that teaches and enforces organizational norms, values, and beliefs.

Definitions of what constitutes a "story" abound. According to Fisher (1984), stories can be defined as any verbal or nonverbal account that has a sequence of events and to which listeners assign meaning. Gabriel (1991) defined stories as "narratives, at times major, at others trivial, which become charged with symbolic significance" (pp. 857–858). According to Hansen and Kahnweiller (1993) stories differ from gossip and other forms of corporate communication in that they possess a setting, a cast of characters, and a plot that involves some sort of crisis. The role an employee plays in an organizational story is akin to that of an actor in a play—the traits, behaviors and natural drives of characters in an organizational story are colored by the storyteller's process. Stories are retold to reflect the storyteller's interpretation. Mitroff and Killmann (1975) posited that every organization has a central story that is "infused into all levels of policy and decision-making" (p. 19).

Although there is a growing body of research on organizational storytelling, little of it examines how stories are created and called upon by organizational member during times of attempted cultural change. Given that stories serve as powerful agents in the co-creation on meaning (Heath & Millar, chap. 1, this volume), turbulent organizational periods are an especially important time to analyze these rhetorical devices. Some work, such as Smith and Eisenberg's (1987) analysis of attempted change at Disneyland, suggested that organizational stories can dictate how change attempts will be construed. Stories are used as interpretative schemes to drive argument practices enacted during a crisis. The strength of a narrative line influences how effectively change can be accomplished. We now present the setting, main characters and the essential plot of this story of organizational change.

AN ORGANIZATIONAL STORY[1]

Auto Tech began in the mid-1970s as a part-time business serving the needs of individuals restoring vintage cars. The owners—a married couple just out of college and sure that working for themselves would be more rewarding than their brief stints in large corporations had been—loved old cars, and frequently went to car shows to "swap" parts with other enthusiasts. Soon after, they began a "parts" business that was housed in one of their parents' basement. They purchased car parts from dealers and sold them to customers they had met at the car shows by mail order. Business was brisk enough to justify hiring others, and the company grew from two-to-six. This formative group developed informal, personal relationships. During a busy time, everyone might work 16-hour days. During slower periods, lunch would last

---

[1]The name of the company and the names of all participants have been changed.

for two hours and work might be ignored in favor of a pick-up basketball game. The owners' son slept in a corner playpen.

Auto Tech prospered. By 1977 business had grown enough to justify a move to warehouse space and to increase the number of employees to 10. By 1994, the company employed more than 100 people, filled over 20,000 square feet of manufacturing space, and generated $7,000,000 in annual sales. Despite the growth, the corporate philosophy retained much of its irreverent egalitarian character. Auto Tech was "fun"; it was like a "family." The owners played the roles of Mom and Pop. High levels of trust and open communication co-existed with a strong work ethic. There was a shared belief that everyone should work together to get the work done. One of the first stories we heard was how one of the owners cruised the building in roller skates. Once when she was running late, she skated into a meeting with bankers to discuss the possibility an expansion loan.

Our association with Auto Tech began when two of the authors conducted communication-training seminars in the plant. For two years we had extensive contact with many of the employees, supervisors, and managers who took our courses. We became friends with many people and we were invited onto the floor to see what the employees were working on. We were familiar figures in the break room. We learned a great deal during this informal period, as organizational problems were addressed in class and personal concerns were brought up in informal conversation. We also participated in many of the organizational events, such as award presentations and parties that happened to be scheduled during "class time." We subsequently submitted a proposal to the Personnel Manager to conduct a long-term analysis of communication patterns at Auto Tech. By the time we began our 2-year long process of formal data collection, we already felt as though we knew the organization fairly well. Data collection included two rounds of interviews with all managers, all supervisors, and a sampling of workers; observation of work on the factory floor; survey questionnaires including network and social support data; and examination of organizational documents. The interviews took place at the beginning and end of the data collection period. In this chapter, we report the results of our interviews with the two owners and the 10 managers who were on the scene at Auto Tech during that two-year period. All interviews followed a protocol of questions asking for descriptions of the culture, relationships, decision-making, change, and support. The interviews were tape-recorded and transcribed; each lasted one-to-two hours. Interview data reported here are supplemented with data from our observations and from organizational documents.

Shortly before we began collecting data, the owners decided to retire and move out-of-state. They wanted the company to continue to grow, but they felt they needed outside expertise to supplement Auto Tech's "home-grown managers." Hence, they hired a professional financial manager to head their existing management team. The resulting transition became a crisis. A company that had little management turnover for ten years, experienced a turnover rate of 50% of the management staff in the next two years. Sales dropped such that there was no corporate profit for two years; some workers in the self-described "happy family" considered starting a union; there was a general sense that something terrible had happened.

Cast of Characters

Nickie and Bill. Owners and founders Nickie and Bill were described as "people people." They were seen as laid-back, and simultaneously serious and fun loving. Stories that were told about them highlighted their generosity (e.g., they once loaned money to a worker so he could post jail bond and they routinely gave people salary advances for car repairs or medical bills); openness (people from all levels of the organization told stories about how they could tell Bill and Nickie anything from job concerns to personal problems); and commitment to others (no layoffs had ever happened at Auto Tech—in Bill's words, "I want these to be good jobs for people"). Nickie was seen as fun loving and caring—the nurturer of the two. Bill was described as fair and involved—the benevolent authority who acted for the good of his people and company. Both were well liked, casual, and were able to make important decisions on the spot. One Halloween as we were beginning data collection, Nickie came to work dressed as Annie Oakley, and spent the day shooting her cap gun in mock gunfights throughout the organization. (Everyone came to work in costume on Halloween).

During the first year of our data collection, Bill and Nickie were physically absent, but workers continued to talk about them as though they were still there. Bill eventually returned as hands-on CEO, and he and Nickie divorced. Because her parents owned part of the company, Nickie continued to own more than half of the company. Hence, even though she had been absent from the plant for nearly two years, Nickie still received phone calls from employees, especially women, who just "needed to talk to her."

James. When Nickie and Bill retired from the day-to-day running of Auto Tech, James was hired as CEO. He was an accountant and he was given responsibility for bringing much needed financial savvy and formal management training to the company. Although James was pleasant, polite and professional, he had little of Bill's "charisma or personality." James was variously described as "stoic," "uptight," "having no sense of humor," "too numbers oriented," "paranoid," and "unable to make quick decisions." James required voluminous data to support recommendations, instituted regular meetings, insisted on formal procedures and protocols, and tried to get people in the front office to adopt a dress code. James was never fully "socialized" as to the unique culture of the business. Nickie acknowledged to us that she and Bill had not taken time to effectively immerse James in the company's culture before they left. Ultimately, James was unsuccessful in his attempt to "rationalize" company operations. By most accounts, he got mired in data, and was slow to make decisions. Bill fired him after one year, but not before James had dismissed several key organizational participants and instituted enough changes to cause great organizational unrest.

Diana and Christie.   Two human resource managers played key roles in our organizational stories. Diana was our original liaison with the organization. Co-workers described her as outgoing, helpful, and well liked. By the time we began our study, however, James had dismissed her for what he termed "inadequate performance of her professional duties." Diana's dismissal caused great turmoil among the workers. After Bill and Nickie left the organization, employees had increasingly turned to her for help and reassurance during the traumatic transition. Her dismissal led some workers to invite union organizers to a meeting at an employee's house. Another long-term employee contacted Bill and Nickie to tell them about the meeting, and the two quickly returned to the plant to show face and allay fears. They stopped the movement to unionize, but James never recovered employee loyalty or respect.

Christie was hired to replace Diana. Christie had extensive personnel experience in two large corporations, and she was hired to "professionalize" the personnel function. Christie considered herself to be a consummate professional, but she liked the informal atmosphere at Auto Tech. By our second round of interviews, she had won the respect of both employees and management.

David.   David had been with the company almost from its inception. He was described to us as a "genius" in research and development. Because he knew the organization and the industry, he was in charge of product development. Coworkers described him as opinionated and powerful. A self-described renegade with waist length hair and cowboy boots, David portrayed his work as play and liked a hands-on approach to problem solving. His title was Chief Operating Officer, but this seemed to be a courtesy—none of our interviewees agreed on where to place him on the organizational chart. He emerged as James' primary antagonist. He felt invulnerable because of his long organizational tenure and his personal ties to Bill. In David's words, "I'm not a numbers man." James fired David three months into our data collection, an act that caused great resentment among employees. James', himself, was fired shortly after David left.

Ian. Ian was head of sales. Like David, he had been with Auto Tech for many years, and had started with them while still in college. In his first interview with us, Ian described Bill as his mentor, and referred to David as his friend. Ian was not as nonconforming or outspoken as David; he cooperated with James on some things while quietly ignoring him on others. When Bill returned as CEO after James was fired, and after Tom resigned, Ian's fortune rose. New managers resented Ian's chummy relationship with Bill and referred to him as the "heir apparent," if Bill retired again. Old managers felt comfortable with Ian, but the newer managers perceived that he did very little work and that he got away with it because he was Bill's "fair-haired boy."

Tom. James hired Tom, the plant manager. Tom had nearly 25 years of supervisory experience, and seemed to understand the "good ol' boy" character of the company. Although he encountered some hostility from people early in his tenure over turf issues, he eventually won over most subordinates and managers. David, who by the end didn't much like anyone, referred to Tom as a "real likable guy." Tom had the outlook of a professional manager, but he was also an astute observer and could adapt to the local parlance. After James was fired, Tom became CEO, and by all accounts was doing a fine job. However, 6 months later, Tom sent a fax to the owners informing them of his resignation due to "personal reasons." Several employees informed us that they thought the personal reason was a widely rumored "affair" with another senior staff member. Both were married. Following Tom's resignation, Bill returned as CEO.

Liza. Liza was hired to be the Marketing Manager, a function that Nickie had handled previously. Liza told us that she was attracted to Auto Tech by its growth potential, opportunity to become an owner, and because she was interested in helping the company develop a more professional appearance. She quickly developed key friendships with several of the managers, especially Christie, Roger and Larry.

Roger. Roger was hired as plant manager after James left and Tom was promoted to CEO. He kept the position after Tom resigned and Bill returned. Roger had management experience, but knew little about cars or the specific production processes at Auto Tech. Affable and a bit insecure, he was likable but was not respected. He was reluctant to admit his ignorance regarding the company's products and procedures and to let the workers teach him things he did not know. He was perceived to make many mistakes because he tried to hide his ignorance. He saw Ian as a threat, and was uncomfortable with Bill. He told us that he felt that he might be fired at any time.

Larry. After James left, Larry was hired to take over as the corporate accountant. Larry was uncomfortable with Bill, and he resented the "managing by wandering around" exercises that Bill required. For example, Larry felt that he was being punished when Bill asked him to help the people in shipping wrap car doors. Bill explained that he wanted to teach new managers how important it was to be "one of the people." Larry was critical of Bill's management style, arguing that "we're like a rocket no one is guiding." Larry left Auto Tech shortly after our last set of interviews.

John. John handled inventory and shipping. He, like Ian, had been with the company for years, and was the oldest of the mangers. John was comfortable with Bill, and handled many of the other management changes by, in his words, "developing a bunker mentality." This meant he'd take care of his job, and stay away from everyone else to avoid as many fights as he could. In our interviews, he was the most guarded and reticent of the managers.

Plot

One Big Happy Family. An analysis of the stories of organizational transition begins with what Auto Tech was before the transition. Auto Tech had an organizational culture that was overwhelmingly egalitarian in its self-understanding (Leichty & Warner, 2001; Quinn & McGrath, 1985). The relations among coworkers had much of the spontaneity and immediacy of communitas as described by Turner (1966). Communitas involves a "relationship between concrete, historical, idiosyncratic individuals. These individuals are not segmentalized into roles and statuses but confront one another ... direct, immediate and total confrontation of human identities" (pp. 131–132). Although Turner (1966) regarded communitas as a transitional state that is present in some degree in the social dramas of all societies, egalitarian culture attempts, as best it can, to "institutionalize" some of the features of communitas.

In the case of Auto Tech, internal distinctions of status by function, seniority and rank were muted. No job within the company was regarded as too beneath one's dignity. When product needed to be shipped quickly, Bill was the first to lend his physical labor to getting the product out the door. Employees who had emergency financial needs had little hesitation about directly requesting temporary loans from Bill and Nickie. The company fit within the quadrant of what Mary Douglas (1982) called high group: High values are placed on group membership, group cohesion, high morale and supportive relationships. Indeed, this case study is interesting in part because Auto Tech was a rather unique organization. As

TABLE 14.1
Cast of Characters

Character	Organizational Role	Organizational Tenure	Cultural Allegiance
Bill	Cofounder, Owner and CEO in stage 3	Stages 1–4*	Egalitarian
Nickie	Cofounder and Retired Owner	Stages 1 & 2	Egalitarian
James	Chief Executive Officer	Stage 2	Hierarchical
David	Chief Operating Officer	Stage 1 and part of Stage 2	Egalitarian
Tom	Plant Manager and CEO after James was fired	Stages 2 & 3	Hierarchical
Diana	First Personnel Director	Stage 1 and part of Stage 2	Egalitarian
Christie	Second Personnel Director	Stages 2–4	Hierarchical
Ian	Sales Manager	Stages 1–4	Egalitarian
Liza	Marketing Director	Stages 3 & 4	Hierarchical
Roger	Plant Manager after Tom was promoted to CEO	Stages 3 & 4	Hierarchical
Larry	Comptroller	Stages 3 & 4	Hierarchical
John	Inventory and Shipping	Stages 1–4	Unknown

Stage 1: From initial contact in 1990–1991. Bill and Nickie ran the company.
Stage 2: James served as CEO, Bill and Nickie "retired" (time elapsed approximately 1 year).
Stage 3: Tom served as CEO (time elapsed = 6 months).
Stage 4: Bill returned from retirement to run the company (through end of study, May 1994).

Coyle (1997) noted, egalitarian cultures are distinctly underrepresented in organizational theory.

Within Auto Tech, this egalitarian corporate-understanding was communicated by the metaphor that "Auto Tech is a like a family." Not only was the company a family business, but many employees had other members of their extended family who also worked at Auto Tech. While there are other possible forms of family culture (e.g., hierarchical, laissez faire, despotic; e.g., Coyle, 1997), in its use by employees of Auto Tech, "family" clearly had egalitarian connotations. When Bill was asked what it meant to say his company was like a family, he said, "when you talk to people you listen to them. . . . You've got to be there among them, you have got to feel like you are one of them, and they are one of you. And understand that the only way you are going to survive is if there aren't lines between manager and labor."

The organizational transition initiated a "perturbation" in this cultural system and its narrative practices. The organizational transition brought about dramatic changes that disrupted or "interrupted the organizational narrative" and an organizational crisis soon ensued. The following account details how the change attempts were construed and how the competing stories themselves affected the trajectory of the crisis. Events were interpreted and reinterpreted to fit with one's preferred organizational story.

The Crisis Stage: The Interrupted Organizational Narrative. In this particular case study, Auto Tech's crisis was not one caused by external events, but was a type of second order change (Watzlawick, Weakland, & Finsch, 1974), experienced as a crisis of legitimacy. The predominant family metaphor was challenged by the decision to hire people with a distinctly different organizational philosophy—the organization as hierarchical system (Coyle, 1997). As Heath and Millar (this volume) noted in their opening chapter, crisis can disrupt normal business activity. Here, the interruption was of the organization's identity or self-definition, as described by organizational members. The crisis called into question employees' understandings of who they were and how they were to relate to each other. As the new managers attempted to structure the organization more formally, the existing narrative lost its coherence or was relegated to a "past but not current reality." Many employees reacted by asserting the moral superiority of the old narrative. They resisted change in both overt and covert ways.

Bartunick (1988) called this process reframing, and argued that reframing begins as a crisis that indicates that present shared understandings are no longer adequate. She noted that the experience of crisis must be strong enough to unfreeze dominant organizational members' present understandings by presenting a major challenge to their validity. Although there was no external crisis, Bill's decision to leave the organization in the hands of someone so radically different was enough to accomplish this unfreezing. Bartunik (1988) further argued that this unfreezing process paralyzes and disorients organizational members who experience it as a series of "deaths and rebirths." Heath and Millar (chap. 1, this volume) observed that organizational stakeholders often respond to crisis with strong emotion, as they fear damage to their interests. Thus, not surprisingly, shock, defensiveness, anger, ambiguity, and confusion are common organizational responses.

Auto Tech's managers' stories detailed ways the family members could count on each other, ways that the family was special, and why their family was best. Many family-like values were stated: informality, closeness, everyone pitching in to get the job done, knowing each other as individuals, working together for a common good. These values lead to expectations. Managers were expected to be accessible and wiser than the average worker. Communication was to be informal. Employees assumed they had a right to understanding and help, with personal as well as with work problems. Hierarchic and status differences were to be muted; workers and managers should work together; in addition, there was to be permanence to the family. People shouldn't be forced to leave the family. If trouble arose, a person should be reassigned until the individual found the "right place." A person should be fired or asked to resign only after prolonged provocation. No one was to be laid off. People knew what to expect from each other. Most of all, people at Auto Tech should have fun when they come together.

During one of our early interviews, David characterized the company this way: "We're a plant that has high employee morale. It's a plant where employees like to come to work and they like to see their friends get hired on here. It's a place I love to be in. I love my job. I guess you're supposed to work at work, but I always thought that coming to work was more like play. People say why don't you do that at home. I say I play at it all day, why would I do that at home?"

Auto Tech's rather homogeneous egalitarian "family culture," certainly a strong culture by any measure (e.g., Deal & Kennedy, 1982), developed around a narrative that portrayed the company as very distinctive and unique. Nickie and Bill were icons of people who got into business because they loved what they were doing. The history included stories about how a love of old cars brought the initial employees of the company together. A small group of committed people had worked together in basements and garages. According to the founding myths, the company experienced phenomenal growth, but the work environment retained its qualities of fun, adventure, and spontaneity: the spirit of communitas.

Although this account may sound alluring, this strong organizational narrative also created difficulties. Strong cultures enable organizational coherence and can motivate sacrifice on behalf of the organization, but strong cultures also tend to be quite inflexible. In the face of cultural stability, all the forces coalesce to move the organization forward—none are available to restrain it or move it in a different direction. Lacking a system of checks and balances, there are no countervailing influences for change or growth. The inertia created by having a "pure" culture, or one set of rationality rules for accepting arguments, inhibits an organization's adaptability. Pure cultures contain the seeds of their own destruction (Quinn & McGrath, 1988; Thompson, Ellis, & Wildavsky, 1990). The egalitarian or consensual culture, for example, if taken to its extreme, becomes an irresponsible country club, characterized by extreme permissiveness, uncontrolled individualism and inappropriate participation.

Bill and Nickie recognized this and attempted to initiate changes that would check the excesses of the organization's egalitarian culture. Hiring James as the CEO was intended to introduce some crucial elements of order, stability and discipline into the cultural mix. Hierarchical cultures value goals, competence, and contractual agreements (Coyle, 1997; Quinn & McGrath, 1988). Tangible output and achievement measure effectiveness. Rational cultures have a high need for control, centralization, and integration.

Our first round of interviews revealed that James had quickly become an icon of the "bureaucratic manager." Long-term employees repeatedly referred to James as "the numbers guy": a person with a low personality quotient who was obsessed with costs, projections and paperwork. Bill wanted James to "prune" the company culture, but he still wanted the company to retain its distinctive egalitarian cultural features. Instead, employees came to see James as the personification of mindless mechanical rationality who was determined to "kill the family." Thus began the clash of the competing narratives: stories about a spoiled and dysfunctional family told by professional managers and of stories of a dying or dead family in stories told by long-term employees. The organizational story became the focal point of the crisis.

Organizational stories not only tell how events come to be identified as a crisis, but they also guide how the crisis will be enacted. They are used to judge the merits of the actions of others, and stories define a context for action that employees use to orient their behaviors (Wilkins, 1983). Stories act as a means of control by maintaining the status quo (Feldman, 1990), and because stories have "morals" they support the actions of one political subgroup or another (Martin, 1982). Because stories can be used to justify actions or feelings, they can be called upon to attack or protect selected people or groups (Morrill, 1995). As meanings are created through the telling and retelling of stories, the analysis of stories gives us a sense of the multiple voices raised in organizational discourse, and allows us to use this discourse to "map" the organization's competing frames. As Wilkins (1984) noted, stories are comprised of details about the organization's current status and serve as a major resource for sense-making practices.

During the crisis stage at Auto Tech, the stories that were told continued to invoke the family metaphor—with a crucial difference. The family saga had taken a tragic turn. Lamentations by the "old-timers" included stories of "how it used to be" compared to how things were now. They told us how people weren't close the way they used to be, and that things weren't the same since Bill had left. James didn't understand. It wasn't fun anymore . . . too many memos and procedures and rules. Managers didn't care. The consistent narrative theme was that the "family was dying" and Auto Tech was becoming just another bureaucratic company.

Old timers' stories were full of the pain of loss—a longing for the days when Mom and Dad were still around. Indeed, this longing had a tangible form: Many managers and workers continued to call Bill and Nickie to handle organizational problems that James was "messing up," very much like children left with a sitter who want to call and get the answer from the "real" Mom or Dad. The "old" managers refused to follow directions, or "do what they're told," because from their perspective, James didn't know "how we do things around here." The old-timers consistently highlighted the difficulty they had working with newcomers who "think they know everything, when they haven't been here long enough to know what they're talking about."

In contrast, when looking at the business practices of the old company, the professional managers tended to see instances of permissiveness, excessive individualism, loose procedures, and high spiritedness that needed to be productively channeled. Tom saw considerable potential, but also saw the need for "order, discipline, and long-term planning." He noted that, "Auto Tech does not have rigid productivity controls, at least not at this time. So whether you are productive or not is a little bit subjective. You can be a very mediocre performer in terms of speed and still have a long-term relationship with Auto Tech."

Likewise, Christie noted that the previous personnel systems had been very informal, "but I don't know if that's the direction James wants to go. I think he wants to get more formal . . . The employees . . . have a very informal chain of command. This one individual needed a loan for what I thought was, well, he had some jail problems and he needed a loan and he approached Nickie. I said I can't believe how comfortable that employee feels with the owner of the place, because I just haven't been exposed to that."

The new managers believed that they had been hired to bring order and rationality to the organization, and from their viewpoint, this was to be accomplished by setting up formal structures and protocols, and standard operating procedures. But, in the eyes of the long-time managers, this view was incomprehensible. They saw the new formality and protocols as squeezing the life out of the organization like a python suffocating its prey. They contended that the new procedures were undermining organizational teamwork, complicating communication, wasting time, and reducing the company's response time to the market. James' "rational" controls were seen as counterproductive, irrational and oppressive.

The changes privileged argument by the numbers—something that old-timers found disquieting. Ian characterized his typical exchange with James this way:

> If you ask about anything, before that conversation is over with, your next job will be to get him something on paper so he can see the numbers in every case. I had to go and buy a new trailer, a company trailer. Sure enough, "I need it on paper." So I put it all on paper. . . There is a hell of a learning curve from flying cropbusters to flying 747s.

Ian went on to talk about communicating by memo:

> It used to be that you walked through the hallways and that's where decisions were made. Now, it's either a meeting or a memo. An analogy I like is going out hunting. We were so seat of the pants, we'd shoot anything that moved. We even shot a couple of hunters. Now I think we're going in the opposite direction to where we're not doing any hunting, and we're not shooting any deer either. We're kind of just sitting around and they finally leave.

As these examples illustrate, stories explicate the competing argument fields present during a crisis. They also identify interactants' positions toward the conflict. Arguments were not generated specifically around positions, but around the people who represent the positions. So, for the old-timers, Larry is cast as villain: cold, unfeeling, and impersonal. According to Nickie, "James is always harping on numbers." The old-timers contrast him with the heroes, Bill and Nickie. "Bill and Nickie are the type that go out in the plant and they're just laid back, happy-go-lucky. In describing James, David said, "Tell me what's going on? How's your family?' James isn't like that. From what I've seen, if he does smile, it's a forced smile. . . . James is the kind of guy you could probably work with for ten years, and never know how many kids he has, how many times he's been married. You wouldn't know if he played tennis or golf or what he likes."

These stories illustrate how the "old" organizational story was challenged by events. For "old-timers" the organizational story no longer seemed to fit. Hence, the organizational family existed only in the past tense. Ironically, the new managers thought the "family" was very much alive. It was throwing a temper tantrum and it needed to be taught a lesson. The first lesson came when Diana the popular personnel director was fired. Some of the workers made noises about unionizing. Bill and Nickie appeared to calm the waters and to support James. About three months later, about two months into our first round of interviews, David was fired. For some long-term employees, this watershed event signified the "Death of the Family."

The first phase of the experiment in cultural grafting failed. Firing David did not cure the problems that James perceived in the organization. Within two months, Bill asked James to resign. Tom was promoted from plant manager to CEO. His tenure began on a more promising note. He gained widespread cooperation from organizational personnel. After all, he was **not** James. He was perceived to be more personable and more patient. Moreover, Tom really knew all about production and how to solve "practical" problems. He had expertise in things that most employees thought were important and really cared about. Tom hired a series of new managers: a replacement for himself as plant manager, a marketing director, and a new company controller. The intensity of the conflicting narratives died down, and it appeared that it might be possible to create a new integrative narrative. However, within six months Tom resigned for "personal reasons." Complications arising from an affair with a senior staff person led to his sudden and unexpected resignation.

Aftermath. Bill decided to throw in the towel on trying to bring in someone from the outside to run the company. He returned to rescue his company and reclaimed the role of CEO. For the "old-timers" who were still left, "Dad" had returned. In short, egalitarian culture had triumphed and the company of the "present" was grafted back onto the narrative of its beginnings. However, things were not the same as they had been before, the cultural struggle continued in less overt forms.

The new managers who had been hired under Tom's tenure felt isolated and oppressed by the restoration of the old order. The new managers told stories about how they were made to feel like children. They argued that their consistently professional expertise was vastly undervalued, and Bill just didn't understand the importance of what they were doing. The new finance manager said, "you have to check with Bill about every decision; he's too emotionally involved in everything. This place treats you like a child." Bill observed that it might take some time, but the newcomers would "have to be brought along" in the Auto Tech Way.

In their stories, new managers defined themselves as family "in-laws" or "step-children," who were not as valued as the "real" children of the organization. The charges of favoritism echoed those of jealous siblings. The four "new kids," Christie, Liza, Roger and Larry all identified Ian as the favored son, and complained that he did not work hard but got all the rewards. Ian was universally seen as the heir apparent. Although he was only in his early 30s, he was one of the few remaining old-timers left among the managers.

Several elements of these stories illustrate how the central metaphor guided enactment processes. First, even the stories told by newcomers revolved around the family theme. The changed organization still clung to the definition of "family"—now a changed family, a family rent with grief and loss, a family struggling to blend the old and new, but a family nonetheless. As the crisis was enacted, not only did the family metaphor guide interpretation, but also the stories we collected exhibited the tension between the "new" way of thinking and the "old." The stories clearly demarcated the competing cultural frames.

Coombs (1999) pointed out that one's interpretation of a crisis guides how one attributes responsibility and assigns blame. One of the most striking elements of our stories was how personal they were. This is what one might expect to find in an egalitarian "family culture" (Ellis, 1998). Arguments were not generated specifically around positions, but around the people who represented the positions. When certain individuals came to personify the problem in narratives, getting rid of those individuals came to be perceived as the solution to the organizational crisis.

The stories also expressed the depth of emotion that living in a crisis creates. Shortly after Bill returned as full-time CEO, the four surviving new mangers formed their own support group. Larry, Christie, Roger, and Liza frequently talked to each other about how bad things were, and devised elaborate games to boost each other's morale. For example, they had 10 positive thinking sayings that they had memorized by number. So, during an especially bad moment, one would flash the other two fingers, or three, to remind the other of a positive thought. John hunkered down and attempted to stay away from everyone during the worst of times. Liza bitterly talked about how Auto Tech was not at all what she was hoping for. Bill returned to a company that was quite different from the one he had left. He talked about the ongoing problems he was having in socializing the management people that he had "inherited."

BEST PRACTICES IN MANAGING ORGANIZATIONAL IDENTITY CRISES

As Feldman (1990) noted, "change and nonchange are always bound up in the change process" (p. 826). Van de Ven and Poole (1988) argued that any theory of change must be able to explain how things remain stable in the light of change. The analysis of organizational stories helps to explain how this change/nonchange process works. The central story changed in ways that incorporated new elements, but it also retained core elements of the original. We submit that, at least in this case, the organizational story itself was central to the process.

Comparisons of the stories of differing organizational groups can reveal the organizational or group definitions of problems and highlight their perceived root causes. In this case, considerable tensions existed across these competing stories, in terms of who the heroes were, where blame should be placed, and what the obvious and acceptable solutions were. Because language defines problems and focuses attention, it also shapes, even constrains, the solutions generated. Stories not only explain the past and the future, they predict likely organizational outcomes.

Based on the tensions exhibited in these narrative accounts, we predicted that one of two events would have to occur in the acute organizational crisis stage: (a) that James, the new CEO, would not succeed in adapting the predominant organizational culture to his preferred blueprint and would either leave on his own or would be asked to leave by one of the owners, or (b) if James stayed for a long period his chief opponents would experience more organizational problems and some of them would leave either voluntarily or involuntarily. We saw James' leaving as the more likely event. Although this did, in fact, occur, we did not anticipate the magnitude of some of the other personnel changes (e.g., David's termination). Once these events did take place, we predicted a merging of the "story values" to help reintegrate organizational understanding and functioning. For example, we expected to continue to hear stories about the "good old days," but with less expectation that all of the elements of these should be current realities.

In our second round of interviews, which occurred after the restoration, we expected to find stories with themes of a blended family. Instead, among the new managers, we found stories about "negligent parents" and "ill-treated step-children." However, there were some glimmerings of stories that contained the kernels of a "blended organizational narrative." For example, there was increased recognition of turning points in the organization's life and there was more awareness that conflict and tension can be useful in helping an organization mature and gain strength. More frequently, narrative description left hearers with the impression that while everything was not perfect, organizational members trusted that in time the "family would heal."

This case study demonstrates the degree to which narrative is not merely something that an organization has, it is something that an organization is. The predominant organizational narrative embodies the organization to its members, especially its employees. If organizations are storytelling systems as Boje (1995) asserted, then an "interrupted narrative" is the essence of an organizational crisis. In this case study, the qualities of equality, spontaneity and immediacy were dramatized and celebrated in the organizational stories that we obtained from the long-term employees. These employees declared that Auto Tech's egalitarian or familial characteristics made Auto Tech a unique and distinctive workplace: a place that they were proud to work for. Indeed, they were willing to sacrifice individual status and prerogatives for the good of the collective. At the same time, the owners of Auto Tech had come to a clear understanding that Auto Tech's egalitarian culture was also stunting the future growth potential of the company.

The continual "seat of the pants" decision making created too much waste. The company lacked the regularized sorts of procedures that would enable it to compete for larger more long-term contracts. In addition, spontaneity and immediacy were often used to soften or avoid individual accountability. Bill and Nickie recognized that some elements of a more hierarchical organizational culture were needed to temper the excesses and instill some discipline in the prevailing egalitarian culture (Leichty & Warner, 2001). They did not want to overthrow the "egalitarian ethos" of their company's culture and replace it with a hierarchical model. Instead, they wanted to introduce a bit of diversity and self-understanding into the company's operating narrative.

The owners recognized that their own style of "charismatic leadership," that is so favored in egalitarian settings (Ellis, 1998), stood in the way of the company's further development. They also correctly anticipated that it would be difficult to institute needed changes in the organization's culture as long as they remained in positions in the company. Hence, they decided to retire and to give a "professional manager" free rein to run the company without their interference. In our analysis, the owners had both good intentions and good intuitions. However, neither good intentions nor good intuitions prevented the development of a crisis or "an event that exceeds normal planning and truly is of the magnitude that the organization's legitimacy is on the line" (Heath, 2001, p. 442).

So why did things go seriously awry? Why did the attempted transition result in a profound organizational identity crisis? The answer seems to be that the owners underestimated the narrative strength of Auto Tech's egalitarian culture. The changes brought about by their abrupt retirements ignited a profound cultural conflict that escalated into a full blown cultural identity crisis. Instead of a controlled reaction, the company experienced a cultural meltdown. In the ensuing struggle, the organizational narrative fractured into competing stories that reinterpreted the past in terms of the present. Instead of moving toward some kind of convergence where a new integrative narrative could be created, the organizational stories became more polarized and rigid. The existing organizational narrative, using the same family metaphor, split into two increasingly polarized, brittle and antagonistic genres. The defenders of the egalitarian culture still recounted the founding cultural myths to us; but pointedly declared that they no longer applied: the company "was no longer a family." In contrast, the management team acknowledged the strength of the "family metaphor," then characterized it as an undisciplined and dysfunctional family. The hardening of narratives was followed by a narrative escalation of atrocity stories by both sides of the conflict.

As a whole, this case suggests some of the following best practices in managing organizational identity, some of which are simply things to avoid.

1. Fostering a "strong" organizational culture in the sense that it is internally consistent, pure or unadulterated usually creates unintended pathologies, especially as it relates to the resilience and long-term viability of the organization. Managers should avoid the seductive temptations of trying to create hegemonic organizational metanarratives.

2. Resilient organizational cultures will admit enough multicultural elements to maintain requisite variety in organizational narratives (Banks, 2000), but will retain sufficient coherence to provide a coherent organizational identity. Some cultural pluralism or variability is advantageous because it provides resources for managing future organizational change.

3. Resilient organizational cultures will generate narratives that acknowledge that the future of an organization is always open. Organizational identity is never finished, permanent, or without ambiguity (i.e., undeveloped potential).

4. Organizations cannot shed their organizational narratives and identities like a snake sheds its skin. An organization can show many different sides to different audiences in the same way that the situated individual does (e.g., Goffman, 1959). However, a differentiated performance repertoire is

only made possible by a coherent sense of individual and/or collective identity. Radical transitions in organizational narrative can create severe organizational identity crises.

5. Necessary updates and changes in organizational narrative should, when possible, be framed within an ongoing narrative of continuity. If a trajectory of changes cannot be framed within an ongoing narrative of change, a crisis in organizational identity becomes likely. It is much more productive to try to update the organizational story, than it is to create a new one from scratch.

6. Planning for organizational transitions will include an analysis of organizational culture and consideration of points 1–5 above.

7. Managing transitions in organizational narrative will also incorporate the recommended steps of crisis recognition, crisis containment and recovery, and postcrisis evaluation and building an institutional memory (Coombs, 1999). Despite the best preparation, some aspects of narrative transitions are not possible to anticipate in advance.

Managing Organizational Images: Crisis Response and Legitimacy Restoration

Joseph Eric Massey
California State University, Fullerton

Although much work on crisis communication focuses on the practical aspects of the management of organizational crisis, little has provided any theoretical contribution to the study of crisis communication (Seeger, Sellnow, & Ulmer, 1998). The purpose of this chapter is partly to fill that void. Two particular theoretical perspectives—organizational image management theory and institutional theory—provide the conceptual framework. These theories are synthesized into a perspective that views crisis management as the management of organizational legitimacy, where legitimacy is defined as the stakeholder perception that an organization is good and has a right to continue operations. Legitimacy is necessary for organizational survival, because stakeholder support for organizational activity is a requirement for organizational success, as many recent organizational crises demonstrate.

The chapter first presents organizational image management and institutional theory, followed by a literature review of organizational legitimacy. We then move to a discussion of organizational crisis as a crisis of legitimacy. To illustrate the relationship between organizational legitimacy and crisis, the case of the NASA Space Shuttle *Challenger* is presented. The chapter concludes with a discussion of the implications of the theoretical model for researchers, students, and practitioners of organizational crisis management.

ORGANIZATIONAL IMAGE MANAGEMENT THEORY

Organizations must sustain an effective image with their stakeholders in order to maximize their chances for success (Garbett, 1988). Although failure is not inevitable when an organization's image is tarnished, it is more likely, as many studies have demonstrated (Baum & Oliver, 1992; Brinson & Benoit, 1999; Dacin, 1997; Englehardt, Sallot, & Springston, 2001; Hearit, 1995; Ice, 1991; Massey, 2001; Ruef & Scott, 1998; cf. Seeger, Sellnow, & Ulmer, 1998).

Organizational image management is a dialogic process in which organizations and stakeholders communicate with one another to co-create the image of the organization. An organization's image is the "shared meanings, attitudes, knowledge, and opinions" of organizational stakeholders, influenced, at least in part, by strategic communications emanating from the organization (Moffitt, 1994, p. 166). Moffitt's work provides support for the argument that image management is a dialogic process—indeed, she argues that sometimes organizations have little influence over the images held by organizational stakeholders. Ginzel, Kramer, and Sutton (1993) further clarify the dialogic process of organizational image management:

> Thus, an organization's image represents a collaborative social construction between organization's top management and the multiple actors who comprise the organizational audiences. A particular interpretation of an organization's image may be proposed by top management, but that interpretation must in turn be endorsed, or at the very least not rejected, by their various audiences if it is to persist. (p. 248)

A Model of Organizational Image Management

Organizational image management is a three-stage process that involves creating, maintaining, and, in some cases, regaining an effective organizational image. First, when an organization begins or is unknown, it must *create* an image of itself with its various stakeholders. According to Garbett (1988) this is difficult because most people are skeptical of the unknown.

Second, if an organization is able to successfully create an image, it must work to *maintain* that image. Image maintenance is an on-going process that requires communication with organizational stakeholders. To successfully maintain an effective image, organizations must seek feedback from stakeholders and adjust their communication strategy accordingly. Again, the process is dialogic: While organizations are strategically communicating with stakeholders to influence perceptions, stakeholders are forming their own ideas about the image of the organization. If an organization fails to monitor and adjust to the feedback provided by stakeholders, successful organizational image management is threatened.

The third stage of the process is *restoration*, and usually occurs because the organization has experienced some sort of a crisis. Not all organizations experience the third stage of the model, but because of the increase in the number (Perrow, 1984; Seeger et al., 1998) and magnitude of crises (Mitroff, Pauchant, & Shrivastava, 1989), many organizations will move to this stage of the model. If an organization moves to this third stage, then it must engage in strategic communication to restore a successful image. If successful, the organization will return to the maintenance stage of image management, but if unsuccessful, the organization could fail or be forced to restructure itself. At a minimum, organizational restructuring involves the development of a new identity, and in extreme cases can result in merger, name change, and other end results that require movement back to the image creation stage of the process. Organizational image management is therefore a cyclical, rather than a linear process, as Fig. 15.1 illustrates.

Organizational image management is a rhetorical process requiring communication strategies designed to establish and maintain a particular corporate image (Coleman, 1990). In a related line of work, organizational communication scholars, particularly George Cheney (Cheney, 1991; Cheney & Christensen, 2001; Cheney & Vibbert, 1987), have examined what they refer to as issue management. According to Cheney and Christensen, issue management "means that the organization attempts to both 'read' the premises and attitudes of its audience *and* work to shape them, often *in advance* of any specific crisis or well-defined debate" (p. 238, emphasis in original). Cheney and Christensen (2001) highlight the rhetorical nature of organizational communication, and also the relationship organizations share with their stakeholders. They stated that:

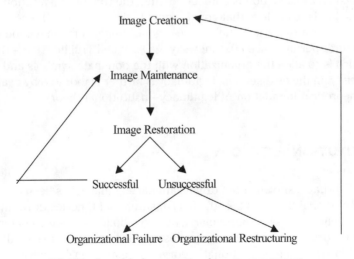

FIG. 15.1. A model of organizational image management.

As many organizations have come to realize, the principal management problem in today's marketplace of goods and ideas is not so much to provide com-
modities and services or to take stands on the salient issues of the day, but to
do these things with a certain distinctiveness that allows the organization to
create and legitimate itself, its particular "profile," and its advantageous position. (p. 241)

Cheney and Christensen's (2001) argument suggests there are at least
two reasons organizations engage in issue, or what I refer to as image management. The first reason is that organizations must attempt to differentiate
themselves from the rest of the pack. The second reason organizations
must engage in image management is to maintain the stakeholder perception that the organization is legitimate. Legitimacy can be defined as "the
degree of cultural support for an organization" (Meyer & Scott, 1983, p. 201).
To achieve legitimacy organizations must develop congruence between
their own actions and the values of the social system in which they operate
(Dowling & Pfeffer, 1975).

Another way of thinking about legitimacy is offered by Bedeian (1989),
who defined legitimacy as a summary or global belief among stakeholders
that an organization is good or has a right to continue operations. Meyer
and Scott (1983) put forth a continuum of organizational legitimacy, ranging
from completely legitimate to completely illegitimate. Completely legitimate organizations have no threat of external (or internal) evaluation,
whereas completely illegitimate organizations potentially face these threats
both internally and externally.

When legitimacy is defined as congruence with the values of the society
in which an organization is embedded, then the role of organizational communication is to achieve that congruence. Notice then, that the perspective
taken here is a rhetorical one, where organizational communication is seen
as cultural performance (Pacanowsky & O'Donnell-Trujillo, 1983)—the goal
of which is to align the organization with the dominate symbols and values
of society. In the next section, legitimacy is further elaborated by examining
the theoretical foundation of legitimacy—institutional theory.

INSTITUTIONAL THEORY

Much of what is known about organizational legitimacy has been developed
by institutional theorists (Scott, 2001). Institutional theories draw attention
to symbolic processes, particularly how symbolic processes confer legitimacy on organizations. This is because, as Eisenberg and Goodall (1993)
stated in reviewing institutional theory, "an institution's survival depends

on public legitimacy, not bottom-line performance, productivity, or effectiveness" (p. 80).

Institutional theory began in the 1940s and was influenced by the work of Weber (1978), Parsons (1956, 1960), Selznick (1949), and Perrow (1970), a student of Selznick. Selznick (1949) argued that the pressure external groups exert on organizations affect the organization's structure and values. Selznick viewed organizations as adaptive organization systems, "affected by the social characteristics of its participants as well as by the varied pressures imposed by its environment" (Scott, 2001, p. 23). Institutionalization is a process where the organization adapts its values to those predominate in its environment. Parsons argued that organizations gain legitimacy to the extent that their actions reflect the cultural values of society (Scott, 2001).

Beginning in the 1970s many of the ideas of institutionalism were revived and led to the development of what is commonly referred to as neo-institutionalism (Meyer & Rowan, 1977, Meyer & Scott, 1983; Zucker, 1977; cf. Powell & DiMaggio, 1991). Scholars in this discipline argue that environments must be viewed, not only in economic and technical terms, but in cultural terms as well (Davis & Powell, 1992; DiMaggio & Powell, 1983). Neo-institutional theory therefore does not differ so much from earlier notions of institutional theory. Neo-institutionalists still argue that the norms of the predominant sociopolitical culture exert significant influence on the organization's behavior (Davis & Powell, 1992).

In an early statement on neo-institutionalism, Meyer and Rowan (1977) argued that in modern societies, formal organizational structures are embedded in highly institutionalized contexts (p. 41). Organizations are therefore compelled to incorporate the programs and policies that have been institutionalized in society. For those organizations that do incorporate the institutionalized practices of society, legitimacy is conferred upon them and their chances for survival are increased. Legitimacy is therefore viewed as a necessary component for organizational survival.

Baum and Powell (1995) further clarified the neo-institutionalist conceptualization of legitimacy. They characterized neo-institutionalism as a "sociopolitical approach, which emphasizes that embeddedness in relational and normative contexts influences an organizational form's legitimacy by signaling its conformity to institutional expectations" (pp. 529–530). Institutionalization is the process whereby organizational practice becomes taken for granted (Davis & Powell, 1992). They further argued that because organizations today "rarely operate in isolation from the state, the professions, and broader societal influences, sociopolitical legitimacy cannot be ignored" (p. 530).

Legitimacy has therefore been viewed by neo-institutionalists as enabling an organization to act by providing a repertoire of cultural and symbolic resources on which to rely. But legitimacy can also be thought of as a constraint on organizational behavior, in that legitimacy determines in large part how an organization should act if it is to survive. As Davis and Powell (1992) stated, "institutional practices and beliefs are translated into both constraints on action and 'tool kits' that can be used to construct and legitimate new courses of action" (p. 354; cf. Swidler, 1986).

The Process of Legitimacy

The question that arises now is just how legitimacy is obtained by organizations. No organization can simply claim legitimacy for itself—rather, legitimacy is something "given" an organization by stakeholders. A stakeholder is a person or group identified as a(n) employee, customer, competitor, regulator, supplier, lender, shareholder, or representative of the media, government, or society in general. Research indicates that an organization's survival depends on its ability to satisfy its various stakeholders (Bedeian, 1987), since "stakeholder granting of legitimacy reduces the potential for organizational death" (Caillouet, 1991, p. 20; cf. Singh, Tucker, & House, 1986).

Like organizational image management, the management of legitimacy is an on-going process that involves gaining, maintaining, and in some cases regaining legitimacy for the organization. Organizations must attempt to create legitimacy when founded. Gaining legitimacy is a proactive activity and involves three primary strategies: conforming to societal expectations, gaining the support of stakeholders, and creating new ideas of what is legitimate behavior (Suchman, 1995).

If legitimacy is established, organizations must work hard to maintain legitimacy. Two issues make the maintenance of legitimacy problematic: stakeholder heterogeneity and structural inertia (Suchman, 1995). Stakeholder heterogeneity refers to the fact that because an organization's audiences are varied and changing, continued satisfaction of these various stakeholders is therefore challenging. Structural inertia refers to the fact that legitimacy itself motivates organizations to maintain stable structures and processes. Structural inertia tends to decrease the organization's ability to adjust to stakeholder demands, decreasing its chances for continued legitimate status. In order to meet these challenges, organizations must (a) be proactive and anticipate stakeholder demands and environmental developments that can cause the organization's legitimacy to be questioned, (b) protect past accomplishments that brought about legitimacy, and (c) generate goodwill and support (Suchman, 1995).

Legitimacy repair is necessary when the organization's actions have been deemed illegitimate by stakeholders. An illegitimate status demands that the organization respond, otherwise organizational failure could result. When attempting to regain legitimacy, organizations have two primary strategies from which to choose: (a) the organization can restructure itself, and (b) the organization can provide some kind of "normalizing account" which will separate the organization from the event that led to illegitimate status (Suchman, 1995). This chapter focuses on the latter—the rhetorical strategies organizations rely on to repair their legitimacy.

ORGANIZATIONAL CRISIS AS A CRISIS OF LEGITIMACY

At no time is organizational legitimacy more salient to an organization than during a crisis, because a crisis involves a threat to organizational legitimacy. A crisis is defined as "a series of events which threaten an organization's legitimacy, and ultimately, its survival" (Caillouet, 1991, p. 6). A difficulty arises for organizations experiencing crisis, however, because as an organization's perceived legitimacy decreases, stakeholders' skepticism of legitimation attempts increases (Ashforth & Gibbs, 1990). That is to say, the more an organization feels that its legitimacy is threatened (as in times of crisis), the more the organization will typically attempt to do to regain its legitimacy in the eyes of its stakeholders. The difficulty facing organizations in times of crisis is that while they are attempting to manage their legitimacy through strategic communication and other activities, stakeholders are likely becoming more and more skeptical of those legitimation endeavors.

Nonetheless, it is imperative that organizations attempt to restore legitimacy through communication and other actions. As Perrow (1984) noted, there are technical and administrative aspects of organizational crisis, and therefore crisis management involves efforts to change both the reality and the interpretation of organizational behavior. The way stakeholders interpret organizational behavior is largely influenced by strategic communication emanating from the organization. After a crisis has occurred, the communication behavior of organizations usually takes the form of accounts.

Scott and Lyman (1968) stated that "an account is a linguistic device employed whenever an action is subjected to valuative inquiry" (p. 46). Accounts are "verbal remedial strategies" (Gonzales, Pederson, Manning, & Wetter, 1990, p. 610) offered by an organization "to minimize blame or stigma when identity-threatening events befall it" (Ginzel et al., 1993). When offering an account, the options available are to either (a) deny the problem, (b) provide an excuse for why the problem occurred, (c) justify the problem, or (d) explain the reasons why the problem occurred (Benoit, 1995a; Scott & Lyman, 1968).

Recently researchers have begun to investigate the effects of account selection on image management (Caillouet, 1991; Coombs, 1995, 2000; Elsbach,

1994; Elsbach & Sutton, 1992; Hearit, 1995; Marcus & Goodman, 1991; Massey, 2001; Tyler, 1997; Watkins-Allen & Caillouet, 1994), and prescriptions have been made regarding which types of accounts are most effective. Coombs (1995) elaborated on this and refers to organizational accounts provided in the wake of crisis as crisis-response strategies. As Coombs (2000) put it, crisis-response strategies are "the messages organizations deliver to stakeholders after a crisis hits" (p. 37). Crisis-response strategies are message repertoires that are designed to repair the organization's legitimate image by influencing stakeholder perceptions. In the next section the crisis response by NASA following the *Challenger* disaster is presented and analyzed.

THE CASE OF NASA AND THE SPACE SHUTTLE *CHALLENGER*

To highlight how legitimation processes occur, a particular example is chosen—the explosion of the Space Shuttle *Challenger* on January 28, 1986. The *Challenger* disaster marked the first time in the history of the National Aeronautics and Space Administration (NASA) that astronauts had been lost in flight. The history of NASA was of a proud and flamboyant organization with a "can-do" attitude. All of that changed on January 28, 1986, and in the aftermath of the explosion in which the Reagan appointed Rogers Commission clearly showed that it was an error of judgment that led to the catastrophe (Martz, 1986, p. 14). To fully understand how this crisis impacted the legitimacy of NASA, it is necessary to trace the history of the organization and to also examine NASA's response to the crisis.

A Brief History of NASA

NASA began in 1958, largely as a response to the former Soviet Union's launching of Sputnik, the first satellite in space. NASA captured the imagination of the American people, who did not want to be second to the Soviets at anything. After only a few years, in 1961, Alan Sheppard became the first American in space. A year later, in 1962, John Glenn became the first American in orbit, and in 1965 Edward White set an American milestone by being the first to walk in space.

But then tragedy struck. On January 27, 1967, a launching-pad fire erupted and killed Gus Grissom, Edward White, and Roger Chaffee, the astronauts aboard the first manned Apollo spacecraft during a test at Cape Kennedy Space Center. For 21 months after the blaze that killed these astronauts, manned flights were suspended. But then, 2½ years later, in 1969, Neil Armstrong and Edwin Aldrin walked on the moon.

From 1969 until 1981, when the first shuttle orbited the earth, NASA continued to perform to the high expectations placed on the organization. NASA was not entirely without blemish, as the Apollo 13 mission and the failure of Skylab illustrate, but overall the organization enjoyed several years of success. According to one report, "in almost three decades, American astronauts and those who had watched them soar so often into space had grown used to success" (Wilford, 1986, p. A7). NASA had successfully created and maintained a legitimate image.

The Space Shuttle

The ideas that launched the Space Shuttle program began to surface in the late 1960s, but it was not until 1981 that the first Space Shuttle, *Columbia*, was launched into space. From 1981 until 1986, there were 24 successful Shuttle missions. Success of the program became so commonplace that the national television stations stopped carrying live coverage of Shuttle lift-offs. Attention returned to the program, however, on January 28, 1986. Seventy-three seconds into the flight of the Space Shuttle *Challenger*, an explosion killed all seven astronauts aboard, which included Christa McAuliffe, the first participant in what was known as the "Teacher in Space Program." Ironically, the Teacher in Space Program was designed to increase public support for space shuttle missions, which had become so commonplace. This, along with other events that were designed to enhance NASA's legitimacy actually created the conditions that led to the disaster (Seeger, 1986).

With many people in the United States and around the world watching, including many schoolchildren who were watching McAuliffe, the *Challenger* exploded and with that explosion came a new view of NASA and of space exploration. According to a Newsweek article, "the nation's view of the space program inexorably changed" (Martz, 1986, p. 14).

In that moment, NASA experienced a crisis of legitimacy (Seeger, 1986). Public support for the organization was compromised. According to Newsweek, the disaster "eroded the National Aeronautics and Space Administration's proud, safety-first tradition" (Martz, 1986, p. 14). Recalling that legitimacy is defined as the degree of cultural support for an organization, it is clear that that support was in jeopardy.

What was potentially more problematic to the organization than the accident itself was the slowly emerging awareness that the astronauts "didn't have to die" (Martz, 1986, p. 14). NASA had pressured the contractors of the Space Shuttle at Morton Thiokol to launch, even though representatives from Morton Thiokol had expressed concerns that the temperature was too cold for a launch. It was determined that faulty decision making led to the disaster, not a flaw in the design of the shuttle itself. According to Seeger

(1986), "NASA's reputation as a rational, successful, and technologically superior institution was immediately suspect" (p. 148).

The Crisis Response

The Reagan Administration responded quickly to attempt to restore the spoiled identity of NASA. President Reagan quickly formed a commission, chaired by William P. Rogers, a former secretary of state. The Rogers Commission consisted of 13 people including Neil Armstrong, the first American to walk on the moon; Sally Ride, the first woman astronaut in space; and Chuck Yeager, the first person to break the sound barrier (McGinley, 1986). The panel was often criticized for being composed of such celebrities that it seemed designed "to capture the imagination of the public and project a squeaky clean, all-America image" (McGinley, 1986, p. 62). The critics notwithstanding, the Rogers Commission fulfilled its responsibility and eventually determined who was at fault for the disaster.

The findings of the Rogers Commission so hurt the legitimacy of NASA that one reporter wrote that "seldom has a U.S. agency fallen so quickly from shining star to scapegoat" (Wellborn, 1986, p. 20). The Commission found that NASA's decision-making procedures and communication systems were seriously flawed (Seeger, 1986). Also, the Commission found that a culture of complacency had developed throughout the successful years of manned space flight at NASA, resulting in a can-do attitude that led to the *Challenger* explosion. As Magnuson (1986) put it, "Americans had soared into space 55 times over 25 years, and their safe return came to be taken for granted" (p. 24), not only by Americans in general, but by NASA officials as well.

The Commission concluded that pressures placed on NASA both internally and externally had led to the disaster. Specifically, funding had been reduced steadily since the late 1960s as NASA's mission became less clear. This reduction in funds led to decisions that were based more on economic efficiency than human survival. NASA then found itself in a double-bind situation, needing first to establish more public approval for its continuation before more funding could be justified. To that end, citizen and teacher in space programs were developed to open up space to common citizens. These pressures eventually led the organization to make decisions that were not in the best interests of the organization, and resulted in the loss of the *Challenger* and its crew.

NASA's handling of the crisis also hurt the organization's image as a public relations specialist (Martz, 1986). Not only did NASA delay a press conference for 5 hours after the explosion, they also confiscated all press video at the scene and ordered all NASA personnel to say nothing to the press concerning the disaster. As Moffett and McGinley (1986) put it, "The agency's muddled handling of the *Challenger* explosion has turned a major human and technological loss into a public-relations fiasco that could [and did] damage the agency's prestige and credibility for years" (p. 23). According to Seeger (1986), "NASA's legitimacy, therefore, suffered not only from the actual failure but from the consequent dialogue which depicted the administrative systems as seriously flawed" (p. 153).

As a result, several immediate effects of a loss of legitimacy resulted including: (a) shuttle flights being grounded for 32 months; (b) Congressional insistence on improvements in management and internal communication systems; (c) increased pressures to utilize unmanned spacecraft when possible; and (d), a loss of business on the part of NASA to other space organizations, including the European Space Agency, which relies on the unmanned Ariane rocket (Wellborn, 1986). Furthermore, insuring the shuttle and its payload became increasingly difficult, and increasingly expensive. As Robert Tirone of Alexander & Alexander, an insurance broker in New York said, "confidence in the shuttle 'has been severely shaken' " (Beck, 1986).

Attempts to Reestablish and Communicate Legitimacy

In the aftermath of the disaster, NASA and other governmental officials attempted to reestablish NASA as a legitimate organization. This was done by both discourse and performance behaviors (Seeger, 1986). Seeger identified four specific activities that were designed to reestablish legitimacy. First, the organization created the aforementioned Rogers Commission, which provided an open investigation of the causes of the accident. Interestingly, as Seeger (1986) pointed out, the results of the Rogers Commission actually served to reduce further the legitimacy of NASA, by highlighting the irrational decision-making processes in place. Second, NASA attempted to shift responsibility for the disaster to specific individuals in NASA and to key personnel at Morton Thiokol and other contractors. Third, NASA attempted to create the perception of rationality within NASA. To do this NASA placed highly visible and competent individuals into the decision-making process, including astronauts and engineers. And finally, NASA began to redefine its performance goals. By limiting the scope of the function of the space shuttle to initially only military payloads meant less performance pressure on NASA.

According to Seeger (1986), reestablishing NASA's long-term legitimacy required both the appearance of rationality and actual performance. Thirty-two months after the explosion of *Challenger*, on September 29, 1988, *Discovery* was launched with five veteran astronauts aboard and safely returned

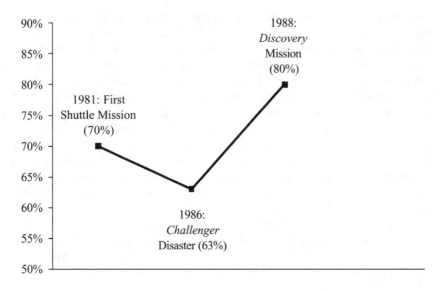

FIG. 15.2. Public support for NASA. From *Public Support for the U.S. Space Program*. Prepared by Yankelovich Partners, Inc., June, 1994. Reprinted with permission.

to earth after a successful mission in space. As Jaroff (1998) stated following the launch of *Discovery*, "The nation's collective sigh of relief could have launched a thousand shuttles" (p. 22).

The case of NASA therefore represents a movement through the three stages of organizational image management as the organization attempted to regain legitimacy. NASA began in the late 1950s and became fully legitimated by achieving the goals its stakeholders had set for it. NASA maintained its legitimacy throughout the 1960s and 1970s and into the 1980s with the introduction of the Space Shuttle program, but experienced a crisis of legitimacy when *Challenger* exploded. NASA's restoration attempts following NASA were not immediately successful, but once Shuttle missions were resumed, stakeholder support for NASA returned. NASA had regained its image as a legitimate organization.

Although no data are available that directly measure NASA's legitimacy, there is research illustrating the impact of the *Challenger* disaster on NASA's legitimate image. Since 1978, Yankelovich and Partners have collected public opinion data for NASA. Although this data represents only one stakeholder group, the U.S. general public, it provides at least limited evidence of the effects of the crisis on NASA's image, and also provides support for the process of legitimation (see Fig. 15.2).

CONCLUSION

This chapter has provided a theoretical model of crisis communication as the management of organizational images. Specifically, the model depicts crisis communication as the proactive, strategic efforts designed to repair organizational legitimacy. Organizational image management theory and institutional theory form the foundation of the theoretical model presented.

NASA's *Challenger* crisis was used as a case to demonstrate the process of image management and the crisis response strategies used to attempt to restore organizational legitimacy. Extant data provide support for the theoretical model and show that NASA was eventually successful in restoring its legitimate image. NASA continues to maintain its legitimacy and public support remains high. Research conducted by Weber Shandwick Worldwide in 2001 found that public support for NASA remains at 80%.

NASA has experienced some setbacks, including problems with the Hubble Telescope and failed missions to Mars, but overall the Agency has enjoyed tremendous success and has not experienced fatalities or other major crises. According to NASA, from 1992–2001 the Space Agency launched 171 missions, 160 of which were successful. In addition to successful Shuttle and other missions, NASA is also being more proactive in its image management strategy. For example, Daniel S. Goldin, Administrator of NASA from 1992 to 2001, vigorously pushed the message that space flight is a risky venture. In a written statement prepared for the 10th anniversary of the *Challenger* disaster Goldin said that even though "safety is the highest priority . . . space flight is inherently dangerous" (Broad, 1996, p. 12), thus preparing stakeholders for any unanticipated accidents.

BEST PRACTICES

The theoretical framework, as well as the case analysis of NASA's crisis response lead to several implications for researchers and practitioners. These are presented as "best practices." First of all, organizations must be proactive in their efforts to create, maintain, and (in the event of crisis) regain a legitimate image. This is achieved largely through symbolic behaviors, therefore communication strategies play a very important role in this process. Second, organizations must engage in a dialogue with stakeholders to successfully manage their image. What was effective last year, or maybe even last month, may not be effective now, and will most likely not be effective in the future. Only by engaging stakeholders in a dialogue can organizations hope to manage their images effectively. Third, image management has become increasingly difficult given the fact that (a) organizations are increasingly multinational; and (b) that new technologies such as the Internet and World Wide Web have changed the fundamental ways that organizations communicate with stakeholders. This requires, therefore, that organizations take an integrated communication approach to image management to ensure that a consistent image is sustained across stakeholder groups and through all channels of communication.

Finally, crisis managers must continue to rely upon communication experts to advise them on how to successfully respond to crisis events. This is accomplished largely by the inclusion of communication representatives on the crisis management team. In so doing, organizations are better able to respond to crisis because they have prepared for the response in advance. As Coombs (1999b) stated, crisis events are unpredictable, but not unexpected. Organizations must prepare for crisis events before they occur, so that if a crisis hits, the organization is able to respond with an open and unified voice that will allow the organization to maintain a consistent, legitimate image.

III

AFTER THE DANCE IS OVER: POSTCRISIS RESPONSE

Robert L. Heath

When does a crisis end? Some purveyors of conventional wisdom reason that the end is marked by the dramatic reduction or absence of media attention. By this logic, when the reporters go home, the crisis is over.

That conventional wisdom may be simplistic. Crisis is a time of ambiguity, uncertainty, and struggle to regain control. The aftermath of crisis may linger for some publics long after media attention has waned. Organizations have many stakeholders that need reassurance that the crisis has ended and that their interests are receiving proper attention. For instance, employees constitute one of the most important audiences in the postcrisis era. They want to be told and reassured that the organization has achieved stability, that it is operating properly.

Chapters in this section explore the ambiguity of crises and communication options needed to bring a crisis to closure. Several premises are examined in this section that can guide and aid executives, including communication managers, as they respond to crises by applying the following best practices:

- Because crisis threatens an organization's social legitimacy, communication strategies need to bring closure to the ambiguity surrounding the organization's performance and right to be trusted to operate properly. Operational change, management tactics, procedures, and statements are all part of an organization's repertoire of strategies to demonstrate that it is responsible, responsive, and ethical in the restoration of its operations.

- Organizations can assert that a crisis is not occurring, did not occur, or has ended. Such assertions require convincing proof because of the ambiguity that characterizes and is unique to each crisis.

- Organizational spokespersons' responses must be sensitive to the markers used by its publics as it asserts that the crisis has ended and that order has been restored.

- Strategies can be used to restore an organization's image. Part of restoration is an acceptance of responsibility for some or all of the crisis. Executive leadership may be reluctant to accept responsibility. They should never be seen as overly recalcitrant in this regard, as they should not think that a facile apology will absolve them of responsibility.

- Each crisis poses one or more rhetorical problem. Restorative measures must be selected and used based on what is a credible interpretation of which sort of rhetorical problem is posed by each crisis.

- Studies of apologia as a crisis response suggest that this tactic can be successful but also can lead an organization into further troubles. The specific apologia must be situationally relevant to the rhetorical problem raised by the crisis and the persons who comment on it.

- Some organizational crises, such as substantial downsizing, are prime facie evidence of management's inability to plan and manage for bad times. Rhetorical responses to such situations must acknowledge the responsibility of management rather than serve as the rationale for the organization's action. Reconciliation is needed by the rhetoric of hiring, "we want you," to the rhetoric of downsizing, "you will have to go for the best interest of the organization." These rhetorical stances are inherently at odds with one another and must be reconciled to the satisfaction of those who are not part of the management team.

- Any public that is asked (told?) to sacrifice for the greater good of some other set of stakeholders is likely to suffer high degrees of cognitive involvement, problem recognition, and constraint. These factors constitute substantial incentives to become an active public which can oppose the efforts of the organization. Rhetorical strategies and management policies need to be selected to reduce and defuse these incentives to opposition lest the manifest themselves in substantial conflict.

- The end of a crisis may be delayed simply because the public relations practitioners cannot respond to the rhetorical problem in a timely and responsible way. The absence of timely and effective response adds to rather than mitigates the crisis damage. This inability to make timely response is further evidence of the organization's ability to exercise ethical and responsive control over itself.

- Communication results from the need for sense making, which is a collective co-created activity. Crises create rhetorical problems that demand that sense be made of decisions and events. The organization suffering the crisis is expected to understand and respond to the various kinds of sense that are being made. Savvy practitioners understand that stakeholders are capable of and motivated to create their own sense of the situation. Responses are likely to be more successful when they acknowledge the mutuality of sense making.

The chapters in this section open consideration to many research questions about the communication strategies for crisis response, including those that follow:

- What markers suggest that a crisis is occurring? What are the markers that can be used to demonstrate that it has ended? To what extent do statements and the evidence offered by the organization satisfy its concerned stakeholders that the crisis is over or never occurred? These questions seem worthy of researchers' attention.
- Organizations are likely to be able to restore their reputation and convince stakeholders that the crisis has ended if they understand the markers held by the stakeholders. Restoration options are limited in number and are likely to be effective only to the extent to which credible and responsible corrective statements and actions are used.
- Under which circumstances is the use of the rhetoric of apology likely to be inappropriate and counter productive?
- Strategies that take a symmetrical approach to individuals which are asked to bear the brunt of a crisis, such as downsizing, can reduce the activists' reaction if they do not seem to privilege some stakeholders to the disadvantage of those who suffered. For instance, when managements receive a bonus for effective downsizing, those laid off are prone to be more angry because they see some parties benefiting by their suffering.
- The relationship between issues and crises needs further clarity. What conditions lead an issue to become a crisis? Likewise, what elements of crisis result in its becoming an issue?

Chapters in this section apply theory, explore case studies, and offer best practices that constitute a sustained argument that crisis is narrative. People experience reality through various narrative frames. Crises, for this reason, are interrupted narratives and require actions and statements that respond ethically to the narrative interpretations that result from dialogue surrounding the crisis.

16

Ambiguity as an Inherent Factor in Organizational Crisis Communication

Timothy L. Sellnow
North Dakota State University

Robert R. Ulmer
University of Arkansas, Little Rock

Tim Conner, president of The Conner Group, a crisis management consulting firm, exhorts organizations facing a crisis to "pay attention to the needs" of the media because "they grind the lens through which society views and judges your company" (English, 1992, p. 12). Much of the communication research focused on organizational crisis supports Conner's practical wisdom. Communication research argues consistently that an early and candid public response to a crisis by the afflicted organization's leadership can minimize the potential damage to the organization's credibility (Marconi, 1992; Schuetz, 1990; Seeger, 1985; Sellnow & Seeger, 1993; Williams & Treadaway, 1992). Yet, the threat, surprise, and urgency surrounding crisis situations often prohibit the identification and communication of such precise and accurate messages (Fink, 1986; Hermann, 1972; Seeger, 1986; Sellnow 1994; Sellnow & Ulmer, 1995; Weick, 1988). Consequently, organizations often appear ambiguous or vague in their crisis communication.

In this study, we investigate the impact of ambiguity in organizational crisis situations and its impact upon the messages intended for the multiple audiences organizations often face when responding to crisis situations. Because few studies of organizational crisis communication have focused on ambiguity, existing research offers little understanding of the role ambiguous messages play in resolving or intensifying crises. Similarly, limited consideration has been devoted to the ethical implications of ambiguous messages during times of crisis. In this chapter, we expand the study of crisis communication to include the role of ambiguity. To do so, first, we delineate the constraints organizations often face during crisis situations. Second, we depict how the nature of organizational communication creates an inherent level of ambiguity that is intensified further by crisis situations. Third, consistent forms of ambiguity in organizational crisis situations are identified and relevant examples are provided. Finally, implications of such ambiguity for the study of organizational crisis communication are provided.

COMMUNICATION CONSTRAINTS
DURING ORGANIZATIONAL CRISES

Crises pose a sudden threat to an organization's social legitimacy, its bottom line, or both (Seeger, 1986). Although warning signs of an impending crisis may exist, the acute phase of the crisis is not typically anticipated (Fink, 1986). Crises are also characterized by a sense of urgency because a failure to respond appropriately and within a reasonable amount of time results in an escalation of the crisis. Hence, an organizational crisis emerges with surprise, threatens the organization's viability, and demands a prompt public response (Hermann, 1972; Seeger, 1986). Furthermore, organizations can face diverse audiences during a crisis—the needs of which may be contradictory.

Schultz and Seeger (1991) contended that the audiences of organizations are diverse and that any assessment of their rhetoric must come from a perspective that is "corporate rather than individual centered" (p. 51). They stated, "While single speakers face multiple audiences, the modern corporation is unique in the degree of audience diversity and nature of their interests" (p. 51). Although a single speaker may wish to appeal to as large an audience as possible, organizations in crisis cannot survive unless they are able to satisfy simultaneously a diverse audience with distinct interests. For example, corporations must maintain the support of customers, employees, stockholders, and regulatory agencies. In crisis situations, the interests and needs of these distinct groups may even be contradictory. Schuetz (1990) explained that companies often structure a complex case in response to a crisis and direct different elements of the case to different audiences. She explained that, in some extreme cases, "companies may advocate new policies and defend old ones in the same messages" (p. 283). In short, the composite corporate audience serves as a constraint to organizations facing crisis situations.

Ironically, organizations have the potential to benefit from crises. Prince (1920) portrayed a crisis as a critical moment "big with destiny" (p. 16). Such destiny is rooted in the organization's ability to "use" the crisis to improve its position in a social hierarchy. Because of the intense media coverage, Marconi (1992) claimed that emphasizing statistical data and examples of public service during times of crisis can actually enhance the company's credibility. Crable and Vibbert (1985) contend that organizations have the right and capacity to participate in the formation of public policy rather than simply being responsive to government. They view crisis as "a moment of decision" where a policy resolution is demanded (p. 6). Rather than being passive in such instances, Crable and Vibbert recommended that organizations consistently engage in "corporate advocacy" or "issue advocacy" so that when issues peak in the public agenda, the organization is prepared to argue for policy decisions that are conducive to their goals. The question for study, then, becomes, what impact does ambiguity have on an organization's attempt to emerge successfully from a crisis situation?

ORGANIZATIONAL AMBIGUITY

Hermann (1963) explained that events which reach a crisis level occur as a surprise for corporations. Because organizational crises are typically unforeseen, organizations as well as regulatory agencies may not be able to fully ascertain the actions that *caused* the crisis until an extensive investigation is completed. In the mean time, the uncertainty surrounding the crisis situation is likely to make communication about causation and responsibility for the crisis ambiguous. Weick (1995) defined ambiguity as "an ongoing stream that supports several different interpretations at the same time" (pp. 91–92). The ambiguity in a crisis situation may, then, enable an organization to emphasize one interpretation of the crisis over another. Specifically, organizations can advocate a perspective or interpretation of crisis events that reflect more favorably on their industry than competing interpretations. Moreover, an organization may enhance the degree of ambiguity in a crisis situation in an effort to *produce* competing views of the crisis situation.

Ambiguity in its extreme form can paralyze an organization; however, we contend that it can be employed strategically by organizations. Ambiguity, whether generated by the organization or inherent to the context of a crisis, in part, enables organizations to communicate seemingly contradictory messages to distinct audiences. Putnam (1981) explained that "organizations are able to manage equivocality by imposing meanings on events; meanings that reduce, maintain, or increase equivocality" (p. 3). Because crises confront an organization with surprise, threat, and short response time (Seeger, 1986), the degree of equivocality during a crisis situation is likely to be intense. Several authors offer explanations of organizational ambiguity that are pertinent to this study.

Williams and Goss (1975) discussed the strategic applications of ambiguity. They contend that:

there are certain contexts where it is better to use vague rather than specific terms, politicians and diplomats have practiced the art of equivocation for centuries, for they have found that success in politics often depends on keeping the opposition guessing and leaving open a wide range of alternatives. (p. 256)

The wide range of alternatives suggested by Williams and Goss is not unique to politicians who incorporate ambiguity into their arguments. Eisenberg (1984) claimed that ambiguity is an essential part of organizing. He stated that strategic ambiguity is actually "essential to organizing because it allows for multiple interpretations to exist among people who contend that they are attending to the same message" (p. 231). Ambiguity, then, serves as a means for organizations to craft a message that may simultaneously appeal to distinct audiences.

The Ethics of Intentional Ambiguity

Johannesen (1990) recognized that "clear communication of intended meaning usually is one major aim of an ethical communicator;" however, he contends that, in some situations, "the intentional creation of ambiguity or vagueness is necessary, accepted, expected as normal, and even ethically justified" (p. 113). Johannesen identified five specific purposes for which he believes ambiguous communication is ethically justified:

1. to heighten receiver attention through puzzlement;
2. to allow flexibility in interpretations of legal concepts;
3. to use ambiguity on secondary issues to allow for more precise understanding and agreement on the primary issue;
4. to promote maximum receiver psychological participation in the communication transaction by letting them create their own relevant meanings;
5. to promote maximum latitude for revision of a position in later dealings with opponents or with constituents by avoiding being "locked-in" to a single absolute stance. (p. 114)

Although any or all of these purposes might be adopted by organizations facing crisis situations, those strategies that better enable the organization to address its multiple audiences are most relevant. For example, flexibility in legal interpretations and positional latitude is vital for organizations that must apologize to consumers, while avoiding legal pitfalls. Similarly, rhetorical messages account for the demands of a diverse audience when they allow factions to formulate their own relevant meanings.

Although the use of ambiguity is ethical in a variety of circumstances, it should be used with caution. Johannesen (1990) stipulated that if ambiguity is unavoidable, speakers should make certain that any use of it is explicit for the audience. Eisenberg (1984) cautioned organizations to consider their ultimate purpose when developing ambiguous messages:

> the use of more or less ambiguity is in itself not good or bad, effective or ineffective; whether a strategy is ethical depends upon the ends to which it is used, and whether it is effective depends upon the goals of the individual communicators. (p. 18)

Sellnow (1993) addressed specifically the implications for organizations using strategic ambiguity in their apologetic arguments during times of crisis. He claimed that ambiguity pervades organizational crisis situations and that recognizing and emphasizing this inherent equivocality in defensive arguments are both acceptable and effective. Yet, he cautions that "If uncertainty is introduced into a crisis situation [by the organization] simply to manipulate the public's perception, such skepticism cannot be condoned" (p. 18). Ambiguity, then, provides an amoral means whereby an organization can appeal to multiple audiences during crisis situations. Ambiguous messages may be deemed unethical, however, if they are not warranted, explicit, and justifiable.

CONSISTENT QUESTIONS FOSTERED BY AMBIGUITY IN ORGANIZATIONAL CRISES

We have identified three questions that consistently arise in organizational crisis communication. These questions focus on the *interpretation* of evidence, the *intent* behind actions leading to the crisis, and the *locus* of responsibility for the crisis. Answers to these questions are inherently ambiguous during crisis situations. The following section analyzes each of these questions in detail.

Questions of Evidence

When an organization's actions, products, or services are named as a likely suspect to be censured in the wake of a crisis, available evidence is likely to be scrutinized by all affected parties, including the afflicted organization. The result is often a complex scientific or legal debate in which the organization contrasts its interpretation of available evidence with that of legal or governmental agencies. For example, when the Food and Drug Administration identified Proctor and Gamble's Rely tampons as a source of toxic shock syndrome, the company hired a team of independent scientists, physicians, microbiologists, and epidemiologists to work with its staff scientists in an effort to challenge the government's findings (Fink, 1986). Because such debates are monitored closely by the media, their content takes on a rhetorical dimension that reaches a broad audience.

Altercations focused on the evidence surrounding a crisis often produce two or more plausible interpretations, thus such rhetoric becomes ambiguous. This interpretation and application, along with scrutiny of tangible research procedures, generate a discourse that Prelli (1989) suggested "is accepted or rejected on grounds of its *reasonableness*—given the issue at stake, the knowledge conditions of the scientific community, and the perceived expertise [ethos] of the makers of the claims" (p. 7). Wander (1976) explained that, from this rhetorical perspective, "science serves as a body of rules by which one version of reality may be legitimated and other, competing versions, discredited" (p. 226). Because such debate is laden with complex scientific or legal terminology and reasoning, the public's role in "deliberation [is] replaced by consumption" (Goodnight, 1982, p. 226). Thus, the complexity of evidence limits the ability of consumers to make judgments about the crisis and to select appropriate reactions to it.

A poignant example of such dispute occurred when Exxon challenged claims that the company was sluggish in its initial reaction to the oil spill in Valdez, Alaska. Exxon argued that it had intended to spray chemical dispersants onto the spill before any oil reached shore, but that it had been stopped by federal, state, and local officials. These officials based their decision, in part, on a study by the National Institute of Health Sciences, which indicated that a chemical in the dispersants Exxon planned to use in Valdez had been shown to cause kidney tumors in laboratory animals (Johnson, 1991). Conversely, Exxon's CEO, W. D. Stevens (1989) insisted that "Dispersants are the most effective, time-tested procedure for treating large oil spills" and that the inability to use them in Valdez made containment of the spill impossible (p. 2). The intricacies of the evidence regarding dispersants were debated for months. This debate left the public with two opposing and viable interpretations of the situation. This contrast resulted in considerable ambiguity for those who followed the story. Similar clashes have made deliberation over legal settlements in the Exxon Valdez disaster long-lasting and contentious.

Debating the merits of available evidence in crisis situations is not necessarily unethical. If, for example, Exxon had accepted the interpretation of those agencies regulating the clean-up, the company would have locked itself into a position of complete responsibility for the spill having reached shore. As a result, the legal consequences and public disapproval of Exxon would have been even more intense than they were. Exxon also consistently placed its arguments about evidence in the context of the oil industry (Johnson & Sellnow, 1995). By doing so, Exxon's claims were directed toward the justifiable end of improving clean-up operations for future spills. Had Exxon criticized the actions of the regulatory agencies in Valdez without offering at least reasonable evidence to support its claims, such criticism would not have been ethically warranted.

Wherever evidence is present, interpretations may vary among receivers. Organizations should not be expected to play a passive role in the interpretation of evidence surrounding crises. However, organizations that engage in such debate should be conscious of their multiple audiences. If consumers feel the organizations should compensate the victims of a crisis, no amount of legal success will ensure the organizations' re-establishment of public favor. Instead, the organization may be forced to go beyond its legal obligations in order to rebuild the trust of its consumers. In short, an organization may win a debate in a legal setting, while distancing itself from the public it depends on to purchase its goods and services.

Questions of Intent

Seeger (1986) equated crisis with a threat to an organization's social legitimacy. He suggested that an organization's legitimacy is based on its ability to establish congruence between the values implied by its actions and the accepted norms within its environment. Such congruence is threatened in crisis situations when an organization's intentions are called into question by consumers, the media, or regulatory agencies. A loss in an organization's social legitimacy occurs if the organization is viewed as "incompetent in fulfilling [its] mission, or when [it has] acted in a manner that exhibits little concern for [its] community by being irresponsible, dishonest, or having broken the law" (Hearit, 1995b, p. 121). To counteract this potential loss of legitimacy, organizations must recast for the public their thoughts and intentions behind the actions that produced or contributed to the crisis. Seeger (1986) contended that this effort to regain social legitimacy is "in part rhetorical and involves offering adequate justifications within a consensus producing dialogue concerning the value of the institution and its activities" (p. 148).

An organization's explanation that, at all points leading to the crisis, its intentions were honorable often requires a degree of ambiguity. Any action by an organization prior to a crisis, regardless of its merit, is likely to be criticized to some extent if it is seen as having contributed to a crisis. As such, an organization is often forced to defend an action that, in retrospect, is seen as the cause of suffering or embarrassment. Organizations frequently suggest that actions leading to a crisis "occurred accidentally" (Benoit, 1995a, p. 73). Such claims create ambiguity when they leave the audience with two competing alternatives: willful disregard for the public's welfare versus a mischance in an otherwise socially responsible system.

The burden, then, rests with the organization as it attempts to persuade its audience that the intent behind such actions was estimable. Chrysler's reaction in 1987 to federal charges of conspiracy to commit odometer fraud serves as an example further illustrating this point.

An investigation into what Chrysler called its "quality assurance program" revealed that Chrysler executives drove cars with the odometers disconnected for 1 day to 5 weeks and that Chrysler replaced odometers on cars showing as much as 100 miles with new ones. Chrysler was also accused of repairing cars that were damaged in accidents and then selling them as new. In all, Chrysler was said to have sold 60,000 previously driven cars as new during 1985 and 1986. The maximum fine facing Chrysler for these charges was $120 million (Sellnow, 1994). A company statement, issued shortly after the indictments became public knowledge, claimed that Chrysler's actions had been misinterpreted: "The U.S. attorney's office is attacking a legitimate quality assurance program, beneficial to consumers, by attempting to apply to the quality testing of new vehicles to a federal statute designed to preclude the rolling back of odometers on used cars" (Peterson, 1987, U.S. charges Chrysler 1A).

In a press conference on July 1, 1987, Lee Iacocca (1994) bluntly admitted that Chrysler's policy of testing cars with the odometers disengaged was "dumb" (p. 109). Worse, he contended, "a few" cars were "damaged in testing badly enough that they probably should not have been sold as new" (p. 109). This action, Iacocca admitted, "went beyond dumb and reached all the way to *stupid*" (p. 109). In his introduction, Iacocca emphasized that his key concern was not with the quality assurance program. In fact, he suggested that if customers would have known their cars were tested by "a qualified Chrysler representative as a quality check" they would have been grateful (p. 110). The concern he established as paramount was customer faith. Iacocca did not debate the technical or legal aspects of the crisis. Instead, he emphasized what he saw as the primary intent of the testing program: making certain that Chrysler customers were purchasing quality automobiles. The fact that the indictments had caused some to question their faith in Chrysler was something that Iacocca wisely sought to resolve. He announced that the company had eliminated the practice of testing cars with odometers disconnected. Second, he outlined a generous compensation program offered to affected customers.

In his press conference, Iacocca insisted that these steps were "not a product recall." Instead, he claimed, "the only thing we're recalling here is our integrity." This remark indicated to listeners that he did not feel the automobiles in the testing program were in any way inferior (Odometer Remarks). In so doing, he kept the focus of his response on rebuilding social legitimacy, rather than replacing shoddy work. Iacocca's explanation that Chrysler's ultimate intent in the quality assurance program was to ensure quality along with his pledge to compensate customers was successful. A Chrysler survey indicated that those with negative feelings about the incident stood at 55% before Iacocca's press conference. A similar survey after the speech indicated that 67% approved of the company's response (Iacocca & Kleinfield, 1988, p. 132).

Two factors make the ethical assessment of such explanations of intent difficult. First, motives and intentions are rooted in the thoughts of the actor. Consequently, it is difficult for observers to know what thoughts and intentions contribute to another individual's actions. Second, in crisis situations, individuals are asked to recreate their thoughts and intentions about previous acts. Thus, the opportunity for revision exists for organizations who seek to answer questions of intent. Any explanation of intent by an organization that is intentionally exaggerated or inaccurate would certainly be unethical.

Organizations suffer the same frailties as individuals in that both are bound by human nature to make mistakes. When such mistakes lead to an organizational crisis, it is reasonable to allow the organization to explain the intentions behind its actions. However, organizations are obligated to ensure that such explanations of intent are accurate.

Questions of Locus

When a crisis occurs, the first reaction of regulatory agencies is to identify its cause and to assign blame (Sellnow & Seeger, 1989). Benoit (1995) explained that "the intensity of a predicament is directly related to its severity and the actor's apparent responsibility for it" (p. 37). For this reason, organizations often rely on rhetorical strategies in order to minimize the intensity of a crisis as well as their responsibility for it.

Because organizations are composed of many employees or members acting in concert, isolating individuals within the organization who are responsible for causing a crisis is difficult—if not impossible. Cheney (1991) explained that organizations tend to " 'decenter' the self, the individual, the acting subject" through the use of language that is "powerfully ambiguous" (p. 5). He observes that individual responsibility is lost in the organization as messages and actions are attributed to the organization as a whole, rather than to the individual speakers or actors. Determining responsibility, then, becomes ambiguous as individuals whose actions produce a crisis defer responsibility to higher levels of authority in the organization. As accusations for blame move up the organizational hierarchy, there is no greater likelihood that an individual will accept blame. Even in cases where the top ranking official in an organization accepts blame for a crisis, she or he typically does so with the understanding that such an acknowledgment is symbolic (Seeger, 1985). In cases of organizational crisis, then, an organization's members are often insulated from blame as society is forced to address an organization's image rather than its people. Consequently, society faces the difficult task of addressing an organization, rather than a group of individuals.

Questions of responsibility also occur when external agents are identified by the afflicted organization as having greater responsibility for the crisis than the organization itself. An organization's success is dependent upon the performance of suppliers, industry standards, legal structures, and economic forces, to name a few. The actions of any such external agency could be crucial to the context of an organizational crisis. Benoit (1995) contended that organizations can, in some circumstances, regain their credibility in a crisis situation by "shifting blame" to such external agencies (p. 73).

Accusations to the organization's external environment introduce a degree of ambiguity into the crisis situation. For example, an organization may contend that an external agency should have resolved a problem before it affected the organization. Simultaneously, the accused agency may contend that the organization should have detected any inadequacies *before* further developing and marketing the materials or services. As a result, the audience is faced with two or more interpretations of the same situation. Each of which may have some merit.

In 1993, Jack in the Box restaurants were charged with causing a food poisoning outbreak that infected hundreds of people and killed three children. In response to this outbreak, Jack in the Box consistently posed arguments that questioned the locus of responsibility both internally and externally.

The crisis began for Jack in the Box when it was alerted by the Washington State Health Department that its restaurants had been identified as a common link in hundreds of E. coli infections—a serious bacterial infection that is life-threatening to children. Jack in the Box was initially hesitant to accept blame for the outbreak. Within a week of its onset, however, the company admitted publicly that the problem was "due to contaminated hamburger" in its restaurants (Press Release, January, 1993, p. 2). Investigations by state and federal agencies indicated that the grill temperatures had been below the state minimum. This state minimum temperature would have been hot enough to destroy E. coli bacteria (Jack in the Box's worst, 1993, p. 35). Jack in the Box posed two questions regarding the locus of responsibility. First, it insisted that the message related to the minimum temperatures had not been communicated effectively throughout the organization. Second, Jack in the Box insisted that a good deal of responsibility for the crisis rested with its meat supplier and the federal government.

Initially, Jack in the Box accused the Washington State Health Department of failing to inform the company of the new minimum cooking temperatures. When an internal investigation revealed that such a message had been received by Jack in the Box's corporate headquarters, Robert Nugent, President of Jack in the Box, released a statement saying, "These items were not previously brought to the attention of appropriate management" (Press Release, February, 1993, p. 2). No individual was publicly identified as having been responsible for the tragic oversight, which resulted in a failure to increase grill temperatures at Jack in the Box restaurants. Instead, Nugent outlined new organization-wide procedures for communicating, filing, and following-up on all regulatory changes in the future. The passive voice used in the only explanation offered for the error falls into a category Cheney (1991) described as "powerfully ambiguous" (p. 5). As Cheney predicts, any individual responsibility for the oversight was *decentered*, leaving only the organization's communication policies to blame.

Jack in the Box also posed a question of locus focusing on meat inspection at the stages that occur prior to the meat being delivered to restaurants. An investigation by Jack in the Box traced the source of the contaminated hamburger to a single supplier, Von's, located on the West Coast and Hawaii. Accordingly, Nugent argued that the crisis originated outside the restaurants and that Von's should share the burden of responsibility. Similarly, Nugent (1993) called for higher standards for meat inspection and better performance by federal meat inspection agents. Nugent's arguments created a form of ambiguity for his audience as he left them to ponder two distinct, but equally reasonable, questions of locus. Were the restaurants at fault for improperly cooking and serving the hamburger? Were the restaurants a victim of shoddy work by their meat supplier and government investigators?

Because decentered communication is prevalent in organizational communication, its presence alone during an organizational crisis does not constitute unethical communication. Yet, if the end of such decentered rhetoric is to avert individual criticism in cases where incompetence or deceit have occurred, such messages fail to meet the ethical standards established in this chapter. Similarly, the identification of external agents whose actions contributed to the crisis is not inappropriate. Because organizations function as open systems, they interact with a myriad of other entities. Such external accusations allow organizations to achieve what Johannesen (1990) called "flexibility in interpretations of legal concepts" (p. 114). If, however, the debate over who is to blame lingers on while victims of the crisis continue to suffer without compensation, one must question whether such ambiguity is warranted. Jack in the Box avoided such questionable behavior by paying the medical expenses of those who were infected at its restaurants even as it continued to question the degree to which it should be held legally responsible for the outbreak (Sellnow & Ulmer, 1995).

The complexity of organizations and the societies in which they exist fragment their responsibility in crisis situations. Recognizing and addressing aspects of shared responsibility enable organizations to promote a realistic interpretation of crises. However, organizations are a vital component of any system in which they operate and, as such, they have an impact on the external agencies that surround them. Hence, any effort by an organization to simplify the cause of a crisis to a point which assigns guilt in its entirety to a external agent or agents should be viewed with great scrutiny.

IMPLICATIONS

Questions of evidence, intent, and degree of responsibility emerge naturally as an organizational crisis unfolds. The answers to these questions are likely to hold some degree of ambiguity. Those who study organizational crisis communication should be sensitive to this tendency. The assumption that organizations should provide a candid and early response to a crisis is, in most cases, inappropriate. Instead, communication critics should strive to determine the degree to which ambiguity is reasonable in the given context of a specific crisis.

Any effort to assess the credibility of ambiguous crisis messages should take into account the complexity of the audience. For example, organizations cannot speak to their customers and the media without having their comments scrutinized by legal parties and regulating agencies. The simple answers that may work best for an organization's patrons may result in harsh legal backlash for the organization. Critics should recognize the vital role ambiguity plays in allowing an organization the flexibility needed to communicate with its multiple audiences.

Organizations can and often do benefit, in the long run, from effectively managing their communication during organizational crises. Ambiguity is a likely component of effective crisis communication. Still, there is ample opportunity for organizations to unethically capitalize on the ambiguity that is present in organizational crisis situations in an effort to avoid deserved sanctions. Critics should acknowledge this potential and scrutinize ambiguous messages accordingly.

When organizations are deceptive in their use of ambiguity during crises, they contribute to what Goodnight (1982) labeled an erosion of the public sphere of argument. Further studies should explore the relationship between ambiguity and the public sphere in all public forms of organizational communication. Foremost, the public stands to benefit from further distinction between contrived and inherent ambiguity in organizational crisis arguments. For, although ambiguity may be a natural byproduct of organizing, it may also be a machination for deceit.

17

Image Restoration Discourse and Crisis Communication

William L. Benoit
University of Missouri

Because our face, image, or reputation is so important to us, when we believe it is threatened, we are motivated to take action to alleviate this concern. Image is important to individuals as well as organizations. Corporations may take both preventive and restorative approaches to cope with image problems. Heath and Nelson (1986) stressed the importance of managing issues before they become image threats. At times, however, corporations must directly respond to corporate crises (see, e.g., Dionisopoulos & Vibbert, 1988). Such crisis management is crucial for a company because, as Brody (1991) asserted, "early response to crises can limit the extent to which organizations are damaged. Prompt, open responses minimize damage potential" (p. 189). At times organizations must produce a message to respond to threats to their good name. And, of course, there are differences in the repair efforts developed by individuals and companies. For example, companies might favor different image repair options than individuals, or might employ strategies in different configurations. Corporations may bring different and greater resources to image repair efforts than individuals. Corporate attorneys may recommend that certain strategies be avoided to prevent or minimize risks of litigation. Despite differences in how image restoration strategies might be selected, combined, or employed, however, the basic image restoration options are the same for both individual and corporate image repair efforts.

In the 12 years since the theory of Image Restoration Discourse was first articulated (Benoit, Gullifor, & Panici, 1991), a considerable body of work has been accumulating. It is time for a retrospective analysis of this research, which is the subject of this chapter.

The way image repair strategies function to repair a damaged reputation can best be understood through an analysis of the nature of attacks, reproaches, or complaints (for an analysis of persuasive attack, see Benoit & Dorries, 1996; Benoit & Harthcock, 1999). Fundamentally, an attack on an image, face, or reputation has two components: (a) An act occurred that is considered offensive, and (b) The accused is held responsible for that action. Only if both conditions are thought to be true by the relevant audience(s) is the accused's reputation at risk.

IMAGE RESTORATION DISCOURSE

For a company's reputation to be threatened, a reprehensible act must have been committed. If nothing bad happened, or if what did happen is not considered offensive, then image is not threatened. Furthermore, before a company should be concerned about negative effects of an act on image, a *salient audience* (or audiences) must be thought to disapprove of the action. If a firm doesn't care that a particular group believes it committed an offensive act, there is no threat to the company's image. Of course, "act" must be construed broadly, including words as well as deeds and encompassing failure to perform expected actions, poor performance of expected actions, and performance of dispreferred or prohibited actions. The point is that an act must be considered offensive by a relevant audience or audiences for image to be threatened.

Second, damage to image requires that the accused be held responsible for the offensive act by the relevant audience(s). No matter what happened or how terrible it was, it is not reasonable to form an unfavorable impression of a company that is *not* believed to be responsible for that act. However, responsibility can appear in many guises: For example, we can be blamed for acts that we performed, ordered, encouraged, facilitated, or permitted to occur.

It is important to realize that for both of these components of a persuasive attack (offensiveness, responsibility) perceptions are more important than reality. The key question is not whether the act was *in fact* offensive, but whether the act is *believed* by the relevant audience(s) to be heinous. If an audience whose opinion is important to the accused considers the act to be offensive, damage to reputation should occur. Similarly, the important point is not whether the accused *in fact* is responsible for the offensive act, but whether the accused is *thought* to be responsible for it by the relevant audience(s). If a person or organization is thought to be responsible for an act perceived as undesirable, image ought to suffer. This does not mean that the "facts" are completely irrelevant; if an act is not offensive, or if the accused is not actually at fault, the accused can attempt to use those ideas to try to repair the damaged image.

Furthermore, offensiveness may be thought of as existing on a continuum. Some offenses are worse than others, and it seems reasonable to assume that the more serious the offense—the more vile the action, the more people harmed by it, the longer or more widespread the negative effects, and so forth—the greater the damage to one's reputation.

Although we can conceive of responsibility as existing on a continuum, blame is probably more likely to be a binary decision (*either* guilty *or* innocent). Still, a firm's reputation may suffer in proportion to the extent to which they are held responsible for the undesirable act (including the extent to which they are believed to have intended the act and its consequences). The greater the (perceived) offensiveness of the act and, perhaps, the greater the (apparent) responsibility of the accused for that act, the greater the damage to the image.

Typology of Image Restoration Strategies

Drawing on past research (Burke, 1970; Scott & Lyman, 1968; Ware & Linkugel, 1973), Benoit (1995a) developed a more complete typology of image repair strategies (see also Benoit, 1997b, 2000) with 5 general strategies and 14 total options (see Table 17.1). Denial and evasion of responsibility address the first component of persuasive attack, rejecting or reducing the accused's responsibility for the act in question. Reducing offensiveness and corrective action, the third and fourth broad category of image restoration, concern the second component of persuasive attack: reducing offensiveness of the act attributed to the accused. The last general strategy, mortification, attempts to restore an image not by disputing the charges, but by asking forgiveness. Each strategy is discussed briefly in this section.

Denial. A person accused of wrong-doing may simply deny committing the offensive action. Whether the accused denies that the offensive act occurred or denies that he or she performed it, either option, if accepted by the audience, should help restore the image of the accused. So, one option for responding to persuasive attack is simply to deny the offensive act. In 1991, Pepsi-Cola accused its chief competitor, Coca-Cola, of requiring its other accounts to pay higher prices, subsidizing its largest customer, McDonald's (see the example below of attacking accuser). Coke replied by denying Pepsi's charges. A letter from Frenette (1991), senior vice president and general manager, stressed that charges that Coke increased prices for some customers but not all "were absolutely false," and that price increases are "universally applied; there were no exceptions" (p. 24). Here, Coca-Cola

TABLE 17.1
Image Restoration Strategies

Strategy	Key Characteristic	Example
Denial		
Simple denial	did not perform act	Coke does not charge McDonald's less
Shift the blame	another performed act	Exxon: Alaska and Coast Guard caused delay
Evasion of Responsibility		
Provocation	responded to act of another	child who broke toy
Defeasibility	lack of information or ability	executive not told meeting moved
Accident	mishap	Sears' unneeded repairs inadvertent
Good Intentions	meant well	Sears: no willful over-charges
Reducing Offensiveness of Event		
Bolstering	stress good traits	Exxon's swift and competent action
Minimization	act not serious	Exxon: few animals killed
Differentiation	act less offensive than similar ones	Nixon: attack Viet-Cong, didn't invade Cambodia
Transcendence	more important considerations	Nixon: new action needed to win war
Attack Accuser	reduce credibility of accuser	Pepsi: Coke charges McDonald's less
Compensation	reimburse victim	disabled movie-goers given free passes
Corrective Action	plan to solve problem/prevent recurrence	AT&T promised to improve service
Mortification	apologize	AT&T apologized for service interruption

Note. From Benoit (1997b). Reprinted with permission.

directly and unequivocally rejects Pepsi-Cola's charges as false: Coke simply did not do what Pepsi had alleged.

A related option is for the accused to attempt to shift the blame. Burke (1970) termed this option *victimage*. This strategy can have advantages over simple denial. First, it provides a target to blame for the wrongful deed. Second, it answers an important question: "Well if you didn't do it, who did?" After the Exxon Valdez oil spill, Rawl, Chair of Exxon, "blamed state officials and the Coast Guard for the delay, charging . . . that the company could not obtain immediate authorization on the scene to begin cleaning up the oil or applying a chemical dispersant" (Mathews & Peterson, 1989, pp. A1–6). If people accepted this version of events, it could help absolve Exxon of guilt for delays in the clean-up (albeit not for the spill).

Evasion of Responsibility. Another general image repair strategy is attempting to evade or reduce responsibility for the offensive act, which has four versions. Scott and Lyman (1968) suggested the accused can claim his or her action was merely a response to another's offensive act, and that their own behavior can be seen as a reasonable reaction to that provocation (they called this strategy scapegoating, but I rename it provocation to avoid confusing it with shifting the blame). If accepted, this rhetorical strategy may shift some or all of the responsibility from the accused, helping to repair his or her image. For example, when a company closes a local plant, and bears the brunt of complaints about that decision, it could argue (assuming it was true) that the move was in response to an increase in taxes and fees.

Another form of evading responsibility is defeasibility (Scott & Lyman, 1968), in which the accused alleges a lack of information about or control over important elements of the situation. Here, the accused claims that because of this lack of information or control, he or she should not be held completely responsible for the offensive act. If accepted, this claim should reduce the responsibility of the accused for the offensive act and help repair the damaged reputation. For instance, a busy executive who missed an important meeting could attempt to justify his or her behavior by claiming that "I was never told that the meeting had been moved up a day." If it is true that the meeting was changed and the executive wasn't informed, he or she lacked crucial information which excuses the absence.

A third option is to claim the offensive action occurred by accident. We have a tendency to hold people responsible for factors that appear to be under their control. If the accused can convince the audience that the act in question happened accidentally, he or she should be held less accountable, and the damage to his or her image should be reduced. After charges of auto repair fraud in California, one response from Sears' Chairman Brennan was to characterize the auto repair mistakes as "inadvertent" rather than intentional (Sears to Drop, 1992, p. 5B).

Fourth, the accused can suggest that the offensive behavior was done with good intentions. Here, the audience is asked to reduce the accused's responsibility for the wrongful behavior because it was performed with good intentions. Those who do improper actions while trying to accomplish good are usually not held as accountable as those who intend to do bad. Another strategy used by Brennan in response to accusations of overcharging its auto repair customers was to stress Sears' good intentions. Brennan (1992) declared that "Sears wants you to know that we would never intentionally violate the trust customers have shown in our company for 105 years" (p. A56). Notice that in this case the strategy of good intentions works well with accident: We have good intentions; any overcharges that may have occurred must be accidental.

Reduce Offensiveness. Rather than deny or reduce responsibility for act, an organization that is accused of wrongful actions can try to reduce the perceived offensiveness of that act. This general image repair strategy has six versions: bolstering, minimization, differentiation, transcendence, attacking one's accuser, and compensation.

First, one may use bolstering to strengthen the audience's positive feelings toward the accused, in order to offset the negative feelings connected with the wrongful act (Ware & Linkugel, 1973). Companies may describe positive characteristics they have or positive acts they have done in the past. Although the amount of negative affect from the accusation remains the same here, increased positive feeling toward the accused may help offset the negative feelings toward the act, creating a net improvement in reputation. Following the Valdez oil spill, Exxon attempted to use bolstering as part of its image repair effort. Chairman Rawl (1989) declared that "Exxon has moved swiftly and competently to minimize the effect this oil will have on the environment, fish, and other wildlife." He declared that this incident "has been receiving our full attention," and expressed his sympathy to "the residents of Valdez and the people of the State of Alaska" (p. A12). Characterizing its actions as "swift" and "competent," its attentions as focused on the incident, and its attitude as sympathetic (*if* accepted by the audience), should bolster its image and help offset damage to its reputation from the oil spill.

A second possibility is to try to minimize the negative feelings associated with the wrongful act. If the audience comes to believe that the act is less offensive than it first appeared, the amount of damage to the accused's reputation should be reduced. After the Valdez oil spill, Exxon officials tried to downplay the extent of the damage. For example, Baker (1989) explained that "On May 19, when Alaska retrieved corpses of tens of thousands of sea birds, hundreds of otters, and dozens of bald eagles, an Exxon official told National Public Radio that Exxon had counted just 300 birds and 70 otters" (p. 8). This appears to be an attempt to portray the damage as less that it appears to be (and possibly less than it actually is), a clear example of minimization.

Third, the accused can employ differentiation (Ware & Linkugel, 1973). Here the accused attempts to distinguish the act he or she performed from other similar but more offensive actions. In comparison, the act performed by the accused may seem to the audience to be less offensive, reducing the negative feelings toward that person. Sears attempted to differentiate its actions, repairing auto parts before they fail, from unneeded repairs (or fraud; Benoit, 1995b).

Fourth, transcendence (Ware & Linkugel, 1973) attempts to place the act in a more favorable context. It can also be useful to simply suggest a different frame of reference. For example, one could attempt to shift the audience's attention to other, allegedly higher values, in order to justify the behavior in question. A positive context may lessen the apparent offensiveness of the act and improve the accused's image. Dow Corning, when accused of having internal documents that revealed the dangers of its breast implants, attempted to transcend this issue by talking about women's desire to have these implants (Brinson & Benoit, 1996).

Fifth, those accused of wrong-doing may decide to attack their accusers. If the accused can damage the credibility of the source of allegations, damage to the accused's image may be limited. Pepsi-Cola attacked Coca-Cola in advertisements aimed at retail outlets (*Nation's Restaurant News*). One advertisement claimed that Coke's pricing policies treated other accounts differently (and worse) than McDonald's: "this year, while coke required national accounts like you to absorb a per-gallon price increase, we hear *there was no change to McDonald's net price*." To make sure the implications were clear, the ad stressed that "Coke's pricing policy is requiring you to subsidize the operations of your largest competitor" (Pepsi-Cola, 1991, p. 34). Here the persuasive attack on Coke is quite clear, and that may reduce the damage from attacks launched by Coke.

In compensation (Schonbach, 1980), the accused offers to reimburse the victim to help mitigate the negative feeling arising from the act. This payment can be goods or services as well as monetary reimbursement. If the compensation is acceptable to the victim, the negative affect from the wrongful act should be eliminated or reduced, improving the accused's image. For example, a group of disabled people were denied admittance to a movie theater. An official later apologized and offered them free passes to a future movie (Rebuffed Moviegoers, 1992). The passes were intended to help compensate them for the offensive act.

Corrective Action. Another general image restoration strategy is corrective action, in which the accused promises to correct the problem. This action can take the form of restoring the state of affairs existing before the offensive action, or promising to prevent the recurrence of the offensive act. A willingness to correct or prevent recurrence of the problem can improve the accused's image. On September 17, 1993, AT&T experienced a breakdown in long distance service to and from New York City. In his attempt to repair AT&T's image, Chairman Allen (1993) relied on corrective action. For example, he stated, "We have already taken corrective and preventive action at the affected facility" and announced that AT&T plans "to spend billions more over the next few years to make them even more reliable" (p. C3). Thus, he promised to make improvements to prevent future problems.

Mortification. Another general strategy for image restoration is to confess and beg forgiveness, which Burke (1970, 1973) labeled mortification. If the audience believes the apology is sincere, they may pardon the wrongful act. Another part of AT&T's response was to apologize, or engage in mortification. Allen (1993) accepted responsibility for the disruption: "I am deeply disturbed that AT&T was responsible for a disruption in communications service." He explicitly accepted full responsibility for the incident. Allen also offered an explicit apology: "I apologize to all of you who were affected, directly or indirectly" (p. C3). Thus, he accepted responsibility for the offensive act and directly apologized to those affected by it.

PREVIOUS RESEARCH ON IMAGE RESTORATION DISCOURSE

This typology has been applied to several instances of image restoration discourse, grouped here into political (Benoit & McHale, 1999; Benoit, Gullifor, & Panici, 1991; Benoit & Nill, 1998; Benoit & Wells, 1998; Kennedy & Benoit, 1997), sports/entertainment (Benoit, 1997a; Benoit & Anderson, 1996; Benoit & Hanczor, 1994; Benoit & Nill, 1998b) and corporate categories. This section describes the work on corporate image repair.

Furthermore, this perspective on image restoration discourse has been applied to corporate image repair. Benoit and Brinson (1994) analyzed AT&T's defense following an interruption of its long-distance service in New York. In September of 1991, AT&T's long distance service in New York City was interrupted. Initially, AT&T tried to shift blame to low-level workers. However, as the complete story emerged, AT&T apologized for the interruption (mortification). Then, bolstered its image (e.g., stressing its commitment to excellence, reporting billions invested in service, and skilled workers). Finally, AT&T promised corrective action. The factors that led to this interruption of long distance service were corrected. Additionally, AT&T promised a comprehensive review of its operations to anticipate and prevent other problems. It also stressed its commitment to providing excellent service and promised to spend billions of dollars to do so. After the initial fumbling attempt to shift the blame, these strategies were well conceived and should have helped restore AT&T's image.

Exxon's response to the Valdez oil spill was analyzed by this theory (Benoit, 1995a). Exxon shifted the blame for the accident to Captain Hazelwood and for the delay in the clean-up to slow authorization from Alaska and the Coast Guard. It attempted to minimize the size of the problem, bolstered its image as a concerned company, and promised corrective action to alleviate any damage. Shifting the blame to Hazelwood may have been helpful (especially after it became known that he had been drinking before the accident). However, the state of Alaska and the Coast Guard were unlikely targets for blame. Exxon's attempts to minimize the extent of the problem were graphically denied by television and newspaper coverage. Similarly, description of a slow and apparently inept clean-up undermined both its attempts to bolster its image and the credibility of its promised corrective action. Thus, Exxon's image restoration campaign was relatively ineffectual. It would have been aided had it discussed policies to prevent the recurrence of this oil spill (it is possible that Exxon's attorneys advised against this option because it could create or exacerbate legal difficulties).

I also analyzed Union Carbide's response to the Bhopal, India, gas leak that killed thousands and injured hundreds of thousands with this theory (Benoit, 1995a). Carbide's primary strategies were bolstering and corrective action. Four specific actions were described: a relief fund, an orphanage, medical supplies, and medical personnel. Although these strategies were appropriate, they failed to address the most important question: What was Union Carbide doing to prevent another tragedy?

Another application of the theory of image restoration to corporate discourse can be found my examination of 3 years of advertising (1990–1992) by Coca-Cola and Pepsi-Cola in a trade publication, *Nation's Restaurant News* (Benoit, 1995a). Each used bolstering in a variety of advertisements, which is hardly surprising. However, Pepsi declared that Coke charged McDonald's less than other customers, so that they were in effect subsidizing their largest competitor. Coke expressly (and effectively) denied these charges. Furthermore, Coke revealed that Pepsi ran its allegations a second time after Coke notified them that the charges were false. Then Coke turned the tables on Pepsi, pointing out that Pepsi used the profits it made from its customers to buy fast food restaurants. Coke pointed out that Pepsi owned 19,500 Taco Bells, Kentucky Fried Chickens, and Pizza Huts. Surely Pepsi's interest in the restaurants it actually owned is far greater than Coke's interest in its largest customer (McDonald's). Thus, Coke and Pepsi both used bolstering and attack accuser, and Coke used simple denial. Pepsi probably should have apologized for its (apparently) false accusations, but did not. Coke's persuasive attack and its persuasive defense were each superior to Pepsi's.

Dow Corning was subjected to harsh criticism over the dangers of its breast implants (Brinson & Benoit, 1996). Its defense went through three phases. Initially, Corning used denial, minimization, bolstering, and attacking one's accuser. As its own damaging internal documents became public, it attempted transcendence. Finally, Corning engaged in mortification and corrective action. Only when it shifted away from its posture of denial to corrective action did criticism of Corning begin to subside.

Another application concerns Sears' response to allegations by the California Department of Consumer Affairs that its repair shops had defrauded consumers through unneeded repairs (Benoit, 1995b). Sears' defense went through two stages. In both, it employed denial, differentiation, bolstering, and minimization. In the first stage, these were coupled with an attack on its accuser. In the second stage, they were used with corrective action. Sears' use of denial and minimization were unpersuasive. Its attempts at bolstering were unrelated to the accusations. Its attack on its accuser was unconvincing. Corrective action was a good idea, but it was simply too little too late.

USAir was attacked in the *New York Times* (Frantz & Blumenthal, 1994) for lack of safety after a crash on September 8, 1994 near Pittsburgh killed 132 people. USAir published three full page advertisements in newspapers: one from management, one from the pilots, and one from flight attendants (Benoit & Czerwinski, 1997). The advertisements used bolstering, denial of unsafe operations, and corrective action including appointment of an Air Force General to oversee safety. This image repair effort was judged as largely ineffectual for three reasons. First, denial conflicted with corrective action—if there was no safety problem, why do corrective action? Second, accusations included delayed repairs, and the fact that three different letters were printed (including one from flight attendants) made it conspicuous that ground crew did not write a letter with assurances of safety. Finally, we thought corrective action was probably better considered pseudo (not real) corrective action; the letters never promised that safety would be improved, only that they would convince us that they were already safe. That is, the "problem" that they promised to correct was (mis-) perceptions of their poorly safety practices.

Television (*Prime Time Live* and *Day One*) and the government (FDA Commissioner Kessler) attacked the tobacco industry, alleging that the companies added nicotine to cigarettes, that cigarettes were addictive, and that the tobacco industry knew this and did so out of greed (Benoit, 1998). The industry responded with testimony in Congress and with newspaper advertising. It primarily used denial (denying that nicotine and cigarettes are addicting, that they add nicotine to cigarettes), but the defense also used bolstering and good intentions, attack accuser, and differentiation (cigarettes are not like heroin, but more like Twinkies). This defense, especially in contrast with the attack, was generally ineffectual. However, both the attack and the defense illustrated how multiple messages can work together, to reinforce main ideas.

Texaco was accused of racism, in part because of a private remark about how African-Americans were like "black jelly beans . . . glued to the bottom of the jar" (Brinson & Benoit, 1999). The company used bolstering, corrective action, mortification, and shifting the blame. The last strategy was interesting, because Texaco shifted blame to a group of employees who were characterized as "bad apples," rather than to a group or entity outside the organization.

These studies suggest that those who desire to restore a tarnished image have a limited number of discursive strategies to achieve this goal. These persuaders used denial, bolstering, shifting the blame, corrective action, and attacking one's accuser frequently. Minimization, differentiation, transcendence, and mortification were also used at times. These strategies were operationalized in many different ways, with varying degrees of success. So, it appears the basic repertoire of image repair strategies is limited, that the theory of image repair discourse identifies those strategies, and that these options are available to those who need to repair their image.

SUGGESTIONS FOR CRISIS COMMUNICATION SITUATIONS

Preparation of Crisis Contingency Plans

Before a crisis occurs, judicious planning may reduce response time as well as missteps in a response to a crisis. Someone should be identified as a "point-person," with the responsibility and authority to prepare for crises and take swift action when they occur. Everyone in the organization should know who has this responsibility, so that others will contact the point person immediately when a crisis arises. Tylenol scored points for swift action in the first poisoning episode (Benoit & Lindsay, 1987), whereas Exxon's reaction appeared slow, which tended to undermine its image repair efforts (Benoit, 1995a).

The point-person should anticipate and prepare for potential crises. Although crises can take a variety of forms, some potential crises can be anticipated. Airlines must realize that crashes occur. Auto makers (not to mention tire manufacturers, like Firestone) should know safety problems are possible. Vendors of food and drink (manufacturers, stores, and restaurants) must know that food poisoning is a possible problem. To the extent those in charge of crisis communication can anticipate possible problems, they can prepare potential responses.

Contingency plans should be reviewed periodically and implemented thoughtfully. It may be that elements of the actual problem differ from the anticipated problem, and therefore the plans will need to be modified accordingly. Still, the contingency plans provide a carefully thought out course of action, making the organization's response easier and quicker to implement. It is easier to make mistakes in judgment when one is rushed and unprepared.

Identification of the Crisis: The Nature of Accusations

When a crisis emerges, it is vital to understand the nature of crisis and the relevant accusation(s). First, what are the accusations or suspicions? Responding to the wrong charges (different accusations from the complaints) could have two detrimental effects. The accusations may be broadened to include the new ones, worsening the image problem. Relevant audiences could also view the response as deceptive (e.g., "What do they mean, 'We didn't sell mislabeled products.' The problem is that they sold *adulterated* products. Who are they trying to fool?"). If one does not clearly know the attacks or suspicions, one cannot hope to effectively nullify them.

Identification of the Relevant Audience(s)

It is also extremely important to clearly identify the relevant audience(s). An important part of persuasion is tailoring one's message(s) to the audience. For example, suppose environmentalists accuse a company of dumping waste. At least five different potential audiences can be identified in this situation. First, the company may, of course, wish to assuage the concerns of their attackers, the environmentalists. However, the opinions of stockholders are important, if they are aware of the controversy. Governmental regulators may fine or otherwise sanction the company. If those who buy the company's goods or services decide to boycott the company because of the attacks, consumers are another potential audience. Local voters could conceivably pass laws restricting the company's business practices. It is important to recognize that the needs and interests of these groups differ widely (e.g., stockholders are concerned with profits; environmentalists with the quality of their local environment; regulators with laws), and thus ideas or persuasive appeals that might be expected to be effective with one group could be utterly worthless with another. Furthermore, some groups may have diverse interests (voters could be concerned with keeping jobs and commerce or with environmental quality), and persuaders may want to attempt to address all of the major concerns.

It is possible that one who is facing an image threat may hope to favorably influence more than one audience. If so, it is probably best to prioritize the audiences, making sure that the most important audience is appeased, and then devoting time and effort to the other audiences as is possible. This may be accomplished with separate, different messages delivered to different groups (while the messages may stress different points, according to the intended audience, it is risky to develop contradictory messages), or by directing different passages or aspects of a message to different audiences. Still, the accused must clearly identify which audience or audiences are the relevant ones. It should be obvious from the environmental example that it is important to try to identify the needs and interests of the relevant audience(s).

Repairing a Tarnished Image

Must the Accused Always Respond to the Charges? The discussion of the theory of image repair discourse presented earlier suggests that understanding the nature of the persuasive attack (accusation) helps understand image repair. Ryan also (1982) emphasized the importance of understanding image restoration events in the context of the specific attacks provoking the face repair work. Ryan is, of course, correct when he asserted that "the critic cannot have a complete understanding of accusation or apology without treating them both" (p. 254). I have stressed that the crisis communicator must know the accusations; but does this mean the charges must always be answered?

First, it is possible to redefine the attack. Senator Kennedy revealed that he had pled guilty to a charge of leaving the scene of an accident, which helped him transform defense of legal actions into a defense of character (Benoit, 1988). If the accused successfully transforms the accusations, he or she will not have to respond to them as they were originally developed. This can, at times, be an effective option. Instead of altering the nature of the accusations, the accused may attempt to refocus attention on other issues entirely as Nixon tried to shift focus away from Watergate (Benoit, 1982) or Clinton away from Whitewater (Benoit & Wells, 1998). Although this maneuver does not always work, or may work only for a time, it is a possibility. If successful in reorienting the audiences' attention, the accused may well be able to successfully ignore some or all of the accusations.

Furthermore, it is possible that all aspects of the accusations may not be equally important to the audiences. Thus, it may not be best to automatically respond to all attacks but to concentrate on those most salient to the audience. It could be a waste of time or even irritating to dwell on attacks that are unimportant to the audience. Additionally, the audience may have forgotten some of the accusations by the time of the response. Of course, if the charges are particularly salient to the audience, or if they are repeated often enough by the attackers, an accused may well be forced to deal with accusations in order to restore his or her reputation. Although Ryan (1982) is correct that the critic must consider the accusations, we must not jump to the conclusion that this means the accused must necessarily respond to (all of) the accusations. It is important to counteract the accusations that are most damaging to the audiences that matter most to the organization.

Suggestions for Effective Image Repair Discourse. First, because image restoration rhetoric is a species (or genre) of persuasive or rhetorical discourse, suggestions for effectiveness may stem from our understanding of persuasion and rhetoric generally as well as from considerations pertaining directly to image restoration. The analysis of the cola wars (Benoit, 1995a) reveals advice applicable to persuasion generally: avoid making false claims; provide adequate support for claims, develop themes throughout a campaign; avoid arguments that may backfire. The tobacco industry tried to argue that cigarettes are no more addicting than Twinkies (Benoit, 1998). Examination of Exxon's discourse on the Valdez oil spill (Benoit, 1995a) suggests that once Exxon made self-serving statements that seemed at odds with other information (their allegedly swift and competent cleanup), this may have damaged Exxon's credibility and undermined other arguments. Coca-Cola's response to Pepsi-Cola's (apparently false) accusations appropriately used a clearly identified and prominent company spokesperson (Benoit, 1995a), while Sears (Benoit, 1995b) at first used a lawyer. However, other suggestions for image repair discourse are more specific to this particular form of rhetoric.

Second, a person or company who is at fault should probably admit this immediately. Apart from the fact that this is morally the correct thing to do, attempting to deny deserved accusations can backfire. A person or organization who (falsely) denies responsibility for offensive actions can suffer substantially damaged credibility when the truth emerges. The risk is that, when the truth emerges, the accused's reputation will not only be damaged by the offensive action but also by lying about responsibility for that act. For example, President Richard Nixon continually denied any knowledge of the Watergate break-in and subsequent cover-up (Benoit, 1982). He ultimately was forced to resign the presidency. Until the Tower Commission Report was issued, President Reagan continued to deny knowledge of the Iran arms sale, and his popularity declined from 63% to 40%. Only after he admitted that he had made a mistake did his reputation begin to improve (Benoit, Gullifor, & Panici, 1991). Although initially attempting to shift the blame, AT&T eventually accepted responsibility for the interruption in long-distance service, and this probably helped restore its image (Benoit & Brinson, 1994). Pepsi should have apologized for making false accusations against Coke (Benoit, 1995a). It is possible that Union Carbide should have accepted some responsibility for the gas leak and apologized for the damage. Of course, an admission of guilt could exacerbate legal difficulties stemming from the offensive act; see Benoit, 1995a). But I cannot recommend that an organization attempt to deny an accurate accusation.

Of course, those accused of wrong-doing may, in fact, be innocent. Coca-Cola argued effectively that Pepsi's charges that Coke's other customers subsidized McDonald's were false (Benoit, 1995a). Tylenol successfully denied that it had been responsible for deaths to its customers (Benoit & Lindsey, 1987). Furthermore, in many cases there is no way for a critic or other observer to determine if, in fact, the accusations are true. Therefore, if it can be sustained, denial can help to restore a tarnished image.

Fourth, at times it is possible to successfully shift the blame. Tylenol successfully shifted the blame for the poisonings to an unknown person, someone insane (Benoit & Lindsey, 1987). If the "true" cause of the problem is someone else (another person, company, or other organization), making that fact clear to the audience should exonerate the one falsely accused of wrong-doing. So, shifting the blame can be an effective image restoration strategy.

However, shifting the blame cannot be viewed as a certain solution to image problems. President Nixon attempted to shift the blame for Watergate to his subordinates (Benoit, 1982). Even if he was correct that they had initiated the break-in and cover-up, he can still be viewed as ultimately responsible for Watergate, because the guilty people were hand picked by Nixon to be his key aides. Similarly, Exxon attempted to shift the blame for the Valdez oil spill to Captain Hazelwood. The captain had been hired and given command of the Valdez by Exxon, so at best Exxon should have to shoulder responsibility with him (Benoit, 1995a). Notice that in contrast to these instances Kennedy cannot be held responsible for the scenic elements, like the bridge and road construction (Benoit, 1988), and Tylenol cannot be held liable for the actions of an insane person (Benoit & Lindsey, 1987). Hence, it is important when shifting the blame to place it on someone or something clearly disassociated from the accused.

Furthermore, Exxon's attempt to shift the blame for delays in the cleanup to the state of Alaska and the Coast Guard was not accepted. This suggests that the scapegoat must not only be disassociated from the accused, but also must be plausibly responsible for the offensive action. Exxon would have been better off to dwell on the environmental factors (cold, calm sea) that hindered the cleanup and were much more plausible targets for the audience (Benoit, 1995a).

Related to this is the strategy of defeasibility. Kennedy suggested that scenic elements beyond his control (a narrow, unlighted bridge without guard rails built at an angle to the road) were responsible for the Chappaquiddick tragedy (Benoit, 1988; Ling, 1972). Perhaps Union Carbide should have argued that faulty equipment was responsible for the gas leak, which could have led directly into plans for preventing the problem's recurrence (Benoit, 1995a). Of course, because it should have properly maintained its equipment, this could not be expected to completely exonerate them (defeasibility can identify needed corrective action, so these two strategies may be more effective when combined). Similarly, if the factors *ought* to have been under one's control, this is a feeble excuse. Still, if factors beyond one's control can be shown to have cause the offensive act, this may alleviate responsibility and help restore a tarnished image.

Fifth, it can be extremely important to report plans to correct and/or prevent recurrence of the problem. While people frequently want to know whom to blame, it is more reassuring to know that steps have been taken to eliminate or avoid future problems. A firm commitment to correct the problem—repair damage and prevent future problems—is an important component of image restoration discourse. This would be especially important for those who admit responsibility. For example, President Reagan announced changes in personnel and procedures to prevent future problems (Benoit et al., 1991). Similarly, AT&T described in some detail plans for insuring reliability (Benoit & Brinson, 1994). Even those who are not guilty of wrong-doing can benefit from plans for preventing recurrence of the problem. For example, although Tylenol denied responsibility for the deaths from poisoned capsules, they introduced tamper-resistant packaging after the first incident and phased out capsules altogether after the second incident (see Benoit & Lindsey, 1987).

Corrective action has two variants. The accused may attempt to rectify or alleviate the effects of the problem, as Exxon attempted to clean up the oil spill and Union Carbide attempted to help victims in Bhopal (Benoit, 1995a). It is also possible to take action to prevent recurrence of the problem, as President Reagan did (finally) in the Iran-Contra affair (Benoit et al., 1991), as Tylenol did after the poisonings (Benoit & Lindsey, 1987), or as AT&T did after the long distance service interruption (Benoit & Brinson, 1994). In some cases it may be difficult or impractical to correct the effects (e.g., the arms had already been sent to Iran; AT&T's customers have already suffered the inconvenience). However, the importance of preventing a recurrence of the problem cannot be overestimated. For example, Union Carbide's statement recounted several actions to alleviate the suffering of victims, but remained silent on the important question of what, if anything, it had done to prevent a similar tragedy. The fact that another leak occurred later (in West Virginia) underlines the importance of this omission (Benoit, 1995a).

Of course, corrective action cannot assure the success of an image restoration effort. For example, although Exxon boasted of "swift" and "competent" actions, reports revealed that these descriptions were inaccurate (Benoit, 1995a). There is a risk that this strategy will fail—if not backfire—if one's actions clearly do not measure up to one's promises. USAir's version of corrective action—trying to correct the "misperception" that the company was actually safe—was also ineffective. The allegations, and their persuasive support, were too strong for USAir to dismiss as they tried. Corrective action should be sincere and plausible to be effective.

Sixth, minimization cannot always be expected to improve one's image. It is quite possible that Exxon's feeble efforts to minimize the amount of damage may have been counterproductive (Benoit, 1995a). When a person (or company) creates a real problem, we expect them to "'fess" up. Trying to make a serious problem seem trivial can be perceived as unethical, irresponsible, and inappropriate.

Seventh, the use of multiple strategies, one of the characteristics of image restoration discourse identified earlier, can be beneficial to the accused. Union Carbide's plans to alleviate suffering were consistent with the attempts at bolstering, portraying the company as concerned with victims of the tragedy (Benoit, 1995a).

However, use of multiple defensive strategies does not automatically help the accused. In Nixon's "Cambodia" address, he used differentiation and transcendence. These strategies may not be inherently inconsistent, but in this speech, they created conflicting impressions (Benoit, 1995a). Similarly, it is possible that in a defense extended over time with several phases the apologist's changing stance could result in charge of inconsistency.

Eighth, analysis of Union Carbide's defensive discourse concerning the tragedy in Bhopal illustrates the effects of topic salience on image restoration. Despite the fact that the public generally held Union Carbide responsible for thousands of deaths in Bhopal, the (American) public still had a favorable overall opinion of the company (Benoit, 1995a). This is probably because events in a distant land are of relatively less importance to the audience than events in close proximity. Hence salience of the victims to the audience is probably an important factor in image restoration. The closer the audience is to the harm, the harder persuaders will probably have to work to restore their images.

Ninth, multiple defenses can work together. Although the tobacco industry's defenses contained inherent weaknesses, at least there was a unified chorus of voices reinforcing key aspects of the defense. Together, they were marginally more effective than they would have been separately. Similarly, USAir presented a united from: The CEO, pilots, and flight attendants all pronounced the airline safe. Of course, had the ground crew joined in with a letter of their own—especially given the fact that some of the allegations concerned deficiencies in repairs—it would have been more effective.

Finally, we must recognize that the powers of persuasion—and the theory of image restoration—are limited. For example, given the mistakes and poor choices made immediately after the accident, there was little that could be done to restore Exxon's image after the Valdez oil spill—other than wait until most consumers had forgotten the incident. Perhaps a firm commitment to preventing similar disasters in the future would have helped more than firing Captain Hazelwood, but the reports of the inept cleanup efforts were a powerful detriment to Exxon's image (Benoit, 1995a). Similarly, President Nixon could have not expected the entire country to rally around his invasion of Cambodia, although he could have arguably contained the damage more effectively (Benoit, 1995a).

CONTRIBUTION TO CRISIS COMMUNICATION THEORY

This chapter reviews the fruits of a research program applying the theory of Image Restoration Discourse to corporate crisis communication. Several specific suggestions are developed for handling crisis communication situations. Recommendations for precrisis preparation are discussed. Whereas a particular crisis is likely to be unexpected, a company can often anticipate the kinds of crises that are the most likely threats to its image. Next, I explain why it is so important to correctly identify the precise nature of the specific threat to an organization's image that emerges in a crisis situation. Third, I argue that there are often multiple audiences in a crisis situation, and identification of the most important audience(s) for the firm is another vital aspect of successful image repair. Finally, nine specific suggestions for successful image repair discourse are drawn out of the review of past research on corporate crisis communication and Image Restoration Theory.

BEST PRACTICES

Review of the research on Image Restoration Discourse has revealed instances in which corporate crisis communicators have responded to crisis situations effectively. I would single out as particularly praiseworthy three of the image repair efforts reviewed here. First, Tylenol's response to the poisoning was exemplary. Despite predictions that the brand name was dead, this company managed to persuasively surmount this obstacle. The fact that the company was not at fault (a madman had poisoned the capsules) and that it responded appropriately made this a successful instance of crisis communication. Second, AT&T (after initial, brief, missteps) provided an effective response to a crisis of its own making. Once again appropriate corrective action helped its image problem. Finally, Coca-Cola's skirmishes with Pepsi-Cola left Coke the winner of these "PR Wars." If there is a "Hall of Shame" in crisis communication, I would nominate Exxon (primarily because management appeared to ignore the oil spill), Sears (for instituting corrective action less than a week after it protested its total innocence), and USAir (for suggesting the only problem that needed correcting was consumers' perceptions of nonexistent problems).

CONCLUSION

This chapter has described the theory of image restoration discourse (Benoit, 1995a) and analyzed research applying this approach to image repair efforts in politics, sports/entertainment, and corporate realms. Then, specific suggestions for those who encounter communication crises are developed, illustrating how this theory can guide practitioners in such situations. Contributions to the theory of crisis communication and best (and worst) practices are also discussed.

18

Exigencies, Explanations, and Executions: Toward a Dynamic Theory of the Crisis Communication Genre

Susan Schultz Huxman
Wichita State University

Since the inception of the study of rhetorical genres, analogies to the study of evolutionary biology have proliferated. Aristotle, the father of rhetorical genres, who was also a noted scientist and taxonomist, advanced the word "species" to describe the types of discourse humans were hardwired to produce and "found" three—*epideictic* (ceremonial discourse), *deliberative* (political discourse), and *forensic* (judicial discourse) (*On Rhetoric*, trans. L. Cooper, 1932). Campbell and Jamieson (1978), early practitioners of generic criticism, argued that: "Biologists speak of the genetic code inherent in the germ plasm[a] of each species. Although there will be variations, that code is the internal dynamic which determines the biological form of the individual member of the species. The internal dynamic of a genre is similar" (pp. 24–25).

Although some scholars (e.g., Conley, 1986) have derided the explanatory power of this comparison, I find the connection useful. If we conceive of rhetorical genres as families of discourse that share a dynamic core of rhetorical choices, it invites scholars to do two things at the very least: (a) excavate carefully the rhetorical terrain that distinguishes a family of discourse in order to yield a more sophisticated analysis of the conventional "markers" of any singular artifact within a genre, (b) be on the look out for rhetorical "hybrids," for though they may temporarily confound an existing classificatory scheme, the hybrid's discovery pushes a generic system to see its parameters as fluid and dynamic, not confining and static.

Some genres are so complex and "high stakes" that they require a special kind of rhetorical maneuvering and critical assessment. One such animal is what Aristotle called an *apologia*—or what we label today as the rhetoric of self-defense, damage-control, image-repair, or crisis management.
This essay aims to: excavate the rhetorical terrain that distinguishes the *apologia* as a hybrid of the classical species of speech; demarcate the various
discoveries of many valuable, but as yet disparate, typologies in the crisis
communication literature; and outline a dynamic theory for the study of *apologia* that is linked to the Aristotelian rhetorical tradition and addresses
how the type of crisis influences the corporate climate/personality profile
and the communication strategies adopted by apologists.

THE "MARKERS" OF APOLOGIA

Even Aristotle was puzzled with how to categorize the speech of self-
defense. Campbell and Huxman (2003) observed that Aristotle never dignified the rhetorical form by giving it separate *species* status, but they noted
that an *apologia* shares features of all three classical genres making it a potent rhetorical hybrid. Specifically, we contended, as *forensic discourse*,
apologists must ask for revised judgments of their past actions. They must
redefine the reality portrayed by their accusers and deal in "*questions of
fact*"—Was an act (misdeed, crime) committed? But apologists are not performing in a courtroom in front of jurors and a judge and so do not seek justice per se. As *deliberative discourse*, apologists must wrest argumentative
control over the alleged misdeed from the hands of their accusers if they
wish to survive and recover politically or economically.

The very definition of *apologia* used by some scholars in the field grant it a
special kind of political power. Hearit (cited in Elwood, 1995b) argued that
"At root within any *kategoria/apologia* exchange is the attempt to assert definitional hegemony or terminological control over the interpretation of an
act" (p. 130). But apologists are not appealing to voters per se, nor aim to
present "*questions of policy*" in problem–solution form to make an expedient
case. As *epideictic discourse*, apologists engage in image repair, seeking to restore their honor by treating "*questions of value*" in front of observers who exercise their voyeur tendencies in what can best be described as a spectacle
of rhetorical grace or awkwardness under fire. But apologists are consumed
with the past, not the present, and the ceremonial expectations of voicing
noncontroversial themes to an audience comprised of a community of believers does not describe the *apologia* either. Its indebtedness to all three genres,
but its allegiance to none, makes the *apologia* a challenging rhetorical hybrid
to create and critique (Campbell & Huxman, 2003, pp. 293–294).

Scholars have returned to the Aristotelian rhetorical tradition to study
the deliberative and epideictic features of presidential military crises. Dow

(1989) echoing Cherwitz and Zagacki (1986) argued there are two types of presidential crisis rhetoric, one emphasizing communal understanding and the other, which strives for policy approval. Campbell and Jamieson (1990) sharpened the straddling of justificatory and consummatory rhetoric in identifying five characteristics of crisis war rhetoric and suggested that when presidents engage in crisis rhetoric designed to forestall impeachment they must resort to a forensic defense. Johnson and Sellnow (1995) examined the deliberative features of crisis in organizations. But none of these works goes so far as to consider *apologia* a hybrid genre sharing components of all three of the classical genres. Such complexity and scope gives the genre rhetorical force because it is grounded in the three questions that are the foundation of all persuasive discourse: fact (the signature of forensic discourse), value (the signature of epideictic discourse), and policy (the signature of deliberative discourse). I argue that even the argumentative resources advanced by Ware and Linkugel (1973), Benoit and Brinson (1994; Benoit, 1995a) and others align with each of these persuasive questions. "Denial" and "Evading Responsibility," for instance, are apologetic resources aligned with a forensic setting. "Bostering" and "Mortification" are apologetic resources aligned with the epideictic setting. "Transcendence" and "Corrective Action" are apologetic resources aligned with the deliberative setting. More connections along these lines are made in the final section of this chapter.

One implication of this discovery for public relations practitioners and academicians alike, is that it invites a scrutiny of how a damage-control campaign plays out in all three arenas simultaneously. For instance, I would argue that the Clinton intern scandal was part tele-spectacle, part bully pulpit and part "exhibit A." Even the most casual observer would note that the President's self-defense took place in "secret" Grand Jury testimony (forensic discourse), in media displays to the public (epideictic discourse), and in the House Judiciary Committee and the Impeachment Debate on Capitol Hill (deliberative discourse). Clinton, himself, alluded to all three venues in his August 17th speech. References to the forensic venue are most common with words like "deposition," "Grand Jury," "evidence," "unlawful action," "law suit," "independent council," "investigation" (repeated 4 times), and "fact" (repeated 3 times). The deliberative genre is invoked with position statements of *transcendence* such as: "It is time to stop the pursuit of personal destruction and the prying into private lives and get on with our national life. Our country has been distracted by this matter for too long ... we have important work to do. Real opportunities to seize. Real problems to solve. Real security matters to face." And yet, strikingly, Clinton closes his address with a reminder of the scandal's epideictic importance. He says, "And so tonight, I ask *you to turn away from the spectacle* [italics added] of the past seven months."

Another example of how a crisis campaign plays out in all three classically inspired arenas simultaneously is the congressional hearings on the Bridgestone/Firestone tire recall case in September 2000. This crisis became the largest product defect case of the past decade, in part, because it implicated three organizations simultaneously: Firestone and its faulty ATX and Wilderness tires; the Ford Explorer and its roll-over tendencies; and the NHTSA and its lack of vigilance over the years as the death toll mounted. As sobering statistics came to light (1400 official complaints, 148 fatalities, 500 injuries), Congress launched a special investigation in late August to "hear testimony regarding the recall" and "examine ways to speed the detection of defective products" (U. S. Senate, 2000, www.senate.gov), wording that underscored the expectation for a rhetorical hybrid.

That directive set the stage for epideictic, forensic, and deliberative discourse, or the *apologia* hybrid. Each organization's apologist (Firestone, Ford, and NHTSA), although facing different charges against them, made strikingly similar statements that began and ended in the epideictic vein ("deep regret," "sympathy," "terrible accidents," "personal responsibility," "valuable lessons," "thank you for this opportunity") made cursory overtures to the forensic venue ("there is no conclusive cause at this time," "personal injury and lawsuits," "the facts will show"), and concentrated primarily on the deliberative arena ("We are undertaking the following actions"). This rhetorical progression was altogether fitting given the location (capitol hill), the audience (legislators), and the charge drafted by the house and senate subcommittees (find remedies). An analysis of the specific strategies used by the major apologists to fulfill the requirements of these classical forms is detailed in a later section of this chapter.

DISPARATE TYPOLOGIES OF CRISES, CULTURES, COMMUNICATIONS

Because Aristotle never dignified *apologia* as a rhetorical form with separate *species* status, our theories of crisis communication tend to disconnect from the classical tradition. Furthermore, much of the current scholarship still constitutes a great divide between public relations and public address scholars. The former preferring to call the genre "crisis management," study corporate communication as a process and draft "crisis plans." The latter preferring to call the genre "*apologia*," study communication as an act and critique speeches. Taken together, much of the current scholarship in crisis communication provides valuable insight on important, but often isolated, characteristics of the high stakes public relations of reputation repair. Three of the many lines of inquiry that have been important to theory building in crisis communication involve enumerating crisis scenarios, describing corporate and personal identities, and naming self-defense strategies.

One fundamental line of inquiry has worked toward identifying the various types of crises, outlining the diverse situational predicaments that put individuals and entities on the defense. For instance, Mitroff and Killman (1984) advanced seven scenarios of corporate "evil," including product tampering, defective product, piracy of product, victim of false accusations, perils of insular thinking, hoax, and cultural insensitivity. Barton (1993, 2001) identified many types of crisis, including terrorism, vicious rumors, product tampering, environmental accident, contaminated product, industrial accident, deceptive advertising, consumer fraud, employee embezzlement, violent crime on the premises, illegal activities, immoral activities, and CEO gaffe. Others like Fearn-Banks (1996) added more distinctive scenarios including, rumor and celebrities and crisis. Bennett (1981) proposed that crisis situations should be plotted on an axis that charts both its seriousness and specificity in order to determine an appropriate defense tactic. The severity of the accusatory climate has also been addressed by such scholars as Barton (2001), Hearit (1995b) and this author (Huxman & Bruce, 1995), the latter advancing five polar conditions related to the nature of charges of wrongdoing, including whether they are major/minor, ambiguous/clear, singular/multiple, precedent/unprecedented, and whether they are transmitted by powerful/powerless sources. All of these studies underscored the importance of the accusatory situation as an exigency (Bitzer, 1969) that frames, if not dictates, apologetic responses and public perception.

A second line of inquiry has functioned to expose the underlying ethos or organizational climate that frames response to crisis. These advancements, although less cohesive as a group than those stemming from the first line of inquiry, nonetheless, offer valuable explanations for how the values embedded in corporate cultures shape their response patterns. For instance, Fisher (1970) argued that four motive states exist in all forms of rhetorical discourse: affirmation, reaffirmation, purification, and subversion. Apologia, or crisis management, he argued, typically stems from the motive of purification. Based on Fisher's work, Ryan (1988) contended that any one of these four motive states might explain the choices rhetors make to repair their image. Kruse (1977) borrowing from Maslow's hierarchy of needs, proposed that one of three motives typify crisis communication: survival, social, or self-actualized states. Hearit (1995b) collapsed this distinction into one overriding motive: the need to regain social legitimacy. Other findings cluster around "postures" (Ware & Linkugel, 1973), "bases of legitimacy" (Harrel, Ware, & Linkugel, 1975), "master stories" (Courtright, 1995; Hurst, 1995), "myths" (Hearit, 1995b), and "personality profiles" (Bridges, 1992; Downs, 1997; Mitroff, 1990). All are interested in examining the various apologetic roles that rhetors project before, during and after the course of their damage-control campaigns.

A third line of inquiry, and clearly a prolific area of research, has involved naming types of recurring communication strategies; examining exactly how corporate entities execute their self-defense. Ware and Linkugel (1973) identified four "factors of self-defense": denial, bolstering, differentiation, and transcendence. Benoit (1995a; Benoit & Brinson, 1994) further subdivided these factors of self-defense, positing five "image restoration strategies": denial, evading responsibility, reducing offensiveness, mortification, and corrective action. Ryan (1982) recalled the classical argument types of fact, definition, quality, and jurisdiction. Cheney (1983) posited three "identification strategies"—association, disassociation, and transcendence. Hearit (1995) identified four "differentiation bifurcations": appearance/reality, opinion/knowledge, individual/group, and act/essence. Sellnow and Ulmer (1995) focused on how and why the strategy of equivocation works for corporate defenders. These researchers share the desire to examine closely the rhetorical choices at the level of the text and are most sensitive to the message dimensions of the *apologia*.

All of these works have contributed enormously to case study examinations of political, religious, celebrity, sports, and corporate *apologia* since the 1970s. And yet these various conceptualizations are limiting because they too often stand alone (Seeger, Sellnow, & Ulmer, 1998); authors rarely cite each other (Benoit, 1995a), nor do they take into account the dynamic between types of crisis, types of personality profiles and types of communication strategies (Coombs, 1999b). This theoretical disconnect is not an indictment of the crisis communication literature per se; it plagues many other areas of communication theory as well, in part, due to the vastness of our field (Craig, 1999). That is no excuse to shrink from a formidable challenge, however. What our theories of crisis communication must continue to address more urgently is *the interaction of situational exigencies, explanatory postures, and argumentative executions*. The motive states of apologists interact with argument types and are framed by situational constraints. The dynamic of this hybrid genre will be preserved when we advance theoretical matrices to capture these elements.

TOWARD A DYNAMIC THEORY OF THE GENRE

If a genre is a collection of "recognizable forms bound together by an internal dynamic" and if a genre is given its character from a "fusion of forms, not by its individual elements" (Campbell & Jamieson, 1978, p. 7), it instructs us to advance frameworks for understanding how the type of crisis influences an apologist's role and the various rhetorical resources the apologist utilizes. This can be accomplished in at least two ways: Mine the existing typologies for more nuanced observations that recall the genre's classical heritage, and show through case study application how exigencies, explanations, and executions coalesce in the *apologia* genre.

In terms of crises typologies, we must move beyond nature and extent of crisis in order to capture its rhetorical features. Remembering that crisis is both an act (an empirical event) and a construct (perceptual and symbolic), we would do well to plot *"crisis severity indices"* that would catalogue such things as *nature, extent, clarity, precedence, visual dimension, power, control of a crisis, and technology and intercultural dimensions of a crisis* (see Table 18.1 below). In this way, scholars can be reminded of their duty to examine *Kategoria* and *Apologia* as a speech set; to treat attack and defense with equal measure as Aristotle instructed. It reminds us too of how powerful situational exigencies are to a genre we call "self-*defense*" and "rapid *response* discourse."

For instance, in terms of crisis control, we know that an airline crash takes on a very different rhetorical challenge for its apologists if the crash is attributable to weather or pilot error. Interestingly, the "paradigm cases" of good crisis management (Johnson & Johnson and the Tylenol Cyanide Poisonings) and bad crisis management (Exxon and the Valdez Oil spill) had everything to do with the corporation's "control" of the crisis or lack thereof. J & J's inability to control a crisis of product sabotage gave their "victim" role legitimacy; Exxon's perceived gross negligence due, in part, to a drunken captain ruled out a victim's stance, heightened the ugliness of the attacks against them, and prompted a "stonewalling" tactic on the part of its CEO. Procter & Gamble had weak control (little culpability) over its satanic rumor crisis; Texaco had strong control (high culpability) over its racial discrimination crisis.

The visual dimension of a crisis is another critical aspect that deserves increased scrutiny. The Firestone–Ford tire recall crisis, the Exxon Valdez spill, the ValuJet crash in the Everglades, the Union Carbide Bhopal gas

TABLE 18.1
Crisis Severity Index

	Weak	Moderate	Strong
Nature of Crisis			
Extent of Crisis			
Clarity of Crisis			
Precedence of Crisis			
Power of Accusers			
Control of Crisis			
Visual Dimension of Crisis			
Technology Dimension of Crisis			
Intercultural Dimension of Crisis			

leak, the Texas A&M bonfire tragedy, the Grucci fireworks explosion all
stand in sharp contrast to Perrier and the benzene contaminant, Intel and
the defective computer chip, Sears and auto-repair fraud, United Way and
employee extortion. In the former cases, the visual dimension is "strong"; in
the latter it is "weak." In the hyper-mediated age in which we live, this index
is especially important. The visual accoutrements of the electronic era have
produced a new model of persuasion, giving rise to a new rhetorical imperative. Erickson (1998) reminded us that visually absorbing images, as opposed to talk, are more likely to capture a spectator's attention and reach
mass audiences, that oral explanations overwhelm and tire listeners, and
that speeches are some of the worst ways to make the news. Eloquence in
any forum is increasingly visual, not verbal.

The Clinton scandal reminds us of the importance of visual dimensions.
More people are likely to remember the visual moments of the Clinton
scandal than any words from a speech, press conference, or jury testimony. Even though Clinton's most memorable words are probably those
uttered in a press conference on January 26th: "I did not have sexual relations with that woman, Miss Lewinsky," we are still more likely to remember it for Clinton's finger-wagging. The Clinton–Lewinsky embrace in the
crowd scene played in slow-motion ad nauseam stands out as the single
most significant image. Clinton's lower-lip biting and folded prayer-like
hands is an image that take a close second in the *apologia* album, as it became the visual imprint for a host of late-night talk shows. A dizzying
array of other images gave the scandal all the telespectacle, excessive display, and persuasive evocation to titillate spectators for some time. Clinton wanted us to "turn away from this spectacle." What for? The visual dimension of the crisis gave the *kategoria-apologia* its most entertaining
qualities. This scandal gave us colorful displays of what is public and what
is morality. We experienced a communal longing for simpler days while
absorbing in near drunken stupor all the graphic details that New Technology could offer. Perhaps the most telling evidence that the Clinton *apologia* should be viewed as epideictic melodrama, a welcome respite from
the demands of daily life, was the collective longing for the story voiced
by many pundits in the wake of ethnic cleansing in Kosovo and school violence in Littleton.

The power of the accusers in a crisis is another critical element often
overlooked in the analysis of damage control campaigns. In presidential crises, Campbell and Jamieson (1990) reminded us that there is enormous difference in the power of the accusers in rhetoric to forestall impeachment
versus a rhetoric of impeachment, the former giving the presidential apologist great latitude in framing a defense and diminishing the voice of Congress, the latter virtually "gagging" the president and elevating the credibility of the Congress to judge and jury.

Dow Chemical refused to respond seriously to the charges of manufacturing an immoral chemical weapon (Napalm) in large measure because the major accusers were college students, not high profile political leaders or even the media. Dow Corning underestimated the power of its accusers—women, mostly housewives with little political clout—to mount an effective legal battle against their defective product, the Dalkon Shield. The Firestone Tire Defect case is especially interesting in this regard. Tread separation on Firestone tires was first reported by a local TV news station in Houston 4 years ago. For the next 3 years, only one TV station in Chicago reported on the tire separation problem, even though the accidents—and lawsuits—were piling up. Still, the national press was virtually silent. Not until July 31st, 2001, did the story finally become national news. After *USA Today* legitimized the story, the media feeding frenzy was on. The death count by now had surpassed 100. On August 9th, Firestone bowed to the pressure and recalled more than 6 million tires (*Brill's Content*, Jan. 2001). In an information age, when even the trivial is magnified, it may appear peculiar that this crisis took so long to surface nationally, except that there was no celebrity victim, no obvious villain, and importantly, no real powerful media accuser until a national newspaper took up the cause.

The power of accusers is often heightened in a crisis when hidden recording devices or other high-tech means are used. To give its story more "punch," NBC DateLine went undercover to air its case about Food Lion and meat packaging contamination. Video of rotted meat being repackaged is revolting, but highly credible. Most viewers believe pictures don't lie. Texaco's racial discrimination crisis ballooned when audio-tapes of executives using racial slurs were produced, even though the tapes garbled key testimony. Bob Knight lost his fight in the court of public opinion and prompted Indiana University to impose sanctions on his behavior when videotape of his throat-hold on one of his basketball players was released to the media and shown repeatedly. The Clinton scandal really became a crisis on the campaign trail when Jennifer Flowers produced an audio-tape of her conversations with the then Arkansas governor. Linda Tripp used a similar strategy to entrap Clinton in the Lewinsky matter. Both of these women had low credibility as accusers until visual and audio evidence was produced. The Internet, in particular, has instantaneously turned the disenchantment of isolated N. I. M. B. Y's into a potent force. The accusations against Intel's defective chip, for instance, started with an Internet group and quickly gained adherents via email. Some websites, such as publiccitizen.org allow the ineffectual single accuser to find like minds and build a large following rather effortlessly.

The precedence of a crisis can be an important mitigating factor too. When the House voted articles of impeachment against Andrew Johnson in 1867, "it created an unprecedented situation. . . . Never before had the constitutional right of the House to impeach been used successfully against a president. Given its unprecedented character, [rhetors] were forced into a contest over the nature of the process ... [they] struggled to determine whether this proceeding was a trial, an inquest, a judicial proceeding, or something else altogether" (Campbell & Jamieson, 1990, p. 147). In the end, the newness of the scenario lessened president Johnson's rhetorical burden considerably.

In the corporate sector, the precedence of a crisis has played a large role. Admittedly, J & J responded effectively to the cyanide poisonings in the Chicago area from their product, Tylenol, but given that product sabotage was such a new type of crisis, that crisis plans for this sort of thing in the corporate sector were virtually nonexistent, analysts were far less critical that J & J had no crisis plan and heaped extensive praise on the company for their decision to mount a multifaceted corrective action plan so early.

Failures in crisis management can be minimized due to this situational factor too. Dow Chemical and its manufacturing of "immoral agents of war," Three Mile-Island and the nuclear power plant failure, and NASA and the Challenger tragedy all were extraordinary, unprecedented crises that must be taken into consideration before labeling their words and actions as disastrous. Conversely, product contaminant, defect, and recall crises are given very little slack by industry analysts because they are not unusual. Without a quick, comprehensive rapid response campaign, companies like Jack-in-the-Box, Odwalla Juice, Perrier, Pepsi, Sara Lee, and many others would have been harshly criticized because there is such strong rhetorical precedence for these scenarios.

Intercultural challenges can also effect the situational climate adversely. Union Carbide exacerbated the Bhopal gas leak tragedy when its American C.E.O. did not understand Indian customs and promptly landed in jail shortly after setting foot on Indian soil. Firestone/Bridgestone contributed to their difficulties in defending themselves on Capitol Hill without understanding the importance of cultivating political support. As a Japanese-owned company, it found itself without allies because its foreign C.E.O. had not even met its congressional representatives in Tennessee!

These various components of the crisis severity index remind us that exigencies are complex and dynamic and impact the rhetorical posture and tactics used by apologists. The index encourages a more sophisticated assessment of the *Kategoria* and allows for a determination of an individual's or a corporation's rhetorical challenge in framing a defense. As both empirical event and symbolic construct, crisis casts a long shadow on a rhetoric of response.

Corporate climate or personality profile is another nuanced component of *apologia* that can be linked specifically to the three Aristotelian genres and packaged with certain communication strategies. Although apologists assume many roles consistent with their personality in responding to crisis, at least three overriding explanatory postures persist. Each is aligned with an Aristotelian "species" or "arena" of discourse as detailed in Tables 18.2, 18.3, & 18.4. As outlined in the "markers of *apologia*" section of the paper, the genre is an amalgam of three classical rhetorical forms. Here, those forms are personified. As a *Pragmatist*, an apologist assumes a political profile that focuses on issues of policy, seeks expedient measures of action, emphasizes the future, and is targeted to "voters" or audiences who leverage action. As a *Friend*, an apologist assumes an expressive profile that focuses on issues of value, seeks to honor self and perhaps dishonor accusers, emphasizes the present moment, and is targeted to "mere observers" or audiences who function as spectators of high drama. As a *Defendant*, an apologist assumes a legal profile that focuses on issues of fact, seeks justice, emphasizes the past, and is targeted to "jurors" or audiences who mete out sanctions. These are not static or schizophrenic postures. Apologists move, often rapidly and seamlessly, from one of these postures to the next. Well-crafted *apologia* showcase that the transference of roles makes for a more sophisticated rhetorical transaction, not a disruptive or insincere one.

TABLE 18.2
Type of Explanations: Pragmatist Posture

PRAGMATIST:	Persona: An apologist who emphasizes a political response
	Aim: Expediency/Inexpedience
	Time: Future
	Issue: Question of Policy
	Audience: Voters

TABLE 18.3
Type of Explanations: Friend Posture

FRIEND:	Persona: An apologist who emphasizes an expressive response
	Aim: Praise or Blame
	Time: Present
	Issue: Question of Value
	Audience: Observers

TABLE 18.4
Type of Explanations: Defendant Posture

DEFENDANT	Persona: An apologist who emphasizes a legal response
	Aim: Justice/Injustice
	Time: Past
	Issue: Question of Fact
	Audience: Jurors

These overarching image projections emphasize one of the enduring rhetorical arenas stipulated by Aristotle. The adoption of any one posture (*friend, defendant, pragmatist*) is largely dependent on the exigency and its various indices as outlined previously. However, these postures are also dependent on the rhetorical predisposition of the apologist. Scholarship on open versus closed organizational cultures (e.g., Bridges, 1992; Downs, 1997; Hurst, 1995) tells us that when in trouble corporations most likely resort to a *rhetoric of inertia*—what was comfortable in communicating to external constituencies before a crisis will most likely be "the path of least resistance" during a crisis.

Further, such profiles, whether adopted by corporate apologists, sport, celebrity, religious, or political apologists are coupled with specific communication strategies to give substance to the form. Twelve such arguments or *executions* are advanced here. The aim here is not to reinvent the work of Ware and Linkugel, Benoit, Ryan, or others in naming apologetic strategies; Rather, it is to simplify the labeling, be more complete than any one existing typology, and cluster strategies in order to track an emergent posture and to capture the dynamic interplay of the genre. The forensic arena is most hospitable to *jurisdiction, stonewalling, denial, and equivocation.* The deliberative arena is compatible with *transcendence, corrective action, extenuating circumstances, and minimization.* The epideictic arena leans toward *confession, bolstering, counterattack, and scapegoating.* See Tables 18.5, 18.6, 18.7.

These response types linked to postures are not fixed associations, but tendencies. Clearly, apologists are not bound to these clusters. The nature of genres is that patterns of usage develop, but never in a rigid, "paint-by-numbers" way that denies a rhetor's unique imprint. And, as already demonstrated, apologists often move from one rhetorical arena to another in the course of a damage control campaign. Concomitantly, the clustering of individual arguments changes as well. Still, a clustering approach to the rhetorical executions of an *apologia* allows the crisis analyst to move beyond description (what responses are used?) to analysis (why are these responses used together?). It recognizes that certain rhetorical choices form

TABLE 18.5
Type of Executions: Deliberative Responses

Political Responses
   —Transcendence
    "There are more important issues . . ."
   —Corrective Action
    "Here's what we are doing so this won't happen again."
   —Extenuating Circumstances
    "Understand we were in an unusual circumstance."
   —Minimization
    "This isn't as bad as it appears."

TABLE 18.6
Type of Executions: Epideictic Responses

Expressive Responses
—Confession
"I'm very sorry."
—Bolstering
"We're like you; we cherish safety . . ."
—Counter-Attack
"Let's look at who's bringing these charges."
—Scapegoating
"We are not to blame; our competitors are."

TABLE 18.7
Type of Executions: Forensic Responses

Legal Responses
—Denial
"We didn't do it."
—Stonewalling
"No comment."
—Jurisdiction
"This is not an issue that can be treated well in the public realm;
it's technical and needs to be sorted out by our legal team."
—Equivocation
"Mistakes were made and it is unclear at this time. . . ."

"constellations" more naturally than other configurations. The typical political responses capture the policy (corrective action, transcendence) and expedient (extenuating circumstances, minimization) expectations of the deliberative genre. The typical expressive responses capture the praise (confession, bolstering) and blame (counterattack, scapegoating) features of the epideictic genre. All of the typical legal responses (denial, stonewalling, jurisdiction, and equivocation) capture the guarded nature of the forensic genre. As a legal team swarms around an apologist, these insular remarks prevail until the "defendant" gets "his day in court."

The major apologists in the Congressional hearings on Firestone's tire recall, Masatoshi Ono, CEO of Bridgestone/Firestone and Jac Nasser CEO of Ford Motor Company, show how these various executions work. Firestone relied heavily on confession and bolstering in Ono's opening and closing remarks in its effort to play "friend" and identify with the values of American citizens. He opened with a remarkably candid and extensive confession: "As chief executive officer, I come before you to apologize to you, the American people and especially to the families who have lost loved ones in these terrible rollover accidents. I also come to accept full and personal responsibility on behalf of Bridgestone/Firestone for the events that led to this hearing. Whenever people are hurt or fatally injured in automobile accidents, it is tragic." In closing, Ono used bolstering: "This year Firestone is observing its 100th anniversary. It is a proud history. Henry Ford used Firestone tires on the original model-T. For 100 years, millions of families have placed their trust and faith in the good people of Firestone. We feel a heavy responsibility to make certain that we are worthy still of your continued trust and confidence." Ono never used the forensic strategies of denial, stonewalling, or jurisdiction, although he once used equivocation ("I am not able to give you a conclusive cause at this time"). In essence, he chose not to play the role of defendant in this setting. The primary strategy Ono used, however, was corrective action. The body of the speech is a laundry list of action items that begins: "On August 8, we met with the NHTSA. . . . On the following day, August 9, Bridgestone/Firestone announced a voluntary safety recall of 6.5 million tires. Since that time, our highest priorities have been to complete the recall as quickly as possible . . ." It is Firestone's pragmatist profile, its allegiance to the deliberative arena, that gives its rhetoric of response its real identity, though its friend profile in the opening and close was crucial in humanizing the organization (www.house.gov/commerce).

Ford, on the other hand, took a decidedly different tack in executing its friend role. It never engaged in confession, but emphasized bolstering to extremes. Strangely, the *apologia* begins with a bolstering sales pitch that fails to acknowledge the severity and extent of the crisis: "Good afternoon. I am Jac Nasser, President and CEO of Ford Motor Company. I have been with Ford Motor Company for more than 30 years in a variety of positions around the world. I am proud of the great contributions Ford Motor Company has made to improving [sic] the standard of living of millions of people around the world. I am driven to make sure that everything we do serves all customers and clearly their safety is uppermost on our minds." Unlike Firestone, Ford adopted the defendant role and used the forensic strategies of denial ("The Explorer is one of the safest SUVs on the road. Proof of this is our exemplary safety record over the last decade. The most recent data from the Department of Transportation show that the Explorer has a lower fatality rate than both the average passenger car and competitive SUV, as shown in Attachment 1.") and jurisdiction. ("This is a tire issue, not a vehicle issue"; "It is important to clarify that there are several types of performance data maintained by tire manufacturers that are not regularly available to auto companies"). Like Firestone, Ford's primary strategy was corrective action ("We have taken extraordinary steps to support this recall and ensure the safety of our customers. We are working relentlessly to find and replace bad tires with good tires") though it also engaged in a tedious use of extenuating circumstances ("Looking back, the first signs of trouble came in Saudi Arabia . . . the tire failures were due to external causes ... Another market where we experienced tire problems is Venezuela. The situation in Venezuela is complicated by the fact that about three-quarters of the tires were locally produced") (www.house.gov/commerce).

By identifying these executions and showing how they align with fitting explanatory postures, one is able to conclude that in this "snapshot" of the damage-control campaign Firestone blended its friend and pragmatist profiles artistically. The crisis was clear, extensive, carried by powerful forces, and was visually compelling. What better way than to express sincere regret and show admirable action. Ford tried to do too much. Nassar used too many strategies for one *apologia* and adopted all three postures perfunctorily. Arguably, Ford's forensic posture was a gamble for this venue. Granted, Ford needed to separate itself from Firestone and to identify the jurisdiction of each company in order to prove its innocence, but its forensic responses (especially denial) appeared strained. And the clarity, severity, and visually compelling nature of the roll-over factor gave the epideictic profile filled with self-congratulations an awkward feel. And yet, Ford was helped enormously by understanding the deliberative arena better than Firestone. Put simply, Ford had allies on Capitol Hill; Firestone did not. That situational exigency alone may have accounted for the rhetorical latitude of their defense.

It is the crisis analyst's job to track the interaction of situational exigencies, explanatory postures and argumentative executions in order to understand the genre's rhetorical force. For instance, when the crisis is marked by uncertainty along several indices, it may foster the adoption of a defendant role framed by the forensic arena and provoke one or more of the four legal responses. When the accusatory climate is marked by clear charges, then such things as the extent, visual dimension, and precedence of the crisis along with the power of the accuser may factor in whether an apologist adopts one role over another and engages in argumentative battle from an expedient, social or legal set of responses. My critical analysis of the Dow chemical company and its crisis concerning napalm production during the Vietnam War revealed that its primary arguments of jurisdiction and denial were an outgrowth of its closed corporate culture and an exigence marked by a clear and extensive crisis event, but unprecedented charges coming from weak accusers. In this case, it would appear that the symbolic features of the crisis "trumped" the empirical features in terms of Dow's adoption of a defendant profile.

The Clinton scandal presents rich opportunities for mining the interaction of situational exigencies, explanatory postures and argumentative executions. Clinton's precrisis empathic posture (open, sensitive, "I feel your pain") gave way to a radically different defensive postcrisis posture (closed, evasive, "I will not dignify that with a response"). What accounted for this about face from amiable friend to embattled defendant? The nature of the crisis itself as Clinton and his team perceived it. This was at first a tiresome (another rumored affair), silly (a White house intern), ambiguous ("He said, she said"), and politically motivated ("vast right-wing conspiracy") charge. What better way to meet the charge then to invoke denial ("I did not have sexual relations with that woman") and jurisdiction ("even Presidents have private lives") and equivocation ("It depends what 'it' means") and frame the event in the forensic arena.

As charges became clearer (DNA on dress) and more serious (articles of impeachment drawn up), the Clinton and Starr forces went into battle for definitional supremacy in the deliberative arena with Starr hammering corrective action (impeachment) while Clinton talked transcendence (giving a State of the Union Address that virtually ignored the furry of scandal). As the crisis deepened and the "noose tightened," a virtual parade of disputants were drawn into the maelstrom to clash about issues of value (Was it an affair or a crime? Was it about morality or the rule of law?) and to debate policy issues (Should he be impeached or censured?) During this stage of the crisis, Clinton desperately tried to play pragmatist; to be commander-in-chief and engage in corrective action on an entirely different issue (Terrorists must pay for their actions; bombing in Africa will commence).

The media, meanwhile, framed the entire "encounter" from the opening act to the final curtain call as a titillating spectacle played out in the epideictic arena. And, ultimately, Clinton was at a loss to address *arete* (moral excellence) the topic required for this stage. His opportunity in the August 17th speech to make a confession, to display human failing and regret, missed the note of sincerity with the passive "*it*" was wrong and "*it* constituted a critical lapse of judgment . . ." [italics added]. His bolstering attempts were surprisingly few and fragmented, with a fleeting reference to "protecting my own family," "taking complete responsibilities for all my actions both public and private," and "answer[ing] questions truthfully." His attempt to appear noble at the end: "I ask you to turn away from the spectacle of the past seven months, to repair the fabric of our national discourse" rings hollow because most of this short speech is devoted to the counterattack of the independent council. In fact, every short paragraph contains at least one such blaming tactic, ranging from "these questions were being asked in a politically inspired law suit . . . ," to "now the investigation itself is under investigation," to "This has gone on too long, cost too much, and hurt too many innocent people," and "stop the pursuit of personal destruction and the prying into private lives." The best expressive display Clinton could muster, reminiscent of a theatrical stage narrator, was his close: "Thank you for *watching*. . . ." [italics added]. In this *apologia*, because blame overshadows praise the friend persona never fully emerged.

CONCLUSION

As a species of speech, *apologia* has an "internal dynamic," a "code" that must be carefully excavated for its distinctive and recurring "markers" to be codified. By reconnecting the study of *apologia* to its classical roots, we can account for its symbolic power and historical persistence. Evidencing traces from all three Aristotelian genres (forensic, deliberative, and epideictic), the rhetoric of self-defense reminds us that: (a) The genre is a reproduction of forensic discourse removed from the legal trappings of the courtroom, but where the litmus test for success is still: "stay low, say little, we will survive." (b) The genre is a high-stakes rhetorical battle in the political arena that apologists cannot afford to lose. Success in this arena requires a "take action, welcome debate, and be rational and methodical" approach. The genre is a public purging of sins and a reaffirmation of the ethical norms of society "dressed up" in theatrical proportions to bring pleasure to spectators; it is the most intimate form of secular discourse. Success in this arena requires a "let it all hang out (remorse, pride, outrage)" approach. The visual media are especially equipped to provide the excess and exaggeration that this type of theatre demands. The psychological appeal of the genre is best summed up by Corbett (1988): "What perversity is there in the human psyche that makes us enjoy the spectacle of human beings desperately trying to answer the charges leveled against them? Maybe secretly, as we read or listen [or watch] [or log-on], we say to ourselves, 'Ah, there but for the grace of God go I' " (p. xi).

As the study of *apologia* itself evolves, it will be important that we emulate the drive of the Ancients for a systematic, coherent body of thought. "The need to deliver an apologia [may be] as old as human history" (Corbett, 1988, p. viii) and "a peculiarity of the human condition" (Hearit, 1995a, p. 118), but its code of situational exigencies, explanatory postures and argumentative executions is a story still in the making.

19

Downsizing or Reduction-in-Force: A Crisis Residual

Kathie Leeper
Concordia College

Layoffs, downsizing, reduction-in-force. Although economic growth and prosperous conditions of the mid 1990s minimized these concepts as concerns, the economic slowdown and recession in addition to the terrorist attacks and response in 2001 quickly brought the reality of layoffs and firings to public attention. As the U.S. economy slid into recession, the number of organizations needing ways to reduce costs by trimming their workforce increased significantly. The unemployed workforce reached new highs for the decade. Economists' forecasts suggested that although companies would "reduce the speed at which they lay off employees, the total number of layoffs would continue to increase" (Claims, 2001).

As organizations identified significant decreases in earnings and evaluated them for their crisis potential, the need for personnel reductions seemed clear. Viewing employees primarily as "costs," management turned to reductions in personnel as a solution when profits suffer. However, some so-called solutions may precipitate secondary crises. Heath (1997) suggested, "A crisis can be an event that creates an issue or keeps it alive or gives it strength" (p. 289). The significant number of layoffs nationwide added strength to this issue.

An organization's decision to downsize or reduce its labor force may decrease labor costs, however, that same action can create an additional issue for employers. They may find a pulling back of trust, commitment, and willingness to invest full effort in the organization by their employees. The downsizing solution may actually precipitate an internal crisis in trust.

299

Whereas trust among stockholders may increase when such announce-
ments suggest increased corporate earnings, trust among a more central
stakeholder, the employee, may clearly be destroyed. Kramer (1996) identified trust as playing a central role in the hierarchical relationship of employees to the organization. This is one of those areas Heath (1988) suggested we need "to plan proactively for new, uncharted public policy
considerations" (p. 1). Because the relationship between an organization
and its employees is vital, this chapter looks at the issue of job loss and
downsizing, or reduction-in-force, from a public relations perspective.

BACKGROUND

The restructuring and downsizing of the late 1980s and 1990s provides some
background for this complex issue. Successful organizations have always focused on cost as a factor in profit growth. And, with the growth of technology
and market demand for profits, restructuring was seen as a means of increasing profits. Statistics suggest that more than 4,000 corporations were restruc-
tured in the 1980s. Wagar (2001) observed, "The decade of the 1990s was
characterized by an almost obsessive preoccupation with downsizing as organizations in North America and around the world cut back on staff at unprecedented rates" (p. 851). Bardwick (1991) identified the pervasiveness of
the problem. "In the 1980s more than 1 million managers and professionals
were cut from the corporate ranks. Another estimate is that number may be
as high as 2 million" (p. 12). But the problem did not stop there. He continued, "111,285 middle managers and executives lost their jobs in all of 1989; in
the first quarter of 1990 alone, the number was 110,152. In 1990, announce-
ments of corporate cuts occurred at twice the 1989 rate" (p. 13). Those losing
their jobs were no longer just at the lowest levels in the organization; many
came from the ranks of middle and top-level managers.

Recognizing a problem and attempting to overcome it, management
turned to language. Employees were not laid off or fired, but were "downsized." Emshoff (1991) explained, "This euphemism (downsizing) for firing
employees emphasizes that they didn't necessarily do a poor job—they
were merely too expensive to maintain as part of the workforce" (p. 4).
Whether the term selected for the actions was cutbacks, layoffs, firings, re-
trenchment, downsizing, or even "rightsizing," the emotional charge and
impact of the situation both inside and outside the organization made this a
serious concern for public relations.

Research in the social sciences has helped identify and explain employee responses. Obviously, the impact on the employee losing the job
will be great. A story of a downsized employee quoted by Kanter et al.
(1992) explained, "To this day, some 20 years later, I still contend that emo-

tional injuries to my pride and self-worth as a result of being fired were much more serious than the physical injuries I sustained as a result of the (motorcycle) accident (requiring a four-month convalescence)" (p. 483). Emotional injury is not often mentioned since it may not affect a company financially.

Leana and Feldman (1990), in an attempt to better understand which aspects of the job can be predicted to have the greatest impact, found that the loss of a valued and interesting job stimulates a more severe stress reaction than does the loss of a less valued job. Their study also suggested that the greatest emotional impact was the reaction to the job loss itself rather than the individual's adjustment to it. Thompson (1992) indicated that employees are likely to feel anger, resentment, and depression, which can affect job performance.

Brockner, Grover, Reed, DeWitt, and O'Malley (1987) found that whether coworkers responded by "distancing themselves from the layoff victims or the organization depends on their prior attachment to the layoff victim" (p. 539). In addition, "if the management of the layoff is of questionable legitimacy, survivors may become critical about the management style in the aftermath of the layoff. This uncertainty may generalize to other issues of considerable importance to employees" (p. 392). These studies suggest that employee responses may be more detrimental to the organization than management may assume.

Curtis (1989) recognized the problems when he said that with downsizing "problems in employee morale, trust, and productivity tend to get worse" (p. 671). He found that downsizing detracts from trust, creates a climate of negative messages going downward, lowered morale, a loss of influence, loss of trust, and more secrecy. In addition, employees experience more fear, anxiety, and guilt. Fergus (1992) also noted, downsizing "can lead to loss of employee morale and damage reputations" (p. 17).

Commitment to the organization also appears to be affected. Brockner, DeWitt, Grover, and Reed (1990) found that employees remaining with the organization often had both reduced work performance as well as lowered commitment to the organization. Brockner, Tyler, and Cooper-Schneider (1992) suggested that when previously committed individuals feel they were treated unfavorably or unfairly within the organization they may show an especially sharp decline in commitment. They tend to be evaluating the justice of the situation in terms of the distributive justice or the outcomes associated with the downsizing such as severance pay. In addition, they evaluate procedural justice—whether a clear explanation exists as to why the specific choices were made.

Research is quite clear, "cutting people to cut costs, if poorly managed, can actually increase some costs," costs that may not be immediately apparent to management, as Kanter, Stein, and Jick (1992) pointed out. The organizational change that occurs results in numerous effects among personnel. Often fear, suspicion, insecurity, and conflicts occur (Curtis, 1989). Thompson (1992) noted, "The financial advantages of downsizing may be negated by a demoralized workforce. Employees are likely to feel anger, resentment, and depression, all of which can affect job performance" (p. 11).

If employees are viewed as "costs," then we should not be surprised at the approach often taken. "A 'folk wisdom' about such cutbacks is that it is better to 'get it all done as quickly as possible,' so employee morale will rebound and workers will not become shell shocked from successive waves of terminations" (Tomasko, 1987, p. 193). Managers may assume that if they don't talk about layoffs until the last possible moment, the organization will experience few effects.

Layoffs and employee termination is a concern that has also received legal attention. Advance notice is mandated by both Federal and, in Canada, provincial governments prior to the termination of large numbers of employees. The United States Office of Personnel Management Web site has issued the guidelines for meeting federal requirements identifying not only for notification but also to "give employees career transition information" because "Ideally, placement efforts should begin long before reduction in force notices are issued." Management must be aware of legal issues involved with employee terminations. However, just because a company can legally take some action, the company cannot assume that all will be well. In fact, Freeman (1984) suggested that public anger will be greater if the law is used to avoid what vital publics consider ethical behavior. The fact remains that the impact on employees cannot be ignored. As Kanter, Stein, and Jick (1992) asserted, corporations "view employees primarily as costs rather than valuing them as assets, and they fail to see the value (in skills or experience) that walks out the door with terminated staff" (pp. 229–230). Not only does this loss of experience cost the organization, but the concept of "employees as costs" is antithetical to a public relations perspective.

RELATIONSHIP TO PUBLIC RELATIONS THEORY

Public relations, according to Cutlip, Center, and Broom (2000), is "the management function that establishes and maintains mutually beneficial relationships between an organization and the publics on whom its success or failure depends" (p. 6). All texts identify employees or internal publics as an important link in public perception of the organization. Newsom, Turk, and Kruckeberg (2000) remind us, "The role of employees is a significant concern in most PR efforts" (p. 110). And Rosenbluth (1992) went so far as to suggest that "Companies must put their people first. Yes, even before their customers" (p. 23). Drucker (1999) echoed this sentiment when he stated,

"The scarcest resources in any organization are *performing people*" (p. 121). Because employees are central, the relationship between an organization and its employees is a public relations issue, especially in times of crisis.

Newsom et al. (2000) noted, however, that difficulties with employees exist. They explained, "The level of employee satisfaction has been low for nearly a decade." This can result in poor interactions with other organizational publics which "can hurt the organization's reputation, since employees are any organization's PR front line" (p. 79).

Possibly the downsizing of the early 1990s has contributed to this. However, employees have been changing also. Today companies have not only production workers but also what Drucker (1999) called the "knowledge worker." This individual is identified not as a subordinate, but as an "associate." Because of the knowledge and ability this individual both brings to the job and develops on the job, Drucker suggested, "knowledge workers must know more about their job than their boss does—or else they are not good at all. In fact, that they know more about their job than anybody else in the organization is part of the definition of knowledge workers" (p. 18). Whereas these individuals depend on the "boss" for those hierarchical issues such as hiring, promotion, and appraisal, these individuals educate that supervisor regarding the specifics of what is being done and needs to be done. As a result, Drucker (1999) suggested that increasingly "full-time employees have to be managed as if they were *volunteers*. They are paid, to be sure. But knowledge workers have mobility. They can leave" (p. 20). Even though they can leave, both the organization and the employee would like to assume a continuing relationship. This requires a different type of management. Drucker suggested, "Increasingly 'employees' have to be managed as 'partners'—and relations are becoming increasingly difficult. It is the definition of a partnership that all partners are equal" (p. 21).

Tomlinson (2000) applied four dimensions of satisfying interpersonal relationships to public relations. These dimensions include investment, commitment, trust, and comfort with relational dialectics. He suggests it is necessary to know and understand these in order for a public relations specialist to build and maintain a relationship.

Although each dimension is important, "trust" stands out as being dependent upon ones perception of and evaluation of characteristics of the "other." Tyler and Kramer (1996) suggested that "organizations have generally experienced declines in their perceived trustworthiness in the eyes of both employees and the members of other organizations" (p. 8). However, as Allen (1995) explained, it may be that "the currency most valued by business leaders has been trust" (p. 13).

Broom, Casey, and Ritchey (2000), studied the concepts and theory of relationships from interpersonal communication to determine if it could be applied to public relations. They explained, "interpersonal communication scholars operationally define relationships as measure of participants' perceptions or as a function of those perceptions" (p. 69). As such, the study of relationships would be based primarily on perceptions. Measurement of relationship, then, would focus on perceptions. Grunig and Huang (2000) suggested that the four features of trust, control mutuality, relational commitment, and relational satisfaction are the "essence of organization-public relationships" (p. 42). These four features, then, can be considered in analyzing the relationship between the organization and employees in the situation where management is considering a reduction-in-force.

For organizations to avoid the potential of a crisis situation, they might heed the advice of Heath (1997). He asserted, "crisis management is an issues management function that entails issues monitoring, strategic planning, and getting the house in order, to try to avoid events that trigger outrage and uncertainty and have the potential of maturing into public policy issues" (pp. 289–290). He explained, "Crisis is about control" (p. 294). Plans to reduce the workforce of an organization would seem to fall into this situation. The concept of control, however, would seem to extend to employees who want a certain level of control over their employment situation. They want to be able to predict that they will have a job at the end of the week, or month, or year. Employees committed and trusting of the organization, however, may be willing to go beyond their own benefit to support the organization. For example, in those situations where hourly employees are asked to reduce hours worked because the organization is facing unusual situations, trusting and supportive employees will often help the organization through the difficulty. If, however, employees find the organization hiring new additional employees and not giving those hours to long term employees, trust and commitment to the organization deteriorates and employees feel used. They voluntarily gave up their personal control and were betrayed.

However, theory and practice offer solutions to the organization. The solution lies in open and honest communication between the organization and its employees. In discussing the Exxon Valdez situation, Heath (1997) stated, "Employees need information, particularly if safety is a factor" (p. 308). Although physical safety would not be an issue in most layoff situations, employees may still define the layoff in terms of their own safety. Information and understanding is essential.

SOLUTIONS

Companies will continue the cycles of increasing and reducing their work forces. A variety of approaches have been tried. Easton (1976) recognized the importance of the issue in *Managing for Negative Growth: A Handbook for*

Practitioners where he stated, "There is no way to carry out a large-scale re-trenchment without causing real injury to many persons. . . . An important aim of the public relations campaign is to halt the progressive deterioration of the relationships between the company and its constituencies" (p. 229). He went on to discuss what happens after employees have left. "The next step is to rebuild the relationships and, if possible, to make them better than before." However in looking at the types and amounts of communication which should occur, he states, "there are times when keeping a low profile is the best tactic" (p. 229). His advice appears to be that the organization should say as little as possible. This is supported by his earlier discussion of downward communication and whether management should be open and "tell everyone in the firm everything there is to know except possibly for those few bits of information that must be kept confidential" or "tell only those very few things each person must know in order to do his particular job, and nothing more" (p. 186). He came to the conclusion that "management need not fear that its people will be shamefully uniformed if it temporarily neglects feeding the formal channels" (p. 188). He suggested that much of the information regularly supplied would be "ignored, and as a result the money spent in the name of full and free communication is partly wasted" (p. 188).

Unfortunately, this has often been the approach taken in downsizing. It is this approach which neglects a public relations perspective. Because reductions will most often come in financially difficult times, guidelines from a public relations perspective are essential. Downsizing must be approached as "issues management" or risk communication to keep employees from creating a type of crisis situation for the organization. The ideal is to manage the communication so that internal publics main trust and involvement.

Brockner et al. (1990) suggested that when employees evaluate management's decision to downsize, they consider several areas. These will include the unusualness of the layoff (the extent to which it violates expectations), avoidability of the layoff, lack of clarity of the decision and basis to keep certain employees and lay off others, unfairness of the decisional basis to keep certain employees and lay off others, perceived adequacy of organizational care in taking care in the event of future layoffs. The perception of fairness would appear to be extremely important to employees. With that perception, it would appear that decisions can be accepted. As a result, these issues should inform managements approach to employees.

Toth and Heath (1992) asserted that "how the organization presents itself and asks its audience to think about itself can be crucial to the impact of the public relations campaign" (p. 42). The organization must be aware of the need for this information campaign for its internal publics.

In the introduction to their chapter, "Employee Communication," Baskin and Aronoff (1992) stated, "Ideal organizational climates are characterized by feelings of trust, confidence, openness, candor, supportiveness, security, satisfaction, involvement, and pride in the organizations" (p. 256). Goodman and Ruch (1981) suggested "Employees must know what's going on in the company. They want to know that management cares about them and that the caring is genuine" (p. 16). With this approach, employees are likely to have the question areas identified by Brockner et al. (1990) clearly answered. The decisions and reasons for those decisions help answer those concerns about fairness. In addition, Finkin (1992) suggested, "Confidence in the organization comes as a result of open communications and leads to the affected parties' cooperation and support of management" (p. 62). As Thompson (1992) offered, "Managers and supervisors should deal with the changing employee attitudes by adopting a policy based on open communication" (p. 11). These plans stress the importance of communicating early and completely with all people involved.

Looking at the importance of employee participation, Jamison and O'Mara (1991) wrote, "At the Heart of any effective participation program are four components: power, knowledge, information, and rewards. Participation works when people are given the power to make certain decisions, the knowledge and skills to make them effective, the necessary information, and meaningful rewards for their effort" (p. 119). Wilcox, Ault, and Agee (1992) stated, "A workforce that respects its management, has pride in its products, and believes it is being treated fairly is a key factor in corporate success" (p. 361). When management satisfies the need for understanding and reduction of uncertainty, employees tend to be more positive toward the organization than negative.

Block (1987), in writing about the issue of empowerment, offered beneficial guidelines when he wrote,

> Sharing as much information as possible is the opposite of the military notion that only those that "need to know" should be informed. Our goal is to let people know of our plans, ideas, and changes as soon as possible. When we are thinking of reorganizing, we tell our people right away instead of waiting until the plan is fully formulated. If a project is running behind schedule, we tell our users we are behind. Most supervisors think part of their role is to shield their subordinates from bad news coming from above. When we shield our people we are acting as their parents and treating them like children. If we are trying to create the mindset that everyone is responsible for the success of this business, then our people need complete information. We need to think of our subordinates and bosses as partners rather than as children or parents. Most of us know that if we withheld information from our partners, we would be putting the relationship at risk. (pp. 90–91)

This approach echoes Heath's (1988) suggestion when dealing with issues of importance it is important for the organization to "Communicate constantly and vigorously with key audiences to build lasting understanding and harmony" (p. 170). Although guidelines appear to be clear that communication is important within the organization, when management faces the threat of what it perceives as a crisis situation, communication may be shut down. Managers, however, must avoid that communication shut down. Instead, it must move toward even more open and frequent communication.

Cutlip et al. (2000) remind us that "the coordination and mediation necessary for dealing with employees today puts the public relations staff, with its communication savvy and skills, square in the middle of managing internal relationships" (p. 288).

Although Seitel (1992) explained that internal "communications must be continuous to reinforce consistently management's interest in its employees" (p. 389), to persuade others to hold the organizational view of reality, challenges of the 1990s have led Seitel and others to recognize that two-way communication is essential with today's employee public. Seitel (2001) explained, "almost everyone wants their ideas to be heard and to have a voice in decision making. This growing 'activist communications' phenomenon must be considered by public relations professionals seeking to win internal goodwill for management" (p. 377).

In planning this communication campaign, it is important to work with Heath's (1988) suggestions for a long-term commitment, timeliness, honesty and coherence, and candor and openness. As these are important for external publics, they are even more important for internal publics. Thus, an open two-way symmetric communication program is essential. In terms of specific recommendations regarding downsizing, Kanter et al. (1992) suggested, "Any company considering downsizing as a solution to its strategic concerns should first think through what its strategic concerns are and then fit downsizing into that context" (p. 288). Matejka (1991) stated, "Employees who feel misused, deceived, baited, or badgered can become angry and strike back at the source of the irritation or at some third party" (p. 145).

, Employees who feel management cares and is helping them locate a new position will probably remain aware and consider the messages management sends. The majority of plans to "ease the pain of reductions in force" (Shattuck, 1991) are designed to keep people involved and help them feel that they have help in finding a new position. The majority of studies suggesting what to do when downsizing recommend that communication remain free and open. Only with sufficient communication will employees begin to feel at ease. According to Jacobs (1991), "Managers can reduce the ill effects of downsizing with clear communication and concrete transition plans" (p. 26).

With these guidelines in mind, it is important to make certain the areas identified by Brockner et al. (1990) are also clear. This means public relations must prepare employees for the possibility of layoffs so that the layoffs are not perceived to be unusual. Communication must also be clear that the layoffs were not avoidable. In addition, the basis for who is kept and who goes must be clear and must appear to be fair to all employees. The final factor identified is the perceived adequacy of organizational care taking in the event of future layoffs. Because these will be the concerns of employees, communication plans for downsizing must focus in these areas.

In terms of specific suggestions Seitel (2001) provided some guidance, "communications must be continuous, respectful, and candid to reinforce a consistent management message" (p. 376). Not only will employees be aware of the communication, but they will also focus on the actions of the organization. This issue was developing as Seitel (1992) pointed out, "Just about every researcher who keeps tabs of employee opinion finds evidence of a 'trust gap' between management and rank-and-file workers" (p. 387). Actions may well speak louder than words. For this reason, it is important to heed Bunning's (1990) suggestion to show the highest level of ethics when downsizing. But even if the organization does, research supports the concept of even more two-way symmetric communication. Shattuck (1991) suggested, "The people left behind need to know from management what they can do to effectively support the terminated employee. . . . Before informing an employee of termination the manager usually briefs the outplacement consultant on the decision" (p. 32). Seitel (1992) explained, "public relations managers must constantly remind line managers that nothing an organization says to its employees can communicate more effectively than what it does to or for them" (p. 260).

Occasionally public relations managers can convince top management with success stories. Downsizing does not need to create undesirable employee reactions if it is handled properly. In her interview with Bell Atlantic's Raymond Smith, Kanter et al. (1992) quoted him as saying, "We've tried to do two things to cushion the blow. The first is to level with people. . . . The second thing we do is to try to make stressful changes like downsizing in a participative manner. . . . After all, almost any organization will succeed if the people feel empowered, are recognized for what they do, and understand the purpose of their jobs" (p. 309).

Kanter et al. (1992) in their discussion of the Bell Atlantic downsizing found, "In our regular employee survey, workers cited our downsizing as one reason for improved morale. They told us that although resources are very tight, Bell Atlantic is now a much better place to work. They said since some of the disaffected, cynical people have left, there is much less time for bureaucracy." . . . "Participants learn that it is vital to understand priorities and know what those priorities are based on, such as the goals of the corporation" (p. 310).

Garfield (1992) wrote, "New story organizations take a more humane approach to lay-offs, and one which incorporates a concern for maintaining the overall health of the organization and ensuring its future. In the new story, there will still be workforce reductions. But instead of engaging in indiscriminate downsizing, simply chopping 10 per cent across the board, new story organizations focus on 'right sizing.' They consider the potential consequences of any layoffs, including loss of collective wisdom and disruptions in important relationships that hold the corporate ecosystem together. They often involve employees in the decision process, thus reducing the impact on morale" (p. 60).

Kanter et al. (1992) suggested, "The best way to bring about change is to let the employees participate in it. That way, they develop insight into the reasons why the change is necessary" (p. 333). As explained, however, "They were not enthusiastic about cutting their own jobs, so in practice the decision was left to the boss. Still, the 'soft' aspects of the organizational change—appreciation, recognition, sharing—were given as much importance as the hard side of reducing the head count" (p. 310).

One manager reported his experience.

> I read everything I could on how to deal with a downsizing, and I decided to break every rule. Give employees a little bit of notice, the experts say. I told them months in advance that their jobs might be eliminated. "Make sure you have a clear picture of what you are going to do" is another homily offered to managers compelled to downsize. I informed employees of what might happen, describing several possible scenarios. In general, my rule of thumb for the actions I took involved one acid test: how would I want to be treated in the same situation. I prided myself on having a participative management style, always asking people who worked for me for their input and showing respect for their ideas. When it came to downsizing, I wouldn't see why this issue was any different from others we had faced. In fact, I told myself, it was *more* personal and *more* important to them than *any* of the others. Why shouldn't they be given all the possibilities so that they'd be able to make the best decisions for themselves? (Kanter et al., 1992, pp. 484–485)

Communication appears to be the solution. In order for internal publics to understand management's decisions, public relations must insure that management has communicated adequately. If the person can be aware of the constraints the organization faces, then understanding and perceptions of reality will have significantly more in common. Public relations' goal is to help management and employees recognize their common interests, develop a shared understanding, and if at all possible, adopt a "win–win" solution to the problem at hand.

CONCLUSION

The process of decreasing workforce size is but one aspect demonstrating a need for internal pubic relations efforts. With workforce composition and expectations changing, internal communication has become even more important. Seitel (2001) explained the importance of openness and honesty with staff as he said, "In today's environment, being candid means treating people with dignity and giving them the opportunity to understand the realities of the marketplace" (p. 378).

As organizations maneuver through the maze of issues and potential crisis situations the expertise of public relations professionals becomes even more important.

Excellent Crisis Communication: Beyond Crisis Plans

Francis J. Marra
Zayed University

Few topics have generated the recent interest and attention of managers as has crisis management and crisis communication. Incidents such as the Exxon Valdez oil spill, the Three Mile Island and Chernobyl nuclear power plant accidents, the chemical leak at Union Carbide's Bhopal, India, manufacturing plant, the Tylenol product tampering incidents, and the *Challenger* space shuttle explosion clearly demonstrated the severity with which crises can affect organizations and their many constituents. The likelihood of an organization experiencing a crisis has become so great that sociologist Charles Perrow categorizes crises as "normal." Perrow (1984) said managers should no longer evaluate *if* an organization will ever face a crisis, but rather when, where, what type, and how large a crisis it will eventually encounter.

When a crisis occurs, many of an organization's publics quickly want to know what happened, when, why, how, and what the effects of the crisis are. These publics are likely to include the organization's employees (current and retired), shareowners, community residents, customers, suppliers, and local, state, and federal government officials and regulatory agencies. Reporters, producers, and other people working in the mass media are another important public that insist on *immediate* information and answers during a crisis.

Organizations that cannot or do not provide information during crises force its relevant publics (particularly employees, customers, and reporters) to turn to other, often less accurate, sources of information. Public relations practitioner Frank Stansberry observed at a regional public relations conference in 1982 that "In the absence of information, misinformation becomes news." Although the facts may later prove these sources wrong, the misperceptions created by these nonorganizational sources during the flurry of media coverage in the initial moments of a crisis may remain with important publics and be difficult, if not impossible, to change. The lasting perceptions created by the inability of an organization to provide accurate information can easily translate into significant organizational losses—employees may quit, customers could switch brands, shareowners might sell their stock, government agencies could increase regulation, and reporters might conduct further investigations.

Many public relations practitioners develop communications plans to help them provide information to their relevant publics during crises. These crisis communication plans often contain comprehensive checklists of what to do during a crisis, names and addresses of relevant people to contact, and outlines of various communications strategies and tactics. In many cases, these plans help public relations practitioners successfully manage the immediate and enormous number of requests for information that accompany a crisis.

Many case studies of crises in the public relations literature indicate the importance of crisis communication plans. Many articles stress the relationship between the presence and use of a practical, functional, and usable crisis communications plan and successful crisis communication. But is this credit deserved? Is excellent crisis communication solely the result of preparing a thorough list of instructions, suggestions, and checklists?

Crisis communications plans are an important part of successful crisis public relations, but *their value appears to be overrated*. Many organizations with comprehensive crisis communications plans, for example, have managed crises poorly, while a number of organizations *without* crisis communication plans have managed crises well.

Almost all of the research in public relations focuses on the *technical* role of communicating during a crisis. Little, if any, research has gone beyond the technical descriptions and applications incorporated in crisis communication plans. A review of the literature and in-depth analyses of several crises revealed crisis communications plans are only a *part* of what determines excellent crisis public relations practice. This suggests public relations practitioners need to expand their technical communication mindset to consider larger organizational variables that are better predictors of excellent crisis public relations.

This parallels the findings of the *Excellence in Public Relations and Communications Management* study led by Dr. James E. Grunig at the University of Maryland (1992). Grunig said excellent public relations requires the *strategic management* of an organization's communication function. Crisis public relations practitioners, therefore, should similarly shift their emphasis from *technicians* who prepare crisis communication materials to *managers* who apply predictive and explanatory crisis public relations theory. Excellent crisis public relations requires communications managers to go beyond the technical elements of crisis communication and consider higher level, theoretical variables that can influence the effectiveness of an organization's crisis public relations efforts.

An analysis of several crises revealed two variables that significantly influenced each organization's response to its crisis. These variables, the autonomy of an organization's public relations staff and its communication culture, emerged as important elements crucial to the success (or lack of success) in managing a crisis.

Two crises in particular provide an in-depth contextual understanding of how autonomy and organizational culture influences crisis public relations. The first crisis involved AT&T and a crisis that occurred on January 15, 1990. An error in a computer program caused AT&T's long distance network to complete only about half of the long distance calls attempted during a 9-hour period. The 1986 cocaine-induced death of University of Maryland basketball player Leonard Bias, and the subsequent investigation of the campus's athletic program, is the focus of the second case study.

Autonomy of the Public Relations Staff

The ability of public relations practitioners to perform their jobs during crises—the amount of power or autonomy they have—is an important explanation and predictor of how well an organization communicates during a crisis. This suggests excellent crisis public relations is, in part, influenced by the amount of autonomy an organization gives its public relations department. Excellent public relations requires the power and authority to *immediately* implement crisis communication tactics. The ability to implement a crisis plan is *not* the same as preparing and having a crisis communication plan at hand. Without an adequate power base, public relations practitioners might be prevented from using communication techniques that could reduce the effects of an organizational crisis.

The AT&T Crisis. The January 15, 1990 long distance crisis at AT&T began at about 2:25 p.m. eastern time. Within 20 minutes, AT&T's Network Operation Center Manager Jim Nelson and his staff knew they had a major crisis in progress. Once Nelson knew the magnitude of the crisis, he immediately called AT&T chief executive officer Robert Allen and the public relations managers assigned to the long distance network.

Independent of Nelson's telephone calls, a reporter from CBS Radio News in New York called AT&T Media Relations Director Herb Linnen in

Washington, D.C. at about 2:40 p.m. to ask why they were having trouble getting through to their Washington, D.C. bureau. The reporter had Linnen's number on file from a 1986 AT&T labor negotiation story. Linnen told the reporter he didn't know about the network disruption, but said he would check to see if the network was experiencing any problems. Linnen immediately called AT&T Director of Corporate Information Walter Murphy at AT&T corporate headquarters in Basking Ridge, New Jersey, who confirmed a problem with the long distance network. The CBS Radio reporter called Linnen back at 2:55 p.m., did a short interview with him, and used the story, with a portion of the Linnen interview, during the 3 p.m. national network news. Thirty-five minutes into the crisis, the media coverage began.

Marilyn Laurie, AT&T's senior vice president for public relations—and her entire public relations staff—instantly knew how they would manage this crisis: "Acknowledge the problem, assume responsibility, volunteer the facts, minimize speculation, and correct inaccurate information" (Murphy, 1990, p. 2). AT&T's public relations strategy emphasized speed and relied on the ability of the public relations staff to release information about the crisis *on their own authority*. Both Laurie and Vice President Bill Mullane said it was crucial to provide information about the crisis as quickly as possible. The public relations battle, they said, is often won or lost during the first 24 hours of a crisis.

Daisy Ottman, an AT&T media relations district manager, said the AT&T public relations staff began working on the network crisis immediately. She said she was able to provide information to reporters within *10 minutes* of the first telephone call she received. Ottman said although at that point in the crisis she barely had any information to give reporters, it was very important to be as candid as possible:

> The kind of information that you give in that standpoint sort of sounds like no information. But it isn't. You acknowledge that you have a problem. If you know what the nature of the problem is, and at this point the problem was undefined, you can certainly say that. You can assure people that the appropriate resources . . . have been brought in, you can assure people that the problem is being worked on. And finally you can tell them what kind of action they should take, such as refrain from calling the affected area . . . [or to] wait a half hour, or keeping trying until you get through. Whatever kind of advice you can give people. All of that is much more helpful than a cold no comment. Or what I think is even worse is not being able to reach a media spokesperson at all. (interview, November 20, 1990)

Other examples showed how AT&T employees typically had an unusual amount of autonomy to act during the crisis. According to Ottman, "The kind of training I had had in [this] organization was such that I felt perfectly competent and perfectly authorized and empowered to do what I had to do" (interview, November 20, 1990). Adele Ambrose, a public relations manager for AT&T's Business Sales Division, said account executives also had the authority to contact their clients as soon as possible:

> Almost without thinking twice about it that night there were all kinds of stories of people going to their customer's office and spending the night there and holding their hand or showing up at the door the next morning to try and explain to them what was going on.... When I was doing some checking a week or so after the crisis was over, one of the national account managers was sitting with one of his customers when he was being interviewed by the *Wall Street Journal*. (interview, October 11, 1990)

A common threat to public relations practitioners' autonomy, especially during a crisis, is their organization's legal department. Potential legal liabilities often cause attorneys to caution against the immediate and frequent communication typically suggested by public relations practitioners. Many chief executive officers accept this legal advice and reduce the autonomy of their public relations staff to communicate during a crisis. The Firestone 500 tire crisis, the Hooker Chemical Love Canal toxic waste crisis, and the Exxon Valdez oil spill crisis are three examples in which the autonomy of public relations staffs were significantly reduced by self-imposed legal constraints.

This potential threat to autonomy, however, was completely absent during the AT&T crisis. AT&T's Marilyn Laurie concisely summarized the relationship between the AT&T legal and public relations departments: "You don't let lawyers run communications. Lawyers are partners at AT&T" (interview, November 20, 1990). This cooperative relationship was reinforced by several AT&T public relations managers, including Linda Evans:

> They provide advice but the decisions have to be made by the managers who have accountability for it. In a personal issue just the other day, I really was wanting the legal department to tell me what to do with it. They said, "This is the advice we're giving you. This is the defensible act, this isn't." (interview, September 28, 1990)

Public Relations Manager Adele Ambrose felt the same way:

> I think we have a fair amount of autonomy. It's their [the legal department's] responsibility to do that [check information] and certainly it's my responsibility to make sure what I'm saying is legally sound. If I had to make a snap decision and was forced against the wall, I don't know that I would call them necessarily, but I also know from the dealings that I have with them everyday what's safe and what isn't. (interview, October 11, 1990)

Neither the public relations nor the legal departments appeared to have a greater power base within AT&T's Executive Committee, the organization's governing body of 11 senior vice presidents and Chief Executive Officer Robert Allen. Public Relations Vice President Bill Mullane said AT&T's chairmen have never automatically favored legal advice more than public relations counsel:

> I think it depends on the argument. It's weighed in heavily. I can go back to the day in 1981 when Charlie Brown, who was the chairman at the time, came to Ed Block who was the [public relations] senior vice president and said, "Read this" and Ed read it. He said, "Can you explain it?" Ed said, "Let me think about it." [And Charlie said,] "If we can't explain it, we won't do it." And that was the divestiture. All the lawyers in the world couldn't have convinced Charlie to do it if you couldn't explain it to the public. (interview, August 30, 1990)

Many AT&T public relations managers said they managed the crisis on their own with little direction or guidance from supervisors or challenges from the legal department. According to several AT&T public relations managers, consulting with company attorneys before the public relations staff released information during the January 15 crisis was an unnecessary step:

> Vice President Bill Mullane: I did not see a lawyer from the time it started until after it was over, other than when I went to get a cup of coffee in the executive area that morning. The general counsel said to me "is everything under control?" I said [it is] as far as I'm concerned. (interview, August 30, 1990)
>
> Public Relations Manager Carol Albright: There's nothing anywhere that says PR has to get [legal approval]. . . . We're not legal experts, but we know what to say and what not to say. I know that when I took all these calls I wasn't thinking in my mind anything about a lawyer that may have been in the room or down the hall. So the legal aspect or the marketing didn't really come in to play for me. (interview, August 30, 1990)
>
> Director of Corporate Information Walter Murphy: It may have been that there should have been some consideration of legal parameters there but there simply was not. It was all happening so quickly that if it were in our minds, and I don't remember off hand that it wasn't, I would assume that it probably was because we run into situations so frequently that there are legal implications and we do consider those. There was no question in anybody's mind that legal considerations would stop us from being forthcoming. (interview, August 30, 1990)

Murphy said all of AT&T's public relations managers have significant autonomy to release information:

Yes. On network outage type of situations. It happened here. In the past couple of months there was a problem that was caused by AT&T that shut down
the commodity exchanges at the World Trade Center in New York City. We
found out from the [public relations] account managers from the NOC [Net-
work Operations Center] and I was in touch with them as to what we ought to
say. We were not calling lawyers or calling [Senior Vice President] Marilyn's
[Laurie] office, or trying to talk to [Vice President Bill] Mullane about what exactly we ought to say. We just said it. (interview, August 30, 1990)

The University of Maryland Crisis. The crisis at the University of Maryland began with the sudden and unexpected death of basketball player Len
Bias on June 19, 1986. Bias collapsed in his dormitory room at 6:30 a.m. after
celebrating through the night with several of his teammates. An unconscious Bias was transported by paramedics to a local hospital where he
was pronounced dead at 8:50 a.m. There were no signs of foul play or obvious reason for Bias's death, but within 8 hours, a Washington, D.C. television station reported Bias had died from cocaine intoxication.

The crisis escalated during the next few days and eventually lasted several months. Bias's use of cocaine resulted in charges that the University of
Maryland was a haven for drug use. Reporters gathering information for detailed stories about Bias's career also discovered the athletic department at
the University of Maryland appeared to exploit its student-athletes. Bias, for
example, was more than 18 months from graduation although he was in his
fourth year at the university. During the spring, 1986 semester, Bias failed
two classes and withdrew from three others. Five of the other 14 players on
the men's basketball team also flunked out of school the previous semester,
but were later reinstated.

University of Maryland Chancellor John Slaughter and his senior administrators decided all requests for information would be handled exclusively
by Director of Public Information Roz Hiebert. They believed funneling information through one person—Hiebert—would prevent inaccurate reporting. On Tuesday, June 24, 5 days after Bias died, Slaughter sent a confidential four paragraph memo to his vice chancellors, provost, deans, directors,
and department chairs that instructed the University of Maryland faculty
and staff to refer all media inquiries to Hiebert. Mercy Coogan, a member of
the university's public relations staff during the crisis, said all inquiries
were handled exclusively by Hiebert:

Roz made it very clear that anybody who called to inquire about it, she
wanted to speak to that reporter directly.... Everything had to be channeled
to her. The problem being, of course, was that she was often not around because she was putting out littler fires all over at various levels. (interview, November 27, 1990)

In-depth interviews with many mid- and senior-level managers at the University of Maryland confirmed that Hiebert rarely delegated important crisis-related tasks to her public relations staff. This, in effect, removed any autonomy by the public relations staff members to release information. Hiebert agreed that she, and not her staff, handled most of the crisis communication responsibilities:

> They set up the rooms. They notified the task force members when a meeting was going to take place and they went out and stood outside the rooms to keep the rooms closed off. Those were their jobs. The rest of all of the Len Bias crisis stuff was handled by me. . . . I had to do all the work. I did *all* the work involved. I wrote all of John Slaughter's speeches. I wrote all of the statements. I set up all of the press conferences. I dealt with, well of course, I dealt with all the media because that's what he wanted and that's what I did and that's the right thing to do in a case like that. It was like a nightmare to do. (interview, September 18, 1990)

The magnitude of the story quickly overwhelmed Hiebert's ability to handle requests for information and interviews. The volume of calls generated by the crisis, combined with her staff's inability to respond to requests for information, prevented Hiebert from handling the enormous number of requests for information as quickly as they needed to be handled. Mark Hyman, a reporter for the *Baltimore Sun*, said using a single spokesperson didn't work:

> It was a big story covered by a number of different news organizations. In fact, a number of different reporters from this newspaper. And Roz had other responsibilities as well as trying to do damage control in the Bias thing. So it was very difficult for her to be available 24 hours a day to accept interview requests and to try to fulfill them. It just wasn't practical. As a result, you could make a request, you could call Roz's office and ask for an interview with person X. And not hear from her for several hours or sometimes until the next day. Because this was a daily breaking news story, that wasn't acceptable. (interview, December 10, 1990)

ABC-TV Assignment Editor Pat Cullen said not giving the University of Maryland's public relations staff the power to release information was a mistake:

> There was nobody from the PR department at the hospital from the University of Maryland [when Bias died]. Nobody at all. There was nobody out at the courthouse for the entire month of August from the University of Maryland

that I saw, at the grand jury. There is no method to deal with the University of Maryland's point of view on any of the things or any of the players that we dealt with. We had to go back to the University of Maryland every time, on each question, on each thing.

There were 15 [television] crews at the high point of that grand jury. Six live trucks. And instead of having somebody there who is monitoring the case and able to speak to it on any given occasion and speaking to the people outside, knowing the press people who are covering the story, knowing what angle they are going for because he's out there as a press person. I mean, even if he doesn't make any statements, there should have been somebody there monitoring us as a press organization. Where are these guys going? Who is talking to whom? Who's ahead of what on what story and what focus is this thing taking? (interview, April 22, 1988)

Hiebert, ironically, suffered the same lack of autonomy from the university's senior administrators that she imposed on her staff. In-depth interviews with all of the senior administrators at the University of Maryland agreed that the decision to release information was often made by the chancellor, his vice chancellors, and the university attorneys—not the public relations department. All of the senior administrators agreed that throughout most of the crisis, the public relations staff, including Hiebert, did not have the autonomy or power to release information or make other relatively important decisions on their own. Although Hiebert released some information on her own authority, she and all of the senior administrators said that the decision to write and distribute statements or press releases came from the chancellor and his staff. The dean of the College of Journalism at the University of Maryland said it typically took three cabinet meetings to decide to issue a press release that the public relations department could and should have handled by itself in minutes. Hiebert said that almost without exception she had all of her material reviewed by the university's legal office. She said she "automatically would show everything to legal that I did in the Bias thing . . . even if it has nothing to do with any legality" (interview, September 18, 1990).

The amount of autonomy public relations practitioners were given within AT&T and the University of Maryland played an important and unmistakable role in how each organization managed its crisis. Public relations practitioners in both organizations had significantly different levels of autonomy in which to perform their job.

People on the AT&T public relations staff had a great deal of autonomy to release information or conduct activities as they deemed necessary. They did not need to have information approved by attorneys or senior public relations practitioners. The AT&T public relations staff made many crisis-related decisions themselves.

The University of Maryland public relations staff, on the other hand, had much less autonomy. Releasing information was much more of a collaborative effort between the director of public relations, the chancellor and his staff, and the University of Maryland attorneys.

The importance of decision making autonomy during crises is supported by research conducted by Roberts and LaPorte (1989). They studied several organizations, such as electric utilities and aircraft carriers "in which accidents have catastrophic potential and which have long histories of nearly error free performance" (p. 1). Pfeiffer (1989), reviewing Roberts and LaPorte's research, said these high reliability organizations perform well because of intense training, open communication, fierce loyalty and dedication, and the ability of "cogs" to make "big wheel" decisions:

> Most organizations consist of people in separate categories: big wheels, cogs, and specialists like accountants or chemical engineers. But the high reliability version is a hybrid, a mix of these roles played by the same individuals under different circumstances. The big wheels are there, but use their power rarely. The chain of command is much in evidence, orders may be barked out, and subordinates behave appropriately as spit-and-polish yes-men. But when tension is running high, all work together as specialists among specialists on an equal footing in a more collegial atmosphere.
>
> The most striking and surprising role change occurs in the white heat of danger, when the entire system threatens to collapse. *Then cogs can become big wheels. Whatever their status in the formal hierarchy, they are trained intensively every day so that—based on their experience—they can take complete command, redirect operations or bring them to a complete halt* [italics added]. (p. 40)

Roberts and LaPorte's research—allowing little cogs to become big wheels—closely parallels the performance and results of the AT&T and University of Maryland crises. The AT&T public relations "cogs" were allowed to make "big wheel" decisions that enabled the company to respond to the crisis and the needs of its publics with minimal delay. The most striking example is the ability of the AT&T public relations staff to talk about the crisis with reporters without supervision or guidance from their supervisors or corporate attorneys.

The University of Maryland, however, did not allow its "cogs" to make similar important decisions. The University of Maryland public relations staff often needed approval from both the entire cabinet (Chancellor John Slaughter and his vice chancellors) as well as from the university attorneys before they could release information to reporters and other relevant publics.

Employees with autonomy to make decisions appears to be an important reason why organizations manage crises effectively. The data from the AT&T and University of Maryland case studies showed organizations benefit from allowing properly trained (public relations) employees to make on-the-spot decisions during crises. The crucial ability to be able to share information as quickly as possible with relevant audiences during a crisis makes it important for an organization's public relations staff to react as quickly as it can. The marked differences between the levels of public relations autonomy between the University of Maryland and AT&T, and the success with which they managed their respective crises, suggests this variable might be an important reason why some organizations manage crises well while other organizations do not. Public relations practitioners must therefore consider autonomy as an important predictor of their ability to gather and release information during a crisis and as a measure of their performance during a crisis.

Organizational Communication Culture

Excellent crisis public relations also requires a supportive organizational communication culture or philosophy. Johnson & Johnson, for example, relied almost entirely on its corporate culture outlined in its well-known credo during its product tampering crises. This organizational statement of beliefs was an important reason Johnson & Johnson handled the crisis as well as it did—especially since the company did *not* have a crisis plan to rely on. Other organizations, such as Exxon and Ford, had inappropriate corporate cultures and ideologies that did not serve them well during their infamous crises (the Valdez and Pinto).

Several researchers, including Ford (1981), Gatewood and Carroll (1981), Mitroff and Kilmann (1984), Pauchant (1988), Pauchant and Mitroff (1988), and Roberts and LaPorte (1989) examined how corporate culture affects organizations' responses to crises. Research by Pauchant (1988) and Pauchant and Mitroff (1988) indicated a strong relationship between an organization's culture and its response to crises. This suggests a similar relationship between a more specific *communication* culture and organizational responses to crises.

The data collected in both the AT&T and the University of Maryland crises supported earlier research conducted by Mitroff and Kilmann (1984):

> The likelihood that an organization will anticipate and respond to an impending corporate tragedy is not just determined by the personality and intellectual capacity of its leaders. Nor is its responsiveness determined primarily by its corporate structure, its business policies, and incentive systems which make up its visible features. Rather, every organization also has an invisible quality, a certain style, a character, a way of doing things that may be more powerful than the dictates of any one person or any formal management system. To understand the essence or soul of an organization requires that we travel far beneath formal organization charts, rule books, employee manuals, machines, and buildings, into the underground world of corporate culture.

This is where we will find the basis for an organization's stance toward the un-thinkable. (p. 63)

The communication cultures present within AT&T and the University of Maryland played an important and unmistakable role in how each organiza-tion managed its crisis. Each organization's communication philosophy clearly influenced its response to its crisis much more than any crisis plan it had previously prepared.

The AT&T Crisis. All of the public relations staff members at AT&T re-ferred in some way to an unwritten, but very powerful, communication cul-ture that dominated their practice of public relations. Interviews with AT&T managers clearly indicated the presence of a well-defined communication culture within the public relations function at AT&T. This culture, said Bill Mullane, a public relations vice president, goes back to the founding of AT&T:

I think the culture comes from the 1890s when Theodore Vail was the first president of our company. He was very PR minded. "If you don't tell the truth about yourself, somebody else will tell it." There's not a person here that's been here any length of time that hasn't come to understand that. Come Sat-urday, I'll have spent 27 years doing media relations at AT&T. We've always behaved that way. It was the culture that I was taught the day I came in. It's the culture that other people are expected to follow. When they don't, we get them out. (interview, August 30, 1990)

AT&T's very proactive and cooperative communications philosophy did not change when the January 15 crisis occurred. Tom Frazee, the public re-lations manager for the affected Network Services Division, said there was "absolutely no doubt" in his mind how he would respond to media inquiries during the crisis (interview, August 30, 1990). Carol Albright, a public rela-tions manager who reported to Frazee, agreed the company's public rela-tions crisis strategy was dictated more by AT&T's communication culture than any crisis communication plan:

There was never any indication that we would hide anything or do anything less than be totally honest and up front with the media. Nobody ever said be-fore, "If we ever have a huge crisis, let's make sure we hide it." No one even thought to do that. It's just part of that culture.

Sseveral senior AT&T public relations managers, including Director of Corporate Information Walter Murphy, also clearly indicated the com-pany's communication culture was the basis for their actions during the crisis:

There simply was no discussion of what it was we ought to do. We just would immediately, as we would normally do, answer press calls with as many of the facts as we then had them. There was no thought given to try to stonewall nor to try sugarcoating this thing. It goes back to what I had said earlier. That this is just the normal way that AT&T public relations and media relations operate. There was not that night any discussion particularly of how we ought to respond to the press. I don't recall even talking to Marilyn Laurie [senior vice president for public relations]. (interview, August 30, 1990)

AT&T's communication culture was evident throughout the crisis. Its very strong communication culture clearly dictated what communication strategies the company would use during its crisis and provided an overall guiding principle for public relations staff members. Few, if any, public relations practitioners at AT&T referred to the company's crisis communication plan (in part because it was being revised at the time of the crisis).

The University of Maryland Crisis. Data collected following the death of basketball star Len Bias showed the communication culture in place at the University of Maryland contributed to its inability to manage its crisis successfully. Although the University of Maryland was more than 130 years old at the time of the Bias crisis, only 5 of the 23 senior administrators interviewed could easily describe the campus's communication philosophy. Four people said the campus had *no* communication culture. When the crisis occurred, Vice Chancellor Brit Kirwan said Chancellor John Slaughter and his senior administrators did not have a well-defined communication philosophy to guide their response. He said they had to start from scratch:

The media attention, of course, was just enormous. . . . The press was all over the place scrutinizing everything they could get their hands on. And I think that one of the first things that the campus had to do was to develop a modus operandi, vis a vis the press, how to interact with the press and how to respond in a way that both protected the institution but gave out some information. (interview, September 20, 1990)

Four senior administrators said that although the university had some communication guidelines and policies, it had no underlying philosophy to turn to for guidance:

Every time a question of public access to information came up . . . [it required] a philosophical debate in the cabinet. . . . You [needed] three cabinet meetings to decide whether by that afternoon you could have an answer for the [Baltimore] *Sun's* reporter. (interview with Reese Cleghorn, dean, College of Journalism, August 22, 1990)

At that time, there was no authority, no strong compelling vision for what the communications strategy should be. It was a bunch of bits and pieces by a set of character actors who played their parts. . . . It's an interesting place in that it has not had a long term tradition of information sharing. (interview with Chuck Sturtz, vice chancellor for administrative affairs, August 20, 1990)

I think it [the University of Maryland] did not have a philosophy or culture, and that in itself is something. (interview with Tim Gilmore, executive assistant to Chancellor John Slaughter, October 23, 1990)

If there is [a communication culture], I can't define it. And maybe that was one of the problems, that we didn't have a well-defined communication culture. (interview with Kathleen Kelly, associate dean, College of Journalism, November 15, 1990)

This weak communication culture caused, in part, the campus to miss important opportunities to foster trust, understanding, credibility, cooperation, and agreement with its important publics. The *Washington Post*, for example, published 63 stories (excluding editorials, letters to the editor, and columns) about the University of Maryland crisis between June 20 and July 31, 1986. Almost half of these stories (30, 48%) did not include a response or comment from a University of Maryland administrator or spokesperson. In addition, almost two thirds of the news stories published in the *Washington Post* during this period (41 stories, 65%), did not include a comment from a University of Maryland administrator or spokesperson in the first 10 paragraphs of the story or until the story "jumped" (was continued) to an inside page of the newspaper from the front page or front page of a section.

By maintaining a defensive and low profile posture with faculty, students, reporters, and other important publics, university administrators missed chances to show they did care—and deeply—for the well-being of the students. Interviews with all of the senior administrators at the University of Maryland strongly indicated these people always placed the best intentions of the students first. Unfortunately, the university's communication culture prevented them from revealing this concern.

Implications

The results from this study offer a number of implications for both managers and crisis management researchers. Among the most important is the need for public relations practitioners to shift their attention from a micro (crisis communication checklists) to a macro (theoretical) level. The relationship between autonomy, communication culture, and crisis communication management suggests public relations practitioners should no longer view crisis communication as limited to a set of technical plans. Instead, the research indicates excellent crisis public relations is best described as a philosophy or process imbedded within specific organizations. Effective crisis public relations, therefore, begins with a supportive organizational philosophy rather than a list of people to call or things to do.

Although studies that demonstrate *how* public relations people should practice crisis public relations are useful, the discipline is now at a point in time where it is important to understand *why* events occur. Future research in crisis public relations should go beyond simple "how to" descriptions that often apply only to a single case. The development and refinement of crisis public relations theory will provide generalizable principles useful to many organizations and individuals.

Excellent crisis public relations is dependent on both autonomy and an organization's communication philosophy. If an organization does not support these characteristics necessary for excellent crisis public relations, a crisis plan, no matter how effective, will not likely work. Unfortunately, few public relations practitioners recognize the important relationship between autonomy, communication culture, and excellent crisis public relations. Many practitioners devote significant resources to produce a crisis communications plan that is destined to fail because the technical strategies contained in the plan contradict the dominant and accepted communication philosophies used by their organization. In other words, a great crisis communications plan won't work if "it's not the way we do things here."

Public relations practitioners, therefore, need to pay special attention to their organization's communication culture. They need to examine the "unconscious personality" of their company. They need to assess the philosophies behind and beyond written policies and job descriptions, and determine how they "normally" communicate. Public relations practitioners who analyze their organization and determine the amount of autonomy they have and understand the communication culture within their organization will have a powerful precrisis predictor of crisis communication success.

21

Issue Management During Sudden Executive Departures: Sensemaking, Enactment and Communication

Kathryn T. Theus
University of Southern Mississippi

In September 1993, CBS television's "Eye To Eye" revisited the events precipitating the sudden resignation of Richard Berendzen, president of The American University. The years since 1990 have not erased wounds suffered by the institution when its chief executive unaccountably began making obscene phone calls to area daycare workers and was arrested. Some of those wounds were inflicted after the president resigned, as the board and interim administration were thrust into a "nonroutine" process of sensemaking. Their enactment of coping strategies and communication during a critical succession period left much to be desired.

Changes in leadership inevitably involve disruptions, even when they are anticipated. In normal circumstances, transition processes are defined. They enable selection, orientation and legitimation of duly empowered successors (Weick, 1988). Presuppositions as to the nature of leadership (should it be dynamic vs. circumspect, collaborative vs. autocratic, etc.) will guide managers as they make decisions about the nature of the affected organization, its operations, and its leadership needs. In abnormal or nonroutine circumstances, the very nature of the presuppositions, themselves, may be affected drastically—especially if the departure of a leader is unexpected or tainted by personal indiscretions, malfeasance, or sudden death.[1]

---

[1]Although sudden departures may differ in nature and may require dissimilar strategies, the essential cognitive situation will be similar: Has a process been identified by which leadership can be transferred? If not, how can a process be initiated, which will empower sensible and sensitive choices that provide for organizational stability?

In such cases, the criteria for sensemaking, enactment, and communication may be at variance with norms; and because significant outcomes may be riding on chosen enactments, the process of succession and change, as well as the events surrounding the need for change, may be subjected to intense public scrutiny. Ashforth and Mael (1989) identified public interpretation of organizational actions as key in motivating decision makers to act.

Sensemaking, Weick (1995) suggested, is a process that precedes, but does not include, interpretation of events. He describes it as grounded in structuring the unknown, forming cognitions, from cues selected from the environment. These stimuli are used to put items into frameworks that enable decision makers to comprehend, understand, explain, attribute, extrapolate, and predict. Dervin (1989) called sensemaking a reflective process by which humans create reality and that observations of reality are socially constructed. To make sense of reality requires exploring all possible options for reaching decisions—proactively. Her definition suggests that reality is better conceptualized in terms of dialogue and that leaders who engage in a dialogic process will be more effective in managing stakeholder affairs.

Enactment cannot be separated from sensemaking easily; it appears to be interwoven with it. Heath (1994) pointed to enactment as a bracketing activity—the process people employ collectively to interpret their environment. "Enactment involves perception and attention. People focus on some element of their environment as they interact with one another about it, and they ignore other aspects. Recurring selections transform into schemata—patterned and predictable ways of perceiving" (p. 8). Morgan (1984) described enactment as subtle or hidden cultural forces that may influence our decision making, thereby reducing sensemaking through conditioning our premises, definitions, communication flow, knowledge, perceptions, and subsequent acts. Heath (1994) added, "Culture is the product of symbolic action through which people create shared frames of reference and make sense" (p. 157). Leaders are to some extent bound to respond to the culture which they help to create. Organizations left leaderless will be constrained to cope with the cultures their former leaders promoted.

A number of factors pose barriers to sensemaking and appropriate enactment for to those who are left to direct an organization suddenly leaderless. First, unanticipated departures will precipitate considerable uncertainty and heightened emotions among those responsible for running the organization (Farquhar, 1989), where uncertainty is defined as information deprivation and concomitant loss of power or control (Crozier & Friedberg, 1980). Ad hoc or newly deputized leaders may question, for example, who should have control over authority, information, and finances (Galbraith, 1974).

As a consequence of this uncertainty, a power vacuum of significant proportions may emerge as access to information and control over its distribution become foci for turf battles. Ad hoc or newly deputized decision makers will often engage in secretive or defensive behaviors to enhance or protect their domains, while communication professionals often will be left out of the loop entirely. These behaviors may have ramifications for internal and external stakeholders—individuals or groups who have a stake in the outcome—resulting in loss of organizational legitimacy and credibility (Theus, 1988) or loss of image (Dutton & Dukerich, 1991).

Destabilization of normal channels for information flow will render sensemaking or enactment more difficult for ad hoc leaders. Hermann (1963) noted that in crises, authority moves to higher levels in the organization, fewer people exercise authority, and the number of occasions when authority is exercised increases. When the organization is tight-looped to start with, crises further constrain the already narrowed information flow through bureaucratic levels (Hage, 1980; Theus, 1991). Such narrowing of communication and feedback networks may prevent access to information, assessment of problems (due to loss expertise), and appropriate response.

Dervin (1989) suggested that optimal sensemaking occurs when communication is symmetric (involves frequent and clear dialogue) between management and internal and external stakeholders. She suggests that a fuller comprehension can be realized only by sharing and confronting many perspectives. "By comparing and trying to understand why and how perspectives differ, humans anchor themselves in an informed sense of their own time-place and become able to take individual and collective actions" (p. 75).

Heath (1994) proposed that a symmetrical relationship exists when stakes are perceived to be equal in worth and parties are willing and able to exercise them. An asymmetrical relationship exists when stakeholders hold stakes of different value or participants are unequally able or willing to grant stakes. The latter often results in reactive enactment and communication, responses that are common in crises (Weick, 1988) and tend to reduce the quality of sensemaking. From the perspective of internal and external publics or stakeholders, tightened central control will create strains between open disclosure, more often viewed as socially responsible organizational behavior and issues of privacy or the withholding of confidential or proprietary information (Theus, 1993). Such potential abridgments of interests will not go unnoticed by those who have a stake in the organization and its success.

The consequences of these multiple effects suggest that sensemaking will be affected adversely when leaders are unexpectedly removed. People will interpret their environments and act, often acting before they think, in order to make sense of uncertain situations (Shrivastava, 1987). Dervin (1989) explained that when decision makers are uncertain, they will call upon "habit paths" (e.g., act by seeking information from those with whom they are in regular contact), in order to bridge gaps and make sense of their situations. Initial actions will set the tone and determine the trajectory of future responses.

Weick (1988) asserted that actions taken, even without reflection, will render crises more controllable. Dervin (1989) critiqued this approach as often counterproductive. Not only will actions narrow alternative response repertoires, but reactive choices may be decidedly dysfunctional. And just as the public nature of actions also makes them harder to undo, explanations that decision makers make for their actions may become justifications that prevent them from perceiving that they may have missed better approaches to problem solving or have escalated organizational stress (Mitroff, Shrivastava, & Udwadia, 1987; Staw, 1980).

The case described in this chapter shows how reactive processes of newly deputized leaders, often resorting to habit paths under conditions of uncertainty, are rationalized as serving expedient functions. It also illustrates how these same enactments often contribute to dysfunctions that disable organizations' responses to crises. The absence of symmetric sensemaking results in leaderships' reduced capacity to restore and retain organizational balance, legitimacy, credibility, and social responsibility. It further suggests that proactive sensemaking and enactments in loosely coupled situations, where information has the opportunity to be generated and is not closely guarded, will yield more salutary outcomes (uncertainty reduction, greater understanding, and lower levels of stress, as well as higher estimations of legitimacy, credibility, and social responsibility) than in tightly coupled and highly specified situations.

The case illustrates how ad hoc leaders will resort to habit paths perceived as safe (even if potentially inappropriate) to solve nonroutine problems. To the extent that they do not disclose their own assessments or actions in order to avoid disapproval of others, or make decisions only because they will be approved by those in power, the more they will miss information needed to manage the situation to lower levels of stress. Dependence upon "safe" avenues may also lead to ethical errors in commission or omission. For example, unwillingness to face public embarrassment may lead ad hoc or newly deputized decision makers to hide facts or give half-truths, which if later disclosed might be labeled "coverup." What was not wrong-doing becomes defined as wrong-doing when justifications for nondisclosure are perceived by stakeholder publics as inappropriate. Communication is a vital concern for sensemaking, as open communication reduces discrepancy in media accounts of organizational issues and causes those organizations to be treated as more socially responsible by journalists (Theus, 1988).

Finally, the case study illustrates problems that arise when no institutionalized means of organizational learning have been provided. As has been found in other types of crises (Pearson & Mitroff, 1993), the process for the selection of a successor often includes no "blame free" process of introspection. Succession plans developed for routine transfers of power often do not serve well following a crisis, in part because of the changed nature of the organization itself (Gilmore, 1988). Once a successor has been chosen, he or she often will select a new team from outside the organization. As a consequence, organizational memory will be lost or, just as often, learning will be avoided because "it is too painful" to reopen old wounds.

By studying one case of a crisis in leadership in depth, it will be possible to examine a process as it unfolded over time (Yin, 1984) as well as communication anomalies that emerged. Further, it will be possible to note additional subtle influences that affected the work of ad hoc leaders and their management teams, because crisis events accentuate dynamics sometimes hidden or absent in routine situations (Eisenhardt, 1989).

METHODOLOGY

The case presented focuses on a crisis-induced change of leadership at a major eastern university. Extensive data were gathered through lengthy interviews, surveys, and document collection in a 3-day period about 1 year after the crisis. The interviews were focused, a special case for studying variations in perceptions and responses from individuals who have been involved in the same situation (Yin, 1984).

Data Sources

Interviewees were selected based on their position within the university, and because of the role they played in the unfolding issue (e.g., the board of trustees chairman and his executive committee; the acting president, university officers and administrative staff; public relations professionals involved in managing the situation; legal counsel, deans, faculty, students, others from middle and lower ranks of the organization; and reporters who created the public record of the issue). Each of 20 interviews lasted 1 to 2 hours in length. A purposive survey of 42 employees drawn from positions at each level of the institution provided external verification for dimensions identified through interviews. In addition, two focus groups, each lasting more than 2 hours, with between 6 to 12 participants were held: one drawn from the organization and one from the surrounding community. Similarly, analysis of institutional documents and news clippings provided a public context for the crisis.

Dimensions explored through qualitative and quantitative data provided insight on enactments, sensemaking, uncertainty, power-relations, organizational structure, and communication during and subsequent to the crisis-induced departure of the organizational leader.

Data Analysis

In order to build theory from this case, it was essential that data be used to construct the issue's history as depicted through interpretations of actions and events from April 6 through December 7, 1990, and to analyze themes to explain the pattern of interpretations and actions. For the identification of themes, both interviews and documents were analyzed and themes recorded as reflected in recurrent topics of discussion or reporting. A theme list was used to isolate how organizational stakeholders interpreted or explained organizational concerns and actions. A case history then was built, based on milestones identified from the themes, as well as from documentary evidence for dates and identification of actors.

In addition, frequencies from the purposive survey were generated to provide some numeric assessment of the prevalence of dimensions present within the community. This information was not used for predictive purposes, but in order to triangulate findings from other sources (Eisenhardt, 1989).

BACKGROUND FOR THE CASE

The president of American University in Washington D.C., over a 10-year span, had been a stunning success in elevating the private institution from acknowledged mediocrity to more competitive standing in areas such as research grants, faculty appointments, and recruitment of students. Campus constituents responding to a purposive survey suggested that the trajectory of American was on the ascent (93%), even though financial resources were no more than adequate (62%), and the most highly qualified students were not beating down the door to be admitted (72%). Nonetheless, American was a comfortable place to be (76%), with not too much discord and with a good deal of intellectual vitality (57%).

The survey also suggested that serious efforts had been taken by the president to create a financial surplus for the university (63%) to increase enrollment (51%), to attract the best students (79%), to serve campus constituents (65%), and to operate the institution efficiently (62%). Focus groups and interviews elaborated these themes. A dean said:

> As a manager, the president had delegated internal decisions to a competent provost and two vice presidents, and fiduciary decisions to his board of trustees. The president saw himself, primarily, as an external person whose task was to bring visibility and resources to the institution. The president wasn't

much of an internal player. He had no staff, and meetings [with deans] were happy talk rather than anything substantive.... I learned very quickly as dean that you didn't go to [the president] with a problem.... He didn't want to hear anything bad. What he wanted from the deans was really two things: he wanted some lines he could turn into sound bites; secondly, he wanted us to carry out his pet projects.... He considered himself a rainmaker.

As for daily working arrangements, lines of authority in the institution resembled an hour glass, with the board of trustees occupying the upper cone, the president representing the conduit, and the provost, vice presidents, deans, and faculty occupying the lower cone. Decision making in the organization was not perceived to be very democratic by campus constituents (68%), with trustees having too much control (72%) and faculty committees having too little responsibility for major decisions (62%). The student body, however, was viewed as an expressive and articulate group, unafraid of censorship (65%).

"The university is not a democracy and it is not an autocracy. It is a manipulatocracy. Ideas have to either naturally bubble up from the bottom or they have to *appear* to bubble up from the bottom ... a manipulation," a top level administrator said.

There existed some stress in reporting relationships in the lower section of the cone, and some of this discontent extended into faculty ranks. According to a faculty member:

There were some claims last year that freedom of speech was inhibited on campus.... While there wasn't a purposeful message from above to below that if you complain you're in trouble, the perception of that in terms of strategic relationships [was] ... that we will be penalized if we complain.

As for the large board (about 50 members when completely constituted), the president hand-picked each highly visible, business-oriented member, and shielded the body from internal university issues and contacts. The board followed the president's recommendations about what actions to approve and disapprove, often with little knowledge of the norms of the organization's culture. Having knowledge primarily of corporate, rather than university culture, the board generally heeded the president's recommendations to the letter. "He did not build a consensual process, and kept the board of trustees and various campus constituencies somewhat isolated from one another," a board member said. "That was the tone of his administration. And most things were controlled through his office."

In fact, the president led the board to believe that only two of the three vice presidents (one for finance and one for development), in addition to himself, should have strong working ties with the board. Described as "out of the loop" was the provost, also a vice president, and by virtue of the university charter designated to become acting president in the absence of the president. The structure provided the provost with little interaction with the board upon which to build a trust-based relationship in the event of a transfer of power. A board member said:

> So these two administrative vice presidents were constantly dealing with the board committees when it came under their purview. The provost dealt less with board committees although there was no barrier to interchange with the provost. It's just that the board didn't deal with academic affairs. But the provost, for instance, was in charge of the budget process, so he dealt with the board at that level. . . . The executive committee in fact, had the power under [its] charter to make most of the decisions for the university rather than take those to the whole board, though that was generally not the case. . . . Issues were reported to the board in a very controlled fashion. . . . Of course, there was a lot of politics involved in all of this.

The vice president for development had the ear of the president and frequently worked with him in designing fund-raising activities. The public relations director reported to the vice president and had no direct line of reporting to the president. Although the public relations office had established good media contacts, and worked to provide faculty with a forum to tell their success stories, little attention was paid to internal communication, about which there were often complaints. A public relations worker said:

> You can't get anything to students (or faculty). It is like a nightmare. In order to get [information] out quickly enough to 5,000 undergraduates and 1,000 graduates (if you are talking about everyone)—getting a letter stamped and mailed—by the time you do that, its been in the paper four days.

Sometimes public relations advice was not heeded by the vice president, even when the issue could cause damaging publicity. A staff member suggested the vice president deferred to the president and board, because of his long-standing friendship with the president.

INTERPRETATIONS OF AND ACTIONS ON PRESIDENTIAL MALFEASANCE

Several distinct phases evolved over the course of the unfolding university crisis, as follows:

Phase 1: Truth About Resignation Not Disclosed
(April 5–20)

When the president of American University announced his resignation during the spring of 1990, effective at the end of the term (some 2 months later), the board's executive committee knowingly allowed the president to provide a false explanation for his stepping down: "Frankly, I am exhausted," his April 10th letter stated. In authorizing the release of the president's statement, *without comment*, the executive committee avoided acknowledging the president had resigned under pressure, and inviting subsequent accusations that it misled publics about the nature of the resignation.

How had the executive committee of the board arrived at this strategy? With whom had the executive committee consulted? Evidence suggests they operated without gathering outside perspectives, but depended upon their own habitual practices of conferring among themselves.

Normally, the president alone would have served as the board's conduit for getting information and advice on dealing with a crisis issue or for gaining access to organization members for input. In the absence of the president, however, the system for delegation of authority and oversight of information broke down. The board's by-laws required 30 days notice for calling a full session and 10 days notice for calling an executive committee session. Such procedures were inappropriate for the kind of crisis American University faced. "You have legal ramifications, you have public relations ramifications. All are very serious. Taking this issue through the standard process is impossible," said a board member. Another elaborated:

> There was no crisis management process that assumed the president would not be functional. The by-laws deal with it by saying if the president isn't able to function, the provost is acting president. But this crisis was a crisis of determining whether the president was able to function or not. And this is not covered in any of the policies, charter, by-laws or the university. So you improvise.

Legal counsel became aware of the situation of Friday, April 6, and the executive committee on April 7. The resignation of the president was secured the next day, according to a board member.

> He [legal counsel] talked to me on Friday at 11:30 a.m. and then there was an executive committee meeting at 2:00 p.m. that day, but I made a decision not to bring it to the executive committee meeting because I didn't know what the facts were. And I was concerned about the PR aspects of this getting out before we knew what was going on.

Other than this group only two or three campus employees knew about the president's behavior, and only then because the police had required their consent to investigate. The executive committee and this inner circle comprised a confidential loop, pledged to secrecy.

The executive committee appeared to have no knowledge of or interest in the vital link that communication played in the daily operations of the lower cone of the university's more organic academic substructure. This was to be expected. The board had never become familiar with the norms of the campus with regard to collaborative decision making. It did not consult the public relations office and discouraged its attempts to assist, even though the public relations director, on learning of the president's sudden resignation, urged the vice president for development (who also had not been told the truth about what was going on), "Tell [the board] they either need to talk to me, or they need to talk to the best PR firm in town." They did neither. A board member later explained its rationale:

> If you don't talk, you can't get in trouble. . . . We said, "we're not going to comment on this until we are ready to comment." That didn't make the press very happy. It was a slow period and they realized they had something interesting to chase here, but that's about what we did.

Even more serious in its implications for continuity of leadership, the board did not give full information to the provost when he was appointed acting president Sunday afternoon, April 8. When the provost inquired as to the nature of the resignation, he was read the president's letter, was discouraged from seeking further information, was told congratulations, and the call was terminated. This, too, reflected the habitual relationship between board and provost, and the board's tendency to avoid the opinion and counsel of outsiders.

When the provost called the president directly, he received no elaboration as to how to proceed. Thus, as the acting president, the provost did not have a clear understanding of whether his authority was vested completely and immediately, or at the end of the term. He took the initiative, however, by calling officers, deans, and campus leaders to inform them of the resignation. Then, to complicate matters, the former president disappeared, literally. The board's executive committee had granted him an immediate leave of absence, but it had not anticipated that he would leave town. This created a significant degree of uncertainty within the inner circle, and also among those attempting to govern with circumscribed information. Rumors had already begun to circulate, and these became exaggerated. A trajectory for the pending revelation of malfeasance had been set.

Meanwhile, the acting president/provost and his team were instructed to carry on "operations as usual," but they faced a difficult task, especially with graduation only 3 weeks away. For example, the enrollment-driven university faced a spring decision date for the entering freshman class, complete with a formal campus gathering that would include prospective parents and students. The acting president, vice president for development, public relations director, and the admissions staff did not know whether the former president might show up to give a scheduled speech. So they could only develop contingency plans. The acting president would speak regardless, they determined. Actions they took were highly dependent upon instinct and habit paths. There were no true precedents for their decisions.

Phase 2: Board and University Distances Itself From Coverup (April 20–End of Spring Term)

On Friday, April 20, only hours before the critical weekend gathering was to transpire, the board chairman told the acting president about the circumstances surrounding the departure of the former president—a full 2 weeks after the problem had been discovered; that is, that police had been successful in tracing an obscene call to the president's private office phone; the executive committee had kept the information confidential to protect the privacy of the president; the board did not know the whereabouts of the president. (It had not yet been discovered by the board that the president, since his resignation, had been undergoing treatment for a sexual disorder at a Baltimore hospital.) He was told that a local television station would soon release a story based on allegations of obscene calls. The acting president was stunned, but relieved that some of the worst rumors had not been correct. (The university itself had not been immune from allegations of malfeasance.)

The public relations director, upon learning the truth, hastened to make the best of a bad situation. Her instinct was to avoid the appearance of being forced into a reactive position, by utilizing a nonblaming and open approach to communicate with the university community and media. She drafted a letter from the board chairman to the university community, which was put in the mail on Friday. (The letter was stacked in libraries and dorms and other public spaces for students to acquire on Monday about the time the mailed versions were to be delivered.) The text, released to media on Monday, April 23, discussed alleged improper behavior and disassociated the institution and the leader's success as a president from his individual circumstances and personal problems:

> I want to emphasize that these allegations concerned personal actions of [the president] and were in no way related to his role as president of the university. No one else in the university community was in any way involved in the alleged improprieties.

Disassociation was the public relations director's suggestion. She also urged the board to come clean on the issue. "She always says when in doubt, tell the truth. That always strikes me as appropriate," a high level administrator said. At the same time, the board formally announced the appointment of the acting president as interim president, and a convocation was scheduled for the entire university community April 27, an event strategically developed to position the acting president as indisputable leader of the campus. The convocation was suggested by the public relations director, who was busily working at damage control. The university senate met the same week to act in support of the provost and in a letter to faculty stated:

> I also communicated our full confidence [to the Board of Trustees] in [the Provost], who has played a major role in the University's growth, as he undertakes the powers and duties of the president.

In early May, a search committee was formed, drawing representation primarily from the board, with several representatives of campus constituencies. It was time to put the awful affair to rest and to move on. No assessment occurred as to how the issue had been managed, however, and the board retained control both of the search process and of the flow of information surrounding what had transpired a month earlier.

Many in the university community remained upset over the events of April and about the manner in which they were informed of the difficulties of the president and the university. Many board members and faculty were especially angry because they first heard of the allegations in news reports. Media reported vigorously as various constituents voiced their dismay. The failure of the institution to disclose the reason behind the resignation of its president was not the subject of comment by journalists, however. This may have been because the president's impact had been great in the community and, therefore, he was treated by the press somewhat sympathetically. Journalists often evoked images of a fallen knight—an idea drawn from the president's own diary, published during his first years as president of American. When the president made an appearance on the Niteline television show with Ted Koppel some weeks later, he disclosed his own perspective on what he termed a temporary stress-induced illness, which he said was related to his own sexual abuse as a child. He apologized to those affected, adding another chapter to a saga that would continue in the media until a summer trial and conviction.

"People always say, 'Did you have a crisis plan?' But written crisis plans always say 'the president will . . .' What do you do when your president's gone?" a public relations staffer said.

Phase III: Former President Seeks Strategic Advantage, Manipulates Board (Summer term—November 2)

Often missteps aired publicly are resolved to the satisfaction of the press as soon as the novelty of an issue becomes less interesting or is superseded by more novel events. This does not mean the issues are resolved. In the case of American University, a second crisis loomed—specifically caused by the manner in which the first crisis was handled by the board. At issue was the former president's status as faculty member at the institution.

The executive committee and its legal counsel had not obtained the former president's resignation as tenured faculty member. A board member explained:

> Legally, we had a contract with [the former president]. There's always the possibility of looking for reasons not to honor the contract based on the behavior of either party. We looked at that. But we did not think it was appropriate from a legal point of view to try to void the contract because of his behavior, nor did we think it was appropriate in terms of the long-term issue of his service to the university.

In fact, in academic institutions, it is the responsibility of the chief academic officer, the provost, not the board, to take initiatives regarding the termination of faculty status of a tenured professor. Because the provost was not included in the original information loop and, therefore, could not give his response to the wording of the former president's resignation letter, the wording did not include language that revoked or even addressed faculty status. When the board accepted the April 10, 1990 letter worded: "consequently, I hereby submit my resignation as President," the tenure contract remained in force. Only a faculty referendum on the issue could then have revoked tenure, once the resignation was accepted.

Apparently, the former president and his legal counsel recognized that tenure might become a bargaining chip for resigning his faculty position. During the summer and fall, many unofficial phone calls and meetings were held between the executive committee, the former president, and legal counsel for both, seeking agreement over whether and how the former president might leave American University. Some board members felt extreme loyalty to the president who appointed them. They followed their former habit paths of honoring relationships established prior to the president's malfeasance. Applying private sector criteria, many felt that compensation above severance pay was appropriate for departing chief executives, regardless of circumstances.

However, most members of the university community did not know about these discussions, nor that tenure remained in force. This reflected prior board secrecy, a habit hard to break. In point of fact, early that summer a board member on the search committee told a faculty senator who wanted to know whether the former president had resigned his faculty status, "It is none of your business." The negotiations continued in secret until the fall, when rumors again began to circulate.

Phase IV: Academic Culture Rejects Board's Value System (November 2–December 7)

When knowledge that the former president had not relinquished his tenure came to light in the fall, just as search criteria for a new president was published, it triggered great dismay. Stakeholders correctly perceived that this circumstance would have significant ramifications for perceptions of safety for students and also for the selection and transfer of authority to a legitimate successor. It also brought into clear focus concern over the degree to which the interim president had been excluded from decision making, and thus the probable omission of campus input and values in reaching a solution.

To make matters worse, on November 2 the campus community learned through the *Washington Post* that the board intended to offer the former president approximately $680,000 to resign his tenure, along with $340,000 specified in his contract as severance pay. (A disgruntled board member leaked the story in precise detail before the board had a chance to inform the campus community of its actions.) The package was equivalent to almost 5% of the school's total endowment. A reporter said a board member told her, "This man gave so much to this institution, we [should] give him even more than we are giving him."

Students, faculty, administration, staff, alumni, and the local community, who had generally given the institution and fallen president the benefit of the doubt, were outraged, not only at the buy-out (a distinctly corporate solution to problems) and the amount, but also at the manner in which they learned of this action.

Immediately, the public relations office braced itself for an onslaught of calls. A reporter said:

> The campus hated the fact they were being dragged through the press. The university was now being completely closed [in its communication style] and things were coming up piecemeal. It's hard reporting on any group when they're in crisis . . . its a sort of structural thing.

Deans threatened to resign if the board proceeded with its intentions. Several hundred students held an impromptu rally, responding to a student's scribbled and posted note, "If you agree with me that this is shit, meet me on the quad at noon." Letters of protest streamed into the interim's office.

Although the interim president had supported a board move to have the former president relinquish his tenure without formal faculty action, he felt that any golden parachute should come from private sources, not from the institution's endowment. "The board hadn't been much of a listener to the campus up until that time, because of the way we were kept apart from the campus [by the former president]," a board member said, explaining its resistance to the interim president's advice. Once the action of the board was known, however, the interim president was joined by his dean of faculty, the chairman of the staff council, deans, faculty, and others in desperately seeking solutions to the perceived inappropriate buyout contemplated by the board. A reporter described what she observed:

> It was my sense that [the interim president] did a very good job of channeling discontent and brokering information. If I had to guess who best began to help the Board of Trustees to understand, he was bringing the message.

Even so, when the interim president began to forcefully confront the board on behalf of enraged stakeholders, he effectively eliminated himself, a trusted campus leader, from consideration for a permanent appointment as president.

Divided in its loyalties and exhausted, exasperated, and surprised by the campus outpouring, ultimately, the board did rescind its buy-out offer; but this action followed the former president's "voluntary" withdrawal from receiving such an offer. On November 26 the former president released a statement that said he would ask to return to teaching after an appropriate leave. With respect to the buyout, he said, "Were I to receive such an offer, I would still prefer to leave it on the table and return to teach." On November 30, a delegation of faculty leaders met with the former president to secure his agreement that he return as a faculty member.

The action of the December 6 board meeting was proforma, and while testimony was given by students and faculty, the board's split decision had already been made. Reflecting on the year-long ordeal, a board member said:

> We were looking at it as a corporate culture issue, not an academic culture issue. . . . It's not unusual when somebody gets in trouble [in a corporation] to support them this way. . . . But academic culture is different. And if you're going to be an effective leader of an academic institution, you have to honor the academic culture. You can't impose a corporate culture on them. And we needed to learn that.

Two days later, the student activist group that organized as a result of the impromptu rally on the quad called for representation of students and faculty on the board of trustees. On December 7, the interim president held a campus-wide meeting to address the events of recent months and to point toward the future of American University, an act that symbolically brought the crisis to a close. By March 1, 1991, a new president had been selected for the institution. And after an extended leave, the former president returned to campus to teach, with only a flurry of media coverage, and with great unease on the part of the campus community.

THE ROLE OF SENSEMAKING, COMMUNICATION, STRUCTURE AND LEARNING: WHAT PRACTITIONERS SHOULD CONSIDER

The story of American University's crisis of leadership continued to unfold for several years. By April 1993 the director of public relations, and the vice president for development, the dean of faculties, and the provost/interim president all had resigned their administrative positions and most had left the university. The newly appointed president had also resigned after little more than a year in office. The institution began a search for a third president in as many years and evidence suggests the institution has not come to terms with the causes nor the effects of the original disruption. An analysis of the case, nevertheless, has suggested several important themes.

Symmetric Sensemaking Should Occur Prior to Enactment. Weick (1988) suggested that enactment renders crises more controllable, and observes that such a statement can be self-affirming because as perceptions of control increase, stress decreases. As a result, people are more likely to notice things they can do something about and feel fewer constraints. They feel they are regaining power, and feel stress with less intensity, making tasks simpler. At the same time, Weick admits that the less adequate the sensemaking, the more likely a crisis will get out of control.

This analysis suggests that *enactment without adequate collaborative sensemaking may render crisis events uncontrollable,* and any perceptions of control will be illusory and misleading. For example, the capacity of legitimate managers to deal with events at American was significantly diminished by the withholding of information and power *by the board.* Initial reactive enactments of the board's executive committee caused the downward trajectory that persisted throughout the affair—by accepting the president's resignation and providing a false explanation, by noting his disappearance and providing no explanation, by appointing an interim president and circumscribing information about the circumstances of the president's resignation, by allowing the terms of the transfer of authority to the interim to be vague, and by bypassing legitimate faculty governance structures in handing down tenure decisions. Enactments, determined in a closed system that constrained consultation, not only increased campus and community anxiety, but compounded problems because faulty assumptions about the executive committee were not aired with the university's management team (interim president, vice presidents, deans, and communication professionals) who could have provided a corrective view—actions that would have placed control where it belonged. Respondents to the survey reinforced this interpretation. They said that actions were taken by university representatives that caused management problems (72%). They agreed that decision makers demonstrated poor communication on the issue (56%) and could have done a lot more to solve the problem (62%). About 72% said they were uncertain whether the administration welcomed information that came unsolicited, and 69% did not believe decision-makers took decisive actions to resolve the problem quickly. Half said the institution only reported 50% of what it wanted released, and did not do so completely and promptly when it did (57%). However, 76% indicated that media did not cause the problems at American, they only reported them.

Tight Coupling Limits Options. The *uncertainty and power vacuum* that emerged at American University escalated in part due to *the tight coupling (and "only a few need to know" approach) that disrupted normal communication channels.* This tight coupling diminished the amount of information otherwise available from internal (employee) and external (stakeholder) feedback. The imposition of the norms of a bureaucratic corporate structure (top-down communication and withholding of information by a dominant elite) exacerbated the chaos that erupted in a usually collegial community. The interim president and the director of public relations (a specialist in the field of public communication) were prevented from timely interaction with their publics and media, because they had little information and no familiarity with the executive committee's operative assumptions. These errors *reduced communication and also diminished expertise for managing the issue.*

Turf-Guarding Erodes Legitimacy and Credibility. The executive committee of the board *unwisely and consistently maintained a course of non-disclosure in order to avoid scrutiny by media or objections of opponents.* Rather than incur a temporary flurry of notoriety, the board opted for a safe course ("no comment") which ultimately created much greater publicity and scorn than had the issue been presented more openly. Decisions that were not on their face patently unethical (because they involved issues of privacy as well as the imposition of norms and routines of a different, in this case corporate, organizational culture). But they became viewed as unethical because of perceived manipulations of decision makers. *The withholding of information by the board inner circle from the interim president and his team—the university's "designated leaders"—vested inappropriate power in the executive committee and removed legitimate power from managers, communication professionals, deans and faculty.* This usurpation contributed to a chaotic downward spiral that ultimately precipitated a second, more serious crisis of public confidence in the organization following the board's offer to buyout the president's contract.

Of course, one cannot determine what the board would have done had it known in advance that campus and community reaction to a buyout would be negative. Many felt the executive committee had little use for campus sentiment. Had the committee known more, it might have managed to present the buyout in a way that would have co-opted key figures and muted negative response.

Board Strategies Discrepant With Organization Culture Will Be Rejected. Corporations solve problems of anomalous executives by quietly providing golden parachutes. This buy-out approach is well within the financial and normative value system of for-profit organizations, and may even be seen as socially responsible under a corporate model. However, such assumptions would be deemed by a poorly funded university as unusual, if not blatantly out of line, as it was viewed at American. *This case suggests that norms guiding decision-makers must conform to norms of the organizational culture, or they will be questioned and rejected as illegitimate by organizational stakeholders.*

Organization Will Perpetuate Its Dysfunction Without Introspection. The American University executive committee and board, throughout its ordeal, failed to consult with those who had a stake in the outcome of the resignation/tenure/buyout situation. *The lack of collaboration, before, during and after the American University crisis prevented the organization from assessing its progress and evaluating its failures. The board's intractability and turf-guarding (commitment to a predetermined course of action) diminished the organization's capacity to restore public confidence.* Only through the search committee, which represented a microcosm of the conflict-ridden institution, were communications attempted between board and campus interests.

FUTURE DIRECTIONS FOR RESEARCH

Sensemaking, communication, structure, and organizational learning appear to be important factors affecting the efficacy of enactments of ad hoc leaders when crises induce or accompany sudden departures of chief executives. Findings reinforce some well-known ideas about organizational adaptation and suggest important new directions for research.

Future studies may wish to explore whether:

- Sudden departures increase the power of information holders and diminish the power of the information deprived, whether or not they hold legitimate positions of authority;
- Norms imposed by interim authority holders must be congruent with norms of the affected organization in order to be deemed legitimate by its members;
- Needs of the organization may be neglected when ad hoc decision makers are bound by loyalty to the former organizational leader;
- High uncertainty in a crisis situation means decision makers will be more likely to save face and protect themselves from accountability through nondisclosure;
- Sure and certain publicity will increase the likelihood that organizations will make timely public statements to address organizational face-saving.

In each of these propositions there appear to be clear links between individual motivations and subsequent organizational effects or responses. Findings from the case suggest other dimensions for investigation:

- When a leader is precipitously and publicly removed from office, especially in the case of a popular leader, will sensemaking through symmetric and collaborative communication provide more efficacious strategies for making decisions?
- Will symmetric communication reduce the potential for abridgments of stakeholder interests through nondisclosure or other perceived ethical or judgment errors.
- Will the development of institutionalized processes of "no fault" reflection about the causes, management and resolution of crises assist organizations in avoiding negative spin-off effects?
- When leaders depart or are removed, will tapping their organizational memory and retaining their organizational learning provide future benefit, even if it hurts to look back?

Answers to such questions may help organizations identify more adaptive processes for sensemaking, enactment, and communication—especially when ad hoc or newly deputized leaders are charged with finding a solution the community can accept, and with identifying a successor to manage the fallout from crises.

Consistent with the spirit of Yin (1984) and Eisenhardt (1989), the story of American University reveals new ideas for theory building, particularly in the domain of organizational communication and its importance for adaptation. The idea that an organization's capacity to communicate is central to its capacity to govern, suggests that organizational leaders, particularly in times of stress, should monitor communication processes. Researchers should ask what motivates ad hoc or newly deputized leaders to look beyond their own worldviews and habit paths, enabling them to communicate about issues symmetrically and openly during periods of stress, and what personal and structural barriers prevent them from doing so.

ACKNOWLEDGMENTS

Interviews with subjects quoted in this study took place at The American University at the invitation of its interim president during the first week of December, 1991. Permission to quote was given on the basis that names and personally revealing information be omitted. Specific citations have not been included in the text nor the bibliography in order to meet the condition of anonymity. Funding for this study was provided by The Lilly Endowment and TIAA/CREF.

References

Aldrich, M. W. (2000, November 27). Tire recall nearing completion. http://dailynews.yahoo.com/h/ap/20001127/bs/tire_deaths_recall_1.html

Allen, M. W., & Caillouet, R. H. (1994). Legitimation endeavors: Impression management strategies used by an organization in crisis. *Communication Monographs, 61,* 44–62.

Allen, R. E. (1993, September 23). Apologies are not enough. *New York Times,* p. C3.

Aristotle. (1932). *On rhetoric* (L. Cooper, Trans.). Englewood Cliffs, NJ: Prentice-Hall.

Ashforth, B., & Mael, F. (1989). Social identity theory and the organization. *Academy of Management Review, 14,* 20–39.

Ashforth, B. E., & Gibbs, B. W. (1990). The double-edge of organizational legitimation. *Organization Science, 1,* 177–294.

Ashmore, M. (1989). *The reflexive thesis: Wrighting sociology of scientific knowledge.* Illinois: University of Chicago Press.

Audi, T., & Dixon, J. (2000, October 6). Documents show Ford was warned about tire thread: Automaker says it acted quickly once it received hard data. http://www.auto.com/autonews/why6_20001006.htm

Axley, S. (1984). Managerial and organizational communication in terms of the conduit metaphor. *Academy of Management Review, 9,* 428–437.

Baatz, E. B. (1994). Corporate Healers, *CIO, 8*(6), 36.

Bailey, S. (2000). Prepared statement for the United States House of Representatives Joint Hearing of the Subcommittee on Telecommunications Trade & Consumer Protection and the Subcommittee on Oversight & Investigations (Sept. 6th). See www.house.gov/commerce.

Baker, R. W. (1989, June 14). Critics fault Exxon's "PR campaign." *Christian Science Monitor,* p. 8.

Banks, S. P. (2000). *Multicultural public relations: A social interpretive approach.* Ames: Iowa State University Press.

Barciela, S. (1996, February 4). "Growth": New buzzword for quality-conscious managers. *Omaha Sunday World-Herald,* p. 13 G.

Bardwick, M. (1991). *Danger in the comfort zone: From boardroom to mailroom—How to break the entitlement habit that's killing American business.* New York: AMACOM.

Barnett, G. A. (1988). Communication and organizational culture. In G. A. Barnett & G. M. Goldhaber (Eds.), *Handbook of organizational communication* (pp. 101–126). Norwood, NJ: Ablex.

Barton, L. (1990, November). Crisis management: selecting communications strategy. *Management Decision, 28,* 5.

Barton, L. (1991). When managers find themselves on the defensive. *Business Forum, 16*(1), 8–13.

Barton, L. (1993). *Crisis in organizations: Managing and communicating in the heat of chaos.* Cincinnati, OH: College Divisions South-Western.

Barton, L. (2001). *Crisis in organizations II.* Cincinnati, OH: South-Western.

Bartunik, J. M. (1988). In R. E. Quinn & K. S. Cameron (Eds.), *Paradox and transformation: Toward a theory of change in organizations and management* (pp. 19–64). Cambridge, MA: Ballinger.

Baskin, O., & Aronoff, C. (1992). *Public relations: The profession and the practice* (3rd ed.). Dubuque, IA: Wm. C. Brown Publishers.

Bateson, G., & Bateson, M. C. (1987). *Angels fear: Towards an epistemology of the sacred.* Toronto: Bantam.

Baum, J. A. C., & Oliver, C. (1992). Institutional embeddedness and the dynamics of organizational populations. *American Sociological Review, 57,* 540–559.

Baum, J. A. C., & Powell. W. W. (1995). Cultivating an institutional ecology of organizations: Comment on Hannan, Carroll, Dundon, and Torres. *American Sociological Review, 60,* 529–538.

Bechler, C. (1994, November). *Using ethnography to understand crisis: Looking beyond the immediate crisis response to ethical and cultural concerns.* Paper presented at the Annual Meeting of the Speech Communication Association, New Orleans, LA.

Bechler, C. (1995a). Future directions in crisis management: A study of public relations practitioners. In A. F. Alkhafaji (Ed.), *Business Research Yearbook: Global Business Perspectives* (pp. 789–793). Lanham, MD: University Press of America.

Bechler, C. (1995b). Looking beyond the immediate crisis response: Analyzing the organizational culture to understand the crisis. *Journal of the Association for Communication Administration, 1,* 1–17.

Beck, B., Greenberg, N. F., Hager, M., Harrison, J., & Underwood, A. (1984, December 17). Could it happen in America? *Newsweek, 104,* 38–44.

Beck, M. (1986, February 10). The starship free enterprise. *Newsweek, 106,* p. 38.

Bedeian, A. G. (1989). *Management.* Chicago: Dryden.

Bennett, A. (1991, June 4). Downscoping doesn't necessarily bring an upswing in corporate profitability. *Wall Street Journal,* p. B-1, B-4.

Bennett, W. L. (1981). Assessing presidential character: Degradation rituals in political campaigns. *Quarterly Journal of Speech, 67,* 310–321.

Benoit, W. L. (1982). Richard M. Nixon's rhetorical strategies in his public statements on Watergate. *Southern Speech Communication Journal, 47,* 192–211.

Benoit, W. L. (1988). Senator Edward M. Kennedy and the Chappaquiddick tragedy. In H. R. Ryan (Ed.), *Oratorical encounters: Selected studies and sources of twentieth-century political accusations and apologies* (pp. 187–200). Westport, CT: Greenwood.

Benoit, W. L. (1995a). *Accounts, excuses, apologies: A theory of image restoration strategies.* Albany: State University of New York Press.

Benoit, W. L. (1995b). An analysis of Sears' repair of its auto repair image: Image restoration discourse in the corporate sector. *Communication Studies, 46,* 89–105.

Benoit, W. L. (1997a). Hugh Grant's image restoration discourse: An actor apologizes. *Communication Quarterly, 45,* 251–267.

Benoit, W. L. (1997b). Image restoration discourse and crisis communication. *Public Relations Review, 23,* 177–186.

Benoit, W. L. (1998). Merchants of death: Persuasive defenses by the tobacco industry. In J. F. Klumpp (Ed.), *Argument in a time of change: Definition, frameworks, and critiques* (pp. 220–225). Annandale, VA: National Communication Association.

Benoit, W. L. (1999). Clinton in the Starr chamber. *American Communication Journal.* http://www.americancomm.org/~aca/acj/acj.html

Benoit, W. L. (2000). Another visit to the theory of image restoration strategies. *Communication Quarterly, 48,* 40–43.

Benoit, W. L., & Anderson, K. K. (1996). Blending politics and entertainment: Dan Quayle versus Murphy Brown. *Southern Communication Journal, 62,* 73–85.

Benoit, W. L., & Brinson, S. L. (1994). AT &T: 'Apologies are not enough.' *Communication Quarterly, 42,* 75–88.

Benoit, W. L., & Czerwinski, A. (1997). A critical analysis of USAir's image repair discourse. *Business Communication Quarterly, 60,* 38–57.

Benoit, W. L., & Dorries, B. (1996). *Dateline NBC*'s persuasive attack of Wal-Mart. *Communication Quarterly, 44,* 463–477.

Benoit, W. L., Gullifor, P., & Panici, D. (1991). Reagan's discourse on the Iran-Contra affair. *Communication Studies, 42,* 272–294.

Benoit, W. L., & Hanczor, R. S. (1994). The Tonya Harding controversy: An analysis of image repair strategies. *Communication Quarterly, 42,* 416–433.

Benoit, W. L., & Harthcock, A. (1999). Attacking the tobacco industry: A rhetorical analysis of advertisements by The Campaign for Tobacco-Free Kids. *Southern Communication Journal, 65,* 66–81.

Benoit, W. L., & Lindsey, J. J. (1987). Argument strategies: Antidote to Tylenol's poisoned image. *Journal of the American Forensic Association, 23,* 136–146.

Benoit, W. L., & McHale, J. P. (1999). Kenneth Starr's image repair discourse viewed in *20/20. Communication Quarterly, 47,* 265–280.

Benoit, W. L., & Nill, D. M. (1998). Oliver Stone's defense of JFK. *Communication Quarterly, 46,* 127–143.

Benoit, W. L., & Wells, W. T. (1998). An analysis of three image restoration discourses on Whitewater. *Journal of Public Advocacy, 3,* 21–37.

Benson, J. A. (1988). Crisis revisited: An analysis of strategies used by Tylenol in the second tampering episode. *Central States Speech Journal, 39*(1), 49–66.

Berg, D. M., & Robb, S. (1992). Crisis Management and the "paradigm case." In E. L. Toth & R. L. Heath (Eds.), *Rhetorical and critical approaches to public relations* (93–109). Hillsdale, NJ: Lawrence Erlbaum Associates.

Berger, P., & Luckmann, T. (1967). *The social construction of reality.* New York: Anchor Books.

Billings, R. S., Milburn, T. W., & Schaalman, M. L. (1980). A model of crisis perception: A theoretical and empirical analysis. *Administrative Science Quarterly, 25,* 300–316.

Birch, J. (1994). New factors in crisis planning and response. *Public Relations Quarterly, 39,* 31–34.

Bitzer, L. (1968). The rhetorical situation. *Philosophy and Rhetoric, 1,* 1–15.

Black, E. (1965). *Rhetorical criticism: A study in method.* New York: Macmillian.

Black, E. (1970). The second persona. *Quarterly Journal of Speech, 56,* 109–119.

Blalock, H. M. (1989). *Power and conflict: Toward a general theory.* Newbury Park, CA: Sage.

Block, P. (1987). *The empowered manager: Positive political skills at work.* San Francisco: Jossey-Bass.

Boffey, P. M. (1984, December 23). Bhopal: The case for poison factories. *Denver Post,* 1D; 12D.

Boje, D. (1991). The storytelling organization: A study of story performance in an office supply firm. *Administrative Science Quarterly, 36,* 106–126.

Boje, D. (1995). Stories of the storytelling organization: A postmodern analysis of Disney in "Tamara-Land." *Academy of Management Journal, 38,* 997–1035.

Bostdorff, D. M. (1991). The presidency and promoted crisis: Reagan, Grenada, and issue management. *Presidential Studies Quarterly, 21,* 737–750.

Bouchard, A. (1992). Freak explosion jolts Baie des Ha Ha. *Public Relations Journal, 48,* 44–48.

Bowers, J. W., & Ochs, D. J. (1971). *The rhetoric of agitation and control.* Reading, MA: Addison-Wesley.

Boxer, P. (1993), Assessment of potential violence in the paranoid worker. *Journal of Occupational Medicine, 35,* 127–131.

Bradford, J. L., & Garrett, D. E. (1995). The effectiveness of corporate communicative responses to accusations of unethical behavior. *Journal of Business Ethics, 14,* 875–892.

Bradsher, K. (2000). 2 Firestone studies in 1999 pointed to tire problems. http://www.nytimes.com/2000/10/02/business/02TIRE.html)

Bradsher, K. (2000, December 19). Firestone Engineers Offer a List of Causes for Faulty Tires. http://www.nytimes.com/2000/12/19/business/19TIRE.html

Braverman, M. (1991). Post-robbery damage control: The human factor. *Bottomline,* March–April, 23–25.

Brennan, E. (1992, June 14). An open letter to Sears customers. *Detroit Free Press,* p. 8G.

Brennan, E. (1992, June 14). An open letter to Sears' customers. *New York Times,* A56.

Bridges, W. P. (1992). *The character of organizations: Using Jungian type in organizational development.* N. P.: Consulting Psychologists.

Briggs, W. (1990). Intercepting interlopers. *Public Relations Journal, 46*(2), 39–40.

Brinson, S. L., & Benoit, W. L. (1996). Dow Corning's image repair strategies in the breast implant crisis. *Communication Quarterly, 44,* 29–41.

Brinson, S. L., & Benoit, W. L. (1999). The tarnished star: Restoring Texaco's damaged public image. *Management Communication Quarterly, 12,* 483–510.

Broad, W. J. (1996, January 28). Risks remain despite NASA's rebuilding. *New York Times,* pp. 1, 12.

Brockner, J., DeWitt, R. L., Grover, S., & Reed, T. (1990). When it is especially important to explain why: Factors affecting the relationship between managers' expectations to a layoff and survivors' reactions to the layoff. *Journal of Experimental Social Psychology, 26,* 389–407.

Brockner, J., Grover, S., Reed, T., DeWitt, R., & O'Malley, M. (1987). Survivors' reactions to layoffs: We get by with a little help for our friends. *Administrative Science Quarterly, 32,* 526–541.

Brockner, J., Tyler, T. R., & Cooper-Schneider, R. (1992). The influence of prior commitment to an institution of reactions to perceived unfairness: The higher they are, the harder they fall. *Administrative Science Quarterly, 37,* 241–261.

Brody, E. W. (1991). *Managing communication processes.* New York: Praeger.

Broom, G. M., Casey, S., & Richey, J. (2000). Concept and theory of organization–public relationships. In J. A. Ledingham & S. D. Brunig (Eds.), *Public relations as relationship management* (pp. 3–22). Mahwah, NJ: Lawrence Erlbaum Associates.

Brown, G. (1990). Building momentum after delayed response. *Public Relations Journal, 46,* 40–41.

Brown, H. (1987). *Society as text: Essays on rhetoric, reason, and reality.* Chicago: University of Chicago Press.

Brummett, B. (1995). Scandalous rhetorics. In W. N. Elwood (Ed.), *Public relations inquiry as rhetorical criticism: Case studies of corporate discourse and social influence* (pp. 13–23). Westport, CT: Praeger.

Buch, K., & Aldridge, J. (1991). O.D. Under conditions of organizational decline. *Organization Developmental Journal, 9*(1), 1–5.

Buckey, K. F. (1984, February 27). Why more corporations may be charged with manslaughter. *Business Week,* p. 62.

Buckey, K. F. (1986, Jan.–Feb.). Corporate criminal liability. *Corporate Board,* p. 147.

Bunning, R. L. (1990). The dynamics of downsizing. *Personnel Journal, 69*(9), 68.

Burger, K. (1995). In a lifeboat without a paddle: The long-term effects of downsizing. *Insurance & Technology, 20*(3), 4.

Burke, K. (1932, August 3). The poet and the passwords. *New Republic, 71,* 310–313.

Burke, K. (1942). The study of symbolic action. *Chimera, 1,* 7–16.

Burke, K. (1950). *Rhetoric of motives.* Berkeley: University of California Press.

Burke, K. (1954). *Permanance and change: An anatomy of purpose.* Los Altos, CA: Hermes.

Burke, K. (1966a). Dramatic form—and: Tracking down implications. *Tulane Drama Review, 10,* 54–63.

Burke, K. (1966b). *Language as symbolic action.* Berkeley: University of California Press.

Burke, K. (1968). *Counter-statement.* Berkeley: University of California Press.

Burke, K. (1969a). *A grammar of motives.* Berkeley: University of California Press.

Burke, K. (1969b). *A rhetoric of motives.* Berkeley: University of California Press.

Burke, K. (1970). *The rhetoric of religion.* Berkeley: University of California Press.

Burke, K. (1973). *The philosophy of literary form* (3rd ed.). Berkeley: University of California Press.

Burke, K. (1983a). Counter-gridlock: An interview with Kenneth Burke. *All Area,* 4–35

Burke, K. (1983b, August 12). Dramatism and logology. *The Literary Supplement,* 859.

Burke, K. (1984). *Attitudes toward history* (3rd ed.). Berkeley: University of California Press.

Burke, K. (1989). Poem. In H. W. Simons & T. Melia (Eds.), *The legacy of Kenneth Burke* (p. 263). Madison: University of Wisconsin Press.

Caillouet, R. H. (1991). *A quest for legitimacy: Impression management strategies used by an organization in crisis.* Unpublished doctoral dissertation.

Calloway, L. (1991). Survival of the fastest: Information technology and corporate crises. *Public Relations Review, 17,* 85–92.

Campbell, K. K., & Huxman, S. S. (2003). *The rhetorical act: Thinking, speaking and writing critically* (3rd ed.). Belmont, CA: Wadsworth/Thompson.

Campbell, K. K., & Jamieson, K. H. (Eds.). (1978). Form and genre in rhetorical criticism: An introduction. In *Form & genre: Shaping rhetorical action* (pp. 9–32). Falls Church, VA: Speech Communication Association.

Campbell, K. K., & Jamieson, K. H. (1990). *Deeds done in words: Presidential rhetoric and the genres of governance.* Chicago, IL: University of Chicago Press.

Campbell, R. (1991). *60 Minutes and the news.* Urbana: University of Illinois Press.

Capra, F. (1988). *Uncommon wisdom: Conversations with remarkable people.* New York: Simon & Schuster.

Carey, A. R., & Parker, S. (1996, January 5, 6, 7). Downsizing 1995. *USA Today,* p. 1A.

Cheney, G. (1983). The rhetoric of identification and the study of organizational communication. *Quarterly Journal of Speech, 69,* 143–158.

Cheney, G. (1991). *Rhetoric in an organizational society: Managing multiple identities.* Columbia, SC: University of South Carolina Press.

Cheney, G. (1992). The corporate person (re)presents itself. In E. L. Toth & R. L. Heath (Eds.), *Rhetorical and critical approaches to public relations* (pp. 165–183). Hillsdale, NJ: Lawrence Erlbaum Associates.

Cheney, G., & Christensen, L. T. (2001). Organizational identity: Linkages between internal and external communication. In F. M. Jablin & L. L. Putnam (Eds.), *The new handbook of organizational communication* (pp. 231–269). Thousand Oaks, CA: Sage.

Cheney, G., & Dionisopoulos, G. N. (1989). Public relations? No, relations with publics: A rhetorical-organizational approach to contemporary corporate communications. In C. H. Botan & V. Hazleton, Jr. (Eds.), *Public relations theory* (pp. 135–157). Hillsdale, NJ: Lawrence Erlbaum Associates.

Cheney, G., & Vibbert, S. L. (1987). Corporate discourse: Public relations and issue management. In F. M. Jablin, L. L. Putnam, K. H. Roberts, & L. W. Porter (Eds.), *Handbook of organizational communication: An interdisciplinary perspective* (pp. 165–194). Newbury Park, CA: Sage.

Cherwitz, R. A., & Zagacki, K. S. (1986). Consummatory versus justificatory crisis rhetoric. *Western Journal of Speech Communication, 50,* 308–316.

Chisolm, P. (1992). Anatomy of a nightmare. *Maclean's, 105,* 42–43.

Cipalla, R. (1993, August). Coping with crisis: What the textbooks don't tell you. *Communication World,* pp. 28–29.

Claims for benefits by jobless decline for 4th week in row. (2001, November 22). *Minneapolis Star Tribune,* p. D3.

Clark, B. (1971). *Group theatre.* New York: Theatre Arts Books.

Clark, D. (1994). *Burkian analysis of the Rainforest Action Network.* Unpublished masters thesis, Texas Tech University.

Clifford, J. (1983). On ethnographic authority. *Representations, 1,* 118–146.

Clinton, W. J. (1998). *Address to the nation* (August 17th).

Clinton, W. J. (1998). *Remarks from Jan. 26th press conference.*

Coleman, J. S. (1990). *Foundations of social theory.* Cambridge, MA: Belknap Press of Harvard University Press.

Collingwood, H. (1992, September 14). Sears gets handed a huge repair bill. *Business Week,* p. 38.

Conley, T. (1986). The linnaen blues: Thoughts on the genre approach. In H. W. Simons & A. A. Aghazarian (Eds.). *Form, genre, and the study of political discourse* (pp. 59–78). Columbia: University of South Carolina.

Conrad, C. (1992). Corporate communication and control. In E. L. Toth & R. L. Heath (Eds.), *Rhetorical and critical approaches to public relations* (pp. 202–204). Hillsdale, NJ: Lawrence Erlbaum Associates.

Coombs, W. T. (1994, July). *Crisis management paradigms: The unfinished agenda.* Paper presented at the annual meeting of the International Communication Association, Sydney, Australia.

Coombs, W. T. (1995). Choosing the right words: The development of guidelines for the selection of the "appropriate" crisis-response strategies. *Management Communication Quarterly, 8,* 447–476.

Coombs, W. T. (1998). An analytic framework for crisis situations: Better responses from a better understanding of the situation. *Journal of Public Relations Research, 10,* 177–191.

Coombs, W. T. (1999). Information and compassion in crisis responses: A test of their effects. *Journal of Public Relations Research, 11*(2), 125–142.

Coombs, W. T. (1999). *Ongoing crisis communication: Planning, managing, and responding.* Thousand Oaks, CA: Sage.

Coombs, W. T. (2000). Designing post-crisis messages: Lessons for crisis-response strategies. *Review of Business, 21*(3/4), 37–41.

Coombs, W. T., Hazleton, V., Holladay, S. J., & Chandler, R. C. (1995). The crisis grid: Theory and application in crisis management. In L. Barton (Ed.), *New avenues in risk and crisis management: Volume IV* (pp. 30–39). Las Vegas, NV: UNLV Small Business Development Center.

Coombs, W. T., & Holladay, S. J. (1995, November). *Communication and attributions in a crisis: An experimental study of crisis communication.* Paper presented at the annual meeting of the Speech Communication Association, San Antonio, Texas.

Coombs, W. T., & Holladay, S. J. (1996). Communication and attributions in a crisis: An experimental study of crisis communication. *Journal of Public Relations Research, 8,* 279–295.

Coombs, W. T., & Holladay, S. J. (2002). Helping crisis managers protect reputational assets: Initial tests of the situational crisis communication theory. *Management Communication Quarterly, 16,* 165–186.

Coombs, W. T., & Schmidt, L. (2000). An empirical analysis of image restoration: Texaco's racism crisis. *Journal of Public Relations Research, 12,* 163–178.

Corbett, E. P. J. (1988). Forward. In H. R. Ryan (Ed.), *Oratorical encounters: Selected studies and. sources of twentieth-century political accusations and apologies* (pp. ix–xi) New York: Greenwood Press.

Couretas, J. (1985, November). Preparing for the worst. *Business Marketing,* 96–100.

Courtright, J. L. (1995). 'I am a scientologist': The image management of identity. In W. N. Elwood (Ed.), *Public relations inquiry as rhetorical criticism* (pp. 69–84). Westport, CT: Praeger.

Courtright, L. L., & Hearit, K. M., (2002). "The good organization speaking well": A paradigm case for institutional reputation management. *Public Relations Review, 28,* 347–360.

Cox, J. R. (1981). Argument and the "definition of the situation." *Central States Speech Journal, 32*, 197–205.

Coyle, D. J. (1997). A cultural theory of organizations. In M. Thompson & R. J. Ellis (Eds.), *Culture matters* (59–78). Boulder, CO: Westview Press.

Crable, R. E., & Vibbert, S. L. (1985). Managing issues and influencing public policy. *Public Relations Review, 11*, 3–16.

Crable, R. E., & Vibbert, S. L. (1986). *Public relations as communication management.* Edina, MN: Bellwether Press.

Craig, R. T. (1999). Communication theory as a field. *Communication Theory, 9*, 119–161.

Croft, A. C. (1992). Delayed action allows informed response. *Public Relations Journal, 48*, 30–32.

Cronen, V. E., Johnson, K. M., & Lannaman, J. W. (1982). Paradoxes, double binds, and reflexive loops: An alternative theoretical perspective. *Family Process, 20*, 91–112.

Cross, M. (1985). *Managing workforce reduction.* New York: Praeger.

Crozier, M., & Friedberg, E. (1980). *Actors and systems.* Illinois: University of Chicago Press.

Curtis, R. L. (1989). Cutbacks, management, and human relations: Meanings for theory and research. *Human Relations, 42*, 671–689.

Cutlip, S. M., Center, A. H., & Broom, G. M. (1985). *Effective public relations* (6th ed.). Englewood Cliffs, NJ: Prentice-Hall.

Cutlip, S. M., Center, A. H., & Broom, G. M. (2000). *Effective public relations* (8th ed.). Upper Saddle River, NJ: Prentice-Hall.

Dacin, M. T. (1997). Isomorphism in context: The power and prescription of institutional norms. *Academy of Management Journal, 40*, 46–81.

Daft, R. L., & Weick, K. E. (1984). Toward a model of organizations as interpretation systems. *Academy of Management Review, 9*, 284–295.

Davis, G. F., & Powell, W. W. (1992). Organization-environment relations. In M. Dunnette & L. M. Hough (Eds.), *Handbook of industrial and organizational psychology* (Vol. 3, 2nd ed., pp. 315–376). Palo Alto, CA: Consulting Psychologists Press.

Deal, T. E., & Kennedy, A. A. (1982). *Corporate cultures: The rites and rituals of corporate life.* New York: Addison Wesley.

Deetz, S. A. (1982). Critical interpretive research in organizational communication. *Western Journal of Speech Communication, 46*, 131–149.

Deming, J. (1991, July). Rescuing workers in violent families. *HR Magazine*, 46–48.

Denbow, C. J., & Culbertson, H. M. (1985). Linking beliefs and diagnosing image. *Public Relations Review, 11*, 29–37.

Dervin, B. (1989). Audience as listener and learner, teacher and confident: The sense-making approach. In R. Rice & C. Atkin (Eds.), *Public communication campaigns* (pp. 71–87). Newbury Park, CA: Sage.

Diamond, S. (1984, December 23). A global question of ethics. *Denver Post,* pp. 1D; 12D.

Dilenschneider, R. L., & Hyde, R. C. (1985, January–February). Crisis communications: Planning for the unplanned. *Business Horizons*, 35–38.

DiMaggio, P. J., & Powell, W. W. (1983). The iron cage revisited: Institutional isomorphism and collective rationality in organizational fields. *American Sociological Review, 48*, 147–160.

Dionisopoulos, G. N., & Vibbert, S. L. (1988). CBS vs. Mobil Oil: Charges of creative bookkeeping in 1979. In H. R. Ryan (Ed.), *Oratorical encounters: Selected studies and sources of twentieth-century political accusations and apologies* (pp. 241–251). New York: Greenwood Press.

Dobbyn, T. (2000, December 11). Agency links 29 more deaths to Firestone Tires. Available online at http://dailynews.yahoo.com/h/nm/20001207/ts/autos_firestone_dc_5. html

Douglas, M. (1982). *In active voice.* Boston, MA: Routledge & Kegan Paul.

Dow, B. (1989). The function of epideictic and deliberative strategies in presidential crisis rhetoric. *Western Journal of Speech Communication, 53*, 294–310.

Dowling, J., & Pfeffer, J. (1975). Organizational legitimacy: Social values and organizational behavior. *Pacific Sociological Review, 18*, 122–136.

Downs, A. (1997). *Beyond the looking glass: Overcoming the seductive culture of corporate narcissism.* New York: AMACOM.

Dozier, D. M., & Ehling, W. P. (1992). Evaluation of public relations programs: What the literature tells us about their effects. In J. E. Grunig (Ed.), *Excellence in public relations and communication management.* Hillsdale, NJ: Lawrence Erlbaum Associates.

Drucker, P. F. (1999). *Management challenges for the 21st century.* New York: HarperCollins.

Druckenmiller, B. (1993, August). Crises provide insights on image. *Business Marketing, 40.*

Duncan, H. D. (1968). *Symbols in society.* London: Oxford University Press.

Dutton, J., & Dukerich, J. (1991). Keeping an eye on the mirror: Image in organizational adaptation. *Academy of Management Journal, 34,* 517–554.

Easton, A. (1976). *Managing for negative growth: A handbook for practitioners.* Reston, VA: Reston.

Edwards, J. (2001, December–January). Wrong turns. *Brill's Content,* 113–115, 168–169.

Egelhoff, W. G., & Sen, F. (1992). An information-processing model of crisis management. *Management Communication Quarterly, 5,* 443–484.

Eisenberg, E. M. (1984). Ambiguity as strategy in organizational communication. *Communication Monographs, 51,* 227–242.

Eisenberg, E. M. (1986). Meaning and interpretation in organizations. *Quarterly Journal of Speech, 72,* 88–113.

Eisenberg, E. M., & Goodall, H. L. (1993). *Organizational communication: Balancing creativity and constraint.* New York: St. Martin's Press.

Eisenhardt, K. (1989). Building theory from case study research. *Academy of Management Review, 14,* 532–550.

Eisenhart, T. (1990). The king of public relations talks damage control. *Business Marketing, 13,* 86–87.

Ellis, R. J. (1998). *The dark side of the left: Illiberal egalitarianism in America.* Lawrence: University of Kansas Press.

Elsasser, J. (1994). The challenge of change. *Public Relations Tactics, 1*(6), 21.

Elsbach, K. D. (1994). Managing organizational legitimacy in the California cattle industry. *Administrative Science Quarterly, 39*(1), 57–88.

Elsbach, K. D., & Sutton, R. I. (1992). Acquiring organizational legitimacy through illegitimate actions: A marriage of institutional and impression management theories. *Academy of Management Journal, 35,* 699–738.

Elwood, W. N. (Ed.). (1995). *Public relations inquiry as rhetorical criticism: Case studies of corporate discourse and social influence.* Westport, CT: Praeger.

Emshoff, J. R., & Denlinger, T. E. (1991). *The new rules of the game: The four key experiences managers must have to thrive in the non-hierarchical '90s and beyond.* New York: HarperBusiness.

Englehardt, K. J., Sallot, L. M., & Springston, J. K. (2001, November). *Compassion without blame: Testing the accident flow chart with the crash of ValuJet flight 592.* Paper presented at the Annual Conference of the National Communication Association, Atlanta, GA.

English, L. (1992, January). Crisis communication. *Business Digest,* p. 13.

Epstein, E. J. (1973). *News from nowhere: Television and the news.* New York: Random House.

Erickson, K. V. (1998). Presidential spectacles: Political illusionism and the rhetoric of travel. *Communication Monographs, 65,* 141–153.

Evans, D. (2000, September 6). Tire maker's resistance a bad choice. *Akron Beacon Journal.* http://ohio.com/bj/business/evans/docs/023746.htm

Fairlie, H. (1989, June 5). Air sickness. *New Republic,* 21.

Farquhar, K. W. (1989). *Employee responses to external executive succession: Attribution and the emergence of leadership.* Unpublished doctoral dissertation. Boston University.

Fearn-Banks, K. (1994, Fall). No resources, no tools, no equipment: Crisis communications after the southern California earthquake. *Public Relations Quarterly, 39,* 23–28.

Fearn-Banks, K. (1996). *Crisis communications. A casebook approach.* Mahwah, NJ: Lawrence Erlbaum Associates.

Feldman, S. P. (1990). Stories as cultural creativity: On the relations between symbolism and politics in organizational change. *Human Relations, 43,* 809–828.

Fergus, J. (1992, March 17). Downsizing is often dangerous. *National Law Journal, 14,* 17.

Fine of $1 million is paid for misleading consumers. (1996, January 4). *Wall Street Journal,* p. B4.

Fink, S. (1986). *Crisis management: Planning for the inevitable.* New York: AMOCOM.

Finkin, E. F. (1992). Effective External Communications in Downsizing. *Journal of Business Strategy, 13,* 62.

Fisher, L., & Briggs, W. (1989). Communicating with employees during a time of tragedy. *Communication World,* 32–35.

Fisher, L. M. (1992, June 12). Accusation of fraud at Sears. *New York Times,* pp. D1, D13.

Fisher, L. M. (1992, June 23). Sears Auto Centers halt commissions after flap. *New York Times,* pp. D1, D6.

Fisher, W. R. (1970). A motive view of communication. *Quarterly Journal of Speech, 27,* 131–139.

Fisher, W. R. (1984). Narration as a human communication paradigm: The case of public moral argument. *Communication Monographs, 51,* 1–22.

Fisher, W. R. (1985). The narrative paradigm: An elaboration. *Communication Monographs, 52,* 347–367.

Fisher, W. R. (1987). *Human communication as narration: Toward a philosophy of reason, value and action.* Columbia: University of South Carolina Press.

Fisher, W. R. (1989). Clarifying the narrative paradigm. *Communication Monographs, 56,* 55–58.

Fix, J. (2000, September 26). Conflict preceded Firestone recall: Ford Venezuela didn't want to share blame. http://www.auto.com/autonews/tire26_20000926.htm

Flecker, S. A. (1990). Getting out the inside story. *Currents, 16*(9), 38–43.

Folger, J. P., Poole M. S., & Stutman, R. K. (1993). *Working through conflict: Strategies for relationships, groups, and organizations.* New York: HarperCollins.

Fombrun, C. J. (1996). *Reputation: Realizing value from the corporate image.* Boston: Harvard Business School Press.

Ford, J. D. (1981). The management of organizational crises. *Business Horizons, 24*(3), 10–16.

Foss, S. K. (1996). *Rhetorical criticism: Exploration & practice* (2nd ed.). Prospect Heights, IL: Waveland Press.

Frame, R. M., Nielsen, W. R., & Pate, L. E. (1989). Creating excellence out of crisis: Organizational transformation at the Chicago Tribune. *Journal of Applied Behavioral Science, 25*(2), 109–122.

Frantz, D., & Blumenthal, R. (1994, November 13). Troubles at USAir: Coincidence or more? A question of safety: A special report. *New York Times,* A1, A18, A19.

Freedman, A. M., & Stevens, A. (1995, May 23). Philip Morris is putting TV journalism on trial in its suit against ABC. *Wall Street Journal,* A1, A10.

Freeman, R. E. (1984). *Strategic management: A stakeholder approach.* Boston, MA: Pitman.

Frenette, C. A. (1991, April 28). Open Letter. *Nation's Restaurant News, 24.*

Gabriel, Y. A. (1991). Turning facts into stories and stories into facts: A hermeneutic exploration of organizational folklore. *Human Relations, 44,* 857–871.

Gabriel, Y. A. (1998). Same old story or changing stories? In D. G. Keenoy & C. Oswick (Eds.), *Discourse and organizations* (pp. 84–103). London: Sage.

Galbraith, J. (1974). Organizational design: An information processing view, *Interfaces, 4,* 28–36.

Garbett, T. (1988). *How to build a corporation's identity and project its image.* Lexington, MA: Lexington Books.

Garfield, C. (1992). *Second to none: How our smartest companies put people first.* Homewood, IL: Business One Irwin.

Gatewood, E., & Carroll, A. B. (1981). The anatomy of corporate social response: The Rely, Firestone 500, and Pinto cases. *Business Horizons, 24,* 9–16.

Geibel, J. (1996). Public relations 911. *Public Relations Tactics, 3*(9), 25–27.

Gergen, K. J., & Gergen, M. M. (1988). Narrative and the self as relationship. In L. Berkowitz (Ed.), *Advances in experimental social psychology* (Vol. 21, pp. 17–56). New York: Academic Press.

Gerhart, M., & Russell, A. M. (1984). *Metaphoric process: The creation of scientific and religious understanding.* Fort Worth: Texas Christian University Press.

Gibbs, E. (2000, September 11). Bridgestone says to rebuild Firestone. Available online at http://dailynews.yahoo.com/h/nm/20000911/bs/autos_bridgestone_dc_64.html

Gibson, D. C. (1991). The communication continuum: A theory of public relations. *Public Relations Review, 17,* 175–183.

Gilmore, T. (1988). *Making a leadership change.* San Francisco, CA: Jossey-Bass.

Ginzel, L. E., Kramer, R. M., & Sutton, R. I. (1993). Organizational impression management as a reciprocal influence process: The neglected role of the organizational audience. In L. L. Cummings & B. M Staw, (Eds.), *Research in organizational behavior: An annual series of analytical essays and critical reviews* (Vol.15, pp. 227–266). Greenwich, CT: JAI Press.

Glaser, J. S. (1994). *The United Way scandal.* New York: Wiley.

Goffman, E. (1959). *The presentation of self in everyday life.* New York: Overlook.

Gonzales, M. H., Pederson, J. H., Manning, D. J., & Wetter, D. W. (1990). Pardon my gaffe: Effects of sex, status, and consequence severity on accounts. *Journal of Personality and Social Psychology, 58,* 610–621.

Goodman, R., & Ruch, R. S. (1981). In the Image of the CEO. *Public Relations Journal, 30,* 14–15, 18–19.

Goodnight, T. G. (1982). The personal, technical, and public spheres of argument: A speculative inquiry into the art of public deliberation. *Journal of the American Forensic Association, 18,* 214–227.

Gottlieb, M. R., & Conkling, L. (1995). *Managing the workplace survivors: Organizational downsizing and the commitment gap.* Westport, CT: Quorum Books.

Gottschalk, J. A. (Ed.). (1993). *Crisis response: Inside stories on managing image under siege.* Detroit, MI: Visible Ink Press.

Graham, J. (1992). Disgruntled employees—ticking time bombs? *Security Management,* 83–85.

Grier, P. (1984, December 26). Poisons in our midst are well-kept secret. *Rocky Mountain News,* p. 81.

Griffin, E. (1994). *A first look at communication theory* (2nd ed.). St. Louis, MO: McGraw-Hill.

Grimaldi, J. V. (December 1, 2000). Climate cited in failure of tires. http://washingtonpost.com/wp-dyn/articles/A8130-2000Nov30.html

Grimaldi, J. V., & Mayer, C. E. (2001, January, 9). Ford, Firestone settle suit, avert high-profile trial. *Washington Post,* 4A.

Grimaldi, J. V., & Skrzycki, C. (September 26, 2000). Firestone, Ford traded blame. *Washington Post,* E01.

Grunig, J. E. (1976, November). Organizations and public relations: Testing a communication theory. *Journalism Monographs, 46.*

Grunig, J. E. (1989). Sierra Club Study Shows Who Become Activists. *Public Relations Review, 15*(3), 3–24.

Grunig, L. A. (1992a). Activism: How it limits the effectiveness of organizations and how excellent public relations departments respond. In J. E. Grunig (Ed.), *Excellence in public relations and communication management* (pp. 503–530). Hillsdale, NJ: Lawrence Erlbaum Associates.

Grunig, J. E. (Ed.). (1992b). *Excellence in public relations and communication management: Contributions to effective organizations.* San Francisco: IABC Foundation of the International Association of Business Communicators.

Grunig, J. E. (1993). Image and substance: From symbolic to behavioral relationships. *Public Relations Review, 19,* 121–139.

Grunig, J. E., & Grunig, L. A. (1992). Models of public relations and communications. In J. E. Grunig (Ed.), *Excellence in public relations and communication management* (pp. 285–326). Hillsdale, NJ: Lawrence Erlbaum Associates.

Grunig, J. E., & Huang, Y. (2000). From organizational effectiveness to relationship indicators: Antecedents of relationships, public relations strategies, and relationship outcomes. In J. A.

Ledingham & S. D. Buning (Eds.), *Public relations as relationship management* (pp. 23–54). Mahwah, NJ: Lawrence Erlbaum Associates.

Grunig, J. E., & Hunt, T. (1984). *Managing public relations.* New York: Holt, Rinehart, and Winston.

Grunig, J. E., & Repper, F. C. (1992). Strategic management, publics, and issues. In J. E. Grunig (Ed.), *Excellence in public relations and communication management* (pp. 117–157). Hillsdale, NJ: Lawrence Erlbaum Associates.

Hage, J. (1980). *Theories of organizations.* New York: Wiley Interscience.

Hainsworth, B. E., & Wilson, L. J. (1992). Strategic program planning. *Public Relations Review, 18,* 9–15.

Hall, J. R. (1991). In the jaws of a crisis. *Directors and Boards, 15*(4), 17–20.

Hallahan, K. (1993). The paradigm struggle and public relations practice, *Public Relations Review, 19,* 197–205.

Harrison, E. B., & Prugh, T. (1989). Assessing the damage: Practitioner perspectives on the Valdez. *Public Relations Journal, 45*(10). 40–45.

Hansen, C. D., & Kahnweiler, W. M. (1993). Storytelling: An instrument for understanding the dynamics of corporate relationships. *Human Relations, 46,* 1391–1409.

Harne, E. G. (1994, May 5). A manager's guide to downsizing. *Security Management, 38,* 20.

Harre, R., & Gillett, G. (1994). *The discursive mind.* Thousand Oaks, CA: Sage.

Harrel, J. B., Ware, B. L. & Linkugel, W. A. (1975). Failure of apology in American politics: Nixon on watergate, *Speech Monographs, 42,* 245–261.

Hart, J., Willihnganz, S. C., & Leichty, G. (1995). The creation of, change in, and tension across narratives during organizational transitions: A longitudinal investigation. In J. Knuf (Ed.), *Proceedings of the third annual Kentucky conference on narrative* (pp. 223–232).

Hart, R., & Burks, D. (1972). Rhetorical sensitivity and social interaction. *Speech Monographs, 30,* 75–91.

Hauser, G. A. (1999). Aristotle on epideictic: The formation of public morality. *Rhetoric Society Quarterly, 29,* 5–23.

Hayes, R. E. (1985). Corporate crisis management as adaptive control. In S. J. Andriole (Ed.), *Corporate crisis management* (pp. 21–37). Princeton, NJ: Petrocelli.

Healey, J. (December 11, 2000). Ford, Firestone says adhesive is linked to bad tires: Theory could clear workers, Explorer. *USA Today,* 1A.

Healy, P. (1996, February 2). State Notes. *The Chronicle of Higher Education,* A26.

Hearit, K. M. (1994). Apologies and public relations crises at Chrysler, Toshiba, and Volvo. *Public Relations Review, 20,* 113–125.

Hearit, K. M. (1995a). Mistakes were made: Organizational apologia and crisis of social legitimacy. *Ccommunication Studies, 46,* 1–17.

Hearit, K. M. (1995b). From 'we didn't do it' to 'it's not our fault': The use of apologia in public relations crises. In W. N. Elwood (Ed.), *Public relations inquiry as rhetorical criticism* (pp. 117–131). Westport, CT: Praeger.

Hearit, K. M. (2001). Corporate apologia: When an organization speaks in defense of itself. In R. L. Heath (Ed.), *Handbook of public relations* (pp. 595–605). Thousand Oaks, CA: Sage.

Hearle, D. G. (1993). Planning for Crisis. In J. A. Gottschalk (Ed.), *Crisis response: Inside stories on managing image under siege* (pp. 397–406). Detroit, MI: Visible Ink Press.

Heath, R. L. (1994). *Management of corporate communication: From interpersonal contacts to external affairs.* Hillsdale, NJ: Lawrence Erlbaum Associates.

Heath, R. L. (1997). *Strategic issues management: Organizations and public policy challenges.* Thousand Oaks, CA: Sage.

Heath, R. L. (2001). Learning from best practices from experience and research. In R. L. Heath (Ed.), *Handbook of public relations* (pp. 441–444). Thousand Oaks, CA: Sage.

Heath, R. L., & Associates (Eds.). (1988). *Strategic issues management.* San Francisco: Jossey-Bass.

Heath, R. L., & Nelson, R. A. (1986). *Issues management: Corporate policymaking in an information society.* Beverly Hills, CA: Sage.

Heibert, R. E. (1991). Public relations as a weapon of modern warfare. *Public Relations Review, 17,* 107–116.

Hellweg, S. (1987). Organizational grapevines: A state of the art review. *Progress in Communication Sciences, 8,* 213–230.

Hendrix, J. A. (1995). *Public relations cases* (3rd ed.). Belmont, CA: Wadsworth Publishing.

Herman, M. (1992, November). Planning for the unpredictable. *Security Management,* 33–37.

Hermann, C. F. (1963). Some consequences of crises which limit the viability of organizations. *Administrative Science Quarterly, 8,* 61–82.

Hermann, C. F. (1972). Threat, time, and surprise: A simulation in international crisis. In C. F. Hermann (Ed.), *International crises insights from behavioral research* (pp. 187–211). New York: Free Press.

Hirokawa, R., & Rost, K. (1992). Effective group decision-making in organizations. *Management Communication Quarterly, 5,* 267–288.

Hobbs, J. D. (1995). Treachery by any other name: A case study of the Toshiba public relations crisis. *Management Communication Quarterly, 8,* 323–346.

Hoff, J. (1984). *People in crisis: Understanding and helping* (2nd ed.). Menlo Park, CA: Addison-Wesley.

Holstein, W. J. (September 11, 2000). Guarding the brand is Job 1. Available online at http://www.usnews.com/usnews/issue/000911/ford.htm

How to win friends. (1989). Exxon's L. G. Rawl must cope with fallout from inadequate crisis communication. *Public Relations Journal,* 42–45

Howard, C., & Matthews, W. (1985). *On deadline: Managing media relations.* Prospect Heights, IL: Waveland Press.

Hurst, D. K. (1995). *Crisis and renewal: Meeting the challenge of organizational change.* Boston, MA: Harvard Business School Press.

Iacocca, L. (1994). Remarks at a press conference concerning odometers. In M. Seeger (Ed.). *"I gotta tell you": Speeches of Lee Iacocca* (pp. 109–113). Detroit, MI: Wayne State University Press.

Iacocca, L., & Kleinfield, S. (1988). *Talking straight.* New York: Bantam Books.

Ice, R. (1991). Corporate publics and rhetorical strategies: The case of Union Carbide's Bhopal Crisis. *Management Communication Quarterly, 4,* 341–362.

Irvine, R. B., & Millar, D. P. (1998). *Crisis communication and management: How to gain and maintain control.* San Francisco, CA: International Association of Business Communicators.

Jablonski, C. K. (1994), *The application of attribution and impression formation theories to public relations: Suggestions for academic research and professional practice.* Paper delivered at the Speech Communication Association convention, New Orleans, LA.

Jack in the Box's worst nightmare. (1993, February 6). *New York Times,* p. 35.

Jacobs, D. L. (1989, March–April). Downsizing without distress. *Management World,* 27.

Jacobs, D. L. (1991). You're outta here: When employees have to be cut, pulling the switch gently and properly will keep costly litigation at bay. *Advertising Age, 62*(18), 26.

Jamison, D., & O'Mara, J. (1991). *Managing workforce 2000: Gaining the diversity advantage.* San Francisco, CA: Jossey-Bass.

Jaroff, L. (1988, October 10). The magic is back. *Time,* pp. 20–25.

Johannesen, R. L. (1990). *Ethics in human communication* (3rd ed.). Prospect Heights, IL: Waveland Press.

Johnson, D. (1991). *Exxon's rhetorical response to the Valdez crisis: An examination of purification strategies.* Unpublished master's thesis, North Dakota State University, Fargo, ND.

Johnson, D., & Sellnow, T. (1995). Deliberative rhetoric as a step in organizational crisis management: Exxon as a case study. *Communication Reports, 8,* 53–60.

Jones, A. S. (1994). Dealing with the fallout when the plant shuts down. *Public Relations Tactics, 1*(6), 1, 8.

Kanter, R. M. (1977). *Men and women of the corporation.* New York: Basic Books.

Kanter, R. M., Stein, B. A., & Jick, T. D. (1992). *The challenge of organizational change: How companies experience it and leaders guide it.* New York: Free Press.

Kates, R. W. (1977). *Managing technological hazard: Research needs and opportunities.* Boulder, CO: Institute of behavioral science, University of Colorado, Monograph no 25.

Katz, A. R. (1987). Checklist: 10 steps to complete crisis planning. *Public Relations Journal, 43,* 46–47.

Kaufmann, J. B., Kesner, I. F., & Hazan, T. L., (1994). The myth of full disclosure: A look at organizational communications during crisis. *Business Horizons, 19,* 29–39

Kennedy, K. A., & Benoit, W. L. (1997). The Newt Gingrich book deal controversy: Self-defense rhetoric. *Southern Communication Journal, 63,* 197–216.

Kiger, P. (2001). Lessons from a crisis: How communication kept a company together. *Workforce, 80*(11), 28.

Kneupper, C. W. (1980). Rhetoric, argument, and social reality: A social constructivist view. *Journal of the American Forensic Association, 16,* 173–181.

Korzybski, A. (1958). *Science and sanity* (4th ed.). Lakeville, CT: The International Non-Aristotelian Library Publishing Company.

Kramer, R. M., (1996). Divergent realities and convergent disappointments in the hierarchic relation: Trust and the intuitive auditor at work. In R. M. Kramer & T. R. Tyler (Eds.), *Trust in organizations: Frontiers of theory and research* (pp. 216–245). Thousand Oaks, CA: Sage.

Krantz, J. (1985). Group process under conditions of organizational decline. *Journal of Applied Behavioral Science, 21,* 1–17.

Kreps, G. L. (1990). *Organizational communication: Theory and practice* (2nd ed.). New York: Longman.

Krippendorf, K. (1989). On the ethics of constructing communication. In B. Dervin, L. Grossberg, B. J. O'Keefe, & E. Wartella (Eds.), *Rethinking communication: Vol. 1* (pp. 66–96). Newbury Park, CA: Sage.

Kruse, N. W. Motivational factors in non-denial apologia. *Central States Speech Journal, 28,* 13–23.

Kurzbard, G., & Siomkos, G. J. (1992). Crafting a damage control plan: Lessons for Perrier. *Journal of Business Strategy, 13*(2), 39–43.

Lakoff, G., & Johnson, M. (1980). *Metaphors we live by.* Chicago, IL: University of Chicago Press.

Lakoff, G., & Turner, M. (1989). *More than cool reason: A field guide to poetic metaphor.* Illinois: University of Chicago Press.

Larson, C. U. (1995). *Persuasion: Reception and responsibility* (7 ed.). Belmont, CA: Wadsworth.

Lauzen, M. M., & Dozier, D. M. (1994). Issues management mediation of linkages between environmental complexity and management of the public relations function. *Journal of Public Relations Research, 6,* 163–184.

Leana, C. R., & Feldman, D. C. (1990). Individual responses to job loss: Empirical findings from two field studies. *Human Relations, 43*(11), 1155–1181.

Leichty, G., & Warner, E. (2001). Cultural topoi: Implications for public relations. In R. L. Heath (Ed.), *Handbook of public relations* (pp. 61–74). Thousand Oaks, CA: Sage.

Leland, J. (1995, May 1). Why the children? *Newsweek,* pp. 48–53.

Leonard, B. (2001). A job well done. *HR Magazine, 46*(12), 34.

Lerbinger, O. (1986). *Managing corporate crises: Strategies for executives.* Boston, MA: Barrington Press.

Lerbinger, O. (1997). *The crisis manager: Facing risk and responsibility.* Mahwah, NJ: Lawrence Erlbaum Associates.

Levine, S. E. (1993, August). Bad news blues. *Bank marketing,* pp. 10–15.

Lin, H-M, Stacks, D. W., & Steinfatt, T. M. (1992). Crisis management planning in corporate Taiwan. *Proceedings of the 9th Annual Intercultural and International Communication Conference.* Miami, FL: University of Miami, 45–48.

Lucaites, J. L., & Condit, C. M. (1985). Re-constructing narrative theory: A functional perspective. *Journal of Communication, 35*(4), 90–108.

Luhmann, N. (1986). The autopoeisis of social systems. In F. Geyer & J. van der Zouwen (Eds.), *Sociocybernetic paradoxes: Observation, control and evolution of self-steering systems* (pp. 172–192). Newbury Park, CA: Sage.

Lukaszewski, J. E., (1987). Checklist: An anatomy of a crisis response. *Public Relations Journal, 43,* 45–46.

Lurie, G. (1991). Ten rules for crisis management. *Leadership & Organization Development Journal, 12,* i–iii.

Maggert, L. (1994). Bowater Incorporated—a lesson in crisis communications. *Public Relations Quarterly, 39*(3), 29–31.

Magnuson, E. (1986, June 9). Fixing NASA. *Time,* pp. 14–25.

Mallozzi, C. (1994, January). Facing the danger zone in crisis communications. *Risk Management,* 34–40.

Manning, P. (1977). *Police work.* Cambridge, MA: MIT Press.

Marconi, J. (1992). *Crisis marketing: When bad things happen to good companies.* Chicago, IL: Probus.

Marcus, A. A., & Goodman, R. S. (1991). Victims and shareholders: The dilemmas of presenting corporate policy during a crisis. *Academy of Management Journal, 34,* 281–305.

Markwood, S. E. (1988). When the television cameras arrive. *NASPA Journal, 25*(3), 209–212.

Martin, J. (1982). Stories as scripts in organizational settings. In A. Hasdorf & A. Isen (Eds.), *Cognitive social psychology* (pp. 255–305). New York: Elsevier-North Holland.

Martin, J., & Powers, M. E. (1983). Truth or corporate propaganda: The value of a good war story. In L. R. Pondy, P. Frost, G. Morgan, & T. Dandritch (Eds.), *Organizational symbolism* (pp. 93–107). Greenwich, CT: JAI Press.

Martz, L. (1986, March 3). A fatal "error of judgment." *Newsweek,* pp. 14–20.

Mason, R. O., Mason, F. M., & Culnan, M. J. (1995). *Ethics of information management.* Thousand Oaks, CA: Sage.

Massey, J. E. (2001). Managing legitimacy: Communication strategies for organizations in crisis. *Journal of Business Communication, 38*(2), 153–183.

Matejka, K. (199). *Why this horse won't drink: How to win and keep employee commitment.* New York: AMACOM.

Mathews, J., & Peterson, C. (1989, March 31). Oil tanker captain fired after failing alcohol test; Exxon blames government for cleanup delay. *Washington Post,* pp. A1, 6.

Matthews, T. (1992, May 11). The siege of LA. *Newsweek,* pp. 30–38.

Maynard, R. (1993). Handling a crisis effectively: Will you be ready if your company comes under scrutiny? Here's how to sharpen your public relations skills. *Nation's Business, 81,* 54–55.

McAuley, E., Duncan, T. E., & Russell, D. W. (1992). Measuring causal attributions: The revised causal dimension scale (CDII). *Personality and Social Psychology Bulletin, 18,* 566–573.

McCroskey, J. C. (1966). *An introduction to rhetorical communication.* Englewood Cliffs, NJ: Prentice-Hall.

McGinley, L. (1986, February 12). Panel probing explosion of Challenger is pressed to prove autonomy in face of strong NASA ties. *Wall Street Journal,* p. 62.

McGuire, W. J. (1989). Theoretical Foundations of Campaigns. In R. E. Rice & C. K. Atkin (Eds.), *Public Communication Campaigns* (pp. 43–68). Newbury Park, CA: Sage.

Metts, S., & Cupach, W. R. (1989). Situational influence on the use of remedial strategies in embarrassing predicaments. *Communication Monographs, 56,* 151–162.

Meyer, E. (2000). Firestone Whistle-blower gains enemies. http://www.ohio.com/dist/nf/008666.htm

Meyer, J. W., & Rowan, B. (1977). Institutionalized organizations: Formal structure as myth and ceremony. *American Journal of Sociology, 83,* 340–363.

Meyer, J. W., & Scott, W. R. (1983). *Organizational environments: Ritual and rationality.* Beverly Hills, CA: Sage.

Meyers, G. C., & Holusha, J. (1986). *When it hits the fan—Managing the nine crises of business.* Boston: Houghton Mifflin.

Milburn, T. W., Schuler, R. S., & Watman, K. H. (1983a). Organizational crisis. Part I: Definition and conceptualization. *Human Relations, 36,* 1141–1160.

Milburn, T. W., Schuler, R. S., & Watman, K. H. (1983b). Organizational crisis. Part II: Strategies and responses. *Human Relations, 36,* 1161–1179.

Mitchell, E. (1993). Weathering the storm. *Public Relations Journal, 49,* 11–15.

Mitroff, I. I. (1986). Prevention: Teaching corporate American to think about crisis prevention. *Journal of Business Studies, 6,* 40–48.

Mitroff, I. I. (1988a). *Break-away thinking: How to challenge your business assumptions (and why you should).* New York: Wiley.

Mitroff, I. I. (1988b). Crisis management: Cutting through the confusion. *Sloan Management Review,* 15–20.

Mitroff, I. I. (1990). *We're so big and powerful nothing bad can happen to us: An investigation of America's crisis prone corporations.* Secaucus, NJ: Carol.

Mitroff, I. I., Harrington, K., & Gai, E. (1996, September). Thinking about the unthinkable. *Across the Board, 33*(8), 44–48.

Mitroff, I. I., & Kilmann, R. (1975). Stories managers tell: A tool for organizational problem solving. *Management Review, 64,* 18–28.

Mitroff, I. I., & Kilmann, R. (1984a). *Corporate tragedies: Product tampering, sabotage and other disasters.* New York: Praeger.

Mitroff, I. I., & Kilmann, R. H. (1984b). Corporate tragedies: Teaching companies to cope with evil. *New Management, 1,* 48–53.

Mitroff, I. I., Pauchant, T., Finney, M., & Pearson, C. M. (1989). Do (some) organizations cause their own crises? The cultural profiles of crisis-prone vs. crisis-prepared organizations. *Industrial Crisis Quarterly, 3,* 269–283.

Mitroff, I. I., Pauchant, T., & Shivastava, P. (1989). Can your company handle a crisis? *Business & Health, 7,* 41–44.

Mitroff, I. I., & Pearson, C. M. (1993). *Crisis management.* San Francisco: Jossey-Bass.

Mitroff, I. I., Shrivastava, P., & Udwadia, F. (1987) Effective crisis management. *Executive, 1,* 283–292.

Moffitt, M. A. (1994). Collapsing and integrating concepts of 'public' and 'image' into a new theory. *Public Relations Review, 20*(2), pp. 159–170.

Moffett, M. A., & McGinley, L. (1986, February 14). NASA, once a master of publicity, fumbles in handling shuttle crisis. *Wall Street Journal,* p. 23.

Morgan, G. (1986). *Images of organization.* Newbury Park, CA: Sage.

Morill, C. (1995). *The executive way: Conflict management in corporations.* Chicago: University of Chicago Press.

Mumby, D. K. (1987). The political function of narrative in organizations. *Communication Monographs, 54,* 113–127.

Murphy, M. (1992). Desperation in Corporate America. *Personnel Journal, 7*(5), 30.

Murphy, P. (1991). How 'bad' PR decisions get made: A roster of faulty judgment heuristics. *Public Relations Review, 17,* 117–129.

Murphy, W. (1990). *Public relations case history: AT&T's network crisis, January 1990.* Unpublished case history written by AT&T's director of corporate information.

Murray, E., & Shohen, S. (February 1992). Lessons from the Tylenol tragedy on surviving a corporate crisis. *Medical Marketing & Media,* 14–15, 18–19.

Nasser, J. (2000). Prepared statement for the United States House of Representatives Joint Hearing of the Subcommittee on Telecommunications Trade & Consumer Protection (September 6). Available online at www.house.gov/commerce.

Nathan, S. (2000, December 7). Tires linked to 29 more deaths lawsuits against Firestone may add Bridgestone. *USA Today,* p. 3b.

Newsom, D., Scott, A., & Turk, J. V. (1992). *This is PR: The realities of public relations* (5th ed.). Belmont, CA: Wadsworth.

Newsom, D., Turk, J. V., & Kruckeberg, D. (2000). *This is pr: The realities of public relations* (7th ed.). Belmont, CA: Wadsworth/Thomson Learning.

Nissen, T. (September 8, 2000). Ford to help pay for tire recall. Available online at http://dailynews.yahoo.com/h/nm/20000908/bs/autos_bridgestone_dc_61.html

Nixon, R. N. (1970). Cambodia: A difficult decision. *Vital Speeches of the Day, 37,* 450–452.

Nowotny, M. R. (1989). Best laid plans vs. reality. *Public Relations Journal, 45,* 17–18.

Nugent, R. J. (1993). *Remarks by R. J. Nugent: President, Jack in the Box, U.S.A. before the United States Senate Subcommittee on Agricultural Research, Forestry, Conservation, and General Legislation.* (Available from Jack in the Box Inc., U.S.A., San Diego, California).

O'Connor, E. S. (1997). Telling decision: The role of narrative in organizational decision-making. In Z. Shapira (Ed.), *Organizational decision-making* (pp. 304–323). New York: Cambridge University Press.

Olaniran, B. A (1993). Integrative approach for managing successful computer-mediated communication technological innovation. *Ohio Speech Journal, 31,* 37–53.

Olaniran, B. A., & Williams, D. E. (2000). Anticipatory model of crisis management: A vigilant response to technological crises. In R. Heath (Ed.), *Handbook of Public Relations* (pp. 581–594). Newbury Park, CA: Sage.

Ong, W. (1993). *Orality and literacy: The technologizing of the word.* London: Routledge.

Ono, M. (2000). Prepared statement for the United States House of Representatives Joint Hearing of the Subcommittee on Telecommunications Trade & Consumer Protection (September 6). Available online at www.house.gov/commerce

Orr, C. J. (1978). How shall we say: "Reality is socially constructed through communication?" *Central States Speech Journal, 29,* 263–274.

Ortony, A. (1975). Why metaphors are necessary and not just nice. *Educational Theory, 25,* 45–53.

Ostrow, S. D. (1991, July). It will happen here. *Bank Marketing,* 24–26.

Overman, S. (1991, November). After the smoke clears. *HR Magazine,* 44–47.

Pacanowsky, M. E., & O'Donnell-Trujillo, N. (1983). Organizational communication as cultural performance. *Communication Monographs, 50,* pp. 126–147.

Parsons, T. (1956). Suggestions for a sociological approach to the theory of organizations. *Administrative Science Quarterly, 1,* 63–85.

Parsons, T. (1960). *Structure and process in modern societies.* New York: Free Press.

Paschall, R. (1992). *Critical incident management.* Chicago: University of Illinois at Chicago Press.

Patterson, G. A. (1992, June 23). Sears's Brennan accepts blame for auto flap. *Wall Street Journal,* pp. B1, B14.

Pauchant, T. C. (1988). *Crisis management and narcissism: A Kohutian perspective.* Unpublished doctoral dissertation, Graduate School of Business Administration, University of Southern California, Los Angeles, CA.

Pauchant, T. C. & Mitroff, I. I. (1988). Crisis prone versus crisis avoiding organizations: Is your company's culture its own worst enemy in creating crises? *Industrial Crisis Quarterly, 2*(1), 53–63.

Pauchant, T. C., & Mitroff, I. I. (1992). *Transforming the crisis-prone organization.* San Francisco, CA: Jossey-Bass.

Peak, M. H. (1995). Employees are our greatest asset and worst headache! *Management Review, 84*(11), 47–52.

Pearce, W. B. (1989). *Communication and the human condition.* Carbondale: Southern Illinois University Press.

Pearson, C. M., & Mitroff, I. I. (1993). From crisis prone to crisis prepared: A framework for crisis management. *Academy of Management Executive, 7,* 48–59.

Pepsi-Cola. (1991, March 11). Accounts payable/receivable. *Nation's Restaurant News,* p. 34.

Perelman, C., & Olbrechts-Tyteca, L. (1969). *The new rhetoric* (J. Wilkinson & P. Weaver, Trans.). Indiana: University of Notre Dame Press.

Perrow, C. (1970). *Organizational analysis: A sociological view*. Belmont, CA: Wadsworth.

Perrow, C. (1984). *Normal accidents: Living with high risk technologies*. New York: Basic Books.

Peters, T., & Waterman, R. H. (1982). *The search for excellence: Lessons from America's best-run companies*. New York: Harper & Row.

Peterson, J. E. (1987, June 25). U.S. charges Chrysler, 2 Execs. *Detroit News*. pp. 1A, 4A.

Pfeiffer, J. (1989). The secret of life at the limits: Cogs become big wheels. *Smithsonian, 20*(4), pp. 38–49.

Pickler, N. (2000, September 12). Transportation secretary to appear. Available online at http://dailynews.yahoo.com/h/ap/20000912/bs/tire_deaths_congress_4.html

Pickler, N. (2000, December 19). Rubber mix source of tire woes. Available online at http://dailynews.yahoo.com/h/ap/20001219/ts/tire_recall_6.html

Pines, W. L. (1985). How to handle a pr crisis: Five dos and five don'ts. *Public Relations Quarterly, 30*(2) 16–19.

Pinsdorf, M. K. (1991a). Flying different skies: How cultures respond to airline disasters. *Public Relations Review, 17,* 37–56.

Pinsdorf, M. K. (1991b) Crashes bare value affecting response success. *Public Relations Journal, 47,* 31–32.

Polkinghorne, D. (1983). *Methodology for the human sciences*. Albany: State University of New York Press.

Powell, W. W., & DiMaggio, P. J. (Eds.) (1991). *The new institutionalism in organizational analysis*. Illinois: University of Chicago Press.

Power, J. (1989, October 15). George Bush shows a new maturity in U.S. statecraft. *Chicago Tribune*, p. 4:3.

Prelli, L. J. (1989). *A rhetoric of science: Inventing scientific discourse*. Columbia: University of South Carolina Press.

Press Release. (1993, January 21). Available from Foodmaker, Inc., San Diego, California.

Press Release. (1993, February 12). Available from Foodmaker, Inc., San Diego, California.

Prince, S. H. (1920). *Catastrophe and social change*. New York: Columbia University Press.

Putnam, L. L., & Fairhurst, G. (2001). Discourse analysis in organizations: Issues and concerns. In F. M. Jablin & L. L. Putnam (Eds.), *New handbook of organizational communication: Advances in theory, research and methods* (pp. 78–136). Thousand Oaks, CA: Sage.

Putnam, L. L. (1981, May). *Equivocal messages in organizations*. Paper presented at the annual meeting of the International Communication Association, Minneapolis, MN.

Quarantelli, E. L. (1988). Disaster crisis management: A summary of research findings. *Journal of Management Studies, 25,* 373–385.

Quinn, R. E., & McGrath, M. R. (1985). The transformation of organizational cultures: A competing values perspective. In P. J. Frost, L. F. Moore, M. R. Louis, C. C. Lundberg, & J. Martin (Eds.), *Organizational culture* (pp. 315–334). Beverly Hills, CA: Sage.

Rainie, H. (1993, May 3). The final days of David Koresh. *US News & World Report*, pp. 25–34.

Ranalli, R. (2000, November 25). Lawyers want to limit secret settlements. Available online at http://www.boston.com/dailyglobe2/330/metro/Lawyers_want_to_limit_secret_settlementsP.shtml

Rawl, L. G. (1989, April 3). An open letter to the public. *New York Times*, p. A12. Also printed in *Washington Post*, p. A5.

Rebuffed moviegoers get apology. (1992, March 31). *Columbia Daily Tribune*, p. 3A.

Reinhardt, C. (1989). How to handle a crisis. *Public Relations Journal, 45,* 43–44.

Renz, M. A. (1992). Communication about environmental risk: An examination of a Minnesota county's communication on incineration. *Journal of Applied Communication Research, 20,* 1–18.

Ressler, J. A. (1982). Crisis communications. *Public Relations Quarterly, 27*(3) 8–10.

Reuters (2000, November 27). Bridgestone/Firestone Tire recall 80 percent done. Available online at http://dailynews.yahoo.com/h/nm/20001207/ts/autos_bridgestone_dc_1.html

Reuters (2000, December 11). Ford, Firestone link adhesive to bad tires. Available online at http://dailynews.yahoo.com/h/nm/20001211/ts/autos_bridgestone_dc_1.html

Richardson, H. L. (1992). Look ahead: Prepare for crises. *Transportation and Distribution, 33*(6), 36–40.

Roberts, K. H., & LaPorte, T. R. (1989, November). *High reliability organizations: The Berkeley Project.* Paper presented to the Second Conference on Industrial and Organizational Crisis Management, New York.

Rogers, R. (1993). Anatomy of a Crisis. In J. A. Gottschalk (Ed.), *Crisis response: Inside stories on managing image under siege* (pp. 123–140). Detroit, MI: Visible Ink Press.

Rosenblatt, R. (1984, December 17). All the world gasped. *Time, 124,* p. 20.

Rosenbluth, H. F. (1992). *The customer comes second.* New York: Morrow.

Roth, T. (1984, December 17). Chemical firms may be facing new regulations. *Wall Street Journal,* p. 4.

Roy, D. (1960). Banana Time: Job satisfaction and informal interaction. *Human Organization, 18,* 156–180.

Ruef, M., & Scott, W. R. (1998) A multidimensional model of organizational legitimacy: Hospital survival in changing institutional environments. *Administrative Science Quarterly, 40,* 1–33.

Ruekert, W. H. (1982). *Kenneth Burke and the drama of human relations* (2nd ed.). Berkeley: University of California Press.

Rumptz, M. T., Leland, R. A., McFaul, S. A., Solinski, R. M., & Pratt, C. B. (1992). A public relations nightmare: Dow Corning offers too little, too late. *Public Relations Quarterly, 37,* 30–32.

Rummelhart, D. E., & Ortony, A. (1977). The representation of knowledge in memory. In R. C. Anderson, R. J. Spiro, & W. E. Montague (Eds.), *Schooling and the acquisition of knowledge* (pp. 99–115). Hillsdale, NJ: Lawrence Erlbaum Associates.

Russell, D. (1982). The causal dimension scale: A measure of how individuals perceive causes. *Journal of Personality and Social Psychology, 42,* 1137–1145.

Russell, R. (1989, June). Workplace violence: A very real threat. *Security, 3,* 8–40.

Ryan, H. R. (1982). *Kategoria* and *apologia*: On their rhetorical criticism as a speech set. *Quarterly Journal of Speech, 68,* 254–261.

Ryan, H. R. (1988). Introduction. In H. R. Ryan (Ed.), *Oratorical encounters: Selected studies and sources of twentieth-century political accusations and apologies* (pp. xvii–xxv). New York: Greenwood Press.

Salancik, G. R. (1977). Commitment and the control of organizational behavior and belief. In B. M. Staw & G. R. Salancik (Eds.), *New directions in organizational behavior* (pp. 1–54). Chicago, IL: St. Clair.

Saunders, M. D. (1988). Eastern's employee communication crisis. *Public Relations Review, 14,* 33–44.

Saunders, M. D. (1992). *Eastern's Armageddon: Labor conflict and the destruction of Eastern Airlines.* Westport, CT: Greenwood Press.

Schonbach, P. (1980). A category system for account phases. *European Journal of Social Psychology, 10,* 195–200.

Schuetz, J. (1990). Corporate advocacy as argumentation. In R. Trapp & J. Schuetz (Eds.), *Perspectives on argumentation* (pp. 272–284). Prospect Heights, IL: Waveland Press.

Schultz, P. D., & Seeger, M. W. (1991). Corporate centered apologia: Iacocca in defense of Chrysler. *Speaker and Gavel, 28,* 50–60.

Scott, M. B., & Lyman, S. M. (1968). Accounts. *American Sociological Review, 33,* 46–62.

Scott, W. R. (2001). *Institutions and organizations.* Thousand Oaks, CA: Sage.

Searle, J. (1995). *The construction of social reality.* New York: Free Press.

Sears opens ad assault to reclaim trust. (1992, June 26). *Journal and Courier,* p. A10.

Sears places ads denying California charges on cars. (1992, June 15). *Wall Street Journal,* p. A5.

Sears to drop incentives in auto service centers. (1992, June 23*). Columbia Daily Tribune*, p. 5B.

Seeger, M. W. (1985). Ghostbusting: Exorcising the great man spirit from the speechwriting debate. *Communication Education, 34,* 353–358.

Seeger, M. W. (1986). The Challenger tragedy and search for legitimacy. *Central States Speech Journal, 37,* 147–157.

Seeger, M. W., Sellnow, T. L., & Ulmer, R. R. (1998). Communication, organization, and crisis. In M. E. Roloff & G. D. Paulson (Eds.), *Communication Yearbook 21,* (pp. 231–275). Thousand Oaks, CA: Sage.

Seitel, F. P. (1992). *The practice of public relations* (5 ed.). New York: Macmillan.

Seitel, F. P. (1995). *The practice of public relations* (6th ed.). Englewood Cliffs, NJ: Prentice Hall.

Seitel, F. P. (2001). *The practice of public relations* (8th ed.). New York: Macmillan.

Sellnow, T. L. (1993). Scientific argument in organizational crisis communication: The case of Exxon. *Argumentation and Advocacy, 30,* 28–42.

Sellnow, T. L. (1994). Speaking in Defense of Chrysler Communication. In M. W. Seeger (Ed.). *"I gotta tell y": Speeches of Lee Iacocca* (pp. 97–188). Detroit, IL: Wayne State University Press.

Sellnow, T. L. & Seeger, M. W. (1989). Crisis messages: Wall street and the Reagan administration after black Monday. *Speaker and Gavel, 26,* 9–18.

Sellnow, T. L., & Ulmer, R. R. (1995). Ambiguous argument as advocacy in organizational crisis communication. *Argumentation and Advocacy, 31,* 138–150.

Selznick, P. (1949). *TVA and the grass roots.* Berkeley, CA: University of California Press.

Sen, F., & Egelhoff, W. G. (1991). Six years and counting: Learning from crisis management at Bhopal. *Public Relations Review, 17,* 69–83.

Sethi, S. P. (1987). Inhuman errors and industrial crisis. *Columbia Journal of World Business, 22,* 101–107.

Seymour, M. (1991). Crafting a crisis communications plan. *Directors and Boards, 15*(4), 26–29.

Shabercoff, P. (1989, March 31). Captain of tanker had been drinking, blood tests show. *New York Times,* pp. A1, A12.

Shallowitz, D. (1987). Preparation needed to handle catastrophes. *Business Insurance, 21*(15), p. 30.

Shattuck, J. D. (1991). Preparing for job separation. *Public Relations Journal, 47*(10), 31–32.

Shell, A. (1994). Life after downsizing: Study outlines new social contract. *Public Relations Tactics, 1*(6), 20.

Sherrell, D., Reidenbach, R. E., Moore, E., Wagle, J., & Spratlin, T. (1985). Exploring consumer response to negative publicity. *Public Relations Review, 11,* 13–28.

Shrivastava, P. (1987). *Bhopal: Anatomy of crisis.* Cambridge, MA: Ballinger.

Shrivastava, P. & Mitroff, I. I. (1987). Strategic management of corporate crisis. *Columbia Journal of World Business, 22,* 5–11.

Shrivastava, P., Mitroff, I. I., Miller, D., & Miglani, A. (1988). Understanding industrial crises. *Journal of Management Studies, 25,* 285–303.

Silva, M. (1995). *Overdrive: Managing in crisis-filled times.* New York: Wiley.

Simon, R. (1986). *Public relations management: A casebook.* Columbus, OH: Publishing Horizons.

Singh, J. V., Tucker, D. J., & House, R. J. (1986). Organizational legitimacy and the liability of newness. *Administrative Science Quarterly, 31,* 171–193.

Siomkos, G., & Shrivastava, P. (1993). Responding to product liability crises. *Long Range Planning, 26*(5), 72–79.

Sklarewitz, N. (1991). Cruise company handles crisis by the book. *Public Relations Journal, 47,* 34–36.

Skrzycki, C. (2000, December 6). Tire Death Toll at 148, Including 4 Since Recall. *Washington Post,* p. E01.

Slatter, S. P. (1984, May–June). The impact of crisis on managerial behavior. *Business Horizons, 27,* 65–68.

Small, W. (1991). Exxon Valdez: How to spend a billion and still get a black eye. *Public Relations Review, 17,* 9–26.

Smart, C., & Vertinsky, I. (1977). Designs for crisis decision units. *Administrative Science Quarterly, 22,* 640–657.

Smircich, L. (1983). Organizations as shared meaning. In L. R. Pondy, P. J. Frost, G. Morgan, & T. Dandridge (Eds.), *Organizational symbolism* (pp. 55–65). Greenwich, CT: JAI.

Smircich, L., & Stubbart, C. (1985). Strategic management in an enacted world. *Academy of Management Review, 10,* 724–736.

Smith, C. (1992). *Media and apocalypse.* Westport, CT: Greenwood Press.

Smith, R. C., & Eisenberg, E. M. (1987). Conflict at Disneyland: A root-metaphor analysis. *Communication Monographs, 54,* 367–380.

Snyder, L. (1983). An anniversary review and critique: The Tylenol crisis. *Public Relations Review, 9,* 24–34.

Soundbites. (1998). *Public Relations Tactics, 5*(5), 4.

Spolin, V. (1963). *Improvisation for the theatre.* Evanston, IL: Northwestern University Press.

Stacks, D. W. (1995). Public relations and travel: A programmed approach to communication in the 1990s. *Southern Public Relations, 1,* 26–29.

Stacks, D. W., Hickson, M. L., & Hill, S. R (1991). *An introduction to communication theory.* Dallas, TX: Holt, Rinehart & Winston.

Stanislavski, C. (1948). *An actor prepares.* New York: Theatre Art Books.

Stanley, G. D. D. (1985). *Managing external issues: Theory and practice.* Greenwich, CT: JAI Press.

Stateman, A. (1997). Around-the-clock crisis help. *Public Relations Tactics, 4*(8), 3.

Stanton, A. (1989). On the home front. *Public Relations Journal, 45,* 15–16.

Staw, B. (1980). Rationality and justification in organizational life. In L. Cummings & B. Staw, (Eds.) *Research in Organizational Behavior. Vol. 2* (pp. 45–80). Greenwich, CT: JAI Press.

Stephenson, D. R. (1984). The sunny side of crisis. *Public Relations Journal, 40,* 16–18.

Stevens, W. D. (1989). *Remarks by: W. D. Stevens: President, Exxon Company, U.S.A. at the Second International Conference on Industrial and Organizational Crisis Management.* (Available from Exxon Company, U.S.A., Houston, Texas).

Stevenson, C. L. (1944). *Ethics and language.* New Haven, CT: Yale University Press.

Stevenson, R. W. (1992, June 17). Sears ducks, then tries to cover. *New York Times,* pp. D1, D4.

Stuart, P. (1992, February). Murder on the job. *Personnel Journal,* 72–83.

Sturges, D. L. (1994). Communicating through crisis: A strategy for organizational survival. *Management Communication Quarterly, 7,* 297–316.

Sturges, D. L., Carrell, B. J., Newsom, D. A., & Barrera, M. (1991). Crisis communication management: The public opinion node and its relationship to environmental nimbus. *SAM Advanced Management Journal, 56*(3), 22–27.

Suchman, M. C. (1995). Managing legitimacy: Strategic and institutional approaches. *Academy of Management Review, 20,* 571–610.

Swidler, A. (1986). Culture in action: Symbols and strategies. *American Sociological Review, 51,* 273–286.

Tabris, M. D. (1984). Crisis management. In B. Cantor (Ed.), *Experts in action: Inside public relations* (pp. 57–73). New York: Longman.

Taylor, M. (2001). Cultural variance as a challenge to global public relations: A case study of the Coca-Cola scare in Europe. *Public Relations Review, 26,* 277–293.

Terkel, S. (1974). *Working: People talk about what they do all day and how they feel about doing it.* New York: Pantheon Books, Random House.

Theus, K. (1988). *Discrepancy: Organizational response to media reporting.* Unpublished doctoral dissertation. University of Maryland.

Theus, K. (1991). Organizational ideology, structure, and communication efficacy: A causal analysis. In J. E. Grunig & L. A. Grunig (Eds.) *Public Relations Research Annual* (Vol. 3, pp. 133–150). Hillsdale, NJ: Lawrence Erlbaum Associates.

Theus, K. (1993a). Academic reputations: The process of formation and decay. *Public Relations Review, 19,* 277–291.

Theus, K. (1993b). Organizations and the media: Structures of miscommunication. *Management Communication Quarterly, 7,* 67–94.

Thomas, J. (1992). Occupational violent crime: Research on an emerging issue. *Journal of Safety Research, 23,* 55–62.

Thomlison, T. D. (2000). An interpersonal primer with implications for public relations. In J. A. Ledingham & S. D. Bruning (Eds.), *Public relations as relationship management* (pp. 177–203). Mahwah, NJ: Lawrence Erlbaum Associates.

Thompson, C. M. (1992). Reorientation eases the pain and loss of downsizing. *HR Focus, 69*(1), 11.

Thompson, M., Ellis, R. J., & Wildavsky, A. (1990). *Cultural theory.* Boulder, CO: Westview.

Thornburg, L. (1992, May). Practical ways to cope with suicide. *HR Magazine,* 62–66.

Tjosvold, D. (1984). Effects of crisis orientation on managers' approach to controversy in decision making. *Academy of Management Journal, 27*(1), 130–138.

Tomasko, R. M. (1987). *Downsizing: Reshaping the corporation for the future.* New York: AMACOM.

Tompkins, P. (1987). Translating organizational theory: Symbolism over substance. In F. Jablin, L. Putnam, K. Roberts, & L. Porter (Eds.), *Handbook of organizational communication* (pp. 70–96). Newbury Park, CA: Sage.

Tortorella, A. J. (1989). Crisis communication; If it had a precedent, it wouldn't be a crisis. *Communication World, 6*(7), 42–43.

Toth E. L., & Heath, R. L. (1992). *Rhetorical and critical approaches to public relations.* Hillsdale, NJ: Lawrence Erlbaum Associates.

Trahan, J. V. (1993). Media relations in the eye of the storm. *Public Relations Quarterly, 38,* 31–32.

Turner, B. A. (1986). Sociological aspects of organizational symbolism. *Organizational Studies, 7,* 101–115.

Tyler, L. (1997). Liability means never being able to say you're sorry. *Management Communication Quarterly, 11,* 51–73.

Tyler, T. R., & Kramer, R. M. (1996). Whither trust? In R. M. Kramer & T. R. Tyler (Eds.), *Trust in organizations* (pp. 1–15). Thousand Oaks, CA: Sage.

Ulmer, R. R., & Sellnow, T. L. (2000). Consistent questions of ambiguity in organizational crisis communication: Jack in the Box as a case study. *Journal of Business Ethics, 25,* 143–155.

Umansky, D. (1993). How to survive and prosper when it hits the fan. *Public Relations Quarterly, 38,* 32–35

Van de Ven, A. H., & Poole, S. M. (1988). Paradoxical requirements for a theory of change. In R. E. Quinn & K. S. Cameron (Eds.), *Paradox and transformation: Toward a theory of change in organization and management* (pp. 19–64). Cambridge, MA: Ballinger.

Vibbert, S. L., & Bostdorff, D. (1992). Issue management and the lawsuit crisis. In C. Conrad (Ed.), *The ethical nexus: Communication, values and organizational decisions* (pp. 103–120). Norwood, NJ: Ablex.

Wagar, T. H. (2001). Consequences of work force reduction: Some employer and union evidence. *Journal of Labor Research, 22*(4), 851.

Wander, P. C. (1976). The rhetoric of science. *Western Speech Communication, 40,* 226–235.

Ware, B. L., & Linkugel, W. A. (1973). They spoke in defense of themselves: On the generic criticism of apologia. *Quarterly Journal of Speech, 59,* 273–283.

Watkins-Allen, M., & Caillouet, R. H. (1994). Legitimation endeavors: Impression management strategies used by an organization in crisis. *Communication Monographs, 61,* pp. 44–62.

Watzlawick, P., Weakland, J., & Finsch, R. (1974). *Change: Principles of problem formation and problem resolution.* New York: W. W. Norton.

Weber, M. (1978). *Economy and society: An outline of interpretive sociology.* Berkeley: University of California Press.

Weick, K. E. (1969). *The social psychology of organizing.* Reading, MA: Addison–Wesley.

Weick, K. E. (1979). *The social psychology of organizing* (2nd ed.). Reading, MA: Addison–Wesley.

Weick, K. E. (1988). Enacted sense-making in crisis situations. *Journal of Management Studies, 25,* 305–317.

Weick, K. E. (1993). *Organizational redesign as improvisation. Organizational change and redesign: ideas and insights for improving performance.* New York: Oxford University Press.

Weick, K. E. (1995). *Sensemaking in organizations.* Thousand Oaks, CA: Sage.

Weinberger, M. G., Romeo, J. B., & Piracha, A. (1991). Negative product safety news: Coverage, Responses, and Effects. *Business Horizons, 34*(3), 23–31.

Weiner, B. (1985). An attributional theory of achievement motivation and emotion. *Psychology Review, 92,* 548–573.

Weiner, B., Amirkan, J., Folkes, V. S., & Verette, J. A. (1987). An attribution analysis of excuse giving: Studies of a naive theory of emotion. *Journal of Personality and Social Psychology, 53,* 316–324.

Weiner, B., Perry, R. P., & Magnusson, J. (1988). An attribution analysis of reactions to stigmas. *Journal of Personality and Social Psychology, 55,* 738–748.

Wellborn, S. N. (1986, March 10). NASA falls from grace. *US News and World Report,* pp. 20–22.

Werner, L. R. (1990). When crisis strikes use a message action plan. *Public Relations Journal, 46,* 30–31.

White, N. (1995, May 26). Local control focus of new grazing plan. Casper (WY) *Star-Tribune,* pp. A1, A2.

Wilcox, D. L., Ault, P. H., & Agee, W. K. (1992). *Public relations: Strategies and tactics* (3rd ed.). New York: HarperCollins.

Wilden, A. (1980). *System and structure: Essays in communication and exchange* (2nd ed.). London: Tavistock.

Wilden, A. (1987). *The rules are no game: The strategy of communication.* London: Routledge & Kegan Paul.

Wilford, J. N. (1986, January 29). Faith in technology is jolted, but there is no going back. *New York Times,* p. A7.

Wilke, J. R., & Scism, L. (1995, August 8). Insurance agents fight an intrusion by banks, but other perils loom. *Wall Street Journal,* p. A1.

Wilkins, A. (1983). Organizational stories as symbols which control the organization. In L. R. Pondy, P. Frost, G. Morgan, & T. Dandridge (Eds.), *Organizational symbolism* (pp. 81–92). Greenwich, CT: JAI Press.

Wilkins, A. (1984). The creation of company cultures: The role of stories and human resource systems. *Human Resource Management, 23,* 41–60.

Williams, D. E., & Olaniran, B. A. (1994). Exxon's decision-making flaws: The hypervigilant response to the Valdez grounding. *Public Relations Review, 20,* 5–18.

Williams, D. E. & Treadaway, G. (1992). Exxon and the Valdez accident: A failure in crisis communication. *Communication Studies, 43,* 56–64.

Williams, M. L., & Goss, B. (1975). Equivocation: Character insurance. *Human Communication Research, 1,* 265–270.

Wilson, E. (1980). *The theatre experience.* New York: McGraw-Hill.

Wilson, S. R., Cruz, M. G., Marshall, L. J., & Rao, N. (1993). An attribution analysis of compliance-gaining interactions. *Communication Monographs, 60,* 352–372.

Wisenblit, J. Z. (1989). Crisis management planning among U.S. corporations: Empirical evidence and a proposed framework. *Advanced Management Journal, 54*(2), 31–41.

Wragg, D. W. (1992) *The public relations handbook.* Oxford, England: Blackwell.

Yankelovich Partners, Inc. (1994, June). *Public support for the United States space program: Results from a national tracking study of registered voters.* Copyright Yankelovich Partners Inc.

Yin, R. (1984). *Case study research.* Beverly Hills, CA: Sage.

Yin, T. (1992, June 12). Sears is accused of billing fraud at auto centers. *Wall Street Journal,* pp. B1, B5.

Zarefsky, D. (1986). *President Johnson's war on poverty.* Tuscaloosa: University of Alabama Press.

Zucker, L. G. (1977). The role of institutionalization in cultural persistence. *American Sociological Review, 42,* 726–743.

Author Index

369

Subject Index